AF556067

DEMOCRACY IN MUSLIM WORLD

DEMOCRACY IN MUSLIM WORLD

Md. Jamal Mustafa

RANDOM PUBLICATIONS

NEW DELHI - 110 002 (INDIA)

Democracy in Muslim World

ISBN 978-93-51117-24-7

Published in 2015 in India by

RANDOM PUBLICATIONS

4376-A/4B, Gali Murari Lal, Ansari Road

New Delhi-110 002

Phone: +9111-43580356, 23289044

E-mail: randomexports@gmail.com; sales@randompublications.com; info@randompublications.com

Reprinted 2026

Type Setting by: Friends Media, Delhi-110089

Preface

Islam is at present the second largest religion in the world. It has more than one billion followers, mostly in the Arab world, Asia, and Sub-Saharan Africa and its numbers are increasing also in Europe and other parts of the World. Recent events such as the Arab spring have given rise to a hope that democracy can spread to the Islamic world. However, there are several reasons to be skeptical. Unlike the Bible's position in Christianity, the Quran is reckoned to be of direct divine origin. Believers in Islam have to obey not only God, but also Muhammad, his messenger. The law of Sharia intervenes in both religious and secular life, including penal punishments and judicial matters, as well as the acts of worship and family life. Muslims are expected to accept the Quran as the word of God, and the Sharia as the regulator of society and daily life. One could argue that with a base of this kind, there is little room for the rights of citizens and freedom of expression, which are key features in the Western pluralistic model of democracy. Both civil liberties and political rights tend to be neglected in the vast majority of Muslim countries today.

However, there are differences within the Islamic world. More secular countries like Bangladesh, Indonesia, and Turkey are better at fulfilling democratic rights than states that practice Sharia, like Saudi Arabia and Iran. Even though there can be different interpretations of Sharia, there is a tendency that the implementation, or even just the acceptance, of Islamic law could mean less emphasis on civil liberties. Sharia can be viewed as an obstacle for democracy in the Muslim world. Several Muslim states can be denoted as having at least to some extent political freedom, such as Bangladesh, Indonesia, Senegal, and Turkey. These countries are not considered best in class when it comes to civil liberties and political freedom. However, there are other factors than religion that influence this picture. Poverty, history, colonialism, and religion should all be taken into account. Turkey chose the way of modernization. The Turkish nationalism under

Kemal Atatürk was also a reaction against Islamic culture and a demand for westernization of society. The new republic dismantled the Turkish Kalifat in 1924, and in 1928 they introduced religious freedom. Turkey thus took a step from the Islamic towards the European culture. Compared to Western standards most Muslim countries of the World tend to have a poor record of democracy. But one should take into account that most of these states are developing countries and have a history of colonialism and violent conflicts. There are Christian countries in many parts of the world who are no better off than the Muslim ones. Deliberations of the Caliphates, most notably the Rashidun Caliphate were not democratic in the modern sense rather, decision-making power lay with a council of notable and trusted companions of Muhammad and representatives of different tribes. According to the Shia understanding, Muhammad named as his successor, his son-in-law and cousin Ali. Therefore the first three of the four elected "Rightly Guided" Caliphs recognized by Sunnis, are considered usurpers, notwithstanding their having been "elected" through some sort of conciliar deliberation. In any case, anyone who investigates Islam will be in no doubt that the notion of democratic participation is clear and adoption from Western ideas and institutions whatever is in agreement with Islamic law and develops Muslim society.

This book focuses on the multifaceted causes of the slow progress in the Muslim world of both modernization and democratization, and suggests remedies grounded in a keen awareness of the challenges facing both Islam and the West.

I thank all members of my team who have helped in the preparation of the book. My special thanks go to "Random Publications" who have published the book.

— Md. Jamal Mustafa

Contents

Chapter 1

Perception of Governance

Perfect Diplomacy

Akhlak-i-Jalali

Muhammad ibn Asad Jalal-al-Din-al-Bawwani (1627-1501 A. D.) the author of this book was attached to the court of Turkoman ruler Uzun Hassan, who at the meridian of his power, had diplomatic relations with Venice and Constantinople, in the West, and Samarqand and Herat in the East. The period of his rule was crowded with political turmoil and administrative anarchy. The character of the people had been adversely affected by lawlessness, and the ethical standards of the rulers and administrators were painfully low.

The main purpose of the writer was to find causes of the prevalent stresses and tensions which had so completely polluted the moral climate in administration, Muhammad ibn Asad was a prolific writer and he wrote on variety of philosophical and mystical subjects in Arabic, but his most famous work is *Lawamie ai-Ishraq fi Makarim-al-Akhlaq* popularly known as Akhlaq-i-Jalali. The book has been frequently printed and widely read in Iran and Indo-Pakistan sub-continent. In 1839 it was translated in English by W. F. Thompson under the title *Practical Philosophy of the Muhammadan People.* The author has made extensive use of the ethical writings of the Greek philosophers and Muslim scholars who preceded him, but every discussion carries a deep stamp of his own genius. His analysis of human nature and character is unquestionably very rich and profound, and constitute a meaningful manifesto to guide men in sorting out issues which are morally right. He believes that man is a vice-regent of God on earth and emulation of divine attributes is his ultimate destiny. This is a difficult assignment and he points out that to fulfil the obligations of vice-regency "two things are necessary, (i) mature wisdom which means perfection in knowledge, (ii) and eminent ability which connotes perfection in practice." Muhammad ibn Asad had a firm conviction that knowledge is meant to serve mankind and unless it is put into practice, human affairs will never be smooth and harmonious. He said, "Knowledge without practice is a burden, and practice without knowledge is a mischief." He has drawn a very comprehensive list of virtues which in his opinion make life socially and morally worth living. These characteristics lend luster, dignity and richness to human behavior and assist human organizations in the realization of their objectives. He has made four broad categories of virtues and labelled them as Wisdom, Courage, Temperance, and Equity, and then under each category he lists certain qualities which ensure the growth of a morally healthy personality.

Wisdom : It means penetration, quickness of intellect, clearness of understanding, facility of acquirement, propriety of discrimination retention, recollection.

Courage : It means magnanimity, collectedness, elevation of purpose, firmness, coolness, stateliness, boldness, endurance, condescension, zeal and mercy.

Temperance Shame : (The author calls it soul's restraint upon itself when aware of intending to commit anything odious, that it may guard against deserving censure. One of the Prophets saying is this, *Shame,* is a compendium of every virtue). Good humour, righteousness, easiness, patience, content, steadiness, piety, regularity, integrity, and liberality.

Equity : It consist of fidelity, union, exactitude, tenderness, brotherhood, gratitude, good fellowship, good faith, cordiality, submission, resignation and devotion.

The above virtues are not merely abstract ethical principles in the opinion of the author. They are meant to be operational instruments for conducting human affairs. For government and administration, Muhammad ibn Asad has added a few other moral responsibilities also. He points out that a free and frequent interaction between governors and governed is essential for justice and cooperation. Any government where people don't have access to rulers is a bureaucratic tyranny. The author of Akhlak-i-Jalali has expressed his opinion on this aspect as follows:

> *For this reason intercourse with our fellow creatures in the way of cooperation is incumbent on us all, or else we*

deviate from the first principle of justice and fall into the path of inequity, like that class of persons who betake themselves to a savage retirement from mankind, and remain altogether aloof from cooperation with their fellow men, loading them however, with the burden of their support and then they call seclusion and consider meritorious in fact it is altogether a state of inequity.

The above statement testifies to the fact that Muhammad ibn Asad feels that meeting people and cooperating with them is an essential characteristic of a good government. In fact this is a quality which can infuse trust, confidence and cooperation in all areas of human relations. He has further clarified the distinction between the righteous and the unrighteous government by saying:-

"He who conducts the righteous government in his rigid adherence to the role of equity, considers his subjects as his children and his friends, placing all covetousness and love of money under the control of judgment. He that conducts the unrighteous government adheres to the principles of force, treats his subjects like beasts of burden, considers them as slaves, and is himself the slave of avarice and passion."

Like other Muslim writers on administrative ethics, Muhammad ibn Asad emphasized in unqualified terms that virtue and rectitude among rulers always have a widespread impact on the subjects. It is a natural tendency among people to emulate their governors.

If a ruler is good, his goodness would be a source of inspiration, but if he is bad, the people unhesitatingly follow the same course. It is therefore vital for the moral uplift of society that administrators should set an example of honesty, justice and integrity. This will give dignity, poise, and solidity to the character of the masses. In Akhlak-i-Jalali this problem of the image of the ruler or administrator has been explained as follows:-

"We are told in holy writ, 'Men resemble their contemporaries even more than their progenitors', and 'Men are of the same religion as their princes.' Hence when the age's guidance is in the hands of a just king everyone directs his course towards equity and the attainment of virtue, on the contrary, the people likewise incline to falsehood, covetousness, and vice of every description."

The qualities which would endear the rulers to the subjects are, seriousness of purpose, rational decision, resolution, endurance, hardwork and incorruptibility. Moreover, authorities in a kingdom are expected to be anxiously concerned about three fundamental principles for the welfare of the state: (i) Financial stability, (ii) kindness and compassion to the people, (iii) and ability to keep away petty-minded people from government offices. Employment in a state, according to the author, should be reserved for people who are talented by nature, and prudent in thought and action. Ibn Asad compiled a code of ten articles, which in his opinion could ensure a sound moral base for administrative behaviour:-

(1) Whatever he holds impossible toward himself he should hold inadmissible towards his people.

(2) Quick justice.

(3) Abstinence from licentious and sensual gratification.

(4) Courtesy and kindness in decision-making.

(5) Faith in the supremacy of the will of God.

(6) Nothing should be done in the opposition to the Message of God.

(7) Mercy and Indulgency.

(8) Should associate with men of righteousness.

(9) Maintaining everyone in the position he deserves.

(10) Officers, soldiers and the people in this relationship should be so balanced that they could not injure each other's interest.

There are many other discussions on morals and manners in Akhlak-i-Jalali, relating to individual and social life, but they don't have such relevance to government and administration. Friendship, family, property, rearing of children, rights and privileges of wives, education of women, rights of parents, meals, etc. are some of the subjects on which the author has dilated in depth.

In short, the treatise is a valuable compendium of ethical values both Islamic and pre-Islamic which the author considers, provide richness and dignity to human character. He insists that without positive moral climate, and universal ethical standards social system decay and wither away. In short, the treatise is of indisputable significance for understanding the practical moral standards of the Muslim people and Thompson is right when on the title page of his translation he calls Akhlak-i-Jalali 'the most esteemed ethical work of Middle Asia'.

According to Erwin Rosenthal, *Jaial-al-Din-al-Dawwani* made extensive use of Nasir-al-Din Tusis *Akhlaq-i-Nasiri,* and to a large extent many of his concepts and discussions were only summaries of Tusi. Al-Dawwani, however, being a theologian, jurist and scholar, has put greater emphasis on traditional Islam. His narrative is free from Greek philosophical influences which so conspicuously dominate Tusi's analysis. His examination of ethical, economic and political problems in a Muslim polity is direct, precise and lucid. A ruler who isolates himself from his fellow men is unjust in his opinion. Rulers, he suggests are 'physicians to the temperament of the world' and their main responsibility is to inculcate righteous opinions, mold convictions of the people, and fashion their disposition in a manner so that good actions could be ensured. In his opinion people are divided into five categories, "good, with good influences on others, good in themselves without influence, bad without bad influence, and finally the opposite of the first group, the bad ones who exert a bad influence."

A ruler's most onerous responsibility is to maintain an equilibrium among all these kinds. That in essence is the purpose of authority in a state and following other works on governmental ethics, he insists that those in authority should have kindness, and compassion and that in selecting state functionaries, rulers should not entrust offices to mean people. Moderation, respect for people's rights, devotion to their welfare, justice and close vigilance over the working of the government and fear of God are the other qualities which give strength and stability to kingdoms. Rosenthal has summed up Al-Dawwani's contributions as follows:-

> *These examples show how Al-Dawwani combines philosophy both ancient and modern with Quran, Hadith and tales as found in the 'Mirrors.' In this way he gives an interesting and colourful account of political thought which is intellectually satisfying and traditionally unobjectionable.*

Counselling for Ministers

Nasaih ul-vuzera vel-Umera : *[The Book of Counsel for Vezirs (Ministers) and Umera (Governors)].*

This small treatise was written by an Ottoman statesman during the later half of the seventeenth century. It's author, Baqqal-Oghlu Sari Hajji Muhammad Pasha was born in Constantinople, but biographical details of his early life are missing from available historical records. In 1671, probably as a teenager, he became an apprentice in the office of the *ruznami je-i-evvel,* an important official of the Treasury department. By hard work, devotion, and knowledge of the financial problems he ultimately became the head of this department. In 1702 Rami Muhammad Pasha, the grand vezir appointed him chief defterdar (Treasurer of the Empire). This was the pinnacle of his professional attainments, but it made the last years of his life extremely uncomfortable. Ottoman administration during this period was a web of unending intrigues, in which all the senior officials of the realm, governors of provinces, courtiers, and members of the royal sergalio were deeply involved. Every senior public servant lived in a state of chronic insecurity. This can be illustrated by the fact that Muhammad Pasha was seven times in and out of his job as a *defterdar* of the empire. His ability and experience were of no consideration to his opponents. Ultimately he fell victim to their jealousy and enmity. By orders of Sultan Ahmad III he was dismissed and imprisoned in the castle of Qavla on the Aegean coast. After sometime in February 1717 he was executed, his head was sent to Constantinople where it was hung on the gate of the Imperial palace.

Writing in Exile : It is assumed that the Book of Counsel for Vezirs and Governors was written during one of the exiles of Muhammad Pasha. The main purpose of the scholar-statesman was to give a detailed account of the political and administrative vicissitudes which had engulfed the empire at that time. Ottoman bureaucracy has always been accorded a place of eminence among the great historical bureaucracies of the world. Its spirit was autocratic, but during the earlier period of the dynasty under capable rulers who presided over an unwieldy empire, which stretched from Constantinople to Egypt and from Algeria to the borders of Persia, it worked efficiently. But this era of territorial expansion and administrative efficiency, ended with the death of Suleyman the Magnificent. After him the fortunes of the empire were in the hands of harem-reared princes who were educated in the cloistered atmosphere of the palace through eunuchs, slave-girls and pages.

War State: The Ottoman empire in essence was a war state. It was one long crusade against the infidel world. As long as the rulers were busy conquering foreign lands administration was efficient and resourceful. Bat once the territorial expansion stopped, there was rapid deterioration in the efficiency and moral standards of the administrators. Revenues which used to flow from booty, ransom, and other spoils of war disappeared, and the empire entered into a period of financial decadence from which it could not recover. While revenues decreased, the luxuries of royalty and its sprawling circles of regal parasites kept on increasing. Ease-loving Sultans, luxuriating courtiers, disgruntled armies, rebellious governors and rapacious bureaucracy completely wrecked the machinery of the government. Bernard Lewis says:

> *"The breakdown in the apparatus of government affected not only the supreme instruments of sovereignly, but also the whole of the bureaucratic and religious institutions all over the Empire. These suffered a catastrophic fall in efficiency and integrity which was accentuated by the growing change in methods of recruitment, training, and promotion. This deterioration is clearly discernible in the Ottoman archives, which reflected vividly and precisely the change from the meticulous, conscientious, and strikingly efficient bureaucratic government of the sixteenth century to the neglect of the seventeenth and collapse of the eighteenth centuries."*

Ottoman administration which under Murad II Muhammad the Conqueror and Salim I, was a source of strength and stability under later weak rulers became an instrument of corruption and exploitation. Sale of public offices became a common feature, and one who paid the highest price would immediately start using his official position unscrupulously for personal gains, because he was not sure when another bidder would replace him.

A contemporary western observer of the time remarked that "the frequent changes of the principal ministers saps silently the foundation of the empire, and gives to the government terrible wounds. Those who are elevated to office, for seeing that this will not long be held, preferring their own enrichment to the interest of empire, let it perish in order to assuage their avarice, and being able to enrich themselves only by unjust means they make use of every means."

Army, which was once one of the finest fighting machines, was reduced only to a pale shadow of its former strength and character. Janissaries which had played a significant role in the creation of the empire, taking advantage of the weakness of the ruling Sultans, had monopolized all positions of power in the state.

Their devotion to the ruling Sultan was only a facade for self-aggrandizement and the non-payment of salaries by the government led them to pillage the land freely and indulge in illegal extortion from the peasantry. The commanders on the frontiers kept false registers to defraud the Treasury at Constantinople. Palace intrigues, corruption, deceit, jealousy and treachery were commonly noticed in every area of politics and administration. Gibb and Bowen have summed up this phase of the Ottoman history in the following words :-

> *"The ruling institution had thus by the eighteenth century, undergone as complete a transformation as was compatible with the maintenance of most of its original forms. Instead of inspiring its members to earn merit by the exercise of talent and virtue, it taught them they must look to corruption for advancement, and might safely neglect duties that should have been concomitant with their privileges. Finally, instead of providing the sultans with an efficient instrument for the preservation and extension of their power, it was now scarcely strong enough to maintain their authority at home, and become an engine of feeble tyranny over those of their subjects that were unable to continue against it."*

It was in this depressing climate of moral and material decadence that Muhammad Pasha wrote his "The Book of Counsel". He admired the political wisdom and high moral standards of administration of Ottoman rule during the fifteenth and sixteenth century. But he felt that in his own time the empire had reached the nadir of its ethical standards. His analysis is illustrated with verses from the Quran Traditions of the Prophet and relevant passages from earlier works on the subject.

The narrative is an index of author's rich and vast experience which he had accumulated as a high-ranking administrator. As defterdar (Chief Treasurer) and as member of the Imperial Divan (Central Cabinet) he had ample opportunity to observe from very close quarters, every branch of administration. Although Muhammad Pasha's main focus was on the Ottoman administration, but in diagnosing the causes of its decline he has pointed out certain basic ethical principles, which can be relevant for administrators, holding positions of power and prestige in any society. In subject matter, Nasaihul-vuzera vel-umera, resembles a great deal with Siyasat Namah and Qabus-namah, although in breadth and depth of analysis it falls short of the earlier works. The treatise is divided into the following nine chapters :-

(1) Explanation regarding the behaviour and habits of the Grand Vezir.

(2) Explanation regarding the official positions and the harmfulness of bribes.

(3) Explanation regarding the behaviour of the Secretary of the Treasury and holders of office.

(4) Explanation regarding the Bektashi Corps.

(5) Explanation regarding the condition of Rayas (the subject peasants and the harmfulness of tyranny and oppression of the poor.

(6) Explanation regarding the state of the Ever-Victorious Frontier and the qualities of commanders.

(7) Explanation concerning avarice and liberality, greed, covetousness, pride, and envy, humility and arrogance, good temper and bad temper and hypocrisy.

(8) Explanation regarding faithful friendship and the harmfulness of calumny and backbiting.

(9) Explanation regarding the state of the Ziamet and Timar (the two principal categories of fiefs in the Ottoman feudal system).

Absence of Facts : Muhammad Pasha, in his narrative does not mention anywhere the moral degeneration of the royal household, or the inexcusable negligence of the Sultans cowards the affairs of the state. As an employee of an autocratic ruler, he probably could not openly criticize the Sultans whose tyranny and pursuits of pleasures had changed the machinery of government into an engine of coercion and exploitation. He opens his first chapter with the following remarks:

> *"Since the Lord without equal, who showers down abundant gifts (may His glory be exalted beyond the reach of imagination) has made that firmly founded dynasty, the surpassing Ottoman Sultanate, to be the refuge of the rulers of the times, and has made their court, which pours out on every hand favours from the ocean of abundance, to be distributor of the sustenance decreed by Providence to the people of the world, it has consequently become a necessary responsibility and obvious obligation of the padishah to fulfil the incumbant gratitude due for their Divine Grace in accordance with the precept." "Everyone of you is a shepherd and everyone is responsible for the flock, he should make affluent the condition of the governed and establish good order in the affairs of the citizens."*

Muhammad Pasha advocates that officials occupying positions of authority must abstain from illegal practices, avoid injustice and remove weeds and thorns of tyranny and corruption. Administrators in his opinion should be free from the baneful attitude of discriminating among people. Rich and poor, high and low, friend and a stranger, all should be treated strictly according to the principles of law and ethics. They must have the moral courage to speak the truth, because truth alone ensures integrity and emancipates human thinking from deceit and suspicion. Hasty use of power is also detrimental to sound administration. In the application of his authority an officer has moral duty to weigh intelligently and rationally pros and cons of every bit of evidence and information. He says :-

"Throughout their period of authority let them treat with equality the humble and the noble, the wealthy and the poor, the learned and the unlearned, the one from far and the one from nearby, the visitor and the neighbour—let them not make use of their power until the evidence is complete—to the glorious padishah let them speak the word of truth without veiling and concealment. For the Prophet of God has said, "words of truth are the best alms."

The Governance

The Ulama, over the centuries, have developed a structure for determining the entire set of rules and regulations arising from the Quran and the Surma (normative practice) of His messenger, Muhammad (PBUH).' This structure is called *fiqh* and is a legal discourse. But this legal discourse has been marginalized and attacked from many quarters, and for that reason few people are aware of the political ideas which the Ulama hold. This chapter attempts to convey certain traditionally held political ideas of the Ulama which will challenge conventional political notions held by some political scientists and students of Islamic civilization.

The Ulama and the Islamic legal discourse *(fiqh)* have been continually and ferociously attacked, even from within the Muslim world, from many quarters from secularists to modernists, reformists to fundamentalists. If these groups have one thing in common, it is a desire for power, and more specifically for state-centred schemes for Muslim progress.

Simply stated, the Ulama stand in their way as modern state centralization has historically been shunned by the Ulama. In fact, the very essence of the Ulama project that edifice erected to determine rules and regulations from the revelation is its decentralization, slow accumulation of positions and argumentation, local dominion, and diffusion. No one person can define and represent the Islamic experience, so the Ulama resist Islam being centralized in the person of the nation-state leader, or in any university or institute. And as for state-centred schemes for progress, in accord with traditional religions, the Ulama do not see progress as a virtue. As Norbert Wiener remarks.

Most of us are too close to the idea of progress to take cognizance either of the fact that this belief belongs only to a small part of recorded history, or of the other fact, that it represents a sharp break with our own religious professions and traditions.

The importance of the nation-state and the concept of progress to the dominant voice of politics in and about the Muslim world, helps explain why the Ulama are portrayed as the enemy or at least as the obstacle, to necessary 'change' and 'development'. But they are not unique in this respect.

Jerry Mander in his book *In the Absence of the Sacred,* quotes Oren Lyons, describing legal procedures of the Iroquois Nation: 'We meet and just keep talking until there's nothing left but the obvious truth, and both (disputing) families agree on the solution'. I was struck by the similarity between this description and that of Lawrence Rosen of a *Qadi* (judge) in a Moroccan town.

For rather than being aimed simply at the invocation of state or religious power, rather than being devoted mainly to the creation of a logically consistent body of legal doctrine, the aim of the *Qadi is* to put people back in the position of being able to negotiate their own permissible relationships without pre-determining just what the outcome of those negotiations ought to be.

What the Ulama share with other traditional knowledge-elites is a desire to preserve a social realm where law is played out in the communal arena with language (or other discursive formats), where not only contention is resolved, but also societal definition and direction is nurtured. This definition and direction comes from the community itself, and not from a media dominated by huge corporations or the government, or from a priestly class of lawyers who design and prosecute laws. In fact, there seems to be no place in their vision for the totalitarian, corporate, legal fiction called the State which we take for granted. The word *Qadi* recalls the Arabic word's meaning of one who settles the affair *(qada),* and Rosen shows how the discretion given to the *gadia* discretion typically criticized by Western observers as laxity allows him to make law a 'metasystem which creates order in a universe that is often experienced in a more disorderly way'.' The disputants are facilitated by the *Qadi* to continue defining the situation until the solution is obvious to all. Consensus developed over time and not coercion, is the central product of this legal activity.

Great Chasm

There is a great chasm between a 'traditional' society, which will mean here a society which organizes itself around divine guidance, and a 'modern' society, which means a society with a state. As we shall see, the concept of state which has fully emerged in the last hundred years or so, and which saturates our field of vision, is alien to many traditional societies and to central activities of Islamic civilization. Yet when we want to investigate politics in Islam, we tend to look for states and at monarchical rulers like caliphs, sultans, and amirs; and when fundamentalists dream, they dream of a powerful, Utopian Islamic State. The fact remains that politics in Islamic civilization is located predominately in quite a different arena, and the Ulama, including Ibn Taymiyyah, traditionally resisted all kinds of forces which might have potentially led to the kind of state powers which we have seen recently.

The dream of an Islamic State seems to include visions of sticks taken to rebellious Muslims, timorous non-Muslims citizens, and autocratic rulers on white horses solving all the prevailing problems. But the preoccupation with caliphate seems entirely modern, arising especially in the face of the humiliation suffered at the hands of nineteenth and twentieth century imperialist powers. Historically, Muslim communities throughout the world established the *Shariah* by themselves, not *ex cathedra,* as the central focus of their community. Glimpses into daily life, chosen from hagiographic accounts of Sufis and their travels, popular poetry, inscriptions, and accounts of peasant revolts, reveal Muslim communities implementing the *Shariah* themselves, striving thereby for a just society. In fact, the very word government *(hukumat)* in Arabic,' as recorded by the lexicographer Ibn Manzur below conveys a negative role for government, not a positive one.

The Arab says *hakam-tu,* I prevented someone and *hakam-tu,* I averted someone with the meaning of I prevented someone and I averted someone. In this category, one says about the *hakim* among people that he is *hakim* because he prevents the oppressor from oppression. Al-Mundhiri reported from Abu Talib that he said about their statement *hakama* Allah among us, that al-Asmai said the root of *hukumat* (government) is averting the oppressor from oppression:

Here the government's role is simply to prevent oppression, because positive political benefits arise directly from practising the *Shariah.* There is no place in this Arab conception of *hukumah* for massive bureaucracies, governmental spending and taxing, standing armies and governments. This conception suggests that government is quite an incidental affair, necessary only to stop the oppressor, and that the real political activity of the community is to be found elsewhere and I suggest that place is the communal arena of the *fiqh*.

The Fiqh in the Political Realm

The Ulama traditionally exercised a distancing from encroaching state power. Indeed, we find great animosity among the Ulama, including fundamentalist favourites like Ibn Taymiyyah, for emerging state power." According to Rosen, the law 'provides a context for the peaceable formation by individuals of their own ties,' so in the classical Islamic theory of the state, law and government were kept largely separate from one another ... By remaining resolutely focused on the individual, the legal establishment forsook the politicization of the law; by avoiding inclusion of the law as an instrument of state policy, the political authorities passed up the opportunity to use law as a vehicle of political centralization.

As with primitive people, Muslims traditionally refused state power over their lives. The kind of distinctions we find between 'then' and 'now', between the largely hidden and suppressed alternative political configurations and our contemporary situations, suggest a fundamental dichotomy. This can be variously characterized as the pre-Columbus era, the last five hundred years (for those concentrating on the civilizations of native peoples) and tradition and modernity (for those emphasizing the sacred, such as the perennialists and traditionalists). But state power is almost invisible, as often is modernity, and so the fundamental dichotomy between anything today (government, media, religion) and then is not always perceived. One way to call attention to modern and state contexts is to draw on analyses which trace the radical changes influencing daily life. Writers like Mumford, Berman, Illich, Feyerabend, and Ellul show us a world where everything is called into question, where the questions of 'why do we do this' and 'why do we think this is normal' assume a particularly poignant note. The popular anti-hero Travis McGee meditates:

> *I get this crazy feeling. Every once in a while I get it. I get the feeling that this is the last time in history when the offbeats like me will have a chance to live free in the nooks and crannies of the huge and rigid structure of an increasingly codified society. Fifty years from now I would be hunted down in the street. They would drill little holes in my skull and make me sensible and reliable and adjusted."*

In Foucault's lecture 'The Political Technology of Individuals'," a fundamental change in politics is seen with the process of defining the 'police' in the seventeenth and eighteenth centuries. He locates a book written in 1779 which is the 'first great systematic program of public health for the modern state'." At the same moment, 'the French Revolution gives the signal for the great national wars of our days ... meeting their conclusion or their climax in huge mass slaughters'.

While for Saint Thomas, the king should imitate God to lead men to the good life, and for Machiavelli, the art of politics is to increase the power of the prince, the aim of the modern state is to 'reinforce the state itself'." This gives rise to a political arithmetic, a statistics which creates a calculus of power, where 'the individual exists insofar as what he does is able to introduce even a minimal change in the strength of the state, either in a positive or in a negative direction ... And sometimes what he has to do for the state is to live, to work, to produce, to consume; and sometimes what he has to do is to die."

Without a calculus of demography, a statistics of population, what we now call politics—state, power, or government—had little to do with the daily life of traditional societies. With the calculus, the individual becomes the business of the state. From before his birth to after his death, the state is concerned with any increase or decrease the individual might confer on its aggregate power. The state has an interest in monitoring and deciding the fate of infants, educating children, intervening to protect them from parental abuse, immunizing them, and so on. What rational opposition can there be, where one must argue today for 'freedom from state interrogation' over 'health' and 'saving lives'?

The desire of the modern state, which is to endlessly interrogate and govern the subject interminably, with forms that need to be filled out, credit card records, and social security numbers, is contrasted with the reticent 'primitive'. Resistance to development is a resistance to this interrogation.

The very idea of 'naked' truth, and truth 'laid bare' rests in a worldview quite opposite to that of the classical Muslim scholars. Now, the truth of someone is that person's failing, sins, and frailties. In the Islamic world, one did not broadcast shortcomings. In his discussion of the metaphor of rinsing the mouth and sniffing water in the process of *taharah* (ritual purity), Ibn al-Arabi reveals the typical emphasis given to this civilizational value. 'Even if his recompense (for speaking of evil),' Ibn al-Arabi comments, 'is in His statement, *[Allah loves not that evil should be noised abroad in public speech, except where injustice has been done],* [4:148], nevertheless silence about it is most excellent."

The resistance of the primitive is well-illustrated in a passage in Munif's novel about the advent of oil exploration in what is now Saudi Arabia, where the bureaucrats say, 'The information we need is simple and necessary, and it is confidential too.' To their long series of questions about his parents, Ibrahim blurts out 'What do you want with my mothers?' And then after even more questions, 'What's wrong with you—can't you talk about anything but my father and mother?' Finally, he cries out, 'God help me—leave me alone!"'

Communities who refuse statehood and states are found throughout the world, from the Penans in Malaysia to the Aborigines in Australia, from Indian nations throughout North, Central, and South America to Kurds and Pathans in South and Southwest Asia. *Cultural Survival Quarterly* reports that three-fourths of the 120 military conflicts in the world in 1987 were native nations defending themselves against nation-state. The ultimate supremacy of the nation-state is not yet established and many communities throughout the world are struggling against it till death. In a world dominated by state powers, and at least—if not more—as influentially by corporations, it is no wonder that the voice of the Ulama is seldom heard.

Caliphal Politics

The classical discussions of caliphate are sparse, overly abstract, and full of hidden agendas. They are not very helpful while questioning how authority is configured in Islamic societies. The voluminous discussions of who is best suited for leadership *(imamah)* during the prayer *(salah),* in contrast, is very helpful.

Should it not then be possible to extrapolate from the discussion of the *salah,* ideas about a larger universe? Is not the ideal leader for the *salah,* the ideal leader for the larger society? Is not the discussion of the criteria for a good leader for the *salah* at the same time a discussion of the good leader of society? If indeed we can examine the *salah* as a microcosm of the Muslim universe, a number of propitious consequences ensue. What I am proposing here is nothing short of an entire re-evaluation of politics in Islam. The entire fundamentalist discourse on the Islamic state in fact arises from the invisible concealment of a traditional world view having its own kind of politics, by a modern world-view of the sovereign state. Let us therefore delve into this matter of politics, because one of the main reasons of examining the *fiqh* discussion of the *salah* as a microcosm for the larger discourse of Islamic communities, which is so propitious, stems from the reassessment of politics which it occasions.

Historically, there is a noticeable absence of sustained and direct discussion on Islamic leadership. The subject matter of kingship or caliphate tended to create treatises at once highly abstract and overly specific. The works of Mawardi, Nizam-ul-mulk, al-Ghazzali, and Ibn Khaldun, for example, when addressing kingship or caliphate, have quite definite agendas to pursue; attacking amid abstract and idealistic verbiage, a powerful woman behind a would-be leader, or simultaneous caliphates, or justifying pinning one's hopes on converting a ravaging Hun. Arkoun lists what Mawardi overlooks:

Al-Mawardi talks neither of the Shiite theory of the designation of the caliph based on a text, nor of the great conflict *(al-fitna)* between Ali and Muawiyyah, nor of Yazid who, according to the Shiite version, had Hussain assassinated at Karbala, nor of the conditions of civil war which initiated the fall of the Umayyeds and the ascendance of the Abbasides, nor of the politics of Mamun toward the Mutazilites and to Shiism, nor that of Mutawakkil for installing Sunnism, nor of the conquest of power by the Buyides.

The actual caliphate was formally abolished by Ataturk in 1925, and even though it was obvious that the caliphate had been an extremely ineffective system for decades, even centuries, the loss of the caliphate had a tremendous impact on Muslims throughout the world. Muslims in India, for example, spontaneously arose and began walking to Turkey to recover their world. Ali Abd al-Raziq's short treatise, published in Egypt in 1933 on government in Islam, arguing that the caliphate is not essential to the Islamic community, quickly brought him major troubles and seemed to many to be salt thrown on their wounds. To this day, many Muslims have put their hopes in a revived caliphate. We have a situation here where there is a dearth of material on Islamic government, together with an inchoate understanding that, against Abd al-Raziq, politics is essential to Islam.

The problem, as I see it, is that there is no state in Islam-state being understood in the Western sense of a sovereign, corporate institution with a reality across time and space, independent of its human constituents or components. When people talk of the 'Islamic theory of state', Ayubi notes,

They are addressing themselves specifically to the problem of government and especially to the conduct of the ruler, and not to the state as a generic category or to the body-politic as a social reality and a legal abstraction ... Even when the Islamic bureaucracy developed and became quite complex, officials and other 'public' personnel appointed to certain jobs or dismissed from them, never signed a contract with the 'State' or any other 'moral personality', but simply with a certain individual employer (al-muwalli).

The issue is not one merely of definition. The concept of a sovereign, corporate nation-state entails absolutism and totalitarianism—no matter how much people in liberal democracies want to believe that their freedom and rights are protected. Traditional scholars spoke of this kind of politics as Thoreau did, where the best government is the least government, or none at all. Ayubi writes that neo-fundamentalists 'invoke the text and quote the source, but in doing so they are highly selective and remarkably innovative. Political precedence is of practically no interest to them; neither is the main body of official jurisprudence, apart from a few exceptions such as Ibn Taimiya.

We tend to equate politics with state and government, and thus when we ask about politics in Islam, we are actually asking about states and governments. At that point, we gather the fairly small series of works, like al-Mawardi's, discussing the caliphate and the sultanate, which digress into discussions about intact testicles and other criteria for leadership, and end up with Abd al-Raziq's ultimate destruction of the whole thing, with his persuasive argument that the Prophet left no system of government and Muslim scholarship never actually addressed the entire issue of how people should be governed.

The moment we disengage 'politics' from 'state', an entirely new situation arises. The many Muslims who were appalled at Abd al-Raziq's position, and at all subsequent liberal positions on government, were right but they were inarticulate (the actual official rebuttal to his work seems to have zeroed in on his use of 'Bolshevik' in a long list of possible governmental systems which could be seen as Islamic). If we ask, 'What governmental system did the prophet leave his community?' the answer is 'the *fiqh* of the *Shariah*'. If the *Shariah* is the politics of the Islamic community, then its entire legal discussion—the *fiqh—is* the expression of politics in Islam. And whereas we have a few hundred pages on the subject matter of caliphate and sultanate, we have perhaps a million pages on the subject matter of *fiqh.*

So if we want to examine Muslim views on leadership, power, relations with the other, differences in communities, structures, and institutions, we would do well to pass over the official statements on caliphates and sultanates and turn instead to the actual arena of political contention and discussion—the *fiqh*. Taking the selection of a leader for the *salah* to be a microcosm of political leadership in Islam unleashes a torrent of positions, arguments, ideas, and terminologies which begin to reflect the historical realities of politics in Islam. At the same time, it offers Muslims an authentic discursive format which allows for an Islamic assessment of politics today. The basic need, then, is to re-evaluate this *fiqh*, both for historical understandings as well as for contemporary problems.

The Jurisprudence

What exactly is the *fiqh?* It is perhaps the most concrete and voluminous monument of Islamic civilization, one format of Muslim understanding *(tafaqquh,* f.q.h.) of the *Shariah*, the rules and regulations of Islam. Although the *fiqh* can become atrophied and reified, static and full of the weight of authority, it is traditionally the living expression of the Muslim community's commitment to realize the guidance of the *Shariah.* For the Muslim, 'right life' is a consequence of right action, and the criterion for right belief is right conduct. Hence the importance of *fiqh.*

The *fiqh* combines concern with both the spiritual and the quotidian, and serves as the arena for political-economic life, regulating activity in the markets, mediating disputes, and determining David Easton's authoritative allocation of value' as well as administering rites of passage (birth, puberty, marriage, death). Its tendency for accumulation means that it preserves centuries of deliberations, discussions, decisions, and debates.

Therefore, the extension of the *fiqh*, and specifically the *fiqh* of *salah*, to the macrocosm allows us to reconstruct a political discourse. The fiqh surrounding the issue of privacy and windows, for example, tells us something about the priorities of Muslim scholars. We can reconstruct that when someone created a window, the neighbour's right of privacy prevailed: the existence of filled-in windows in traditional Muslim cities is the physical sign of the following event. Someone opens up a window to improve his house, and a neighbour begins to worry that the window looks into his house, disturbing his privacy; they take their case to the *Qadi* (from the Arabic root q.d.y. as we saw, meaning to settle or resolve). The *Qadi* seeks *sulh*, harmony among disputants, and so he brings along a builder to the site. If indeed the window 'harms'—from the axiomatic *Hadith* `There shall be no harming, nor being harmed', *la darar wa là darar*—the window is boarded up. I suggest that in this process, the traditional politics for Muslim societies is seen.

In this process, obedience to the revelation is manifested within community relationships. This is why a break between spirituality, as expressed in obedience to the revelation, and politics, as depicted in interactions in communities, is inconceivable in traditional Islam. Let us look now explicitly at spirituality and politics.

Administrative Morality

In an imperfect world, it has been man's eternal yearning to create perfect institutions. The ideal of the Caliph-Imam as a vice regent of the Prophet, and the head of the newly formed community of believers, was one of such efforts. It was meant to create a political institution, which would be free from moral bankruptcies commonly associated with politics. The institution in its original spirit did not last for long time. Its failure could be attributed to the fact that the Arabs before the inception of Islam had very little experience in the political organization of a large community. Tribal organization to which they had been accustomed from times immemorial was not suited to the centralized governmental machinery of a territorially integrated state. But even a bigger cause could be that the moral ideals, which supported the Caliphal edifice were difficult to attain in practical politics. The result was the office of the Caliph became a subject of acute controversy, and Muslim scholars of various schools of thought wrote almost a library of literature on the subject. The hold of the ideal over the popular imagination was however such, that in spite of repeated setbacks, people's faith in it was never shaken. This glaring incompatibility between the ideal and the reality kept gnawing at the soul of the Muslim community. Muslims in many lands suffered from the crisis of the conscience throughout their history.

Recession of Ideals

After the Pious Caliphate, the ideal receded from the field of practical politics, and the Muslim state was modeled on the pre-Islamic political and administrative practices of the newly conquered non-Arab lands. Religious and moral aspects of the Caliphate were reduced merely to a superficial embellishment, and political and administrative behaviour of the Muslim rulers was completely denuded of the spirit which had motivated the immediate successors of the Prophet on the seat of Caliphate-Imamate. In every Muslim dynasty, with a few exceptions, majority of the rulers were corrupt and incompetent. Most of them were guilty of moral turpitude, and under their rule public life in a Muslim community was thoroughly contaminated with vices of despotism, oppression and ethical irregularities.

Widespread exploitation of the masses was a common feature, monarchs and state functionaries indulged in ethical lawlessness without any compunction of the soul. There were some great rulers, no doubt, who lived up to the great religious ideals of Islam, but such periods in Islamic history were always short-lived. The general tenor of the government and administration in a Muslim state remained far removed from the pristine values and beliefs of the doctrine. Shariah was the law of the land, but the functionaries who administered it were so utterly subservient to the will of the rulers that no independent judgement or interpretation could be expected of them. *Ulamas* (religious scholar) who in theory were the custodians of the high ethical standards in public life, were corrupted and majority of them lived as spineless minions of the state. The Caliphate was changed into sultanate, which was another name for military dictatorship. The society became a loose confederation of feudal estates, wherein the feudal lord and the tax collector were always on the rampage. So far as welfare of the masses was concerned, the spectacle of government and administration was depressing and disheartening.

It was in these circumstances that Muslim statesmen and scholars turned to "wisdom literature" and wrote some of the classics, which have enthralled students of Islamic studies for centuries. That most of the writers were statesmen and administrators should not surprise anybody, because the cream of talent in a Muslim kingdom always gravitated towards the court of the ruling prince. Attachment to the retinue of the ruler of the day was the highest certificate of merit that a scholar or a professional in any trade could have. Their primary responsibility was to ensure the welfare of the prince in all walks of life. The court was the nerve center of the realm and for an observant eye there was enough material to draw a comprehensive picture of the prevalent moral and political climate in the kingdom. Not all, but some of them used this accumulated knowledge to compile books on counsels for the kings, or general dissertations on the art of governing men. Some of these works have won permanent place in Islamic culture and literature. There is always something refreshing in them, although the expression might not be so absorbing and cultivated. According to Reuben Levy, these works constituted the Islamic version of the Eastern tradition of "wisdom literature manifested in such scriptural books as Job, and Proverbs, and frequently also in Sanskrit literature."

Wide Canvass : These statesmen-scholars used a very wide canvas to portray the dynamics of socio-political and religious issues with which they wrestled their mind and soul. Their approach was both diagnostic and prescriptive. They explored in depth the causes of the malaise, which had hit the Islamic civilization, and then in the light of precepts enunciated by the Quran, the Traditions of the Prophet, and the lives of great kings of the past, they drew certain guidelines which in their opinion could open vistas of rectitude for a world which had been so badly corrupted and demoralized.

To explain their point of view they also made extensive use of anecdotal literature of many cultures. Each one of these works is a harmonious blend of facts and fables, out of which the authors have drawn shrewd and insightful conclusions. To dispel the tedium and monotony of their ethical sermons, they also make a frequent use of Persian and Arabic verses which are relevant to a principle or situation being examined. Stylistically these books lack the elegance and beauty of a good prose work, but they are remarkable for the breadth of wisdom, and depth of human insight. But more than anything else they provide a lucid account of the religio-political conditions of the Muslim society in which their authors lived.

Moral and political failures of the rulers, and the inertia and helplessness of the people are depicted in a frank and candid manner. The range of topics discussed is also very wide. Justice, probity, duties and responsibilities of kingship, public morality, princely manners, statescraft, religious sects, political factions, dynastic squabbles, administrative failures, social foibles, economic problems, military matters, are all fit subjects for such works. Very often authors unroll detailed exposition of human nature, and relate it to the discrepancies and fallacies they notice in social life and political organization. They are also an immeasurable storehouse of wit and wisdom. Their pages glitter with social maxims, spicy half-truths, and brilliantly spun anecdotes. At appropriate occasion people's habits, customs and eccentricities are also uncovered with great perspicacity.

In short, everything which has bearing on human behaviour is examined in one form or another. In spite of the exuberance of their wisdom, however, note of caution is warranted for a student who approaches them for critical appreciation. Firstly it is to be understood that these works were not written by historians with a keen and anxious eye on the authenticity of fact. They were written by statesmen and administrators, out of their life long experiences, observations and hearsay, and very little care was expended to verify the historicity of the details. One has to be particularly careful about the anecdotes attributed to great personages of the past, because most of them seem to have been derived from untrustworthy sources. The integration of the materials also at various points is unscientific, and a reader tends to feel the strain of monotony as he goes through certain portions. But these deficiencies do not delete anything from the tremendous value they have for a student of government and administration in Islam, and the amount of pleasure they have afforded generation after generation of readers in many Muslim lands. They are free from rhetoric and abstruse constructions, commonly associated with Arabic or Persian prose. The beauty of diction is not there, but the style is simple and direct.

In this book nine classic books of the Islamic wisdom literature have been reviewed, but only those portions have been subjected to review which specifically pertain to the issues relating to ethical behaviour in politics and administration of a Muslim state. As mentioned earlier these works, though small, have an encyclopaedic range of subjects. But for our purpose only those elements have been skimmed which either portray the degeneration in which the Muslim society had sunk, or provide guidelines to understand the ethical contours of administrative machinery in a Muslim state.

Civility and Morality : There are two treatises with the same title written by two different scholars. The first was written by Ibn Adi (d 976 A.D.) a Syrian Christian scholar. Ibn Adi's book is basically a collection of ideas borrowed from the Greek ethical thought. There is nothing specific relating to rulers and administrators, but from his narrative an impressive list can be prepared to indicate virtues of good disposition and vices of corrupt behaviour.

The list is as follows:

I. Virtues of Good Dispositions

1. Continence
2. Self-control
3. Dignity
4. Mercy
5. Trustworthiness
6. Humility
7. Truth of speech
8. Generosity
9. Aspiration
10. Steadfastness in adversity
11. Frugality
12. Tranquility
13. Love
14. Fulfillment of promise
15. Keeping a secret
16. Cheerfulness
17. Good intention
18. Courage
19. Great ambition

II. Vices in Corrupt Behaviour

1.	Dissoluteness	11.	Secret hate
2.	Greediness	12.	Avarice
3.	Shabbiness	13.	Cowardice
4.	Levity	14.	Envy
5.	Awkwardness	15.	Treachery
6.	Excessive love	16.	Perfidy
7.	Pitilessness	17.	Divulging a secret
8.	Sternness	18.	Impatience in misfortune
9.	Falsehood	19.	Smallness of ambition
10.	Deceit	20.	Injustice

The virtues listed above according to Ibn Adi are essential for the perfection of human character. They are cultivated by rigorous training of mind and soul and depend to a large extent on the depth and comprehension, that one possesses about the world. Self-discipline and abstinence from harmful pleasures of life are advocated as instruments of moral rectitude.

The second treatise was written by Abu Ali Ahmad Ibn Muhammed ibn Maskawaiha (d. 1030 A.D.). The author of this treatise lived during the military dictatorship of the Buwaihid who had put Abbaside Caliphs under their forced protection. They captured Baghdad in 945 A.D. and remained the indisputable rulers of the Eastern Caliphate for 110 years. Ibn Maskawaiha was secretary of Al-Muhallabi, the Prime Minister of Muizz-al-Dawla the Buwaihid prince who conquered Baghdad. *Tahzih-al-Akhlaq* (The Correction of Disposition) is considered to be an outstanding work on the philosophy of ethics in Islam. The author believed that human conduct is built by restraint, courage and judiciousness. The fruit of righteousness stems out of integrity.In other words, integrity connotes translation of worthiness, truth, and goodness into human action. They constitute a moral conquest over falsehood and evil. At another place Ibn Maskawaiha has listed four fundamental qualities which are vital for higher ethical standards and has contrasted them with four evils which constitute the bane of morality.

(i)	wisdom	——	ignorance
(ii)	purity	——	greed
(iii)	courage	——	cowardice
(iv)	righteousness	——	violence

Wisdom, a Virtue : Wisdom is a virtue of human soul by which men comprehend the existing things in the light of the words of God. It is a quality by which distinction is made between desirable and undesirable actions. Purity is an instrument of self-discipline. It is a thoughtful use of human desires and soundness of judgment. Righteousness is a sense of justice by which excesses and deficiencies are eliminated and a fair course of action is adopted. Anger, conceit, vanity, jesting, boastfulness, perfidy, unfairness, laying up treasures, are counted among the diseases of the human soul. Courage and judiciousness are advocated as antidotes to these evils. He pleads for restraint on desires and appetites. Courage is not merely a weapon to defend one's body and material possession, it is also a strength of mind by which evil propensities of self have to be conquered. Judiciousness stems out of wisdom cultivated through study and reflection.

It is therefore incumbent upon all right-thinking people and seekers of truth and righteousness to search for knowledge in all directions. A person who has decided to discipline his soul, and wishes to avoid risks of moral defilement must, according to Ibn Maskawaiha, set before himself the following objectives :-

1. He had striven to maintain what we would call personal integrity. This he defined as the preference (ithar) for what is worthy (al-haqq) over what is futile in beliefs; for what is true (al-sidq) over what is false in statements; and for what is good (al-khair) over what is evil (al-sharr) in actions.
2. He had emphasized the continuous struggle that he needed to keep up between his essential manhood (al-mar) and his animal nature.
3. He had felt the importance of adhering to the Law (al-Shariah) and of recognizing the necessity of its functions.
4. He had endeavoured to remember agreements and to fulfill them, particularly any agreement that he had made with Allah.
5. He had shown little confidence in men, and this he accomplished by avoiding familiarity with them.
6. He had cultivated the love of the beautiful for its own sake and for no other reason.
7. He had appreciated the value of silence in times of agitation, until reason would direct him.
8. He had striven to continue any state of mind that was beneficial until it would become a habit.

9. He had approved taking the initiative in things that were creditable.
10. He had found that whole-hearted sympathy was necessary in order to work on any important undertaking without distraction.
11. He had felt that the fear of death and of poverty could be counteracted by doing what was still possible and by not being indolent.
12. He had casted out from his mind such anxieties as were aroused by sayings of the base, and he had tried to suppress his desire at night to plan something against them.
13. He had come to realize that he must be inured to wealth or to poverty, and to liberality or to contempt.
14. He had tried to remember times of sickness when he was in health, and occasions of joy and pleasure when anger was apt to arise, so that there might be less injustice and transgression.
15. He had rejoiced in times of trust, appreciating the goodness of hope and confidence in Allah, turning his whole heart to him.

He further points out that greatest happiness of man depends on the manifestation of the innate excellencies of the human soul. The happiness of one man is linked with the happiness of the rest. Mutual assistance in other words is the essence of social health and stability. In pursuit of happiness, each individual should be a torch-bearer for the perfection of others. It is for this reason that Ibn Maskawiha points out that virtue cannot be practiced in isolation. Asceticism, in his opinion is wrong and inimical to individual and social happiness. In essence ethics is an instrument of self-discipline and a method for character-building.

Books for Counselling:

Qabusnamh (Book of Qabus) or Andarz-nama (Book of Counsel)

It was composed by Kay Kaus ibn Iskandar ibn Qabus in 375/1082 A.D. The author was the Ziyarid ruler of Tabristan. He was endowed with profound wisdom and literary attainments which are amply manifested in the said treatise. At the age of sixty-three Kay Kaus thought to capture in book form his life-long experiences as a ruler and administrator for the guidance of his son Gilanshah. The purpose was to outline eventualities which are likely to befall rulers of men, and to suggest ways and means to tide over difficulties which so often crop up due to the chronic uncertainty of political conditions. John Alden Williams has given the following sketch of the purpose with which Kay Kaus decided to write his experiences in the form of a book of counsel for the rulers.

In the advice of Kay Kaus ibn Iskandar the Ziyari ruler of a little kingdom in the Caspian provinces of Persia, to his son, Gilanshah, we have a valuable insight into Islamic kingship as it appeared to a Muslim king in the eleventh century. Kay Kaus is a professional member of the ruling class, and an affectionate father, who wishes to pass his knowledge to his sons. He is very conscious that even if a king cannot have lordly morals, he must appear to have them. He knows that a king must sometimes tell lies and kill, but it is not expedient to get a name for it. Virtue, or its appearance, is useful; it is one of the means by which a king in his civilization must try to secure his power.

Kay Kaus had the ability to wield sword and pen with equal dexterity. The book has enjoyed great popularity in the annals of Persian literature. Wit, wisdom, frankness, conviction, directness of expression, and richness of experience constitute the highlights of the work.

The *Qabus-nama* consists of forty-four chapters and a preface. The contents of the book provide ample evidence that the royal author was deeply concerned about the growing malpractices in the administration of the country. The first thirty-four chapters are related to the general principles of moral life. They range from obedience to God to the uses of astrology, mathematics, and poetic arts. It is in the later chapters that Kay Kaus turns his attention to the affairs of kingship and administration. Chapter thirty seven deals with services of the kings. Thirty eight is on the qualities of the courtier, the thirty ninth deals with the secretaries of the state and secretarial art; the fortieth chapter is on the qualities of the wazir ; the forty first on the duties and responsibilities of generals; the forty second on the qualifications and duties of the king; forty third deals with farmers and agriculture, and forty fourth discusses generosity. The pervading spirit of all his analyses is emphasis on the cultivation of virtues and excellencies which have been preached by Islam, Kay Kaus is of the opinion that rational and practical side of religion should be a vital element in understanding Islam. Browne remarks :-

> *"The author's ideas display a curious mixture of craft and simplicity, of scepticism and piety. Thus he dwells on the ethical, as apart from the spiritual value of prayer, fasting, and other religious exercises as means to cleanliness, humility, and temperance; and advocates conformity with the laws of Islam, because there is no stronger bond than the Commonwealth of Islam."*

The whole of the work is replete with worldly wisdom some of which at least has great relevance even to our own times. The book throws a flood of light on the state of affairs in the Muslim civilization as it existed during the Middle Ages. It advocates lofty ethical principles, which would be above greed and expediency. He is convinced that human society cannot exist without some kind of governmental organization, because man's bewildering propensities for evil need an effective machinery of control. "Now man has need of government and regulation; without direction he is brutal (uncivilized)." Government in turn depends upon authority, the way it is organized, the manner in which it is used in decision-making, and the image which people hold about it. Kay Kaus has laid down certain principles which must be strictly adhered to if authority has to make any impact on affairs of men. A person making authoritative decisions should "be neither harsh, nor sharp tempered, nor devoid of clemency (yet be not so entirely yielding as to be swallowed upon on account of your softness) and never be so morose that you are not to be won over."

Worldly Wisdom : Browne has summarized the worldly wisdom of *Qabus-nama* in these words:-

> *His worldly maxims are shrewd, and wonderfully modern at times. He expatiates on the advantages of a smooth tongue, bids his son learn wisdom from fools, and cautions him against over-modesty, "for," says he 'many men fail of their objects through bashfulness.' His remarks on truthfulness are delightful. But do thou, O son, says he, 'be specious, but not a liar: make thyself famous as a speaker of truth, so that if at some time thou shoudst tell a lie, men may accept it as true from thee.' He also cautions his son against making statements which, though true, are likely to be disbelieved, and cannot be easily proved; for, says he, 'why should one make a statement, even if it be true, which it needs four months and the testimony of two hundred respectable witnesses to prove?*

He is also of the opinion that in adopting a particular course of action, a man on the seat of authority should not act arbitrarily. Even with the maximum of learning and knowledge, it is always desirable to consult someone. Over-confidence in one's own abilities and judgment is symptomatic of arrogance, a quality quite unbecoming of those who have been entrusted with authority to preside over the destiny of human organizations. He says:-

Therefore, be not puffed up with your own learning, however learned you may be. And if any task befalls you, even if you have the capacity to perform it, do not rely entirely on your own judgment, for he who relies entirely on his own judgment ever regrets it. Never be ashamed of asking advice, consulting old men of understanding and well-disposed friends. Even Muhammad despite his wisdom and his prophethood, after becoming the examplifier and agent of God's work was told by him 'Consult them in the matter, O Muhammad' (Quran 3, V, 153).

He further adds that it does not behoove a man in authority to be "any degree careless over the duties of justice and governmental control and from treating overlightly anything essential to these matters." One must also be watchful that offices are not bestowed on "impecunious or impoverished men," and he compares such appointments to a dry canal which will not water fields and gardens until it is saturated with moisture. Meaning that a poverty-stricken man, if installed to a position of power, is most susceptible to dishonest dealings. Probably knowing that such a rule cannot be meticulously followed, Kai Kaus mentions that authority should be maintained with firmness and spiteful disregard of it, should not be tolerated.

Those who willfully disobey legitimate commands deserve exemplary punishment. But in order to avoid an ugly situation, those who wield authority have certain professional and ethical obligations. Their commands should be precise, clear and decisive. Their tone and intention should be firm and unambiguous. Their reputation should be such that people will not hesitate to repose confidence in their decision. Men of authority are custodians of the realm and it would be ridiculous to have someone take custody of the custodians or to have a guard for the guardians. He says :-

"The orders, then, of both kings and viziers must be unequivocal and their commands decisive, if their authority is to remain firmly established and their interest to prosper. Next, drink no intoxicant liquor, out of such drinking there arise carelessness, laxity and injustice Allah protect us from a wine-bibling vizier and wanton governor ! If it is the king who indulges in wine, decay soon pervades the realm. Therefore keep a watch on yourself and conform to what I have told you ; the vizier is the custodian of realm and it would be a very ugly matter if the custodian should need another to have a custody of him."

Kai Kaus, in order to substantiate his contention narrates an anecdote, relating to a confrontation between an old woman and King Masud of Ghazni. The woman had lodged a complaint against a governor, who had refused to pay heed to the King's letter, which the woman had taken to him. Thc King decided to write a second letter, but the woman refused to carry it saying that such a letter had already been taken to the governor which had failed to redress her grievance. The King said "What am I to do?" The woman replied, "Your course of action here is simple. Maintain your authority in such a fashion that your instructions will be acted upon or else resign your authority and let another possess it leaving you to occupy yourself with your pleasures. Thus mankind will cease to be held fettered in the miseries of tyranny." In other words, an ineffectual authority is a gateway to tyranny, and a state where authority fails to get compliance forfeits its right to exist. Therefore authority requires strict control and vigilance from one who holds it. In other words an authority which is not used effectively is worse than anarchy because under cover of law officers will indulge in illegal extortions and the time would come when the country would be depopulated. An oppressive authority leads to decay and desolation and it is therefore extremely inexpedient to show any negligence in this matter.

Political Authority : After having established the necessity of political and administrative authority, our author goes on to elucidate ethical equipment of those who govern men. These ethical principles are spread over all the forty four chapters of the book. They are more or less the ones which have universally been applauded as pertinent guidelines for righteous action. In his opinion wisdom and virtue should be in inseparable partnership in life. If a person is wise, but the moral side of his character is tainted, he cannot be a success in life. He says :

> *If you have wisdom, therefore acquire virtue for wisdom without virtue is like a man without clothes or a person without a face or a body without a soul. Indeed there is a proverb to the effect that 'virtue is the visage of the mind.'*

The world is not meant for fools although they are in abundance, but nor are the wise of any good if their wisdom is denuded of ethical lustre and dignity. Kai Kaus gives primacy to wisdom and virtue, because both are qualities, which are acquired and not inherited. He quotes an Arabic proverb which says, "Honour lies in the mind and in acquired worth, not in origin and noble birth," and then mentions Socrates, who in his opinion, once said "that there is no treasure better than virtue; no honour more glorious than knowledge, no ornament more beautiful than modesty and no enemy worse than an evil disposition." An accomplished person is judged by his frank and fair disposition. Duplicity destroys trust, and if trust is gone other qualities can be of no avail. Profession, must synchronize with action. Any incongruity between the two can have a damaging effect on individual's integrity. Kai Kaus says :-

> *"Once having made a profession of your beneficence, however, let not your actions contradict it. Do not say one thing with your tongue and harbor a contrary thought in your heart, lest you reveal yourself to be one who displays wheat but sells barley."*

He maintains that it is a great virtue to be generous and benevolent, and believes that malice is a bane of the human soul, and it leads to spiritual impoverishment and social humiliation. He is however not very sure about modesty which according to an Arabic saying is bracketed with faith. He believes that modesty may be good, but "yet it may frequently happen that bashfulness is a misfortune to men. Do not therefore be so shamefaced as to cause failure or injury to your own interests. There are many occasions when boldness must be exercised to ensure that your purposes may be achieved."

It is through speech that most of the qualities of human character are manifested for the rest of the world. It behooves, therefore of those who make public policies and issue statements to be watchful of what they say. Language helps understanding, facilitates communication, and is the one and only effective carrier of information. Wrong choice of words can infuriate another person, inflict unnecessary humiliation, and damage human relations. Command over words is a powerful weapon, but one ought to be discrete in their use. Kai Kaus has divided words and their uses into the following four categories: those neither to be understood nor uttered, those to be both understood and uttered, those to be understood though not uttered. Those which are neither to be uttered nor understood are they that contain some peril to the faith.

Noblest Category : The noblest category from the point of view of our author is the one "which contains those words which can be both understood and uttered." It is a matter of common knowledge that loose or sharp-tongued persons could be a source of great social and organizational tensions. They can breed resentment, and considerable apprehension and dissatisfaction both for superordinates and subordinates. Therefore one who is discrete in the choice of words is ethically fortified against many evils. Words should not be used for uttering falsehood, because lying according to our author "is a form of madness." Another quality which can morally strengthen a decision-maker is to abstain from action unless the matter has been subjected to reflection and deliberation. Haste breeds waste—wastage of time, wastage of energies and wastage of resources. For some ignorant persons haste is synonymous with efficiency. This in reality is a sign of imprudence and irrationality. Many ills have befallen administrators and men of authority, who pronounced their judgements in haste. More often than not it can lead to injustice and tyranny. Anything which is done in a hurry carries an element of uncertainty; it reduces precision and determination which give authority in a state its effectiveness. He says :-

"Both in speech and action, be weighty and deliberate."

According to Kai-Kaus, quarrelsome and contentious persons are also ethically weak. They are mostly stubborn and irreconcilable in their attitudes. No group or organization can tolerate such members for a long time. It is extremely unbecoming of a man of authority shouldering vast responsibilities for decision-making to quarrel frequently. In this way he will not only lose respect, but become a source of many petty squabbles which lead to stress and tension. Quarrelsomeness very often stems from arrogance, which as all accounts agree, is a reprehensible quality from any ethical standard. He has depicted the evil consequences of such an attitude as follows : quarrelling is not indulged in by men of dignity, but rather by women and children. If a quarrel should on any occasion break out between you and another, do not utter all that you could say, but so conduct your quarrel as to leave a loophole for reconciliation.

Don't be completely irreconcilable and stubborn; considering stubbornness and irreconcilability as the characteristics of persons of little worth. Realize that humility is the best of qualities, one of God's blessing which no one envies. Do not with every word you address to others say 'O man'; this repetition of 'O Man without reason detracts from a person's dignity as a man, Extravagance and excess have also been listed as evils which ruin the moral fiber of human beings.

According to Kai Kaus, extravagance is the cause of poverty and all misguided persons, who tread this path have suffered in the long run. Anybody indulging in it is an enemy of his own interests. He uses the term with its widest connotations. Extravagance in his opinion does not merely mean indiscrete spending and thoughtless disbursement of funds. Excess in all spheres—eating, drinking, speaking and working—is bad because it makes one deviate from the path of moderation and rectitude. In his opinion one who indulges in excess "harms the spirit and deadens the living mind." He says :-

> *"You observe that the life of a lamp is generated by oil; if you pour oil into the lamp without measure and limit, so that it overflows the spout of the container and passes beyond the tip of the wick, it immediately extinguishes the lamp. Oil itself then becomes the cause of lamp's extinction, although had it been present in moderate quantity it would have been the means of keeping it alight once there was an excess of it, it became the means of lamp's extinction.*

Man in charge of public affairs is supposed to have a good reputation. According to our author ill-repute begets shame, disgust and frustration. One should not be swearer of oath because people tend to lose faith in a person, who takes oath frequently. Riches and power cannot safeguard an incumbent of high office from evils of bad reputation. The best course is to create an image of trustworthiness because all right-thinking people shun the company of a liar. One should abstain from misleading others, and also be watchful that he himself is not misled. A person who has acquired this characteristic is certainly going to win the trust and confidence of those around him. A good reputation, particularly for trustworthiness is the Philosopher's Stone, which would make an individual an embodiment of sterling qualities. Unbridled appetites also spoil reputation.

Generosity of Mind : Generosity of mind is a quality, which mitigates the rigidities of law. It is true that without law political systems and administrative organizations cannot exist. But obsessively legalistic views could also be extremely detrimental to peace and harmony in the affairs of men. One should be an administrator of law and not its captive, and in administering rules, according to Kai-Kaus, the most dignified thing is not to punish people for trivial mistakes, and if a petitioner comes the best course would be to forgive him. If at all a person is to be punished and there is no escape from it, the penalty should be strictly in proportion to the gravity of the offense, and if possible may be a little less than what is entailed by law. Clemency and mercy are virtues of high merit. An officer who is not generous in his attitude creates tension and ill-feelings among persons subjected to his jurisdiction. A person who holds money higher than honour is doomed to ignominy. Avarice and insatiable lust for wealth are enemies of honourable conduct, and one who indulges in dishonourable deeds brings destruction on those who are held in esteem and honour.

It is a common characteristic of men working in governmental hierarchies, or may be it is a common feature of human endeavors in all avenues of life, that they want to have accelerated promotions. They want to attain highest rank overnight, and impatience is writ large over all their activities. Subordination is galling to them, and by swiftest means they want to get the highest position available. Kai Kaus thinks it is unethical and he says :

> *"Until you have borne the drudgery of subordinate position, you will never attain to the comforts of high ranks."*

There is considerable truth in the remarks of our author because many ills in human organizations stem from ambivalent behaviour of overambitious persons. They make life for others irksome, have no peace and equanimity in their own lives, and very often intrigues and frictions which lead to the disenchantment of the participants can easily be attributed to them.

In Chapter VIII, Kai Kaus has listed forty two counsels which Nushirwan (the just) gave to his son. Some of those which are relevant for men in authority and who hold in custody the welfare of the people can be listed as follows :-

1. The great man who looks upon himself as small is the great man of the age.
2. There is no meaner person in the world than he to whom appeal is made for help and though able to grant it refuses.
3. If you desire to remain free of unhappiness be not envious.
4. If you desire to command men's respect then exercise justice.
5. If you want not to be disillusioned, do not regard an undone task as having been done.
6. If you do not wish to be stricken with shame do not remove what you have not yourself deposited; and if you desire not to be mocked behind your back, respect them that are subordinate to you.
7. If you desire to be included in the numbers of honourable men, give covetousness no place in your heart.
8. If you desire to be a man of justice be generous as far as lies in your power towards them that are subordinate to you; and if you desire your heart never to be stricken a blow which no remedy can heal, never engage in agreement with fools.
9. If you wish to retain men's esteem, learn how to esteem other men.
10. If you wish for effectiveness in your tongue then restrain the rapacity of your hand.

The *Qabus-nama* was written at a time when the political authority of the Abbaside Caliphate had almost been extinguished. The Commanders of the faithful still wielded a supranational spiritual authority, but it was facing growing challenges from new sects and heretical cults. The author makes a strong and stirring advocacy of Sunni Islam. Therefore there are a wide ranging discussions on theological matters which point out that a ruler in order to cultivate wisdom must follow the word of God meticulously. He made a fervent plea for effective governmental authority, but at the same time pointed out that it could only be established if the people living under its jurisdiction were happy and prosperous. Extortion and recklessness in his opinion perpetuate tyranny, seal the wellspring of justice and would ultimately spell ruin and desolation for the kingdom. Authority should not be an intoxicant, and rulers of men should be equipped with six qualities, "awesomeness, justice, generosity, respect for law, gravity and truthfulness" The four basic factors which maintain peace, order and stability in a kingdom, according to Kai Kaus are authority, army, finance, and prosperity, and they are all interdependent.

Tradition Politics

Siyasat-nama

Nizam-al-Mulk (d. 685/1090), the author of this treatise was Prime Minister for more than thirty years of two Seljuq monarchs, Alp Arslan (d, A.D.-1072) and Malikshah (d. A.D.-1092). This was a period of acute ideological stress and political lawlessness in the Muslim world. In this stormy climate the Seljuqs had been able to establish a stable kingdom by conquering Khwarizm, Tabaristan and Persian Iraq. Their rule touched the highest watermark of economic prosperity, political stability, and intellectual development during the reign of Nizam-al-Mulk. He enjoyed unlimited power and through his prudence, sagacity and diplomacy was able to maintain peace and tranquility in the kingdom. His role as a statesman and administrator in one of the most critical periods of Islamic history has been summed up as follows :-

> *"As a great Iranian Vizir he conspicuously exemplifies the chief minister's role of mediator between a despot, in this instance, an alien Turk and his Persian subjects—he enhanced the dignity and prestige of the Seljuqs by inculcating canons of royal behaviour and etiquette, and he tempered military harshness with lessons in judicious clemency and conciliation. He built up Seljuq powers with the Sultan as the keystone in an integrated administration."*

Hitti calls him "one of the ornaments of the political history of Islam. His political and administrative achievements were great, no doubt, but in Islamic history his reputation primarily rests' on scholarship and his generous patronage of art and letters. He was particularly anxious to encourage scholars and theologians, for whom he established *madrasas* (Institutes of Studies) in all the major cities of the kingdom. Nizamiyah colleges, named after him were built in Nishapur and Baghdad between 1065-67.

At these institutions instruction was imparted by leading intellectual and religious luminaries of the day. Al-Ghazzali, one of the greatest theological thinkers of Islam, taught at both the academies. The Nizamiyah college in Baghdad was a rendezvous for famous preachers; for nearly two centuries, and disappeared only when it was merged in a new college founded by Caliph Mustansir (A.D. 1226-62). According to Goldziher the foundation of Nizamiyah college was an "epoch-making advance" in the development of higher learning in Islam. Nizam-al-Mulk was not only a patron of scholars, he was himself endowed with scholarly qualities of very high order which have earned for his *Siyasat-nama* a place of eminence among the great prose works of Persian literature. E. G. Browne has summed up the significance of this book in the following words:-

> *The* Siyasat-nama *is, in my opinion, one of the most valuable and interesting prose works which exist in Persia, both because of the quantity of historical anecdotes which it contains, and because it embodies the views on government of one of the greatest Prime Ministers whom the East has produced—a Minister whose strength and wisdom is no way better proved than by the chaos and internecine strife which succeeded his death."*

The work was written at the behest of Malikshah. It is divided into fifty chapters, thirty nine of which were completed at the time of its original submission to the king, but later eleven more chapters were added on subjects relating to government and religious controversies, which were threatening the unity and solidarity of Islam. The declining years of the great statesmen when he made up his mind to revise and enlarge his work were beclouded with gloom and distress. He had become a victim of court and *harem* intrigues, which ultimately cost him his life. John Alden Williams has depicted the last years of the aged and shaken Prime Minister in the following words:-

> *About 1091 the aged minister began to write again, and now his words had an urgent note. Times had changed. Much of his earlier advice had not been heeded, and Malikshah's favourite wife was his enemy. The Sultan was engaged in a quarrel with the Caliph, and had also come under the influence of adventurers and heretics. The elder statesman outlined the dangers that particularly threatened the Seljuq empire, and the states like it. Before the addition to his book could be presented to Malikshah, however, Nizam-al-Mulk was dismissed from office. In A.H. 485/A.D. 1092 he was murdered by Ismaili assassins in circumstances suggesting that they may have been sent with the knowledge of the Sultan or his queen.*

The author's main purpose was to write a basic source book on the art of governing men. It was an effort to examine the political and administrative dimensions of a despotic form of government, a system which was extremely susceptible to abuse of authority and corruption.

Rich Scholarship

Muslim scholarship has always been very rich in religious literature and history. Scholars have always found in religion and history an immeasurable reservoir of wisdom and human experience. Religion was the revealed word of God, while history was a resplendent stockroom of events which if intelligently and objectively analyzed could be a tremendous source of guidance and enlightenment. Nizam-al-Mulk's knowledge of both these sources was deep and profound and in collecting the substance of *Siyasat-nama*, he relied heavily upon them. At the conclusion of his work he has made the following remark:-

> *So ends this book of the Rules for Kings. Your humble servant was previously commanded to compile a volume on this subject, and he carried out the command. At the time he composed thirty nine chapters extempore, and submitted them to the Lofty Throne (may Allah exalt it.) They were found acceptable. However, that was merely an epitome. Later he expounded at his leisure, and wrote chapters and related stories on a variety of subjects, expounding everything in the clearest and simplest language. Let him not listen to what others say, but read this book constantly; he will never be wearied by reading this book, for it contains advice, wisdom, proverbs,*

> *interpretation of the Quran, tradition of the Prophet (upon him be peace; stories of prophets, memoirs of saints, and tales of just kings, it tells of the lives of the departed and deeds of the living.*

The instrument of instructions from the king which commanded the author to compile this work pointed out that the administration of the kingdom was decaying, and that he should find out reasons for that sorry state of affairs, and search out remedies against evils which had destroyed peace and harmony in the working of the government.

The purpose of commissioning the seasoned statesman to write such a treatise was that out of his long administrative experience and knowledge of history and religion he should produce a manual, which would ensure stability in politics and honesty in administration. In short, the book was to be a digest of political wisdom and knowledge about administration so that decision-makers in both fields could make ethical and rational judgments. As he proceeded with his compilation, Nizam-al-Mulk widened the scope of his assignment, and made frequent comments on the state of affairs of Muslim societies in his own time. Whenever opportunity arose he unhesitatingly uncovered the evils of contemporary government and administration.

There is, however, a basic deficiency in the book that it only makes comments, but does not give any clue about the actual machinery of the government. The book also gives an impression of having been written in a hurry. As the author himself confesses, the first thirty nine chapters were written extempore, as such, in spite of his experience, wisdom and breadth of comprehension, which are abundantly reflected in every chapter, they lack the depth and authenticity of historical research. Pieces of advice and anecdotes relating to noble qualities of the past rulers have not been coherently organized. The scope of the book, however, is fairly wide.

The writer has collected large numbers of maxims on good government, and discusses in reasonable detail duties and responsibilities of state functionaries, both at the center and in the field. In analyzing various issues he draws extensively on the storehouse of experiences, which he had accumulated during thirty years of service as a leading administrator of the Muslim world. In his opinion a Muslim ruler should be physically handsome, his character good and untainted, courage undiminished, justice perineal, and warlike qualities unquestioned. Nizam-al-Mulk's advocacy of absolute monarchical rule is understandable, because that was the accepted ideology of the day, but he repeatedly insists that all authority should be exercised within the boundaries of Shariah (religion). He firmly believes that religion is a powerful antidote against those corrupting elements which are rooted in human nature.

Since the rule in most cases are not conversant with religious law, he insists that while making public policies they should show special deference to the opinions of the doctors of law. Companionship of the learned assures sound judgment and rulers can fulfil their religious, moral and temporal obligations effectively. He says:-

> *It is incumbent upon the king to inquire into religious matters, to be acquainted with the divine precepts and prohibitions and put them into practice, and to obey the commands of God (be he exalted); it is his duty to respect doctors of religion and pay their salaries out of the treasury, and he should honour pious and abstentious men. Furthermore, it is fitting that once or twice a week he should invite religious elders to his presence and hear from them the commands of the Truth, he should listen for the interpretations of the Quran and traditions of the Prophet (may Allah pray for him and give him peace) and he should hear stories about just kings and tales of the Prophets (upon them be peace). During that time he should free his mind from worldly cares and give his ears and attention to them . . . then the way of prudence and rectitude in both spiritual and temporal affairs will be opened to him.*

Knowledge of Religion

Knowledge of religion has always been considered an essential quality for rulers in Islam. It is deemed to be a remedy against vanity, jealousy and numerous other kinds of evil. It insures equity, probity, and justice. Nizam-al-Mulk had to insist more on religion because he lived during one of the most critical periods of the religious history of Islam. All kinds of heretical doctrines were trying to sap the original simplicity and purity of Islam. In *Siyasat-nama* he has devoted six chapters to these heretical doctrines.

He examines their origin, principles, practices, and undesirable consequences, which result from them in the body politic. He had deep-seated hatred for Ismailes, and Batnis, and bitterly opposed the employment of Jews, Christians, and Zoroastrians in government service. He argues, representatives of these communities, because of their affluence formed a great source of corruption in the realm. In his opinion, since the non-Muslim minorities were rich, they could easily buy public offices. Probably the chain of his famous Nizamiya colleges in the kingdom was meant to remedy this defect. Graduates of these institutions were religious scholars, but they were primarily trained to fill administrative positions in the government. They were expected to keep the people on the "Straight Path" Vladimir Minorsky says:-

In the *Siyasat-nama* of Nizam-al-Mulk we have a document of first importance setting forth the program which combined the force of the Turks with the administrative methods of the Sassanids and the great Abbasid Caliphs. The system of spies, of messengers, and of troops skilfully assorted from different elements was harmonized with the founding of the religious colleges, those nurseries of administrators who were to watch over the rectitude of the path followed by their flocks.

He was convinced that if the rulers and officials do not conform to the same religion, administration suffers from chronic distrust and unrest.

Heavy Responsibility

Nizam-al-Mulk feels that governing of men is a very heavy responsibility ; particularly personal rule of despotic kings entails special obligation. Any ruler who has usurped despotic powers must exercise constant vigilance over the conduct of his functionaries otherwise the state would be under permanent threat of dissolution. Rulers must have proper machinery to collect information about the activities of public officials and they should have the courage and honesty to punish them for all omissions and abuse of authority. He recommends an effective network of central intelligence, which would keep a watch over the actions and affairs of all senior officers. He relates a story of Nushirwan (The Just) the pre-Islamic Iranian king, who attributed financial and moral degeneration of his kingdom to the negligence of his father who had failed to keep himself well-informed about the shameless embezzlements of his civil servants. A king should appoint informers in every part of the country, because that is the only way to safeguard people against oppression. Information received from such sources should reach the king directly.

The author is fully aware of the delicate nature of such spying and reporting on public officials and would therefore advise the rulers that agents of central intelligence should be persons of unimpeachable integrity and honesty so that what they report is not subject to any suspicion. An arrangement of this kind would enable the king "to know every event that takes place and will be able to give his orders as appropriate, meeting out unexpected reward, punishment or commendation to the persons concerned." Nizam-al-Mulk is of the opinion however, that information culled out of the secret reports of the informants should be anxiously examined, before any decision is based on it. Every report needs to be dissected with patience and understood with care. The Quran says : "O you who believe, if a wicked man brings you tidings, verify it lest you smite some people in ignorance and then repent of what you did.'

After giving the above citation from the Holy Book, Nizam-al-Mulk says:-

> *"So one should not be precipitate for precipitancy brings regret, and regret is of no avail. . . . Elders of religion have said, 'Haste is from Satan, deliberation is from the Merciful. Works undone can be done, but that which is done cannot be retrieved."*

Like other writers on ethics and administration, Nizam-al-Mulk has emphasized justice, honesty, accessibility to complainants and generosity of mind as the best moral equipment for rulers of men. Justice in his opinion is the corner-stone of political and administrative stability. Injustice wrecks state and ruins peace and prosperity of the people. He deems that it is the personal responsibility of the head of the government to see that the legal institutions are strong and not discriminatory in the administration of justice. Law should not make any distinction between high and low, and the entire official world should give ungrudging support to judges in their daily work. If anything contrary to this principle happens it is symptomatic of decadence. He says :-

Dignity of Judiciary

All other officers must strengthen the hand of the judge and uphold the dignity of the courts. If anyone makes excesses and fails to appear in court, however exalted he may be, he must be forcibly compelled to be present. For in the time of The Companions of the Prophet (upon him be peace and blessings) justice was dispensed in person and not delegated to anyone else, so that there could be no scope for injustice. In every age from the time of Adam (peace be upon him) until now, in every nation and every country men have practiced equity, justice and striven after righteousness, and when this has been so, dynasties have endured the generations.

Justice bridles the evil intentions of the oppressors, and protects and preserves the rights of the oppressed. Governments are judged by the means they adopt to eradicate evildoers and the remedies they provide to victims of injustice. He believes that "sound judgment is a better thing to have than a powerful army."

Honesty is universally recognized as a vital requirement for good, effective and efficient administration. Corruption has been a cause of ruin of many establishments. Nizam-al-Mulk has not made a scientific or psychological inquiry into its causes, but he emphatically points out that unchecked corruption is a sign of political ailment. In a climate of distrust; effective implementation of public policy is simply impossible. Nizam-al-Mulk has suggested special watchfulness on tax collectors, who in his opinion are the biggest source of corruption. Every tax collector who is in charge of a revenue district should be given strict instructions not to harass the peasantry by untimely demands and additional extortions.

In his dealings with the public he should be guided by civility and courtesy. If a tax collector has taken a bribe, the best course would be to reclaim the money from him, deprive him of his office and ban all future government employments to him. In view of the universality of corruption, he recommends exemplary punishment for the culprits. He narrates the story of an officer who was beheaded by King Altiginm because he took some hay and a chicken from a peasant. Honesty among senior officers is of particular significance because juniors are very likely to be influenced by their behavior. He points out that if an officer of the rank of wazir is corrupt, the other officials will behave likewise or may be worse.

Accessibility of common people to the chambers of administrative decision-making to complain against wrongs suffered at the hand of public servants has been acclaimed as one of the cardinal characteristics of Islamic code of ethics for administrators. It is a virtue which insures rectitude in administration, and generates popular trust and confidence in government. Even the most despotic governments require the cooperation of the people, but if the latter do not have the right to complain against administrative decisions, no cooperation will be forthcoming. It is for this reason that Nizam-al-Mulk at several places in his treatise has warned the rulers against inaccessibility of government functionaries to aggrieved persons. He says:-

> *"It is absolutely necessary that on two days in the week the king should sit for the redress of wrongs, to extract recompense from the oppressor, to give justice and to*

listen to the words of the subjects with his own ears, without any intermediary. ... I have read in the books of the ancients the most of the non-Arab (Persian) kings used to put up a high platform and sit up there on horseback so that they could see all the complainants gathered about, and they would redress the grievances of everyone. The reason for this was that where the king sits in a place protected by gates, locks, vestibules and screens, self-interested and oppressive persons can keep people back and not let them go before the King."

He cites the example of Nushirwan, who, in order to save the people from palace guards and other officers had hung a chain with bells, which any complainant could pull and seek redress of grievances. If the people have no access to the rulers, the only other alternative under despotic rule for people to undo wrongs is to strive through conspiracies and revolts. Generosity and large-heartedness are also advocated as essential characteristics for those who wield political or administrative authority in a state. They eliminate fear from the mind of a common man and enable him to give maximum compliance and loyalty to the state.

Significant Features

Nizam-al-Mulk has listed certain other features of good administration, which in his opinion, ensure peace and stability in a kingdom. He feels that collectors and other field officers should be transferred every two or three years. He does not want officers to be entrenched at one place for a long time, because the longer they stay at one place, greater the chances of their becoming a source of tyranny and maladministration.

They are likely to become corrupt and indifferent to the interest of the masses. He further recommends that the King should not appoint his personal friends as officials of the state, nor should the officers be included in the circle of his intimate friends. By virtue of their closeness and friendship with the ruler, they become arrogant and practice oppression and high-handedness. He also believes that the best way to avoid abuse of administrative authority is to introduce participative approach in decision-making. Holding consultations on affairs is a sign of sound judgment, high intelligence, and foresight. Every person has some knowledge and in every branch of knowledge one knows more and others less. One may have knowledge and never have put it into practice or tested it. Everybody in the world agrees that there has never been any mortal wiser than the Prophet . . . and Gabriel (upon him be peace) often used to visit him, bringing inspiration and giving news of things past and things to come ... in spite of all this perfection, in spite of all his miracles, God (be He exalted) said to him (in the Quran 3:153) (Consult them in affairs) 'O Muhammad, where you do any work, or when you are confronted with an important matter, confer with your companions.'

Some Advices : At another place he has mentioned that it is very unbecoming of seniors to reprimand their juniors publicly. Loss of honour leaves a dent in one's ego and an individual with a damaged self-respect can never be honest and efficient. It diminishes goodwill in organizations; as such the best course according to our author is to overlook a mistake, if it is committed for the first time. Administration is an onerous job. It taxes all human faculties, therefore, those who are involved in it deserve every possible encouragement. Their achievements and services should be properly rewarded. A disgruntled bureaucracy can do a lot of damage to the peace and security of a country. There should be no wastage of talent in society. Each capable person has a right to ask for appointment according to his abilities, so that he could earn his livelihood. Another fallacy which continuously erodes administration, is lopsided distribution of work. He warns against assignment of two or more positions to one person or one position to two persons. In both cases performance is bound to be faulty and inefficient. He says :-

> *Enlightened monarchs and clever ministers have never in any age given two appointments to one man or one appointment to two men, with the result that their affairs were always conducted with efficiency and lustre. When two appointments are given to one man, one of the tasks is always inefficiently and faultily performed; and in fact, you will usually find that the man who has two functions fails in both of them, and is constantly suffering censure and uneasiness on account of his shortcomings. And further, whenever two men are given a single post each transfers (his responsibility) to the other and the work remains for forever undone.*

Counselling the Rulers

Kitab Nasihat-al-Muluk : This book was written by Abu Hamid Muhammad-al-Ghazzali (d. 505/1111) who ranks among the greatest theologians of Islamic history. The work was originally composed in Persian and later translated into Arabic. Scholars have claimed that several popular writings attributed to Ghazzali are spurious, but none has contested the authenticity of Nasihat-al-Muluk. The treatise was written at the behest of Sultan ibn Malikshah sometime between 499/1105 and 505/1111. Ghazzali lived during he Seljuq period and his thought and mind were greatly influenced by the state of affairs prevailing at that time in the Muslim world. After complete mastery of the canon law theology, and mysticism, Ghazzali studied critically the writings of those, who vehemently opposed the orthodox view of Islam. He also read Batinite and rationalist philosophers with special interest and anxiety.

In this way he kept the spectrum of his philosophical and spiritual inquiries very wide and whatever he wrote or discussed was always imbued with precision and profundity. He considered *aql* (intelligence or reason) as one of the supreme graces of man and included it among the greatest gifts of God. It was his belief that all religious doctrines except the fundamentals like the existence of God, revelation and prophethood could be substantiated through basic reason. In religion his greatest work was *Ihya Ulum al Din.* (Revivification of the Sciences of Religion).

In 1106 he was asked by Sultan Sanjar of Khurasan to resume teaching in the Nizamiyah College at Nishapur. In 1109 he retired to Tus and spent the rest of his life as a mystic. He died on the 18th of December 1111 at the age of 53. It is said that *Nasihat-al-Muluk* was compiled during his retirement shortly before death.

In all his ethical writings, al Ghazzali preaches that men become perfect only by emulating attributes of God in their character. He wrote:-

> *"The perfection of the worshipper as well as his happiness lies in imitating the qualities of Allah the Most High and in adorning himself with the meanings of His attributes and of His names ... in that measure of course that may be considered within his right."*

He contends that there are all kinds of failures and frailties associated with human character, but most evils result when ambition and anger dominate man's disposition. Ambition in his opinion is a source of "shamelessness, wickedness, extravagance, stinginess, hypocrisy, defamation, impudence, folly, greed cupidity, flattery, envy, rancour, gluttony, and lewedness. Anger induces men to indulge in rashness, excessive spending, haughtiness, boasting, arrogance, self-admiration, derision, making light of others, disdain, mischief, abuse." In order to mitigate the effect of these vices, al Ghazzali has mentioned qualities like "chastity, contentment, abstinence, fear of God, piety cheerfulness, a comely appearance, modesty, ingenuity, courage, generosity, self-control, fortitude, clemency, endurance, forgiveness, stability, genius, bravery and gravity" which in his opinion if harmoniously blended can produce an ideal human character.

"Al-Ghazzali was a keen and anxious student of human behaviour and tried to explore psychological and social causes of men's actions in organized society. In his opinion each action is composed of four factors, i.e., *Khawatir* (affections of mind), *raghbia* (inclination), *itiqad* (intellectual conviction), and *irada* (will). In other words:-

Khawatir,	*Raghbia,*
(Affections of the mind)	(inclination)
ad, Irada,	*Amal,*
(intellectual conviction)	(will produce) (action)

In his Ihya-al-Ulum-al-Din, Al-Ghazzali compares human heart to a fortress, which has to be guarded against satanic intrusions. Anger, desire, envy, and greed are the main gates through which Shaitan (Satan) leads his hordes of evil to attack this fortress. Religion and reason are the primary defences against such inroads. If they are weak, Satan and his evil forces have every chance of being triumphant in human life. So far as moral accomplishments are concerned, he has divided humanity into four groups :-

(1) "The first are those who are heedless who do not distinguish truth, from folly and beautiful from the base."

(2) "Those who know well enough the baseness of what is base, but they do not become habituated to good conduct because they consider that their evil conduct is something enjoyable."

(3) "Those (who) actually approve of base dispositions maintaining that they are necessary, right and beautiful."

(4) "The fourth kind are those, who along with what accompanies corrupt belief and practise, see also a sort of virtue in their very excess of evil and the destruction of lives."

Moral Values and Precepts : Moral values and precepts constitute a universal antidote against error and evil, but men belonging to the fourth category are so wicked that no amount of persuasion could convince them about the aims and objectives of righteous action. Morality in his opinion is a skill or a habit of mind which can be cultivated only by conscious efforts. It consumes time, and requires absorbing interest, but once an aptitude for ethical conduct is developed then it flows effortlessly into all channels of human affairs. In his Ihya, Al-Ghazzali has made the following remarks:-

> *"This question of moral progress is precisely like progress in the arts, for if anyone wishes to acquire skill in calligraphy, for instance, he must exercise the necessary mental perseverance. He must engage in what the skillful writer gives him to do, which is the production of a well-written line. At first this will be a matter of requirement and of imitation. And afterwards he must not cease to give his attention to making this well-written line until his aptitude in doing so is established, and until his skill becomes actually a mental quality. In the end he will do naturally and easily what was at first an arduous effort. The time however, will be good which he had made good, first with conscious effort, but in the end quite naturally. This is all because of mental capacity to receive an impression"*

Nasihat-al-Muluk, which is strictly a treatise on administrative ethics, is replete with Al-Ghazzali's depth of understanding about human character and behaviour. It also shows the sad spectacle of political lawlessness and administrative anarchy which was rampant all over the Muslim world at that time. There are nostalgic references to glories of Muslim and non-Muslim past when justice and equity reigned supreme in human affairs. He complained bitterly of the wickedness of the people and the luxuriant and comfort-seeking existence of rulers. He was convinced that Islamic society was unhinged because unethical character of politics and administration had destroyed its moral moorings. Another reason which in his opinion had wrecked peace and order was that political authority was either too weak or too lenient. He was convinced that wickedness could only be eradicated by firmness. He says:-

> *"The reason why we are saying so much on this subject is that our present age is an exceedingly wicked one. The people are wicked and the Sultans are preoccupied with the lower world. With wicked people things cannot be set right through tolerance and indulgence . . . power to inspire awe and maintain discipline are essential, if the individual is to be able to go about his business and if the people are to have security from one another, peoples' outlook has been corrupted and in which they have all grown wicked in both deed and intention."*

Bitter Experience : The wickedness of the people, the torn fabric of once powerful caliphal authority of the Abbasides, deep ideological frictions which plagued the Muslim world, and worries of his declining years, made Al-Ghazzali a mystic during the last phase of his life. The *batinis* under the leadership of their teacher the Fatimide-al-Mustansir (1035-1094 A.D.) and Nazarites led by Hassan-al-Sabbah (d. 1129) with his spiritual and military headquarters at Almout, challenged the righteousness of Sunnite doctrine which was the official creed of the Abbasides and the Seljuks, and used all subversive means to dismantle their political hegemony. There was chronic insecurity of life and property, and anarchy and lawlessness were almost endemic. In such a socio-political climate, mysticism with its negative approach to worldly gains, and human ambitions, had every chance of capturing the imagination of scholars and intellectuals. Therefore it is not surprising that Al-Ghazzali in his retirement preached mystical ethics. Nasihat-al-Muluk is replete with admonitions, anecdotes, aphorisms, which furnish an eloquent testimony to the deep-seated mystical proclivities of its author. He believed that ghoulish enticements of the world hamper man's salvation. It was common among mystics to believe that lust for worldly gains and insatiable appetites grievously injure the welfare of mankind. Al-Ghazzali says :-

> *"You should understand that a stopping place is not a fixed abode, and that man is in this world in the role of a traveller, the mother's womb being his first stop and the grave his last stop." In order to substantiate his contention about the transitory nature of human life and treacherous ways of the world he has given ten analogies to create awareness about them :-*

1. This is to explain the spell of this World. God's Apostle said, "Hold aloof from the world for she is a worse spellbinder than Harut and Marut. The beginning of her spell is that appears to you in such a way that you suppose her to be stationary and fixed in relations to you; for you look at her, and she is the universe itself yet she is continually fleeting from you.
2. She resembles a worthless woman who is vicious and importunate and lures men to her in order to make them her loves, then takes them to her house and destroys them.
3. She is like an ugly old hag who masks her face, but has put on fine clothes and done herself up ornately. Men see her from afar and are enchanted with her, but when they remove her veil they are dismayed to find such ugliness.

4. He will then understand that this world resembles the route of a traveller, starting from the cradle ending at the grave, and with a given number of stages in between.
5. You should understand that this world, in the pleasures which her sons get from her and again in the disgrace which in the after-life they suffer because of her, is like a person who eats rich and sweet food in such excess as to ruin the stomach.
6. Jesus declared that the seeker of this world is like the drinker of sea-water, the more he consumes the thirstier he becomes and he will continue drinking until he perishes and he will never be cured of that thirst.
7. This is that a person who comes into this world resembles one who goes as a guest to a home of a host, whose custom is to keep his mansion always adorned for guests and to invite them in parties. The host places before them a tray of jewels and gold, and a silver censor with aloes wood and incense for giving fragrance, but they leave, the tray and censor for the next party when it arrives.
8. This world's inhabitants, in their preoccupation with its affairs and forgetfulness of the world to come, resemble a ship's passengers, who on reaching an island go ashore to perform the natural functions and rituals ablutions. The ship's officers call out "Let nobody take too long or get busy with anything except the ablutions as the ship is to sail soon."

Thoughts embodied in the above analogies form the crux of Iranian and Arabic mystical literature. Many of their connotations are inimical to the basic principles of Islam. Mystical ethics is vastly different from Islamic ethics in the sense that Islam insists on purity of thought and action, preaches that, life of sin and vice is destructive, enjoins virtue and righteousness, but does not advocate asceticism. Its approach is positive and activates the believers to appreciate and enjoy the fruits of this world, but in doing so they should abstain from excesses and injustice which lead to immoral acts.

The frame of reference of Nasihat-al-Muluk is predominantly mystical. Moreover the treatise has focused most of its attention on the kings. There are only passing references to administrators and other state functionaries. Some pages have been devoted to the role and qualities of Wazirs (Prime Ministers) and Dabirs (Secretaries), but the author does not provide a comprehensive picture of the ethical basis of these offices.

For instance, in his chapter on secretaries, Al-Ghazzali has put more emphasis on the shape and form of a pen to be used by a secretary than on the qualities of head and heart which would mold his character as an administrator. The chapter on Wazirate, however, though short, has some references to the ethical foundation of this office. His exposition of the moral qualities of kingship are detailed and exhaustive and this has accorded the book a respectable place in Islamic literature. From this material a student of administrative ethics in Islam, can glean valuable guidelines to crystalize moral basis of government and administration in an Islamic society. The qualities depicted no doubt were meant for the princes, but they could be equally relevant to the character and behaviour of the functionaries who executed their policies.

Foundation Rock : According to Al-Ghazzali, authority is the foundation rock over which the super-structure of a politically organized society is built. Authority ensures stability and prosperity for the realm, but it is a delicate instrument. It is both a bane and a bliss. If exercised righteously and with care, wisdom and prudence it can be a source of eternal blessings, but abuse or misuse of authority can damage peace and order in a country. He says:-

> *"This is that (the ruler) should first of all understand the importance and also the danger of authority entrusted to him. In authority there is a great blessing, since he who "exercises it righteously obtains unsurpassed happiness, but if any (ruler) fails to do so he incurs torment unsurpassed only by the torment for unbelief, ... Such being the case there is no greater blessing than God's grant to a person of the office of ruler and Sultan, whereby an hour of his life is raised (to be equivalent) to the whole life of any other persons, but if he shows no appreciation of this blessing and gives himself over to tyranny and passion, there is a terrible wish that God on High will count him as an enemy."*

He makes reference to the two traditions of the Holy Prophet in which a serious warning has been administered to those who have been given the responsibility to preside over the destiny of a Muslim community. The Prophet said "If any man is granted authority over the Muslims and does not look upon them as he would look upon members of his own household, tell him he will get his place in Hell." "Two persons in my community will be denied my intercession ; the tyrant and the innovator, who practices such exaggeration in religion that it goes beyond the limit."

There is, however, a slight contradiction in Al-Ghazzali's approach to authority. He begins his analysis by pointing out that exercise of authority within the boundaries of ethics and religion is the greatest benediction of God. An hour spent in the righteous use of authority is equal to the whole life of other human beings, but a little later in the same chapter, he takes considerable pains to explain that all authority, just or unjust is subject to divine admonishment. He says:-

> *"Hudhayfah (ibu-al-Yaman) used to say: 'I never praise any holder of authority. Whether virtuous or wicked. When asked why, he replied that it was because he had heard God's Apostle declare : "On the Resurrection Day, all holders of authority will be brought in: whether unjust or just. All will be stationed on the (bridge called) Sirat, and God on High will inspire the Sirat to shake them off in one sharp shake; for there will not be a single one among, them who has not judged unjustly taken a bribe when trying a case, or lent his ear overmuch to one contestant. All will fall off the Sirat, and all will go down the Hell for seventy years, at the end of which they will reach their final resting place."*

Mystical Suspicion : Mystical suspicion and derision of worldly possessions could be the reason for this outright condemnation of all kinds of authority. Whatever might have been the reason, Al-Ghazzali's earlier statement that righteous use of authority brings unsurpassed happiness and ensures salvation hereafter is the true ethical basis of authority of Islam.

Justice and equity according to Al-Ghazzali constitute prominent branches of the true Faith. Injustice and inequity are vices for which there is no atonement. The unjust Sultan is warned against severe torments, and a prince who collects taxes from his subjects and does not practice impartiality between the strong and the weak, and is arbitrary in his judgments will have to pocket odium of God. Justice in his opinion entails strict adherence to the laws of God. A ruler, whether he inflicts punishment or shows compassion must exercise discretion. Excessive compassion is as bad as excessive punishment because both are contrary to principles of justice. He quotes the following tradition of the Holy Prophet:-

> *"God's Apostle stated that on the Resurrection Day, holders of authority will be brought in and told 'You were shepherds of my sheep', (One will be asked) 'Why did you award a penalty and inflict a punishment on so-*

> *and-so in excess of what I bade you?' He will reply: 'O Lord God, in wrath because they were offending against you and he will be told, Why should your wrath exceed Mine?' Another will be asked 'Why did you inflict a punishment falling short of what I bade you?' He will reply 'O Lord God I did so out of compassion' and he will be told 'Why should you be more compassionate than I am? Their God on High will order them to be shown the corners of Hell."*

A ruler should refrain from injustice and it is incumbent upon him to exercise constant vigilance over the behaviour of his soldiers and civil servants. If he is just, and his employees are unjust, the conditions of society will never improve and he would be held responsible for their misdeeds. Justice becomes effective and meaningful only if the entire governmental machinery is pervaded with judiciousness and all state employees make justice a permanent feature of their professional ethics. Al-Ghazzali is of the opinion that if the chief holder of authority is just and endowed with excellencies of character, there is every possibility that these traits will be emulated by his subordinates. He points out that Shaqiq-al-Balkhi, a learned ascetic once told Harun-al-Rashid the Abbaside Caliph, "You are a fountain and the other officials (who help you to govern) the world are the streams (which flow from it). If the fountain is clear, there can be no damage from silt in the channels; if the fountain is turbid, there will be no hope (of maintaining) the channels." Unjust officials have a tendency to hood-wink the rulers and more often than not they indulge in tactics and use strategies by which injustice is portrayed as justice. Such functionaries are the greatest enemies of state and their evil intentions spell destructions of the realm.

Passion and Anger : Passion and anger render the prospects of justice bleak, and it therefore befits a ruler who is in search of just laws to avoid them as much as he can. Intellect should be the guardian of those passions which blur human vision, and hamper perception of reality in its true perspective. Outward appearances are often deceptive and in order to do justice men are advised to comprehend things as they really are Al-Ghazzali sums up his views on this subject as follows:

> *"To sum up (the ruler) must act justly towards his subjects and (at the same time) keep his staff, household, and sons on the path of justice. Nobody, however, can do this unless he first observes justice inside himself. Now justice consists of restraining tyrannous instincts,*

> *passions and anger in order to make them the prisoners of reason and religion, and not letting reason become the prisoner of tyrannous instincts, passions and anger .... reason is the army of God on High, and that passion and anger are the army of the Devil. How can a man who keeps God's army captive in the hands of the Devil's army act justly towards others .... you should understand and be assured of this, O Sultan, that justice springs from perfection of the intellect and that perfection of the intellect means that you see things as they really are and perceive the facts of their inner reality without being deceived by their outward appearance."*

After justice Al-Ghazzali expects men of authority to be humble in disposition. He is conscious of the fact that authority has the tendency to become a narcotic of human mind. It makes people proud and arrogant and pride and arrogance impel holders of authority to become angry and revengeful very fast. These undesirable characteristics deprive human personality of that eternal lustre that stems out of humility and modesty. Anger which in his opinion is a manifestation of pride is a "blight of the intellect". As an antidote to the natural inclination of pride among men of authority, Al-Ghazzali advocates forgiveness, generosity and forbearance.

These qualities in his opinion distinguish men from beasts. In this connection he makes a reference to the tradition of the Holy Prophet in which he mentioned three things for the perfection of faith. They are : "not to form a wrong intention when angered, not to set aside what is right when pleased, and not to take more than what is right when powerful." In order to further support his contention he mentions another saying of God's Apostle in which forbearance and forgiveness have been considered as good as fasting and prayer for the purity of human mind and soul.

Significant Principles : Redress of the grievances of the masses is another principle of governmental ethics, which has been emphasized by Al-Ghazzali in a great deal. He insists that if a ruler disregards public petitions; he is treading a dangerous path which can pose immeasurable hazards. He brackets redress of people's complaints with religious duties. For a healthy polity a ruler must have a network of effective espionage by which he can uncover people's reactions to governmental policies.

Accessibility of officials to complainants has always been considered one of the fundamental principles of administrative ethics in Islam.

Practically all writers on the subject have accorded this quality a high place in the professional and moral equipment of public officials, Al-Ghazzali says:-

> *"The Arabs (have a saying); that nothing is more damaging to the subjects and more prejudicial and sinister for the king than royal inacessibility and seclusion; and that nothing impresses the hearts of the subjects and officials more, than ease of access to the king. For when the subjects know that the king is easily approachable it will be impossible for the officials to oppress one another. Through making himself readily accessible, the king will acquire information about all the affairs of which he must never be heedless of the prestige of the monarchy is to be maintained and if he himself is to reign undisturbed."*

Oppressive rule of inaccessible officials destroys peace and prosperity and ultimately political fabric is torn into shreds.

In Islam religion and politics are inseparably integrated. It is essential for a political authority to safeguard interests of religion from internal and external attacks, and watch the conduct of the subjects so that sanctity of religion is not tainted by eccentric distortions and heretical practices. As has been noticed earlier Al-Ghazzali lived at a time when Muslim lands were plagued with religious dissensions and established Sunnite doctrine was being virulently questioned by many new sects in Islam. Therefore safety of religion was a matter of deep concern for Al-Ghazzali. In Nasihat-ul-Muluk he repeatedly emphasizes that kings must take special care to eradicate heresies from their jurisdictions. A ruler under all circumstances, in his opinion, should abide strictly to laws of *sharia,* and his image among masses should be that of a devout and conscientious adherent of religion. He must adopt stern measures against those, who deviate from the established order, because this is the only way by which he can acquire reputation as a defender of the faith. He says :-

> *"The quality which kings most need is correct religion because monarchy and religion are like brothers. (The king) needs it equally whether he be healthy or sick. He must be diligent in matters of religion, performing the duties at the proper times avoiding eccentricity and heretical innovation and shunning unjust and immoral actions. If he hears that any person in his territory is suspect as regards religion, he must summon him and*

interrogate him until he repents or else punish him or exile him from the territory; in this way the kingdom will be purged of eccentrics and heretical innovators, and Islam will be strong. He must keep the border lands populated by sending garrisons, strive to increase the power of Islam, and keep the Prophets Sunnah fresh and vigorous."

Evil Traits : All human beings have certain evil traits like envy, ambition, spite, cupidity, and love of pleasure and it is one of the primary duties of a ruler to adopt such effective measures by which these vices can be contained. This is a vital service which can be done by men presiding over socially organized entities for the cause of human welfare. A weak authority can as much be a cause of ruin as tyrannous authority, and a competent ruler always avoids both extremes from his actions. Piety, equity, and awareness of the interests of the people are advocated as essential characteristics of those who administer human affairs. Since rulers don't have divine vision, they are advised to exercise special vigilance over behaviour of their administrators. This would minimize chances of corruption and other baneful practices commonly associated with administration. Umar I, the Second Caliph after the Holy Prophet, in one of his sermons said:

"O People! In the time of the Prophet the divine inspiration used to come down, and through that inspiration he used to know men's outward acts and inward thoughts, both good and bad. Now the inspiration has ceased and we view every person by his public behaviour; but God the Strong and Glorious is well aware of men's secret motives. I try to ensure that neither I nor my assistants and revenue officers ever take anything from the people (wrongfully) nor ever give (anything to anybody wrongfully)."

Al-Ghazzali is convinced that corruption, nepotism, and favouritism result from negligence, irrational mildness and constant slackness of rulers. If a ruler personally supervises administration and anxiously looks into affairs relating to the welfare of his people the impact of these vices could be reduced considerably. If the king is upright, his subjects and officials will be upright, but if he is dishonest, negligent and comfort-seeking, people living under his jurisdiction and officers implementing his policies will soon become slothful and corrupt.

Al-Ghazzali has devoted a separate chapter on magnanimity which in his opinion is a sterling quality for rulers and administrators.

Magnanimity is an antithesis of low-mindedness. He defines the term as "self-restraint and courage and self-respect and self-knowledge, but the numerous anecdotes that follow these definitions, show that the term is used to connote large-heartedness and generosity. Particularly if a person is blessed with munificence, he should not hesitate to provide financial and material succour to others. He quotes thc saying of Umar ibn al Khattab who said, "Take good care not to be mean-minded, for I have seen nothing more degrading in men than low-mindedness." Reference is also made to aphormism of a sage who said, "The essence of greatness is taking pains and the essence of error is haste ; the essence of depravity is miserliness". Another sage said, "If men open their hands to give generously their faces will shine luminously".

Divine Gift : According to Al-Ghazzali, political authority as embodied in kings and governors is a divine gift and a trust. Application of this gift for the general good requires cultivation of certain graces such as intelligence, knowledge, sharpness of mind, ability to perceive things, perfect physique, literary taste, horsemanship application to work and courage, together with boldness, deliberation, good temper, impartiality towards the weak and the strong, friendliness, magnanimity, maintaining toleration and moderation, judgement and, foresight in business, frequent reading of the reports of early Muslims, and constant attention to the biographies of the kings, and inquiry concerning the activities of the kings of old, because the present world is the continuation of the empire of the forerunners.

He further refers to the letter which Yuman the Dastur wrote to Anushirvan in which he advised the king to promulgate justice, use intelligence, exercise patience, and practice modesty and to abstain from envy, arrogance, narrow-mindedness, and malice.

At another place he mentions Sufyan (al-) Thawri who said that permanent happiness of men depends on intelligence and knowledge and cultivation of such excellencies as "chastity, courtesy, absteniousness, honesty, truthfulness, modesty, compassion, kind-heartedness, fidelity, patience, tact and equanimity."

Divine Politics

Akhlaq-i-Nasiri

Akhlaq-i-Nasiri. Its author Nasiruddin-Tusi (1201-1276 A.D.) was born ninety years after the death of Al-Ghazzali. He was attached to the court of Assasins Chief Ala-al-Din (1220-1255) at Alamut. Like the rest of the writers who preceded him, Tusi was convinced that salvation of mankind lies in establishing a political system which is divine in origin. He calls it Siyasat-i-Rabbani, (Divine Politics). He elaborated his views on this point as follows :-

> *"There is no state more ruinous than that which means the abandonment of the divine administration (siyasat-i-rabbani) and the wasting of his favours. That is the very essence of unrighteousness, for it is ingratitude for his benefits and a denial of which is the equivalent of unbelief. For the true content of oppression is the placing of things at wrong places. Thus the manager becomes the managed, the King becomes the subject and the lord becomes the slave."*

Al-Tusi lists absent-mindedness, rashness, cupidity, and oppression as the bane of human conduct. In his opinion human soul is motivated in all actions by three faculties, i.e., reason, appetite, and temper. Reason distinguishes between good and evil, appetite helps acquisition of goods and physical pleasures and temper helps man to defend himself against injury. Man in his opinion can be reasonable, but he has also the tendency to succumb to a very low level of irrationality also. In order to attain high level of perfection, it is essential to curb appetite and discipline one's temper. Al-Tusi believes that men have many things in common with animals, and morality is meant to minimize the role of animality in human affairs. Lust and unbridled aspirations to satisfy bodily desires reduce man to the level of a beast. They hinder healthy development of human personality and as such it is essential to safeguard oneself against such a degradation. He says:

> *"It may be said in regard to what man has in common with animals and other forms of life, that if his animal nature prevails over him and his inclination is in that direction, he will be degraded from his proper rank to that of the order of beasts or even lower. For the Quran says "They are like the brutes. Yea, they go more astray." (VII : 178). He reaches the place, for example, where he longs to gain the pleasures and the desires of the body, those for which the bodily sense and powers are eager and have a craving—such as things to eat, things to drink, things to wear, and marriages. The result is that the power of beast soon gets the upper hand. Or his development is similarly curtailed if he takes to violence and assault and vengeance, which are the fruits of anger having sway."*

Sole Objective : Al-Tusi, following other moral philosophers in Islam insists that the sole objective of human existence is the perfection of man's soul. *Nafs-i-natiqa* (soul) in his opinion has two powers—the power of knowledge and the power of action. Knowledge entails comprehension of the known world and mastery of arts and sciences relating to it. Action relates to human capacity to harmonize—variegated powers of self in a manner that they do not try to dominate each other.

Everything good or bad has been entrusted to the custody of man. Preferences are all his own, and if he is careful and vigilant he can control evil propensities, and through his watchfulness he can direct them for personal and social goodness. If his control is casual or relaxed, or his powers deficient, he will be left destitute of moral purpose in life. He has illustrated his point as follows :-

> *"Others said that the situation of mankind with reference to these selves is more like that of a man mounted on a powerful horse, when with a dog he goes out to hunt. If the authority is with the man he will employ his riding animal and his hunting animal with discretion. He will be attentive to what is necessary for the well-being of all of them in time of danger, and he will make arrangements for what food is needed for them all in just measure. Thus as companions in eating and drinking and in other matters of subsistence, they will be maintained according to the needs of their respective natures. But if the riding beast has his own way and does not recognize the authority of the rider, then he will start to run wherever he sees the best grass. In roughness of gait, in straying from the road, and in making speed at the wrong place, he will give great annoyance to himself and his companions . . . Also if the hunting animal has its own way, at the time when it sees the prey it will lead the riding animal and its rider in that direction as fast as it can, with resultant hardship and fear of destruction, as has been mentioned. It is even probable that in the course of the encounter, when fighting with the animal that is hunted, it will itself be wounded and worn out that it will perish. But if the two beasts are subject to the rider who knows what is best and who has the right to command, they will be saved from these misfortunes and accidents."*

Al-Tusi warns against excesses. In his opinion any deviation from accepted standard can unhinge a situation. Overdoing is one way of excess and neglecting the other. Men, in order to live a healthy, moral existence must avoid both.

Virtue is moderation, while evil resides on both extremes. Wisdom, bravery, purity and righteousness are midway virtues in his opinion, and their extremes on both sides he has analyzed as follows :-

> *"To be absent-minded is on the side of excess, for it is the employing of powers of thought on what is not necessary, or to a greater extent than is fitting. Some call this self-deception or being like a large over-ripe cucumber. To be ignorant or stupid is to err on the side of carelessness or neglect, in voluntarily failing to make use of the power of thought, not because of any physical limitation."*
>
> *"Rashness, which is from excess, is always ready to start something which it is not seemly to start, whereas cowardice, which is on the side of insufficiency, is avoiding things which it is not commendable to avoid."*
>
> *"Cupidity, which is on the side of excess, is greed for pleasures beyond measures that is proper, whereas the abating of passion which is on the side of deficiency, is lack of initiative in seeking necessary pleasures, or such as reason and law permit—when this indifference is voluntary and is not due to physical limitation."*
>
> *"Oppression, which is on the side of excess, is the acquirement of the means of living by methods that are reprehensible, whereas living oppressed, which is on the side of deficiency, consists in affording opportunity to anyone who is seeking the means of living by methods of violence and plunder, i.e., in submitting to their being taken without justification and merely because they are themselves object."*

Reputed Treatise

Al Fakhri

The author of the book Muhammad Ali son of Tabataba (Rapid Talker) wrote this book in 1302 A.D. in honour of Prince Fakhr-ad-din Isa son of Ibrahim. The treatise enjoyed wide reputation for authenticity and scholarship among the later Muslim scholars. It was first translated into French in 1910 and later the Arabic text was published in 1921.

The English translation of the work was done by C.E.J. Whitting in 1947. The author in his introduction has given reasons for the compilation of this book. His main purpose was to provide a compendium of knowledge for kings and rulers because their ignorance, lack of historical perspectives and indifference to the interest of the subjects, in his opinion, constituted one of the fundamental causes of the ruin of kingdoms. The ministers, he points out, always felt happy under a prince who was not knowledgeable, because that would facilitate their monopoly of power in the state.

A monarch with knowledge and will of his own was always considered a threat to the prerogatives of a minister. The immediate cause for writing this treatise was the desire on the part of the author to furnish a manual of statecraft to his patron from whom he received kindness and hospitality.

Significant Elements

The book has been divided into two parts. In the first part he has listed certain special characteristics which form an indisputable, moral and intellectual equipment of a ruler and establish his superiority over his subjects. The second part gives a chronological account of dynasties which ruled the Muslim empire during different periods of history. It is the first part of the book which is relevant for our purpose because in it the author has elucidated his ideals about the ethical foundations of a Muslim polity.

The narrative, like other books on the same subject, is embellished with verses from the Quran. Traditions of the Holy Prophet, anecdotes from the lives of rulers, who were just and generous in their attitudes towards the subject. The author has abstained from theoretical discussions regarding the origin of power, and the nature of religious and temporal authority in Islam. He says, "it (book) has been composed only to deal with systems of government and conventions useful in current affairs and in conflicts which occur, in the rule of subjects, safety of the realm and improvement of manners and conduct."

Knowledge, intelligence and justice are the first set of qualities which according to Al Fakhri, can help a ruler or administrator to escape from errors of judgment. To be governed by an ignorant ruler in his opinion is the worst tragedy that could happen in a society. Knowledge that he envisions for just and efficient and kind-hearted rulers is not a specialized knowledge of arts and sciences. What he expects of them is a general familiarity with different areas of learning, so that they can coordinate matters of public policy with insight.

Specialization in his opinion leads to obscurity of thought and narrowness of mind, both of which are detrimental to efficiency and comprehension. They must have enough understanding so that they can enter into dialogue with experts. A ruler or administrator must have breadth of vision and sufficient understanding so that his subordinates will not be able to deceive him. Knowledge, however, in his view is culture-bound, because polities derive their strength or weakness from the socio-religious and philosophical climate in which they are nurtured. Knowledge imbibed by men in authority will also differ according to their personal proclivities, but the author of Al Fakhri believes that over a period of time each social system develops its own ethos and ethical principles which are always deemed to be essential for intelligent and effective administration of the realm. He says :-

> *"The studies of the rulers of Persia were laws, moral precepts, literature, history, geometry and the like. The studies of the rulers of Islam were philology, grammar, lexicography, poetry and history, so much so that an error in speech was one of the most objectionable faults in the royal dignity, and man's rank might be advanced with them by a single anecdote, a single verse of poetry nay a single idiomatic word. As for Mongols, all these studies were rejected and other studies were popular with them—economics, accountancy, for balancing the budget and the estimates of revenue and expenditure, medicines, and astrology to choose occasions."*

Fear of God : Like other Muslim thinkers Al Fakhri advocates that fear of God is the foundation-rock for a stable moral character and most of the sterling qualities of human behaviour, and other ethical excellencies stem from it. He believes that rulers tend to be irate and full of hatred. But in his opinion these are ignoble qualities which lead to moral degeneration. A ruler should show love and concern for his subjects rather than pity. If a ruler or administrator has nothing but pity for his people, the society will be full of disenchantment and bitterness. In a population which is alienated a ruler will, never be able to get proper affection and cooperation. He says:

> *How can a ruler attain his desire in major affairs of state, and achieve his intended objects, save through the willing cooperation of his subjects? What wisdom is there in that ? Is there aught in it some embitterment of the ruler's life, the decerebrating of his subjects against him and the estrangement of them from him ?*

Feelings of Conciliation : Bonds of the rulers and the subjects have to be cemented by feelings of conciliation. These feelings in his opinion, are cultivated only through clemency and forgiving attitude of the administrators. Generosity of mind, spaciousness of thought are qualities which are of invaluable significance in winning the hearts of people. Al Fakhri has enumerated ten basic qualities which could insure peace, order, and prosperity of the kingdom. They are,

(1) to spare bloodshed,
(2) to guard property,
(3) to protect morals,
(4) to prevent disasters,
(5) to restrain evil-doers and troublemakers,
(6) to check the extortion which follows from civil war and unrest,
(7) to study the affairs of the subjects in depth and detail,
(8) to reward good and punish evil,
(9) to exercise constant vigilance and
(10) to manifest unending care.

These prerequisites are vital determinants of legitimacy in a political system. A ruler who entirely relies on his independent judgment, will miss the depth of understanding and richness of information and alternatives which are produced by-consultation. The author mentions that if the Prophet used to consult his companions so often in handling the affairs of the community, he sees no reasons why the rest of the Muslim rulers should claim immunity from it. On the question of consultation enjoined upon the Prophet by God, Al Fakhri has summed up the views of the various schools of thought in Islam as follows:-

> *The theologians disagree as to whether God, Most High, commanded his messenger to seek advice despite the help and advice given to him by Him. On that there are four views. First, that he was ordered to consult the companions to win their loyalty and secure their willing cooperation. Secondly, that he was ordered to consult them in war, so that the correct view might be confirmed for him, and he act accordingly. Thirdly, that he was ordered to consult them because of the useful and advantageous (counsel) they possessed. Fourthly, that he was only ordered to consult them in order that people might copy him and this I hold, is the best view and the most correct.*

Thus, according to Al Fakhri, consultation in decision-making creates confidence, disarms resistance, and once the people are convinced of the integrity of the ruler they develop the natural tendency to emulate him. Impetuosity, and ennui are very unbecoming characteristics in a ruler. They bring nothing but humiliation. It is one of the supreme ethical responsibilities of the ruler to protect people from oppression and strengthen the hands of the weak so that he can fight battles of life with success. "Among the duties of a ruler to his subjects is restraining the stronger from (oppressing) the weaker, giving the lowly justice against the powerful, establishing the rule of law among them, maintaining their rights as they should be maintained, helping the dejected, answering any of them who cries for aid, and holding the scales of justice equal between the most distant of them and the nearest, the lowliest and the mightiest."

It is indisputable that the ethical standards of the government to a large extent depend on the moral values of the administrators who run the affairs of the state. As such recruitment should not be left to chance. It must be based on sound judgement. Al Fakhri mentions the practice of a ruler who used to publicize the name of a person who was a potential candidate for a position of responsibility. In this way he used to feel the pulse of popular reaction to the future appointee. In the light of information thus collected he used to finalize his decision. He had informers who used to mix with the common people in disguise and collect information on such matters.

Firmness and strength of character are qualities which are always applauded in the art of governing men. Firmness, however, has to be based on reason and compassion. Indiscriminate persecution or high-handedness would never be considered as signs of firmness. Such excesses should be distasteful to a ruler, unless they are necessitated by some unavoidable emergency. Obsessive firmness is symptomatic of arrogance which creates a climate of frustration in society. Pride in ones ancestry does not help in politics. One should feel proud of one's own attainments in civility, culture and knowledge.

Faulty View : People tend to take a simple but faulty view of administration. They categorize administration into five kinds: of the home, the village, the city, the army, and the state. They believe that "he who administers his home well, will administer his village well, he who administers his village well, will administer his city well, he who administers his city well, will administer an army well, and he who administers an army well, will administer a state well." Al Fakhri believes this oversimplified analysis deceptive because many whose domestic affairs are well administered are poor administrators of the affairs of the state, and those whose administration of public affairs is superb are weak and inefficient in administering domestic affairs. The role of sword and pen has been a subject of deep controversy among Muslim scholars on politics and administration. Sword symbolizes military establishment and coercive power of the state, while pen stands for civilian machinery which is created to administer affairs of kingdom in peace time. Al Fakhri has summed up this controversy as follows :-

> *The realm is guarded by the sword and administered with the pen. People disagree about the sword and the pen, as to which of the two is superior, and takes precedence. Some think that the pen has it over the sword, and urge in support of their view that the sword guards the pen, and so stands to it as a guardian and servant. Others think the sword superior, and urge that the pen serves the sword because it provides the soldiers with their pay, and so it is a servant to it. Others say that they are equal and that neither of them can function without the other. They say a realm is fertilized by generosity, populated by justice, secured by common sense, protected by courage, and administered by leadership.*

The author of Al Fakhri is fully aware of the critical nature of power in politics. He thinks it is a delicate instrument which has to be wielded with care and utmost anxiety. He says that "the practice of power is more difficult than (to obtain) power itself." Power has to be exercised with patience and fortitude. If power passes into the hands of an impatient person, there is every possibility of its being abused and misused. A seeker of power must also have the ability to discriminate and should also be endowed with talent and insight to make sound judgement. It would be better if he is aware of the vicissitudes of life, and the ebb and flow of human fortunes during different eras of history. Power without tact and grace is a crude weapon which can be extremely dangerous for civilization. A person holding power must be able to cajole his enemy with tact and hide his secret with grace. Power corrupts where an individual becomes over-confident, and refuses to seek advise from others. One's own commonsense alone cannot resolve complexities of politics and administration. It requires constant reinforcement from the genius of others, in the form of consultation.

The most competent ruler according to Al Fakhri is one "whose work rules his play, and whose judgement overrides his desire, whose deeds express his intentions, whose will does not counter his luck, nor anger his cunning." One of the qualities of a competent ruler is, his ability for self-examination. It is a common frailty among rulers that they always try to camouflage their failures. A ruler with a high ethical standard would readily subject himself to public scrutiny and speedily accept his failures and deficiencies. Self-assessment and self-realization are characteristics which clarify vision. A ruler ought to be a personification of affability, his kindness proverbial and manners exemplary. If the attitude and habits of the governors and the governed synchronize, systems tend to be stable and prosperous. People cannot blame the acts of rulers if their own life and character are imbued with the same spirit. It is also essential for administrative efficiency that the decision-maker be in a position to anticipate dangers. An administrator who lacks these qualities is patently incompetent.

Another matter which requires special consideration of rulers is the verification of information received from government informants. It is a matter of common knowledge that kingdoms have suffered grievous wrongs at the hands of corrupt and selfish spies. Rulers have committed egregious blunders in relying for their judgements on wrong information. For you have to judge that which appears (in the open) while God judges the hidden. Dislike on behalf of your subjects, what you dislike for yourself. Conceal the shame of others and God will conceal for you that which you wish concealed. Be not in a hurry to believe the informer, for he is dishonest even though he may give good advice.

Since there were long periods of anarchy in Islamic history Muslim political thinkers had always deep concerned about peace and stability. Many of them concluded that only a strong and powerful ruler could provide security of life and property to his people. They unhesitatingly acknowledged that even if the ruler was unjust, his rule should be preferred to one who was just but weak. The latter in their opinion was unable to protect the fundamental rights of his subjects because his weakness made him susceptible to exploitations by self-seeking nobles and other vested interests in the realm. People were victimized by overambitious and unscrupulous fortune-hunters, and instead of suffering the despotic rule of one they would be subjected to many despots. Al Fakhri has made the following remarks on this controversy:-

> *They have disagreed as to the unjust ruler and the weak just ruler. They (mostly) prefer the strong unjust, arguing that the unjust powerful (ruler) guards his subjects against "vested interests" (and protects them by his*

> *power) from others than himself. His pride preserves them from being damaged by others than himself. So his subjects are in the position of who one is spared damage by all men but suffer damage by one. The weak just (ruler) neglects (the interest of) his subjects, and everyone has authority over them, and every hoof tramples them, so that they are in the position of one who is spared damage by one and suffers damage by all.*

Compendium of History, Philosophy and Sociology

Muqaddima

Ibn Khaldun, the author of the *Muqaddima,* ranks among the greatest historians of the world. The book is basically on the philosophy of history, and has never been included in the literature on political or administrative ethics. It is a compendium of history, philosophy and sociology, and unquestionably the greatest work of Muslim scholarship which has won universal recognition for depth, comprehension, and creative insight into all organized affairs of men. Ibn Khaldun dealt at length on all theoretical and practical aspects of government and administration, and in doing so he has not failed to uncover ethical dimensions of the art of governing men. He emphasized that human life is a playground of good and evil, and evil propensities in organized moral communities are manifested, in the form of aggression and injustice. Governmental authority, in his opinion, is the only force which can save social systems from evil consequences of injustice and aggression. He says :-

> *Mutual aggression of people in towns and cities is averted by the authorities and the government, which hold back the masses under their control from attacks and aggression upon each other. They are thus prevented by the influence of force and governmental authority from mutual injustice, save much injustice as comes from the ruler himself.*

Ibn Khaldun is perceptive enough to know that governmental authority equipped with the coercive power of the state is necessary to ward off dangers of subversion from within and destruction from outside. But at the same time he is fully aware that all bureaucratic structures have a built-in tendency to abuse this authority. It is not uncommon for guardians of justice and equity to commit brazen acts of injustice and inequity. How to guard against the guardians is a prominent theme of Ibn Khaldun's great work, and it is in this connection that he has unrolled the discussion on administrative ethics. His feelings are that although evil is ingrained in human nature, but still more often than not, men prefer doing good than pursuing actions which are morally reprehensible. Politics and public morality in his opinion should be inseparable from the affairs of organized communities. He says :-

> *"The existence of (royal authority without the simultaneous existence of) the perfecting details would be like the existence of a person with his limbs cut off, or it would be like appearing naked before people."*

The Perfection

The emphasis all along in his great work is on perfection of Islamic principles of ethics. Prudence, wisdom, kindness, justice, fortitude, and honesty are repeatedly mentioned as glories of human conduct which give continuity and stability to moral communities. They ensure peace and order in kingdoms and give moral legitimacy to governmental authority. He says that 'politics is concerned with the administration of home or city in accordance with ethical and philosophical requirements, for the purpose of directing the masses toward a behaviour that will result in the preservation and permanence of the human species.' He insists that lawgivers must live up to the spirit of the religious laws because they are good for both here and hereafter, and they are free from foibles and frailities so commonly associated, with man-made laws. To articulate his views still further Ibn Khaldun has reproduced a long letter written by an Abbaside general Tahir ibn-al Hussayan to his son Abdallah b. Tahir when the latter was appointed governor of ar-Raqqah Egypt by Al-Mamun.

He speaks admiringly of the contents of this letter and mentions that Al-Mamun was so impressed by the depth and wisdom of the subject matter that he ordered that the letter be circulated among all officials stationed in various regions of the empire. Tahir starts this letter with usual exhortations of a devout Muslim, impressing upon his son the need to cultivate the fear of God and never to be forgetful of the fact that ultimately he would be accountable to Him for all his deeds and misdeeds, and one who holds authority over people, shoulders a grave responsibility. One of the primary duties of a God-fearing administrator is to preserve law and order, avoid brutality, protect the life and property of his subjects and to see that God's laws are not violated. It is also incumbent upon rulers of men not to allow their prejudices to interfere in the administration, and that they should set an example of moral rectitude so that people can repose confidence in their leadership. He says :-

> *"Do not be swayed from Justice according to your likes and dislikes, either on behalf of a person close to you or on behalf of one remote to you—In addition when people notice your (religious attitude) they will have respect for your rule and reverence for your government."*

Those who are charged with the authority to govern men, have primary responsibility to exercise constant vigilance over the behaviour of their subordinates. A negligence in this direction has been the cause of ruin for many a ruler. It is a universal phenomenon that delegated authority, which is not investigated and supervised constantly, has a tendency to exploit people, and once a situation like that arises, kingdoms tumble very fast towards decadence. Tahir is unequivocal in his statement that this is the most important task of one who has been entrusted with the sole responsibility of governing and guiding the masses. This is the only way to preserve the spirit of the religion in the life and character of a polity. At the same time it is essential that the wrong-doers should not go without punishment which should be according to principles ordained by God. Rank and status of culprits should not interfere in the dispensation of justice. Even postponement of punishment can have an impairing effect on public opinion. Justice deferred is no justice.

Anger, deceit and levity are some of the evils which administrators must avoid in their actions. Tahir makes significant remarks about arrogance which is common vice among those whose authority is unchecked. An authority which has no ethical base is unislamic. Authority according to Islam is only a means to an end and not an end in itself. The ultimate authority belongs to God. Human beings hold it only as a trust. This accountability to the ultimate source is a recognized principle of Quranic law. He says:-

> *Beware of saying: "I am in authority. I may do what I want to do. This soon reveals a lack of sense on your part and little certainty of the one and only God. Let your intention with regard to (God) and your certainty of Him be sincere. You should know that royal authority belongs to God. He gives it to whomever he wants to give, and takes it away from whomever he wants to take it away."*

Divine Retribution : According to Tahir, men occupying high positions in government are subject to divine retribution more than anybody else, because their actions can make or mar the fortunes of millions living in their jurisdiction. They probably don't know that by not using authority in a righteous manner they are being guilty of stark ingratitude to God who confers power as a special privilege on a selected few. The only way one can repay this gratitude is by dispensing justice and working ceaselessly for the welfare of the subjects and curbing greed and lust which inhibit ethical performance. He administers a special note of warning against extravagance and ostentatious living of state functionaries.

Avarice and insincerity of officers, always have a disenchanting effect on social life in a community. Generosity, he preaches, is a balmy quality and its constant practice ensures trust and confidence in administration. Tahir has depicted the relationship between the ruler and his subjects in the following words:-

> *"You should know that by your appointment, you were made treasurer, guardian and shepherd. The people under your jurisdiction are called subjects (raiyah flock) because you are their shepherd and overseer. Therefore accept from them what they give you of their affluence, and use it for the administration of their affairs, for their welfare and for providing for their needs. Employ for them understanding skilled and experienced men, who have theoretical knowledge of, and are able to act with, political wisdom and moderation. Give them good salaries. This is one of the duties incumbent upon you in connection with the task from which you have been entrusted."*

The above remarks show that the writer was fully aware of the significant role which the selection of personnel plays in creating a healthy administrative climate. Understanding, experience, knowledge, political wisdom and moderation are some of the salient qualities, which he thinks are essential for good administrators. On the other hand it is the responsibility of the government to see that salary structure is rational so that administrators can have adequate income to maintain a certain respectable standard of living.

Financially dissatisfied public service can play havoc with the fortunes of the people. Adequate salary is not an absolute safeguard against corruption or dishonesty, but it can certainly reduce its intensity considerably. Tahir also advocates effective intelligence service as another safeguard against excesses of officials. This would keep the government well-informed about the behaviour, style of life and other activities of officers working in the field.

Another theme which Tahir has developed at length is the accessibility of the ruler to his subjects, particularly the poor ones who don't have the means to find ready access to the regular law courts. If these simmering grievances of the people are not corrected, they can ruin the stability of thc kingdom. He says :-

> *Devote yourself to looking after the affairs of the poor and indigent, those who are not able to bring before you complaints about injustices they have suffered, and other lowly persons, who do not know that they may ask for their rights. Inquire about these people in all secrecy, and put good men among your subjects in charge of them. Command them to report to you their needs and conditions, so that you will be able to look into the measures through which God might improve their affairs.*

Even if officials are legally accessible to the public, many of them have the tendency to adopt such measures which would discourage a visitor from visiting public offices. Either there are restrictions on the number of interviews one can have with an official or there are so many barriers of security and secrecy, that petitioners have neither the courage nor the means to surmount them. In order to make accessibility meaningful Tahir suggests that, 'let people frequently come to see you and show them your face. Let not your guards hinder them. Be humble towards them. Show them your smiling countenance. 'Be lenient with them when (you put) questions and speak to them, Be benevolent to them in your generosity and bounty.'

And lastly it is the duty of the government to keep a constant watch on the accumulation of wealth and property by state officers and no effort should be spared in exercising vigilance on their faithfulness, straightforwardness and support for the government. Very often, it also happens that one has an access to an officer, but the latter's attitude would be so scowling and arrogant,' that the complainant would never be able to unburden all his grievances. It is unbecoming of an officer to give an interview to an aggrieved person, and then to give such a shabby treatment, that he may not turn up again with any complaint.

Chapter 2

Ideal Governance Traditions

It is extremely misleading to apply non-Islamic terms to Islamic concepts and institutions. The ideology of Islam has a social orientation peculiar to itself, different in many respects from that of the Modern West, and can be successfully interpreted only within its own context and in its own terminology. Any departure from this principle invariably tends to obscure the attitude of Islamic Law toward many of the burning issues of our time.

Welfare State

The concept of "Welfare State" is a quantitative concept and not a qualitative concept. This has important Connotations for Afro-Asian countries, having their own sense of destiny. Also, it is in this context, that we must view the disenchantment or disillusionment which is felt in Britain about the 'Welfare State'. This disillusionment arises primarily from the awareness of the fact that the British system now no longer produces 'Empire Builders.' the ears stands on hearing such words as 'Empire' and 'Empire Building'. But these are used here only as a concept and also perhaps to catch the attention of the reader. The 'Empire' in the modern world is akin to the 'Area of Influence' or a 'Block'. Was it not Allen Dulles who had said:-

> *"Our conflict is world wide and we must intervene in order to protect our global interests."*

We should not, however, blame Mr. Dulles for what he says. Every great power in any time would have had to same interests. In fact in the history of the world, one cannot find a great country which has also not been an empire building country. There are numerous references to this phenomenon in the poetry of Dr. Muhammad Iqbal.

It must, however, be understood that the word 'Empire' has a different connotation in Islam, that what this word is commonly understood to imply. The Quran says:-

> *"You are the best community that has been sent forth unto mankind: you enjoin the Right and forbid the Wrong: and you have faith in the Laws of God"*
>
> *(Al-Quran 3:110)*

Allama Muhammad Asad commenting on this issue says:-

> *"This is the moral justification of the aggressive activism of Islam, a justification of the early Islamic conquests and of its so-called 'imperialism'. For Islam was 'imperialist', if you insist on this term; but this kind of Imperialism was not prompted by love of domination, it had nothing to do with economic or national selfishness, nothing with the greed to increase Muslim comforts at other peoples' cost; nor has it ever meant the coercion of non-believers into the fold of Islam. It has only meant as it means today, the construction of a worldly frame for the best possible spiritual development of man. For, according to the teachings of Islam moral knowledge automatically forces moral responsibility upon man. A mere Platonic discernment between Right and Wrong, without the urge to promote Right and to destroy Wrong, is a gross immorality in itself. In Islam, morality lives and dies with the human endeavour to establish its victory upon earth."*

Right to Conquer : If one goes back in history, one finds Aristotle preaching to his disciples, one of whom came to be known to the world as Alexander of Macedon that Greeks as a civilized nation had a right to conquer and civilize the barbarians and, if need be, to destroy them. The 'State' is nothing but a sum total of the ideology, aspirations and hopes of a people. These act and react to produce (that is, if these actions and reactions occur in the right direction and are of sufficient force) a prototype personality to whom the name of 'Empire Builder' is given.

This 'Empire Builder', acts on one hand on the ideology, aspirations and hopes and on the other on the education, culture and religion of his people. This action and reaction produces the needed personality-type i.e. the person which ideally reflects the image of a nation. When a nation has succeeded in producing the needed personality-type in adequate numbers, their actions and reactions on the previous blocks of the model would tend to lead to the fulfillment of a nation. The name 'Empire has been given to this state of fulfillment.

Let us put some flash on our 'Empire Builder'. What type of man is he? To do this, we must first select a 'State'. Let us select Great Britain for this purpose which has been after all most recent of the 'Empires'. In a somewhat lighter vein, we may find a caricature of the Britain 'Empire Builder' in Major Thompson the dynamic impact of the others can be gauged in the following quotations:-

> *"He (John Jacob) was remarkable man, possessing both physical and moral courage to an extraordinary degree. Whatever he thought was right and just he would do it....I seldom get above three hours sleep in the twenty-four, and the work will kill me which I do not regret, for I have proved and established principles and built foundations on which other will be able to work"*

> *"In August, as the situation steadily deteriorated, John Nicholson rose from his bed, though in a raging fever, and headed south for Attack with sixty Pathan horsemen, leaving orders for 150 levies to follow him on foot. Riding hard through the night, he reached the Indus with about half his horsemen, in the early hours of the morning, and dashed up to the gate of the fortress. Rousing the garrison from their sleep, he demanded that the gates be opened for him, and when this was done ordered that the men arrest their mutinous leaders. For some moments the situation looked ugly, and if the Sikhs had set on him Nicholson could not possibly have escaped with his life. But he was of the stuff that great heroes are made (twenty years later mothers in the Punjab would threaten their naughty children that 'Nikal Seyh' would get them) and his language and presence made a shattering impression. The Sikhs were cowed, and did as they were told; Nicholson took over the fort and prepared it for a siege, then, leaving it under a loyal commander, began scouring the countryside with his cavalry, putting down disorder whenever he found it".*

John Nicholson had once written to Henry Lawrence:-

> *"I feel I am little fit for regulation work, and I can never sacrifice common-sense or justice, or the interest of a people or the country to red-tape"*

Empire Builders

Some of these 'Empire Builder' were vain and proud while others were modest and considerate, but all possessed one quality which was their complete devotion to duty, and above all a cultivated sense of self-righteousness. Now we come to the Islamic Empire, the memory of whose glorious past has haunted the Muslims throughout the ages. It is the memory of dynamic Islam which rose like a storm from the wilds of Arabia and enveloped the world in a short span of 125 years, pulling down from their high pedestal gods who had ruled over man since the beginning of history, up- rooting centuries old institutions and superstitions and replacing all civilization that had been built on enslavement of humanity.

Who were these people then, who created this greatest of the empires, the Muslim 'Empire Builder' in addition to the above mentioned qualities of the British 'Empire Builder', had one more advantage, that was his devotion was not to man-made ideals but to the concept of 'Tauheed', which enabled him, while remaining fully involved in the affairs of this world, to cultivate a sense of detachment and spirit of sacrifice for other fellow beings. Belief in Tauheed meant that their devotion to Allah was absolutely complete; that is they had no fear but that of Allah and fear of Allah means consciousness of the disadvantages of acting against laws of God given to man through the Quran. These people in the Muslim terminology are called 'Mumin' and 'Muttaqi' and only these are fit to be the rulers and administrators in an Islamic State.

In the affairs of the nations, it is mot important to maintain a balance between socio-economic ideology and the spiritual ideology. It was in fact this balance which for the first time in the history of world was presented by Islam. It is felt that the present Chinese Cultural Revolution initiated by Mao Tsetung is nothing but an arrangement to fill the gap which has arisen between the great economic ideology of China and the lack of a supporting spiritual ideology. It will not be out of place to mention once again Allama Asad who says:-

> *"It was the religious teaching of the Quran that gave a solid foundation and the life-example of the Prophet Muhammad (Peace and Blessings be upon him) that became a band of steel around that grand social structure. The Roman Empire had no such spiritual element to keep it together; and therefore it broke down so rapidly."*

It is most important to appreciate that imitation — physical or ideological — is a most dangerous course for any nation to follow "and only very superficial people can believe that is possible to imitate a civilization in its external appearance without being at the same time effected by its spirit. A civilization is not an empty form, but a living energy. The moment we begin to accept the form, its inherent currents and dynamic influences set to work in ourselves and mould slowly, imperceptibly, our whole mental attitude."

It is in perfect appreciation of this experience that the Prophet said:-

"Who imitates other people becomes one of them"

Also there is feeling among the intellectuals of the Afro-Asian countries that the ideals of 'Welfare State' are purposely being imposed upon the developing countries by the West. The Western Powers, it is felt, are interested in extending 'Welfare State' to the developing countries, with a view to counteract the popular political reactions in these countries in the overall interests of their 'Global Strategy' and diverting these countries from their drive towards real economic viability based on a sound and self-expanding infrastructure of capital and technology. It is also feared that Western concept of 'organized welfare' leads to a crisis of identity and that its organized propagation by West aims at creating an 'awareness' leading to general dissatisfaction, frustration and drift. This state of affairs, then naturally diverts the attention of developing countries from nation building tasks of real importance.

Scholars have laid much emphasis on Islamic Charity'. His idea of a 'Modern welfare state' being a heaven of charity, though having some superficial similarity with some limited functions of an Islamic State, is practically an antithesis of Islamic concept, simply for the reason that this idea of charity results in building a makeshift barricade against the emergence of a true Islamic order. The countries of Asia and Africa need a revolutionary concept if they aspire for self-sufficiency and real independence. Only such a concept can extol them to an honourable position in the community of nations. The changes in social structure may be drastic, violent or evolutionary. But makeshift concepts or patchwork ideas simply would serve no real purpose.

The scholars while advancing their ideas of charity so vehemently overlooks the revolutionary concept of Islam in human, economic and social structure. Islam in its pristine ideology, does not envisage society composed of 'haves' and 'have nots', where a vast majority of people are perpetually degraded to the position of beggars, asking for alms from a minority of charitable and benevolent ruling class. This is diametrically opposed to Islamic principles of Akhuwwat and 'Musawat' and hinders any real progress of the society. It is a concept born out of western capitalism and neo-colonialism. Islamic concept, as can be understood from the Quran and authentic hadith, aims at building a classless society obeying the laws of the Quran:-

> *"And what do you understand what the Era of faith is; again, what do you understand what the Era of faith is? It is the Era in which no man shall have any control over any other man; and the reign in that Era shall be entirely of Allah's Laws." (Al-Quran 82:17,18,19)*

Thus a country, aspiring to become an Islamic State, must declare its faith and pledge at the very outset to create such classless society governed by the Laws of Quran, as illustrated by the life of the Last Messenger of Allah (peace and blessings be upon him) and his four closest companions, Khulafa-i-Rashideen. It will be a waste of time and energies for Muslims to grope in the dark labyrinth of Western political and social theories. All charitable activities in an Islamic state are meant to cover the interim period till the conditions of a true Islamic society are reached and to meet exigencies of curing maldistribution of wealth. Allama Muhammad Asad commenting on the following hadith says:-

> *"The faithful are like one man, if his eye suffers, his whole body suffers; and if his head suffers, his whole body suffers. You will recognise the faithful by their mutual compassion, love and sympathy. They are like one body; if one of its part is ill, the whole body suffers from sleeplessness and fever".*

Sociological Lesson : "This, then, is the deepest sociological lesson of Islam: there can be no happiness and strength in a society that permits some of its members to suffer undeserved want, while others have more than they need. If the whole society suffers privations owing to extraordinary circumstances (as, for instance, happened to the Muslim community in the early days of Islam), such privations may become the source of spiritual strength and, through it, of future greatness. But if the available resources of a community are so unevenly distributed that certain groups within it live in affluence while the majority of the people are forced to use up all their energies in search of their daily bread. Poverty becomes the most dangerous enemy of spiritual progress, and occasionally drives whole community away from.

God-consciousness and into the arms of soul-destroying materialism. It is undoubtedly this that the Prophet had in mind when he uttered the warning words:-

> *Poverty may sometimes turn into unbelief (Kufr).*
> *Poverty in the midst of plenty is a negation of the very principle of brotherhood by which Islam stands and falls."*

The scholar have suggested the collection of 'Zakat' by Union Councils. In Islam 'Zakat' is a central responsibility and obligation and must be collected centrally by an Islamic State. Furthermore, if a state is not Islamic in its positive basic concept by virtue of its declarations and actions, it cannot collect 'Zakat' whether centrally or through such agencies as Union Councils, as it no longer remains obligatory on Muslims to pay 'Zakat' to an un- Islamic State, no matter whether it is entirely composed of people paying lip-service to Islam.

In this connection, it is also important to note that:-

> *"Behold, God has bought of the Faithful their persons and their possessions, offering them Paradise in return".*
> *(Al-Quran 9:111)*

Government's Rights

It follows, therefore, that a government ruling in the name of Allah and His Prophet and in obedience to the Law of Islam has the right to call upon all the resources of the citizens —including their personal possessions and even their lives— whenever the interests of the community and the security of the state demand such an effort. In other words, the government is entitled (a) to impose, over and above the Zakat- tax immutably laid down in Quran and Sunnah, any additional taxes and levies that may be deemed necessary for the welfare of the community, (b) to impose, whenever necessary, restrictions on private ownership of certain kinds of properties, means of production, or natural resources with a view to their being administered by the state as public utilities, and (c) to subject all able-bodied citizens to compulsory military service in defence of the state.

It will not be out of place to point out here that most of the present day problems of concept in Muslim world are the outcome of attempts to amalgamate. Western pseudo-social and political theories with wrong notions of Islam. This will lead us nowhere. The absolute truth of Islam does not accept any compromise with man-made fallacies.

> *"Accept Islam in its entirely"* *(Al-Quran 2:208)*

Acceptance in Totality

Either we shall have to accept Islam in its full application to our social and political life or reject it totally and be damned. There is no midway. There is a very big difference between a state run by Muslims of today and a true Islamic State. We have to discard many legacies of Muslim Monarchism and Western Imperialism in order to become an Islamic State. The Quran provides us the required sound basic concept of such a state without hankering after alien and doubtful ideologies.

The great scholar of Islam, Allama Muhammad Asad said that : "We should not underestimate the difficulties that will confront us should we decide to give to our polity the contents and forms demanded by Islam. For one thing, it is not an easy task to achieve a truly Islamic polity after the centuries of debasement and slavery which have sapped the strength of the Muslim community and undermined its social morale. During the period of their political decay, the Muslims have lost a good deal of their cultural self-confidence as well, and many of them find it difficult today to avoid thinking in Western terms of 'state and nation' and to think in Islamic terms instead. They blindly follow Western patterns of thought in the naive belief that every thing which comes from the West must be more 'up-to-date' than anything which they, the Muslims, could produce out of themselves; and this conviction leads them to an irresponsible application of Western political concepts to all that happens in their own society. On the other hand, many conservative Muslims who, in word and deed, insist on the maintenance of all traditional forms and, consequently, oppose the Westernization of their community, base their opposition not so much on the real values of Islam as on the social conventions evolved in the centuries of our decadence.

Their minds seem to work on the assumption that Islam and the conventions of Muslim society are one and the same thing (which every thinking person knows is an utterly false assumption) and that, therefore, everything that implies a departure from the conventions evolved in the course of our history — both with regard to our social habits and our approach to the problems of state and government — goes against Islam; and that, therefore, it would be the duty of an Islamic state to give permanence and legal sanction to all the social forms in which we have hitherto been living. In other words, these conservative elements within our society seem to take it for granted that the survival of Islam depends on the maintenance of the very conditions which, because of their sterile rigidity, now make it impossible for Muslims to live in accordance with the true tenets of

Islam....Apart from the difficulties arising from our own cultural decadence and the centuries-old stagnation of Muslim thought, any attempt to reorganize our countries on truly Islamic lines invariably arouses apprehensions in the non-Muslim world and causes ;it to place all manner of obstructions, direct and indirect, in our way towards this ideal.

Ever since the Crusades, Islam has been misrepresented in the West, and a deep distrust — almost hatred — of all Islamic propositions has become part and parcel of the Western cultural heritage. The Westerners see in the tenets of Islam not only a denial of many of the fundamental beliefs of their own religion but also a political threat. Under the influence of their historical memories, of the centuries of passionate warfare between the Muslim world and Europe, they attribute to Islam — quite unjustifiably — an inherent hostility towards all non-Muslims; and so they fear that revival of the Islamic spirit, as manifested in the idea of the Islamic state, might revive the slumbering strength of the Muslims and drive them to new aggressive adventures in the direction of the West. To counteract such a possible tendency, the Westerners are doing their utmost to prevent a resurgence of political power in Muslim countries and a restoration of Islam to its erstwhile dominant position in Muslim social and intellectual life. Their means of combat are not merely political; they are cultural as well. Through the instrumentality of Western Schools and of Western-oriented methods of education in the Muslim world, the distrust of Islam as a social doctrine is being systematically planted in the minds of the younger generation of Muslim men and women; and the principal weapon in this campaign to discredit Islam is being supplied, unconsciously, by the reactionary elements within our own society".

Communication of Law

Legal Literalism

Ibn Arabi is not specifically pointing to some outwardly 'reformable' defect in the teaching and transmission of the law in his time, nor to the fraudulent pretensions or normal defects of particular individuals. Rather, he is primary alluding here to the fundamental—and in our present circumstances, humanly inescapable—problem that the just, appropriate application and interpretation of the traditional sources concerning the divine commands and their historical application by the Prophet usually require a far deeper understanding of both their ultimate contexts and intentions and the relevant factors in each particular case than can be expected of any but the rarest individuals, those whose every action is divinely inspired and protected from error. As he remarks, more openly in section II-7 below, those truly qualified `authorities' (the true *wulat)* in any age, whether or not they outwardly rule, are none other than the divinely guided 'saints'—i.e., the *awliya* (a term drawn from the same Arabic root as the words translated as `authority' in these passages, and having explicit connotations of spiritual authority *[wilaya]* that are not readily conveyed by the term `saint' in Western languages). (James Winston Morris, in Michel Chodkiewicz (ed.) (1988). *Les Illuminations de La Mecque* (Paris: Sindbad).

Let us examine the methodological basis for Ibn al-Arabi's *fiqh,* and then two cases of that method in practice. Ibn al-Arabi describes his colleagues as *ummal,* those entrusted to act, among the Ulama, those who know.' As with all the technical words used by Ibn al-Arabi, this finds sufficient description in the Arab language, which is not the growing and changing language of Arabic but the language of the Quran. Ibn Manzur says about the word *amil,* which is the singular of *ummal,* 'The *amil* is the one who is put in charge [w.l.y., *cf. wilayah* and *awliya*] *of* someone's affairs, his wealth, his property, and his works.'

The actual self of the true *amil is* invisible, because the activity one sees is rather that of the one on whose behalf the *amil* negotiates or contracts or speaks. Hence, the description of the 'people put in charge', the *awliya: When they are seen, Allah is remembered.'*

Another word describing people who give a certain kind of command *is umara (amr, a.m.r.),* where when 'they' command, 'He' commands. The superimposition of commands comes about with literal transmission. They are, Ibn al-Arabi says, *umara* who hear the divine Word and give it back just as they heard it, word by word. He says. This [reward] does not occur except to one who propagates the revelation from the Quran or Sunna with the words which it came in. And this does not happen except for the transmitters of the revelation, among the reciters and transmitters of *Hadith,* and for the legal scholars; but not for the one who transmits the *Hadith* according to meaning (that is, not literally), like Sufyan al-Thawri and others believed in doing.

The problem with such transmission is that what is being transmitted is one's own understanding of a particular *Hadith.* Such a transmitter has, in fact, falsely claimed to be a messenger himself. In great contrast, the *amil* transmits the word directly, without intervention and without adding his own ideas or understandings.

The ones who propagate the revelation as they heard it, and give back the message as they heard it, the reciters and transmitters of *Hadith, 'they* will assemble at the row of the messengers, on them peace." Because it is easy to transmit literally and exactly, and because it is difficult to be a prophet and carry the burdens of caring for a community, Ibn al-Arabi links the *Hadith, There will be a people on the day* of *judgement the prophets will be jealous of* to this situation.'

Thus, the importance of literal transmission. Besides this literal transmission which allows one to assemble with the prophets, there is another prophet-like activity. That activity is *ijtihad,* which looks like the creation of Law, while we know and accept as a tenet that the creation of *Shariah* ended with Muhammad. Given that the decision of the *mujtahid* (one who does *ijtihad)* is confirmed by the *Shariah,* given that new law is impossible, and given that, *There is no messenger after me, nor prophet,* Ibn al-Arabi categorizes that act of the *mujtahid* as giving him the degree of the prophets but without giving them Law. He says,

Allah honoured His messenger by making his people witnesses to the nations of prophets as He made the prophets witnesses to their nations. Then He made this nation special, meaning its Ulama, by making Law for them *ijtihad* of the legal properties *[ahkam,* singular *hukm],* and by determining as the *hukm* what their *ijtihad* leads them to.

Then,

Such a one in this nation would not be a prophet, as he is not a prophet through revelation sent down. But Allah made law for the Ulama of this nation their *ijtihad,* just as He said to His Prophet, *So that you would judge [h.k.m.] among the people by what Allah showed you [4:105];* the *mujtahid* does not judge except by what Allah shows him in his *ijtihad.* One characteristic of *ijtihad* is that the right determination gets extra reward and the wrong determination still gets one reward. The standard text for this situation is found in *Subul al-Salam,* from Amr Ibn al-As, that 'He heard the messenger of Allah (PBUH) saying, When the *hakim [h.k.m.]* determines the *hukm,* that is [interjects the author of *Subul al-Salam],* when he wants to determine the *hukm,* based on his word, let him do *ijtihad,* because *ijtihad* is done before the *hukm* [is determined], then if he hits the mark, he gets two rewards, and when he determines the *hukm* and does *ijtihad* and errs, that is, is not consistent with what the *hukm* is with Allah, then he gets one reward'.

There is also a lesser known *Hadith*. In *Musnad* Ibn Hanbal 2:187, *haddathana* [it was told to us in the form of a *Hadith* by] Abd-Allah *haddathani* [it was told to me in the form of a *Hadith* by] my father [Ahmad ibn Hanbal] *haddathana* Hassan *haddathana* Ibn Lehyah *haddathana* Amr Ibn al-As who reported that he said, 'I he [...] and the messenger of Allah came and he said, When the *qadi* judges [q.d.y.] and does *ijtihad,* and hits the mark, he has ten rewards; and when he does *ijtihad* and errs, he has one or two rewards.'

One of the ways Ibn al-Arabi explains this characteristic is found in his *fiqh* discussion of the prayer during the eclipse. He crosses over from the outward legal positions to the inward truths to show that if 'the *mujtahid* errs, he is at the level of the one who is in the concealed area of the eclipsed area. There is no burden on him; he is given one reward.' But there are those who, in full daylight, still refuse the light. About them, he says,

But if the revealed text appears to him, and he leaves it in favour of his own opinion *[ray]* of his *qiyas* [deduction], manifesting his false allegation, there is no excuse for him before Allah, and he has offended.

Continuing, he says,

Most of this comes about with the legal scholars following those who said to them, 'Do not follow us blindly, but follow the *Hadith* which comes to you, if it opposes what we have determined as *hukm* [legal property], because the *Hadith is* our *madhhab* [way, school]. We do not determine anything except by the evidence which appears to us, and which appears to us to be evidence; we do not make requisite anything other than that. We have not made requisite on you all following us, but we have made requisite on you to be petitioners of us. These eclipsed legal scholars refuse the text itself. They do not appreciate that as the moment changes, the situation changes, and the legal properties change accordingly. Ibn al-Arabi says,

During every moment, during a single event, the *hukm* [legal property] alters according to the *mujtahid.* Because of this, [Imam] Malik used to say, when someone asked him [for a legal decision] about an event, 'Did it occur?' If he said, 'No', he would say 'I will not give a *fatwa* [legal opinion].' If he said, 'Yes', he would give a *fatwa* at that moment according to what his evidence gave him. The blind follower [q.l.d.] of the legal scholars of our times has decided that he has fulfilled the duty of his following his leader by following the *Hadith* which his Imam commanded him, and his blind following of the *hukm,* despite finding something which opposes. So he disobeys Allah, in His word, *So take what the messenger gives you, and adhere to it [59:7],* and he disobeys the messenger, in his word, *So obey him,* because he [Muhammad] did not say anything except from a command of his Lord. And he disobeys his Imam, in his word, 'Take the *Hadith* when it is sent to you, and scorn my word.'

They 'are in eclipse perpetually, endless for them until the day of judgement. They are not with Allah, nor are they with His messenger, nor with their Imam. Of them Allah and His messenger and their Imams have washed their hands and they have no proof in respect to Allah. So let them see who gathers with these!

First Case : Respect for the literal words and phrases of the revelation involves respect for the silences as well. Ibn al-Arabi condemns the silences of the revelation being filled in with arrogant noise, often justified as *qiyas* (analogical deduction). There are two kinds of *mujtahids,* he says at one point. One predominates declaring taboo and the other predominates lifting difficulties (where the word is *haraj,* about which Ibn Manzur says, 'You are in *haraj,* that is, in tightness and constriction', and based on the verse, *We did not make any haraj on you all in the religion [22:28], by adhering to the verses and by returning to the root [asl]."* The latter 'is according to Allah closer to Allah and greater in level than the one who predominates declaring taboo, as taboo is an accidental thing which occurs randomly on the *asl.*'

Given this, in the absence of taboo declared by the revealed text, one should return to the root. The first issue is about purification for the circumambulation of the Kaaba." Ibn al-Arabi's position is, 'The circumambulation is permitted without *wudu* [a form of purification] for the man and the woman, unless the woman is a menstruant, based on the mention of the revealed text about it."' The restriction is only on the menstruant, 'and not every worship makes as a precondition for it this outward purification [of *wudu*].' So, in the absence of a text for non-menstruants, men and women, Ibn al-Arabi's position is to return to the root; then, we find that everything in existence has a face towards Allah, and in this respect, it is pure.

There is not in existence, according to the real determination, anything but The Pure, because the name *al-quddus* [The Holy] *is* associated with existence, and this is confirmed by His statement, 'To Him returns the entirety of the affair, so worship Him and rely on Him; your Lord is not Unaware of what you are doing' [11:123].

Here, Ibn al-Arabi glosses the Quranic phrase 'what you are doing'. He says it refers to 'your interference between Allah and His creatures'.

The word he uses, *tafriq (f.r.q.),* carries negative connotations, where Ibn Manzur says, *farraqa* (differentiation) for something good *is farq* (difference), and *farraqa* for something bad is *tafriq* (interference). Therefore, Ibn al-Arabi says, 'It is not appropriate to intervene between the creature and his Master except to enter in between the creature and the Master for good *[khayr].'* The negative intervention he is talking about is our speaking unfavourably about creation; the only proper intervention is interference for the good. He tells the following anecdote to demonstrate this. Ibn al-Arabi says,

'I met one of the Itinerants on the seashore, between Murcia and Manarah [in Tunis], and he said to me, I met in this place some one of the Truthful Substitutes when he was walking along the edge of the ocean; I greeted him and he returned the greeting. In the country was a great oppressive tyrant. I said to him, O you, have you seen what oppression there *is* in the country? He looked at me very angrily, and said to me: Do not say anything but the Good.' Ibn al-Arabi explains, 'Because of this, Allah has made intercession Law and accepts legal excuses'. This is then linked to impurity. 'Impurity is an accidental thing, designated with Law-property; but purity is an essential thing'. Therefore, if there is an accidental property which emerges at some moment, then every other moment remains in its root property, which is purity.

Unfortunately, 'the legal scholars have been heedless of this, flailing at it, but they do not get it. We have already explained that one does not get into a disobedience completely, if one is a believer'. Ibn al-Arabi explains that the situation of the believer who does something bad is described as, *One who mixed a wholesome act with another which was bad [9:102].* The bad is the bad but the wholesome act is the faith of the believer (the *iman* of the *mumin),* because there is no disobedience by the believer except faith that accompanies it, which tells the believer that it is something disobedient. Hence, the 'faith which knows it is a disobedience is actually an obedience to Allah'.

This conclusion combines with Ibn al-Arabi's *fiqh* position on praying behind a bad-doing leader, which focuses on the standard legal question which is based on the paradigmatic case of the Muslims praying behind al-Hajjaj and whether their prayers would be accepted. Ibn al-Arabi says that, of course, one cannot pray behind a bad-doing leader; but let us look at the legal facts. When al-Hajjaj does *wudu* for the *salah* and follows every condition for the validity of the *salah,* how can the name 'bad-doer' apply at that moment? Furthermore, `al-Hajjaj and others in the context of their bad-doing are believers obeying their faith' that what bad they are doing is disobedience.

Ibn al-Arabi sums up the situation as follows :

> *The most amazing thing about this issue is that we are commanded to have a fine impression of people, forbidden to have a bad impression of people. We saw one whom we knew to be a bad-doer, who did* wudu, *and did the* salah, *so how could we apply to him the name of bad-doer during the moment of his worship? And how much more is the fine impression than the bad impression of him in doing it? We have no knowledge of the future for him, and we do not see what Allah did in the past with him, and the* hukm *[determinative property] belongs to the* waqt *[moment] of obedience which he is upon, being involved [right then] in obedience. So the fine impression is prior.*

Then, Ibn al-Arabi tells a story which is a warning to smug piety. He mentioned that someone 'firm in his religion told me about a man who was a legal scholar and a theologian who was a profligate of *nafs* [self].' This is a clue to the audience that this man struggled with his self (cf. *mujahidah),* and it is the terms of the struggle, not the discreet outcomes, which is of significance.

He said to me, 'I came upon him in a gathering where wine was being circulated, and he was drinking with the rest. The drink was finished, and it was said to him, "Send someone to fetch us some drink". He said to them, "I shall not to do it!

I have not decided upon disobedience completely. For me between the cups there is a turning for forgiveness, and I do not wait for the next cup, so when the cup gets in my hands, I wait and ask whether my Lord will give me success and I will leave it, or He will desert me and I will drink it".' Like this are the Ulama, may Allah have mercy on them! This knowledgeable man died while there was in his heart a disappointment that he did not meet me, but he did meet me, but he did not recognize me, and he asked me about myself, and he had love for me, may Allah have mercy on him. That was in Murcia in the year 585.

Concluding this section, Ibn al-Arabi tells another anecdote about a spiritual encounter' he had. He says,

> *I witnessed the Real in my innermost being during a* waqiah *[spiritual encounter], and He said to me, 'Tell My worshippers what I designated as My generosity to the believer: the good rewarded with ten like it up to seven hundred as many, and the bad with only one like it. The*

> *bad act does not oppose faith in its being a bad act. So why would My worshipper despair of My mercy?* My mercy pervades everything *[7:156], and* I am according to the impression of My worshipper of Me, so let the impression of Me be Good!'

Second Case : The particular spiritual position of the believer presents certain legal, *fiqh* consequences. One of them is examined in the issue of praying over a person who has committed suicide. 'Should the one who killed himself be prayed over or not? There is one who said he should be prayed over, and there is one who said he should not be prayed over. For the first I argue.'

To support this position, Ibn al-Arabi addresses the background situation of intercession. As usual, he finishes his enumeration of the Ulama's outward legal positions with their inward complement, which he calls *itibar,* a crossover. He says here, 'A crossover for this section is that as Allah has permitted intercession in the *salah* over the dead, we know that Allah approves of that, and that the petition for him is accepted.' But we have the seemingly obvious *Hadith* which at first glance seems to refute that background. It is reported that *The one who kills himself abides in the fire, abiding therein ever,* and that *The Garden is forbidden him.* People take that to mean that *salah* over the suicide should not be done, but Ibn al-Arabi works from another text which will challenge that first glance understanding.

One key text precedes the text above and has the phrase, *My worshipper rushes to me on his own,* where 'rushes', Ibn al-Arabi says, is an allusion to other texts, which are always taken positively. He says, 'The wisdom alluded to, here in this issue, is the word of Allah, *My worshipper [abd] rushes to Me by himself; I forbid him the Garden.* There is an allusion here and a reality, and the allusion is to *They race* [to the Good, 3:114] and *They are foremost* [in seeking forgiveness, 57:21] and *Who approaches Me an inch, I approach him a yard*—all positive images. The root word 'rushes' includes the concept of taking one's own initiative. This contrasts with the usual situation, where Allah 'makes for him a specific limit [of lifespan]. But [the suicide] tries to hasten the meeting and *rushes* to Him before having come to that limit'. Now, this entire text, with rushing and with being forbidden the Garden, is in a differentiated mode *(tafsil),* and for that reason, it is possible—in the *fiqh* sense—to return to the undifferentiated mode, which is the root, the *asl* or *usul* (plural, roots). It can, he says, 'be brought toward the face which is best for the believer, for helping him out, with the *usul,*' and that 'is a priority'."

When the text is differentiated, that is, made specific and detailed, such as, 'As for His statement about the one who killed himself by iron, or poison, or throwing himself from a mountain', then one can argue that, [I]t is not said in the *Hadith* whether they are believers or something else [and this leaves the way open for debate], so one may advance a likelihood; and if the likely is going to be introduced, we return to the usul [basic, general, undifferentiated] texts, where we see that faith has dominion of power which, because of it, the ever-abiding without end in the fire is not possible. So we know, certainly, that the revelation must be reporting that about those who associate partners with Allah *[mushriks],* is designated that they will be punished forever, so he said, *Who kills himself with iron, among the mushriks, his iron in his hand will take him to the innermost fire of Jahannam, everlastingly, abiding therein everlastingly.* That is, this type of punishment is his determination in the fire. Like that, *Who drinks poison, and kills himself, sips it in the fire of Jahannam everlastingly, abiding therein everlastingly,* that is, that is the kind of punishment he is punished with, this *kafir* [ingrate]. And it is reported that *Who kills himself with something is punished with it.*

Now, since we know that the believer's faith cannot be ultimately opposed, so we know that the text above must apply to the *mushrik,* 'even if the revelation did not specify, in this report, the sort [of person] itself, yet because the *Shariah* proofs are taken from many different perspectives, one of them coming together with another, in order to strengthen one by another, as *the believer is to the believers like the brick* wall, so one strengthens another.' Also differentiated is the vision of the divine. We know that 'the folk of the Garden see their Lord with a blessed vision, after they have entered the garden, as the report says about the calling to the garden—*When the people take their places in the Garden they are called to a vision.'*

Ibn al-Arabi is going to separate the two events, the taking of their places in the Garden and their being called to a vision. He argues, then that it is possible that,

> Allah has specified that, for this one who rushes to Him himself by killing himself, His word *I have forbidden him the Garden* may be before meeting Him; the blessed vision preceded the suicide meeting of Allah, and *then* he would enter the Garden, because the suicide saw that Allah was more merciful than the situation he was in, the circumstances which were the cause for him of this rushing. Otherwise, he would not have imagined that the repose with Allah would be better than the punishment which he was in when he rushes *to Him.*

To back up this argument, Ibn al-Arabi recalls the *Hadith* we just saw: *I am according to the impression of My worshipper of Me; so let the impression of Me be Good.*

Allah says, *ana inda zann abdi bi, fa-l-yazunna bi khayr [I am according to the impression of My worshipper of Me; so let the impression of Me be Good],* and the suicide, if he is a believer, has a Good impression of his Lord. It was the Good impression of his Lord that made him kill himself. This is more suitable, that one attribute to him the phrasing of this divine report. Well, there is no revealed text which clearly states a contradiction to this *tawil* [interpretation], even if it seems far-fetched; may the observer in his observation keep far away from the stipulated roots which would contradict this *tawil* with eternal wretchedness [for him]! So if he is present in it and balances it, he will recognize what we say about it. In the authentic report, there is *They will exit who have in their hearts the least, least of a grain of mustard of faith,* and nothing else remains except what we said about it. Allah did not say in this report anything but that he *forbade him the Garden,* only.

In effect, it is the job of the legal scholar (the observer above) to argue the best possible case, in this case, for the suicide. Ibn al-Arabi admits that his interpretation is far-fetched, but the argument is nevertheless logical and complies with the technical rules of the fiqh.

So if we argue for the chastisement, then the Garden is something forbidden to him that he enters without chastisement, like with the person of great sins. The report is a text for the suicide and others, among the people of great sins—they are upon the *hukm* [property] of [divine] volition, because *the man written down in the scrolls will not enter the fire,* even though he is one of the ones of great sins, if there was nothing with him but *la ilaha* in all his Islam in his period of life in the world. The reason for the [extreme threat] is so that one would realize that the carrying out of the threat against the suicide is for before entering into the Garden, that he will not be forgiven suicide. But Allah is more Generous than that the carrying out the threat be imputed to Him; rather imputed to Him should be His volition and the preponderance of Generosity. It is as one of the Arabs (desert Arabs) described it:

inna idha awad-tu-hu (IV) aw wa d-tu-hu (I)
la-akhlifu iadi
wa unjizu mawidi
When I vow or swear
I may go against my threat
But I would carry out my promise.

There is no mention in the revealed text about the threat *[iad,* root w.d.], but there is a mention about the promise *[wad w.d.]: Never think that Allah would go against His promise [to His messengers] [14:47].* The *iad* is specifically used for bad [e.g., a threat], but *wad* may be either good or bad. This argument is entirely justified linguistically. Ibn Manzur says about the root *w.d.*

Al-Azhari said, In the *Arab* discourse, *wad-tu [I* promised] the man good, and *wada-tu (I* threatened) him bad. If they do not want to mention good, they say, *wad-tu* and do not insert the *a,* and when they do not want to mention bad, they say, *awad-tu* and do not omit the *a.* There is a verse from Amir ibn Tufayl:

inna in awad-tu-hu aw wad-tu-hu

la-akhlifu iadi

was unjizu mawidi.

There are many who may object to Ibn al-Arabi's legal discourse, but it is not because he is not literal or firmly grounded in the revealed texts or does not follow the rules of legal discourse. But instead there seems to be another reason. Ibn al-Arabi's extreme literalism in the first case served to restore the essential quality of creation-purity. In the second case, he pushed literalism to the extreme and forced interpretations which he admitted were far-fetched. Why? To intercede positively for the eternal soul of a believer. We have quite the opposite legal discourse (if one can even use this term) today: a number of Islamicists who will identify impurity and pollution as essential and general traits of creation. Far-fetched interpretations are used to serve that purpose, but none are profferred to help out the believers.

Perennial Situation

That such a situation is perennial is suggested by Ibn al-Arabi's discussion of the addition during the prayer call of the morning *salah,* 'The *salah* is better than sleeping!' Some legal scholars argued that it was something introduced by Umar, so it is not strictly speaking Sunna (normative prophetic practice). But Ibn al-Arabi says, 'as for our position, we ourselves argue for it as being Shariah, even though it is an act of Umar, because the revelation determined it in his word, Who *practises a practice [Sunna] which is fine, [and it is practised after him, he gets its reward and the like of the reward of theirs, without diminishing their rewards at all],* and we have no doubt that it is a fine Sunna [practice], so it is appropriate to express it as the Shariah'. And then, 'Anyone who dislikes it, dislikes it only from fanaticism *[taassub]*. Who argues that, does not to do justice to it. We take refuge in Allah from the havoc of the egos!'

Ibn al-Arabi and Ijtihad

Frank E. Vogel remarked that Western studies of Islamic law have 'often omitted, justifiably or not, any consideration of the law's application'. This has led to confusion about concepts such as the 'closed gates of *ijtihad'*, where, as Wael B. Hallaq noted, we get 'the oddity that scholars should declare *ijtihad* non-existent, while they at the very same time acclaim certain *fuqaha* of their own age as *mujtahids,* exercising *ijtihad.'* Although Vogel gives an intriguing outline of an approach which should be used to address this and other issues, I believe there is much more than what meets the historical eye. Discussions about *ijtihad* are in fact indications of deeply held political positions. Solving the question of *ijtihad* is, therefore, beyond the scope of a narrowly conceived historicity.

Vogel lists three 'peculiar tenets associated with the theory of *qada',* which make the application of law problematic, but which also more deeply evince a radical and uncompromising world-view. First is the tenet that the *qadi* be a *mujtahid,* one able to do *ijtihad.* Second is that 'nothing but the revealed texts and the concrete facts of the case ought to constrain the *qadi's* conscience.

And third that there can be no reversals or appeals of decisions based on *ijtihad* of the *Qadi.* Vogel's notes that Ibn al-Muqaffa and others must have perceived that if 'this conception of *qada*—so idealistic, individualistic, multifarious, and unpredictable—were given full scope, Islamic legal systems would face great practical difficulty'. Vogel, and a great number of legal scholars over the centuries, favour an 'Islamic legal system' over idealizing conceptions. There are thinkers, however, who do not do so, particularly Ibn al-Arabi, and it is their concept of *ijtihad* which we examine here.

Vogel correctly links this idealizing conception of *qada* to an endemic tension between the sultan and the state, which wants a standardized, centralized, and codified system of law that can be practiced universally and then I would propagate it to every city of the cities of the Muslims, and I would command them to practice it, and they would not refer to anything else.' Imam Malik said, 'Do not do so, O Amir of the believers, because the people have had handed over to them positions, and they heard *Hadith* and they examined reports, and each people takes what was handed over to them, and they yield to Allah with it, so leave the people alone and what they choose for themselves in every country.' The desire of the ruler is to codify laws. The kind of application of *Shariah* which Malik conceived is impossible for emerging states. The state is interested in one answer not multiplicity, in one mass not diversity, in efficiency and not variance. One tentative contact between those scholars who would aid the state in codification occurred within two centuries of the death of the Prophet. Vogel describes it as follows:

> [Ibn al-Muqaffa] recommended to the caliph that the latter examine all of the conflicting rulings on each issue, select among them, and then codify his choices into a written law. This proposal was defeated, and with it a bid that the ruler—wielding the authority *of siyasah* [political power] with its breadth, flexibility, responsiveness to utility, and, above all, powers of compulsion—should seize control of legislation and thereby replace the Ulama and their rigorously individualistic and conscience-based *ijtihad.*

However, other contacts succeeded a thousand years ago and the superstructure of *fiqh* became autonomous and fixed. The contact was genuine compromise. The sultans wanted a codified law which would place all the authority and legitimacy of Islam at their disposal, creating a system of law which would be efficient and centralized, maximizing of utility and concentrating all discipline and punishment under the sultan's or state's hand. The Ulama wanted a *fiqh* which could be responsive to the highly diverse cultures and situations the Muslims found themselves in; a system which would maintain a hierarchy of knowledge, not a hierarchy of property or be subjugated to demands of efficiency over appropriateness; and a place in a community which sought their knowledge, tradition, and authority. The compromise reached was the 'closed door of *ijtihad*'.

The Ulama severely constricted their massive *fiqh* superstructure until it was reduced to 589 issues.' They agreed that for these 589 issues they will proffer one position, which would be the representative position of their *madhhab,* school of jurisprudence. No one would be able to switch from one school to another and no one would be able to reopen the legal discourse first set by the founding Imams, even on evidence. They got the door shut on flagrant abuse of legal power by the sultan, while the latter got a codified law and a large degree of *siyasah.*

But it is my argument that many of the Ulama, and especially the Sufi scholars," were quite conscious of the sultan's and later the state's designs on Islamic law, and that they supported a conception of *qada* which, while causing great practical difficulty, was nevertheless essential to the meaningful life exhorted in Islam. They struggled explicitly to keep the authority of practising *ijtihad* located indigenously, and away from state power.

What is at stake in this debate? For Ibn al-Arabi, the denial of *ijtihad* amounts to nothing less than the denial of Allah's continuing, living solicitude and the mission of the Prophet as a mercy to the worlds. In one passage where Ibn al-Arabi talks about what we are calling the closed doors of *ijtihad,* he draws out in the starkest terms imaginable, the true location of *hukm,* which means property, ruling, and decision. The *hukm,* he says, belongs to Allah, not the intellect. When we do not know the property of a thing, we must rely on Allah. This act of relying on Allah is *ijtihad,* and entails becoming 'like the corpse in the hands of the washer', which is a definition of being an *abd* (a bondsman or slave) to Allah. When the *abd* achieves this radical passivity, it is as when Muhammad believed that he threw the sand, at the Battle of Badr, but it was Allah who throws—You *did not throw, when you threw, but Allah threw (8:17),* a verse which negates one thing, affirms one thing, and then affirms another thing.

Let us examine one of Ibn al-Arabi's discussions on this issue, found in his chapter on mysteries of *taharah* (purity), when he discusses wiping the shoes for *wudu,* when travelling, but with the added situation that there is a hole in the shoe. Ibn al-Arabi is going to use this particular *fiqh* issue (one of the *589)* to demonstrate, again thematically, that it is Allah who Acts, something which orthodox and conventional Ulama would entirely endorse, but in a way, which if they perceive, they would find highly dangerous. In particular, Allah Acts; the *Shariah* has confirmed the *hukm* of the one who does *ijtihad;* so h/He a/Acts.

As with all of Ibn al-Arabi's works, the original, fixed and transcendentalized Arab language is used; this is not the living language of Arabic. I use Ibn Manzur.'s (d. *711/1311) Lisan al-Arab* to access this language. The first word we need is *khuff.* Ibn Manzur says, 'A person's *khuff is* what touches the ground from the *batin* [bottom] of one's *qadam'.* About *khafa (kh.f.y.),* a word that will be crucial for this passage, Ibn Manzur says, 'The *khafa* of the lightning is its sparks.

And to kh.f.y. something is to make it *zahir* [topside, outward, manifest], appear [z.h.r] and to bring it out. One says the downpour [kh.f.y.] the mice, when it brought them out from their burrows. Imru al-qays said, describing horses [racing across the desert], *khafa-hunna [the horses] brought them out [the mice] from their burrows).'* And al-Lahyani said, 'If you keep the secret, we will not kh.f.y. it'. His word,

We will not kh.f.y. it is, 'We will not make it *zahir'*. And the recitation of His word, *'Verily the Hour is coming, but I shall kh.f.y. it' (20:15),* means, 'I shall make it *zahir'*, which al-Lahyani related from al-Kasai, Muhammad Ibn Sahl, and from Saiyd Ibn Zubayr. And kh.f.y. something is to keep it concealed; kh.f.y. also means to make it *zahir,* and the two are opposites. And *akhfaytu* (kh.f.y. 'I concealed') something means *satartu-hu (s.t.r.,* 'I veiled it').

Ibn al-Arabi says,

As for the *hukm* in the *batin* [inwardness], we call shoes *khuff* because of *khafa,* as the shoes completely veils [s.t.r.] the foot. So when the shoe is torn, and something of the foot becomes *zahir* [exposed], then wipe that part of the foot which is *zahir,* and wipe the shoe. And that only as long as it can be called a shoe-inevitably with this condition. Here is a strange mystery for the one with sharp understanding. The *khafa is* also the *zahir!* Imru al-Qays says, *khafa-hunna out of their tunnels,* that is, they brought them out and they made them *zahir*.

So in this passage we have the shoe connected to the word *khafa,* which includes the meaning of veiling something, with its act of veiling being the same definition used by al-Layth in Ibn Manzur's dictionary. We then have some part of the foot emerging, with the verb here being *zahara,* which is related linguistically to *zahir,* which is the antonym of *batin,* meaning contextually top and bottom or outward and inward. Ibn al-Arabi then noted the mysterious—but linguistically-based—connection *of khafy* and *zahir*.

Continuing, we find this:

> *We argue for wiping what emerges, because we were commanded in the Book of Allah to wipe the feet, so when something of the foot emerges, we wipe it.*

As for the inward realm, the outwardness of the Shariah is a veil *[sitr]* over a reality of the *hukm* of unity *[Tauhid],* in relating everything to Allah. So, if everything is related to Allah, who is then left to be charged with performing the *Shariah*? Ibn al-Arabi has a series of answers to this question which he explores throughout the *Futuhat,* but the fact is that certain kinds of descriptions of *Tauhid* (oneness of God) are offensive, requiring an *adab* (courtesy) which attributes all good to Allah and all bad to oneself.

Then, Ibn al-Arabi says:

> *So the* taharah *concerning the Shariah is connected and it is that you associate the* Tauhid *of it with the fact, that you see it as a* hukm *of Allah in His creation, not a* hukm

> *of the things which belong to creation, like administrative wisdom. We saw that the outwardness of the* Shariah *veils the reality of* Tauhid. *This reality of* Tauhid *is related to the 'radical ambiguity of existence'. William Chittick writes that, 'the Quranic verse that Ibn al-Arabi cites more often than any other to show the radical ambiguity of existence was revealed after the battle of Badr, which turned in favour of the Muslims when the Prophet picked up a handful of sand and threw it in the direction of the enemy. Concerning the Prophet's throwing of this sand, the Quran says* You did not throw when you threw, but God threw [8:17].' *What this means in this passage is that the* taharah *of wiping of the shoe proceeds whether the veil is purified, the shoes or the foot recalling the authentic* Hadith *of Allah that* Verily I become the foot of the abd [worshipper] with which he walks."

The word *abd* here is crucial, because it is the same station of *abd* which characterized Muhammad and which is recited in one version of the testimony: 'I testify that Muhammad is His *abd* and His messenger'. The station of this kind of *abd* is one which negates any semblance of independence and Lordship, and which consequently affirms that the speech *(kalam)* is Allah's, not Muhammad's. Another instance of this is the *abd* in this verse: *So they found one of Our abds [abdan min ibadina] on whom We had bestowed a Mercy from Us, and We taught him knowledge from Our presence [ladunna], (18:66),* where the *abd* is characterized as having knowledge not acquired by his own efforts, but as having knowledge directly and immediately bestowed on him by Allah.

So, now we have a situation where the act of *taharah* on this shoe/ foot discloses a radical ambiguity of existence. Now we come to *ijtihad.* So, the *shar* is a *hukm* of Allah, not a *hukm* of the *aql* [intellect], as some of them believe. Therefore, the vision [Cyj of *taharah* of the Shariah is based on Allah, One, Real. Because of this, it is not appropriate to contest the *hukm* of the *mujtahid,* as the *shar* [Law], which is a *hukm* of Allah, has already affirmed that *hukm* of the *mujtahid:* it is the *shar* of Allah to affirm whomever. This *[ijtihad]* is an issue in which all the experts of the schools of jurisprudence are falling into the forbidding, without calling to mind what we have pointed out, despite their knowing it. But they have been heedless of calling it to mind, so they have offended proper courtesy toward Allah in that, while the courteous among the worshippers of Allah succeed. So the one who faulted the *mujtahid* himself has in fact faulted the Real in what He affirmed as *hukm.*

The tearing of the shoe, which is outward, corresponds to the tearing of the Shariah, which is also outward. Hence;

If the *shar is* torn, it becomes *zahir* in some issue as one of the properties of unity which would remove a property of the *shar* completely, transferring the *hukm* to a *taharah* of that unity which is effecting a removal of a *hukm* of the *Shariah,* just as one who relates all acts to Allah, from every perspective, does not concern himself with what becomes *zahir* as a consequence, whether contradictory or harmonious.

What is needed is purification from this problem; the *Shariah* becomes torn and at some point ceases to be called Shariah, as happens with torn shoes. But as long as the name 'shoe' does apply, wipe over the part which emerges. Ibn al-Arabi says,

That is explicated, for that unity designated for this issue, is the perspective made *shar,* and this is that one say, *But Allah has created you and what you know.* So the practices of the creation belong to Allah, despite the fact that they are related to us. But they are not related to Allah from every perspective, so they do not affect the wiping. The *hukm* about that would be as we have determined it.

In what preceded, the contours of Ibn al-Arabi's opposition to the use of *qiyas* (analogy)" also appear which we will consider briefly below. Simply stated, the interpretation and the application of the *shar* can never admit of purely human intervention, such as logic and analogy.

This is Ibn al-Arabi's discussion of *ijtihad,* and it is found even today. But one need not demand the entirety of this conception of *ijtihad* to still see a lively tradition of *ijtihad* in the face of the state of Islam. If we focus less on the state and the official proclamations of its Ulama and more on the lived reality of Muslims, we see a different situation with *ijtihad.*

Jurisprudence

From one perspective of application of Law, the concept of there being closed gates of *ijtihad* is indeed odd. By relying on stultifying descriptions of a static legal discourse, Western scholars have missed the actual function of Islam in communities. The enumeration of the 'sources of legal injunctions' (usul *al-ahkam),* or 'sources of legal discourse' (usul *al fiqh)* was the conventional series of four: Quran,

Sunna, scholarly consensus, and analogy *(qiyas).* The process of legal reasoning was the conventional one of searching the Quran for an explicit reading, then looking at the Sunna if there was nothing in the Quran, and then falling 'back on scholarly consensus, and if no consensus existed, then resorting to the extension of an explicit command by analogy.

This process is a methodology reached after the fact. In fact, the entire enterprise of the *usul al fiqh is* highly contentious. As with most *post hoc* histories, it is difficult to re-evaluate the early history of the development of *fiqh* without the received version colouring our views. There was, and still is, no clear and obvious hierarchy in the first two sources. The Sunna gives stoning for adultery, the Quran whipping. The Quran makes circumambulation of the Kaaba merely permissible, the Sunna seems to make it obligatory. The Quran seems to have the feet wiped for wudu, as we shall see, but the Sunna is for washing. The list goes on: it is simply not obvious how the Quran and Sunna are to be taken, harmonized, or ranked. Adding the next two sources, consensus (ujma)—(whose consensus? when and where?)—and analogy, only adds to the confusion.

This *post hoc* method, tortuous in its implications, was obviously in dire need of personal interpretations, but the gates of *ijtihad* had been closed centuries before, so the hapless Muslim is constrained. I was startled to realize that the same description of the process of Islamic law which I had learned and absorbed years ago, after four years of direct study of the books of *fiqh,* simply looked bizarre. But putting aside the received histories and the powerfully argued *al-Risalah* of the founding father Imam Shafii, and concentrating on the actual case by case debates, I was able to re-evaluate the history. It did take me a while to determine why that conventional description was so jarring: it is because the phenomenon being described is two-fold, but the description is one-sided. As Vogel pointed out, Western studies of Islam often omitted the law's application, possibly because of the linkages with the state of Islam and Ulama, to the exclusion of the masses and unofficial, underground expressions of faith (such as Sufi shrine activity).

Islamic law has two sides. There is the *fiqh,* which is the superstructure of interpretation erected on the revealed text. This superstructure sorts and classifies the determinative properties *(ahkam,* singular *hukm)* of the revealed text into categories such as lawful/unlawful; obligatory, recommended, neutral, disliked, and forbidden; generally addressed and specifically addressed, abrogated and abrogating; and so on.

And then there *is qada,* the 'settling of affairs', as we saw described by Lawrence Rosen. The *fiqh* and *qada* are two separate activities. *Ijtihad* is done everywhere and always, despite talk of its closed gates. The establishment of the *qiblah,* the direction of the Kaaba in Mecca, is a process of *ijtihad,* as the legal scholars always said. Accepting the *qiblah* of a particular mosque without personally assessing the *qiblah* on one's own is following another's authority *(taqlid).* Many mosques have an old architectural *qiblah* which those doing the *salah* today may ignore, turning instead in a direction perceived by *ijtihad* to be more truly the *qiblah.* In this example, the requirement to establish the *qiblah is* absolute: there is no room for *ijtihad* here to determine whether or not you must establish a *qiblah.* But the actual process of establishing the *qiblah is ijtihad.* Put these two together—the *fiqh* of the *qiblah* and the *qada* of determining it—and one can see why statements about there being no *ijtihad,* or a need for more, sound strange. There are two sides to Islamic law, and there are two types of *ijtihad:* there is the *ijtihad* of the *fiqh,* which has been severely restricted, and there is the *ijtihad* of the *qada,* which is constant in practice (at least in healthy communities). This misunderstanding arises from not recognizing *fiqh* and *qada as* two different things and stems from not appreciating the concept of *hukm,* (a thing's property). The way to see how Islamic law operates is to focus on *hukm.* This word means property, with related meanings of ruling, decision, judgement. But the value of seeing *hukm* as property, and not as ruling or judgement is this: the divine name *hakim is* the 'one who establishes the property' of something; and *Allah says al-haqq (33;4),* meaning the truth of a matter is what Allah says about it. So the key process of *fiqh* is understanding the *din,* religion, which recalls its Quranic derivation—*tafaqquh fil-din* (cf. 9:122)—and that is examining the entirety of novel things and issues and circumstances and assigning them their name," which means giving things their *hukm.*

Naming

What the *Qadi,* who Rosen describes, does is help disputants put names and properties on to their concerns. He is helping them to create a 'metasystem which creates order in a universe that is often experienced in a more disorderly way.

'Knowledge in this scheme is knowing the *hukm* of a thing. And knowing the *hukm* first requires knowing names. In a preceding passage, Ibn al-Arabi said, 'And that only as long as it can be called a shoe inevitably with this condition.' *Shariah* refrains run throughout the *Futuhat,* with Ibn al-Arabi always insisting on careful definition of names. As long as you have a shoe, the *taharah* of wiping over them is possible. Ibn al-Arabi does not propound the more stringent rules relating to tattered shoes—whether the holes involved are one or three inches wide, and so on.

Ibn al-Arabi propounds the easiest position, which is as long as you can call the thing a shoe, it is possible to wipe it. When what is seen is not a shoe but tattered rags, for example, then the *hukm* of wiping it is no longer possible. The importance of names is described by Chodkiewicz in this way: In the *Futuhat,* Ibn al-Arabi casually recounts an anecdote that might conceivably serve as an exergue to the remarks that follow. The hero of the anecdote is Malik, the Imam founder of one of the four principal schools of Sunni jurisprudence.

Malik b. Anas was asked: 'What is your opinion about the lawfulness of the flesh of the water pig *[khinzir al-ma:* an expression that refers to cetaceans in general, but dolphins in particular]?' He replied, '*[fa-afta:* a judicial consultation, not a simple exchange of words] that it was illegal'. An objection was made: 'Does this animal not belong to the family of marine animals [literally, 'fish', whose flesh is lawful]?' 'Certainly', he said, 'but you called it a pig *[khinzir].*'

Some might be tempted to class this ambiguous cetacean among the taxonomic fantasies of a maniacal casuistry. But Ibn al-Arabi's mention of it on two different occasions shows it to be something completely different for him. What is in question here is the authority of the name *[hukm al-ism]* and the secret of naming *[tasmiya],* which leads us to the very heart of Ibn al-Arabi's hermeneutics.

Most of the application of Law is getting definitions straight. As we saw above, the foundation of interpretation is language, and specifically the language of the Arab. Ironically enough, it is remarkable how liberating a literal reading of the textual tradition is. The *fiqh* approaches each issue with a thorough and exhaustive examination of every relevant piece of information. Was the command made specific for a particular audience, or a particular situation? Are there preconditions? What is the entire range of the key word in question? When did the command appear, and in what context? Debate and discussion fill pages upon pages for each detail. The liberating aspect is that the entire discursive system is designed to answer quite simply this question: What minimum does this command of Allah's require of us?

As we saw, the *hakim* is the one who determines the *hukm* or property of a thing. Today in South and Southeast Asia, the word *hakim* is used for a traditional doctor. The word still retains its meaning, however, where the *hakim* as doctor seeks to determine the property of a person, to identify the constitution *(mizaj)* and to prescribe the medicine/food needed to restore the balance *(mizan).* That this is not a closed system is clear from the fact that historically, the *hakims* did not restrict themselves to the paucity of prophetic statements about explicitly health-related matters, described as 'Prophetic Medicine' *(tibb al-nabawi),* but instead incorporated Greek *(Yunani)* medicine into an Islamic discourse on health and disease.

If we note that the word 'information' may be glossed as `data put information', we can see how the *hakim* operates. The data is data, but the information is the way that data is filed and put into forms, and it is that process that is 'Islamic'.' So the important part is identifying novel things, *(hukm);* the central practice is taking new people with new problems and identifying the *hukm* over them and prescribing accordingly. Once the *hukm* is discovered, the remedy is indicated. Once the *qiblah is* determined, the direction one faces is indicated.

The reason then why the Ulama (at least some of them) resisted the sultan and state is precisely because the state wants to seize the identification process by codifying and standardizing highly diverse human behaviour into narrowly defined and static categories. The *Qadi* who insists that each case is unique, is not efficient, and the state can have none of that. The entire project of the Ulama does not fit ideas of progress and efficiency which pervade typical development and social change paradigms. Also, as opposed to a precedent- and adversarial-based legal system, fairness and justice are not seen as predictable outcomes based on repeatable events nor as the result of a dialectical process, but rather as the process of arriving at a unique description of a situation which restores a universe of harmony for the disputants, the *Qadi's* role being that of facilitator. This is, too, a system which resists efficiency, as does the constant use of *shura* (consultation) for explicitly political affairs. No one could say that the Quaker or Amish systems of *shura* are efficient: but they are remarkably effective.

Another indication that the project of the Ulama resists centralization and state power is found in its rejection of 'one-man Islam' which involves a denigration of the slow, gradual, and cumulative nature of the Ulama project and its substitution with a single perspective of reform that will solve all problems. Nuh Ha Mim Keller, the translator of *Umdat al Salik,* remarks that 'each school [of jurisprudence] does not merely comprise the work of a single Imam, but rather represents a large collectivity of scholars whose research in sacred Law and its ancillary disciplines has been characterized by considerable division of labour and specialization over a very long period of time. . . . The result of this division of labour has been a body of legal texts that are arguably superior in evidence, detail, range, and in sheer usefulness to virtually any recent attempt to present Islam as a unified system of human life.'

The basic methodology of Ibn al-Arabi and the non-state Ulama stems from a concern with the literal, linguistic meaning of the text. Ibn al-Arabi goes further, being more literal and more keyed into linguistic possibilities than most of the Ulama. Chodkiewicz notes Ibn al-Arabi's 'concern for considering each of God's words and silences', but understands that this 'is certainly not sufficient to convince his adversaries of his orthodoxy'. In fact, 'Nothing better illustrates the impossibility of satisfying the *Ulama al-zahir* by rigorous fidelity to the *zahir* or Quranic text than the reading that Ibn al-Arabi does of the famous verse [42:11] *Laysa ka-mithlihi shayun.'* This verse, which means 'There is nothing which is H/his similar', has *ka* which must be explained. Chodkiewicz comments that Qushayri and al-Razi, among others, take the particle *ka* as *li-l-mubalagha* (having an intensifying function), something like, 'There is nothing at all which is His similar'.

But while Ibn al-Arabi takes this meaning throughout the *Futuhat,* he also reads another linguistic possibility of this verse. Chodkiewicz says, 'Ibn al-Arabi completes it by another one, which is its exact opposite. God does not speak to say nothing: the particle *ka* can thus also preserve all the force of its normal meaning. And the verse thus means: "There is nothing like His similar"—an interpretation that, for the *fuqaha, is* supremely blasphemous.'

In his commentary on this verse (42:11), al-Razi affirms the 'problem' of accepting the Quran literally. He says, 'The *zahir* [obvious, literal] meaning of this verse has different modes; one says the intent of verse is to reject something similar to Allah, but the *zahir* requires the affirmation of something similar to Allah, because the *zahir* necessitates rejecting something similar to His similar, not something similar to Him.' Al-Razi, Ibn Hisham in *Mughni al-Labib,* and Ibn Aqil respond to this problem by citing the Arab usage of *ka* in the statement *ka-mithlika la yabkhulu,* that is, the likes of you would not be miserly, so we deny miserliness by your similar, and the Arab means denying miserliness by you, as al-Razi says it. Ibn Manzur sums up the problem by saying, *Laysa ka-mithlihi shayun* means *laysa mithlahu,* and it could mean nothing but that, because if it is not said like that, this verse would affirm that He has a similar.

The Ulama who promoted particular meanings of this verse did so for well-documented reasons. Al-Razi, for example, was concerned with the Jahmiyyah or Jabriyyah school of theology which over-abstracted divine attributes and tailored his argument to refute them. But the intellectual rigour of the Ulama is such that ideas, even ideas the author is utterly opposed to, are presented straightforwardly. For example, in the long discussion of the issue of washing or wiping the feet during *wudu* presented by al-Razi, one could not discern which of the many arguments he presents would be approved of and which would be disapproved of, until he inserts his own comments directly onto the argument.

Another example of this is with the issue of a woman leading the *salah* when there are men present. There are arguments for and against. Abu Thawr, for example, takes the positive argument that the revealed text, 'Let him lead who is best at reciting *[aqra]* the Quran' is general, not specific to men. Ibn al-Arabi, as another example, takes the positive argument that leading a *salah is imamah* (leadership) and that *imamah is* a sub-set of being *kamal* (complete) (such that all complete people can be Imams, but not all Imams are complete), and since we know from an authentic *Hadith* that among the complete people are Maryam and Asiyah (the wife of Pharoah), we know that *imamah* of women is permitted.

The only against argument proffered is that the Prophet (PBUH) *is* supposed to have said, 'Woman shall not lead man'. Now the majority of legal scholars through the ages have not accepted the *imamah* of women over men. When they argue, they generally leave aside the for arguments for this case. As for the against argument, scholars like al-Nawawi, Ibn Hajar, and al-Bayhaqi admit the *Hadith,* 'Woman shall not lead men', is weak (and therefore cannot be used as evidence), but then say, 'But we [still] do not permit the imamah of woman over men'.

Added to the for arguments is the case of Umm Waraqah, who was commanded by the Prophet himself to be the Imam of her household in which there were men. Al-Darqutni, in an effort to divert this argument, goes to great lengths to fabricate a scenario where the men run out to the mosque before Umm Waraqah starts leading the prayer. Al-Bayhaqi tries to divert the argument by saying that the best rows for women are the back ones; this is a non-argument, because the woman may as well lead from the back rows or between the men's and the women's rows.

Ibn al-Arabi's acceptance of the position of those Ulama who permit the woman leading men is based on the literal, outward, *fiqh* evidence.

This is the basis of accepting one or another position. He is also able to delve into the inward or spiritual explanations for the outward truth. The inward affirmation of the outward position is found in crossing over from the outward to the inward. This he does by crossing over Man to *aql* and Woman to *nafs*," explaining that it is permissible for the *nafs* to lead the *aql* (but that is not permissible for *hawan-caprice,* which is crossed over to the kafir—to lead the *salah*). In this context, gender is inwardly determined; a female gender inwardly may exist in a male sex outwardly. More accurately, genders operate in a yin-yang mode.

One wonders what Muslim communities would look like if they took some of the positions held over the ages by the Ulama, especially those not linked into state power. One can imagine far-reaching corrections and readjustments which could be made without extensive *ijtihad.*

Logic and Analogy

One of the ways in which positions such as this one, which forbids the leadership of women over men, gain sway, is by a storming of culture (paternalistic) over the legal text. The flexibility of opinion and cultural input into the legal discourse meant that the strict textual approach to *fiqh* and contextual approach to *qada* succumbed to sultanic forces. The kind of legal reasoning that emerges, then, seeks to cut off what Allah pronounced *(mantiq)* and fill in what Allah was silent about (*maskut*). In his strict rejection of all *qiyas* which is not explicitly *ijtihad,* Ibn al-Arabi recognizes the dangers of extending, through analogy, explicit commands into realms of silence. There is a firm boundary separating the *mantiq* and the *maskut*, and to breach the line is to take Lordship on oneself. To silence what was spoken and to vocalize what was silent is to assume Lordship. The *abd,* in complete contrast, seeks to be utterly passive and receptive to Allah's command, like the corpse in the washer's hands.

One of Ibn al-Arabi's arguments against *qiyas* is found in his discussion of *tayammum* (preparing for *salah* by dusting the hands and face). To understand how *qiyas* is related to the issues surrounding *tayammum,* we need to understand how Ibn al-Arabi crosses over (cf. *itibar)* a *hukm* from the outwardness to the inwardness. The most felicitous folk, Ibn al-Arabi says, are those who follow the *hukm* of Allah in the outwardness and also in the inwardness. For Ibn al-Arabi, each *hukm* has an outer and one or more corresponding inner dimensions. First, the linguistic base. About *itibar* and *ibrah ('b.r.),* Ibn Manzur says, 'The *ibr* [crossing] of the arroyo.' And 'in the *Hadith* of Abu Dharr there is, What were the *suhufu Musa* [books of Moses]?

He said, They were all *ibarahs.* That is, they were like admonishments which people would heed and would put into practice.' Also `in the *Hadith* of Ibn Sirin, he said, I do *[itibar]* of *Hadith,* the meaning of which is that he crosses over ('b.r.) the perspective of the *Hadith* as he crosses it over with the Quran by its interpretation; for example, "the crow" is crossed over to the *fasiq* [bad man], and the rib to the woman, because the Prophet called the crow *fasiq* and declared the woman like the rib. The likes of that is done with allusions and nouns.' (The word *itibar* is the thing crossed over, in the Greek sense of metaphor.)

Ibn al-Arabi says,

A taharah of sight for example, for the inwardness, is considering things through the eye of *itibar,* so one's eyes will not chase after distractions. The likes of this are not for any but the one who has realized the performance of the *taharah* set down by revelation in [different] places, each one of them. Allah said, *In this is an ibrah for the ones having sight [3:13].* He made the *ibrah* with 'sight' because it is the secondary cause that leads to the inward, which is that to which the eye of insight crosses over. It is like this for each of the bodily parts.

Receptivity to divine speech *and* silence are necessary. This makes most kinds of analogical deduction, *(qiyas)* illegitimate.

One of Ibn al-Arabi's discussions about *qiyas* is found in his justification for taking the position that *tayammum is* not a substitute for purification. In this case of *tayammum,* the key properties in his discussion are water, dust, earth, knowledge, and *taqlid.* Water is crossed over to knowledge for those with insight, and if one examines the Quran, the water which animates dry earth and causes plants to grow is fluidly crossed over to knowledge which inspires the hard heart and causes good fruit to be produced. Dust and earth are humble, reminding the one with insight that we are dust to dust, and that the earth was made humble. Then, the *hukm* of *tayammum* is crossed over to situations where water—knowledge—is not found, or cannot be used. For Ibn al-Arabi, *tayammum* is not a substitute for *wudu* or *ghusl,* as the Ulama believe, but a *taharah* set down in the Shariah in its own right. For Ibn al-Arabi, the only way to approach Allah in the *munajah* with Him," which is the *salah,* is to do *taharah* with water or with dust. Because each is set down by the *shar* (Law-giver), there is no question of denigrating *taharah* with dust simply because dust is not a linguistic or rational form of purification.

Therefore, in the absence of knowledge, *taqlid* is required. For Ibnal-Arabi *taqlid* is certainly not following the authority of one of the experts of opinion, but of one of the 'people of remembrance' or *ahl dhikr,* which means the one who can tell the person without knowledge that this or that is indeed the *hukm* of Allah, or of His messenger. Ibn al-Arabi says this:

> *Our position is that* tayammum is *not a substitute but rather a* taharah *set down by* shar, *specified and designated for a specific state; the One who revealed it revealed the use of water for this specified worship, and it is Allah, and his Messenger, so it is not a substitute. Rather, it is based on an extraction of the property for this issue, from a revealed text mentioned in the Book or Sunna, encompassing the property for this issue in a synopsis of that discourse. It is the* fiqh *of the* din. *He said,* Let a contingent from every expedition remain behind to apply themselves *[cf.* tafaqquh] to the din and admonish the people when they return to them that thus they may learn to guard themselves [against evil] *19:122]-and we do not need* qiyas *for that!*

Taking a standard argument, that we have no revealed text regulating beating one's father with a stick, and that we need to extend the 'Say not *uff* to them' (17:23) to cover beating with a stick, Ibn al-Arabi says this:

> *We say that we do not have the exercise of declaring the property over the* shar *[Law-giver] concerning anything, even among the things it is permitted that we be responsible for—no declaring of the property, especially not in the likes of this. If there had not been mentioned explicitly in the revelation something other than this [saying of* uff] qiyas *would not have been made required of us, and we do not augment it by the saying of* uff. *Rather we make as* hukm *what He mentioned, and it is His statement,* treat with kindness your parents [17:23]—so *the address is undifferentiated; we extract from this synopsis the* hukm *about everything which is not a kindness. Beating with a stick is not one of the kindnesses which has been commanded by the revelation in our relationships with our parents. So we did not make as* hukm *anything but the revealed text, and we do not need* qiyas.

The *din* is perfected, and it is not permitted to add to it, just as subtracting from it is not permitted. So the one who beat his father with a stick has not treated him kindly, and the one who did not treat kindly his parents has rejected what Allah commanded of him, that he practise kindness toward his parents. And the one who opposed the word of his parents, and did what his parents do not approve of, something which is permissible for him to leave off, has in fact been disrespectful to them both. And it has been established that disrespect to parents is one of the great sins. Because of this, we argued that the *taharah* with dust—and it *is tayammum*—is not a substitute. Rather it is set down by *shar,* just as *taharah* with water was made *shar.*

Besides the peril one places oneself in with breaching boundaries between what Allah has stated explicitly and what He has not stated, between the *mantiq* and the *maskut,* societies yield to pressures to make Islam a culture. Thus, the patriarchy and racism found in culture is extended analogically to Islam.

The contest over *ijtihad* revolves around the role the intellect will play in determining rulings. For Ibn al-Arabi, *ijtihad* requires an *abd* who is so effaced that in effect the *hukm* discovered is the *hukm* of Allah. Novelty does not faze the *abd,* because in fact 'Every moment He is upon some task' *(kulla yawmin huwa fi shanin, 55:29),* nor the *Qadi* who sees each case as novel and unique. Whether desire for standardization and codification is natural or state-induced, the fact remains that the complacency this produces is antithetical to the perpetual receptivity—even confusion—required by the radical ambiguity of existence.

Spiritual Dimensions

The attack on the *fiqh* by modern movements, such as fundamentalism, includes an attack on spiritual things as well. Western scholarship on Islam is beginning to recognize that traditionally, the majority of the Ulama participated in one or more *Sufi* paths.' For them, the concept of *ilm,* of sapiential knowledge, meant an integration between virtue, praxis, knowledge, and sanctity, just as it meant the integration of law and spirituality. One problem which disturbs contemporary Muslim life, is that of the separation of law from spirituality and vice versa. There are Muslims who elevate their spiritual life beyond the concerns of their daily lives and discard law as an essentially mundane, rigid, and trivializing discipline. Then there are Muslims who have reified the law, taking a static and arid lump of rulings as the last word on a dead revelation. I would like to explore here the world-view which maintained an integration of law and spirituality and offer encouragement to those who work for a reintegration of *Shariah, fiqh,* and spirituality.

The world-view which sustained the traditional Sufi scholars posited the following scenario. The essence of Islam is the Shariah. The messenger of Allah, Muhammad, was sent as a mercy to the worlds and a demonstrator of the *Shariah*. The *fiqh* is the application of the *Shariah* to different times and places based on deeply and vigorously debated rules and methodologies (e.g., *the usul al fiqh).* Spirituality is sought and expressed within the confines of the *Shariah* boundaries. This world-view maintained Islamic communities through hundreds of years. It is my hope that by engaging the areas of law and spirituality, once again, in an integrated discursive system like the *fiqh* we may achieve some degree of integration, where our physical and worldly lives are perfected through our imaginal and spiritual lives; or to say it another way, our spiritual lives are perfected through our physical lives.

Divine Guidance

The classical Ulama have a very clear idea of how divine guidance is to be applied and realized in communities. The importance of knowledge of language is seen in such works as the fourteenth century Ibn Manzur's *Lisan al-Arab,* where he creates, Nuh-like, an ark to contain the words in circulation during the time of the Prophet and massive works identifying his Companions. In it, as many details of their lives as possible are assembled to enable the *Hadith* scholar to evaluate chains of transmission which testify to a very particular structure of knowing—developed and maintained by an amorphous knowledge elite, the Ulama. Their vision is by no means the only possible vision—its formal structure did not appear until three or more generations after the death of the Prophet. So while that vision is often either assumed as obvious, or rejected equally out of hand, I prefer to identify its implicit values and its normative force. Once we recognize its normative position, we immediately begin to identify its challengers. Three groups especially have been seen by the Ulama as threatening and illegitimate.

The Khawarij, Batiniyyah, and Ibahiyyah Types

These three groups are present today, so one may speak of types. First is the Khawarij challenge. Historically, this is the group which sought a radical Islam, shorn of its cultural, linguistic, and human accoutrements. It is this group which could contemplate the murder of Uthman, draw a definition of 'Muslim' so tight as to wage war on slackers or Muslims not up to their standards. This group in its later incarnations could destroy the tombs of the Prophet and companions, as the Wahhabis did. Their orientation towards the future and their vision of movement and progress make this type peculiarly modern. Their ideology makes it desirable to erase centuries of learning and tradition (going directly to Quran and Sunna, they ignore and denigrate centuries of Muslim scholarship). This type, as it manifests itself in modern fundamentalism, creates clear lines of battle, quickly and surely defining its enemies (Jews, tradition-bound Muslims, Americans), seeks rapid development and success (throwing derision at the traditional responses of *sabr* [patience], and the other worldliness of Sufis), and mocks the sacred, whether in art, attire, housing, or occupation.

Ibn Manzur emphasizes their tendency to restrict and make the religion hard and harsh. Among the Khawarij, there is another group called Hurrayrah—a name based on their locale. Ibn Manzur says, 'al-Harura is a place outside of Kufah to which is related the Hurrayrah, belonging to the Khawarij, because al-Harura was the first place they founded their community, and the place where they declared their authority after they opposed Ali.' He then goes on to describe how the word is adjectivally used: 'The linguistic extension is, "Someone is Harurawi." ' He then quotes al-Jawhari, who said, 'al-Harura is a name of a village.'

The word also appears in a *Hadith* from Aishah when she was questioned about the menstruant making up the *salah*. Ibn Manzur says, 'She replied, "Are you a Hurrayrah?" They are the Hurrayrah belonging to the Khawarij who fought against Ali. On their part they used to make harsh that which in the religion was an easing, so when Aishah saw this woman making the affairs of menstruation harsher, she compared her to the Hurrayrah. They make their affairs harsher in many of their issues, and they torment themselves with them. It is said they want to oppose the Surma and leave the [local] community just as they left the [larger] community of the believers.'

Groups which make their religion more difficult and demanding in order to distinguish themselves from the larger body of Muslims fit this type. A second group are the Batiniyyah, a word based on *batin,* the inward, who denigrate the body and the material. Ibn al-Arabi describes their error in this passage:

> *Know that Allah addressed humankind in his totality and did not honour his outwardness over his inwardness, nor his inwardness over his outwardness. They are dedicated, the ones who invite people [to the religion], most of them, to knowledge of the* ahkam *[legal properties] of the* shar *(cf.* Shariah*) in their outwardness, but are heedless of the* ahkam *set down by revelation in*

> *their inwardness, except for the few, and they are folk on Allah's path. They investigate that, outwardly and inwardly. There is no* hukm *[legal property] which they determine according to the revelation, for their outwardnesses, except they see that that* hukm *has a relationship to their inwardnesses. They take, in that way, the entirety of the* ahkam *of the revealed religions. They worship Allah with that which He made* shar *for them, outwardly and inwardly, and they succeed where the majority fail.*

Continuing, Ibn al-Arabi says,

Three groups arose, one misled and another making others misled. One takes the *ahkam* of the *Shariah* and discharges them for their inwardnesses, and they leave nothing of the *ahkam* of the *Shariah* for their outwardnesses. They are called Batiniyyah, and they are, in that, in different schools. Imam Abu Hamid [al-Ghazali] indicated, in his book *Kitab al-Mustazhiri* refuting them, something of their schools and explained their errors therein.

Summing up, Ibn al-Arabi says,

Felicity is with outward folk. They are diametrically opposite inward folk. But felicity, all felicity, is with the group who combine the outward and inward; they are Ulama (knowers) of Allah and His *ahkam.'*

Although there is a historical identification by Sunnis of the Ismailis as the Batiniyyahs, this tendency is found among many scholarly and progressive Muslims, who have intellectualized, abstracted, and made philosophical and symbolic, their approach to the sacred text. A third group may be called the Ibahiyyah, the ones who make everything permissible, denying divine punishment, and relativizing all actions. The Khawarij voice is the fundamentalist voice which commands a great audience, and not just because of the Western media. The secularist or liberal voice, which has elements of Batiniyyah and Ibahiyyah, gets its amplification from a cosy relationship with liberalist yearnings in the West and political power in the East.

Since one could hardly imagine a Muslim who claimed not to believe in the fundamentals of Islam, fundamentalist is not a very apt description. Let me introduce the term 'technist' for the Khawarij tendency as it appears today. A technist is a Muslim who believes fervently that the historical decline of Muslims is due to a problem of technique: if only Muslims had correctly applied such and such a technique, they would not be suffering today in Bosnia, Somalia, Palestine, and elsewhere. And if only Muslims would apply another technique (e.g., 'be as brothers unto one another', or apply the *hijab,* or the *hudud* as in the Hudud Ordinances in Pakistan), we would be as successful as the Israelis or Americans or Japanese. The ultimate in technist thinking is the notion that the Quran is a constitution, reducing, as only technists can do, a sacred text into a tremendously unidimensional and flat document.

One consequence of the text produced by the technists is that they have in effect co-opted the revelation and the *fiqh,* Well-meaning Muslims, Sufis and spiritualists, lay and non-academically trained Muslims alike, tend to accept the technist arrogation of the texts without challenge. Believing themselves bereft of *Hadith* and the Quran, they forsake the text and search elsewhere for solutions to the problems facing their communities.

The contemporary Batiniyyah and Ibahiyyah viewpoints have accepted the primacy of the modern world-view. Now, in order to live in this world, they must derive a means of handling the Islamic text. The means derived often revolve around a rejection of literal and narrow-minded interpretations and an emphasis on a moral and ethical Islam distanced from its historical roots.

Views of Technists

The views of technists concerning man and caliphate, for example, are utterly modern. For centuries the Quranic commentaries restricted the entire caliphate complex, described in the Quran, to Adam and the other prophets. Suddenly, due to the attractiveness of an all-powerful modern Western man, technists were saying that we are all supposed to assume caliphate. This ultra-modern sleight of hand allows technical Islamicists to paint an Islamic facade over newly industrializing countries' efforts to gain power and prestige, to treat nuclear weapons as a simple Islamic progression from swords and arrows, and to explain why modern Muslims are wielding such power over environments and peoples whereas traditional Muslims were wallowing in passive and unaggressive relationships with others and with nature.

Nation States

If their nation-states are caught in neo-colonial nets, then it must be because the leaders are not ideal. Logically, if you could install ideal leaders, you would avoid all problems. So the search for a caliph who will forcefully implement the *Shariah*—whose politics must be absolute because they are linked to absolute religion—preoccupies the technists.

Ironically, the traditional view is that caliphate is preceded by absolute servanthood to the divine, such that the only person qualified to lead is the one who is so effaced that the divine rules through him as a marionette is led by the puppeteer. One recalls the admonishment to His messenger in the Quran, It is *not you who killed them: it was Allah who killed them; and you did not throw when you threw, but Allah threw (8:17).* Ibn al-Arabi's metaphor for this is the *Hadith qudsi,* that is, a *Hadith* of Allah's words, '. . . I am his ear with which he hears . . .'

For centuries the scholars of commentary have interpreted (13:11) *Verily Allah does not change what is with a people until they change themselves* as meaning, 'Verily Allah does not change what is with a people [by way of good] [to bad] until they change themselves [by doing bad, and so become deserving of punishment]'. For example, al-Razi's commentary on this part of the verse is as follows.

As for His statement, may He be exalted, *Verily Allah does not change what is with a people until they change what is with themselves,* the word of all the commentators indicates that the meaning of *will not change is* what *is* with them by way of good fortune to the descent of vengenance, unless there are among them people of disobedience and wickedness. Al-Qadi said, there is no other possible meaning except this one ... since He, may He be exalted, begins with good fortune in *din* [religious matters] and *dunya* [worldly matters], and then blesses in that whom He will ... Al-Qadi [also] raises the issue that He does not visit punishment on the children of the polytheists due their fathers since they have yet not changed what is with themselves by way of good fortune.

Today, of course, the interpretation is quite the opposite, implying that if only we will change ourselves—become punctual, brotherly, and technically correct—God will make us successful, like the Americans or the Japanese. These modern technical interpreters are not literal, nor do they have any special claims to authencity. They entirely dispense with the connecting chain *(silsilah)* which links ourselves to the prophetic period, seeking to tear out the revealed data onto their supposed *tabula rasa.* In fact, by claiming to consider only the Quran and Sunna—which they do not do literally nor very well—they ignore the inevitable cultural baggage they bring. And this baggage, quite clearly, was packed in the West. By sweeping away centuries of Islamic civilization, they claim to approach the texts literally. They reject previous scholarships, legal schools, and spiritual paths.

They claim to take just from the Quran and Sunna, effectively denying the interpretive process and so erect for themselves an unassailable stance. The way to challenge this stance is to demonstrate that they do indeed, bring with them their modern baggage, their televisions and computers, their ache for industrial power and prestige, and their frustration with female suffrage and universal education, thereby coming to conclusions utterly at odds with a thousand years and more of commentary on the Quran.

It is impossible to give credence to someone who takes a Quranic verse, especially in translation, and says 'so and so' is what it means. To be authentic, a discussion of a verse or a *Hadith* must be prefaced by references to classical commentaries. This does not necessarily preclude novel interpretations, but it discourages the arrogance of believing that fourteen centuries of devoted Muslim scholarship missed something we only now see. The answer of how Quranic verses have to be understood and interpreted is that it is all contextual and interpretive. It is the Muslims who are striving to respond to the divine commands, to live a life of sacred obedience, to produce on earth-as much as He wills—a just society. The way we accomplish what is good, is by engaging at every step our understanding of the divine revelation. *Fiqh,* then, is one of the means we have of following, of engaging, the guidance of the Quran and Sunna. The *fiqh* has its rules of engagement, its courtesies, and protocols for disagreement, its systems of logic and demonstration; it has its rules of citation and chains of authority which are evaluated intellectually, not charismatically.

The Islamic life is not a technique. Nor is it an abstract ethics, a vague desire to 'do good'. It is rather the manifestation of guidance, the strides we take for ourselves and in society to follow the straight path. One beauty of Islamic civilization is that so many scholars have expressed a number of positions and interpretations. While this dismays the technist, it emboldens those who wish to realize the general divine command for their particular situation.

One example of a *fiqh* discussion which rejects the reifying and reductionist machinations of technists can be found in the following case. For this issue, the imamah (prayer leadership) of a child, Ibn al-Arabi examines three different positions and gives a metaphor for each position.' There is quite clearly no one position which is absolutely better than the others. The issue is not one of the right answer, but one of delving more deeply into the case in order to find appreciation at the higher levels, instead of moving down to a least common denominator. In fact, in order to quiet inevitable conflicts in Muslim communities, some suggest we ignore the details of Islam and hold firmly to the bigger picture. Frithj of Schuon denounces this kind of exoteric ecumenism, writing that :

> *When a man seeks to escape from 'dogmatic narrowness' it is essential that it should be 'upwards' and not 'downwards': dogmatic form is transcended by fathoming its depths and contemplating its universal content, and not by denying it in the name of a pretentious and iconoclastic 'ideal' of 'pure truth'.*

Or worse, as James Cutsinger adds, 'in the name of a tolerance whose chief objective is of a strictly social or political sort'. Schuon's metaphor is the false ecumenism where, 'to reconcile two adversaries, one strangles them both, which is certainly the best way to make peace.'

Ibn al-Arabi's discussion follows :

> *The [scholars of the* fiqh] *disagree about the leadership of the child,* sabiy [s.b.y.] *who is not mature, even though he is a reciter of the Quran. Some people permit that absolutely, and some people forbid that absolutely, and some people permit it for the supererogatory prayers, but not for the required* salah.

The crossover [from the outward ritual to the inward truth, but not vice versa] of the matter for that is, that one says, 'So and so childishly tends [s.b.y.] to something' when he inclines to it, and since the child inclines toward the property of Nature, and is swayed by his individual desires, he is called a child; meaning, he is inclined to his cravings. He is without maturity in respect to intellect, which is required for the prescription of the Law. Nature, in its standing, is without the intellect, so it is not correct for Nature to have priority, nor for the one who inclines to Nature to have priority, even if he is inclining to Nature by rights, so in fact Nature has the position of the one behind, and indeed [the one who inclines to Nature] is behind, and the one who is behind shall not be a leader standing in front: it is the opposite of what the property of leadership is about.

So the one who considered *this* crossover did not permit the leadership of the child even if he is a reciter. And the one who considered the fact of his having memorized *hamil [h.m.l.]* the Quran, understood the leadership to be that of the Quran, not of the child-leadership to be subject to being followed on account of the Quran, so he permitted the leadership of the child. He said, 'We gave him jurisdiction as a child' [19:12]—i.e., jurisdiction of leadership—and They said" 'How shall we talk to one who is in the cradle, as a child'? [The newborn infant Jesus] said, 'I am a slave of Allah; He gave me the Book and made me a prophet [19:29-30]—and Prophethood is the position of leadership, despite his being called a child.

And the one who saw the worship of the child to be a free—will worship in the absence of a prescription of the Law requiring him to do it—and who saw that the supererogatory prayers are a freely-willed act of worship, he permitted the *salah* of the child as the leader for the supererogatory prayers, but not the required prayer, due to the supererogatory prayers' relation to free-will.

Thus, without seeking to create a new position, Ibn al-Arabi instead examines previous decisions and describes what Allah had disclosed for him about the truths behind the different positions. In fact, in the thousands of pages of text expounding Ibn al-Arabi's special understanding of the *fiqh* positions, he enumerates the various positions held historically by the *Ulama* but usually indicates which of those positions he himself prefers and then illuminates the 'crossover' (from outward ritual to inward truth) involved in each case. As a result, one gains from this kind of study of the *fiqh* a deep understanding of the physical manifestation of following the commands, and at the same time bridges the inward and outward aspects of the revelation, affirming at once the necessity and value of strict obedience to the outward realm of ritual while grounding and authenticating the inward spirituality of the believer.

Charter for Governance

A modern writer defines constitution as "codes which aspire to regulate the allocations of functions, powers and duties among the various agencies and offices of the government...." When we apply it, to a document which was signed within a few months of the Hijrah of the Prophet (PBUH), fourteen hundred years ago, we do not get the exact sense and meaning given to it by either the Prophet (PBUH) himself or those to whom the document was being given. He had called, the Document under study, as:-

"A Writing from Muhammad, the Prophet of Allah."

It could also mean a letter and a document, the last being the most appropriate. This settles one thing. It was neither a 'treaty' nor an agreement, because it was "From Muhammad, the Prophet of Allah," and not an agreement between him and others. They had no objection in receiving it as a Charter laying down the Code of Life for Yathrib. They also accepted his position as "The Prophet of Allah," even though some of them desired to retain their attachment to the religion they already professed. They had, as a matter of fact, no option but to accept it or else live in Yathrib as aliens.

A few points need to be borne in mind while studying this Document. First, that the Document must be placed chronologically before any of the other objects is studied. This is necessary, because of two reasons. The first reason is that unless its period is determined it will not be possible to determine the object for which it was promulgated. We have referred to the immediate object of this Document as the Defence of Yathrib in the last Chapter. The Document is of a permanent nature. There must, therefore, have been other reasons which are of a lasting nature. The Constitution, if we consider it as such, of the first Islamic State, brought into existence by the Prophet (PBUH) himself has to remain, in most respects, if not all, a model Constitution for all states established by Muslims. We, therefore, feel that it needs studying from a number of angles.

It is important to bear in mind that the Document was dictated by the Prophet of Allah (PBUH). He had been receiving Sublime Guidance, for thirteen years, from Allah. A person of his calibre would not issue a document of this nature without an adequate and a set purpose. Furthermore a person of his knowledge, experience and capabilities would not issue a self–contained document piece meal. If a document is issued by installments it loses consistency and results in being misunderstood. His actions subsequent to the issue of this Document have also great relevancy. They show, if he was in the habit of tackling problems in a consistent or a disjointed manner.

It must be kept in mind that he is The Law Giver and laws given by him have stood the test of time. Persons who create and promulgate laws have to consider problems from all angles, otherwise their laws fail to receive such reception as desired. There has to be logic and consistency in the words and actions of men placed in the position he occupied. Written documents become out of date if they are void of consistency. Lastly, it has to be borne in mind that this Document was issued under certain conditions. Therefore, to gauge its proper importance we must bear in mind all the time, the circumstances which necessitated its issue. These have been discussed briefly.

We have referred to the Document as a Constitutional Charter.

"The form and nature of a constitution are dictated by the relationship prevailing among the various sections or classes of people." There was no organized group with whom the Prophet (PBUH) could have executed a treaty or an agreement. Hence we find that it was neither a treaty nor an agreement. It is important to bear in mind its heading, which also forms the very first Clause.

The heading needs to be given in full.

> *"This Document (writing) is from Muhammad The Prophet of Allah (PBUH) to Quraysh and Yathribite Believers and those who will follow them and fight alongside with them. They will form ONE UMMAH to the exclusion of others."*

Primarily the Document has been issued to administer the affairs of Muhajir and Ansar Believers. Its jurisdiction is then extended to those who live and fight Jihad under the leadership of these Muhajir and Ansar Believers. Leadership has been given to the entire Muslim community. The Prophet (PBUH) has not spoken of his leadership. This point has great significance for future generations of Believers.

The manner of promulgation of the Charter may also have a bearing on the circumstances at the time of its issue and the keenness of the recipients to be favoured by inclusion in the Ummah. From the wording and placing of concessions to various tribes, it creates the impression that the dictation of the Charter took place in an open Darbar, and as the Arab custom was and still is, those to whom a clause did not apply they spoke up to be included and at once another clause was dictated for inclusion.

The Document was issued within a few months of the Hijrah of the Prophet (PBUH) which took place in July or August 622 A.C. This is the period when, "a few years earlier, the reign of the grandson of Nousherwan was extended to the Hellespont and the Nile, the ancient limits of the Persian monarchy; the Christians of East were scandalized by the worship of fire and the impious doctrine of the two principles; the Magi were no less intolerant than the bishops, and the martyrdom of some native Persians, who had deserted the religion of Zoroaster was conceived to be the prelude of a fierce and general persecution. The oppressive laws of Justinian, the adversaries of the Church were made the enemies of the state; the alliance of the Jews, Nestorians and Jacobites, had contributed to the success of Chosroes, and his partial favour to the sectaries, provoked the hatred and fears of Catholic clergy."

The Persian monarch was so full of arrogance that, as his predecessors used to carry away the gods of the defeated, back to Persia, he carried away to his capital the Holy Cross from Jerusalem. The situation, however, altered, within a few years as predicted in the Quran. Byzantium, "rallied under Heraclius, who had led his troops in 624 A.C., into the heart of Iran. Chosroes was deposed and executed by his own subjects, and Heraclius recovered the Cross".

It meant a great deal for the prestige of the Emperor. To have brought back Holy Cross, the symbol of true Christianity, to Jerusalem, where the Jews were supposed to have been instrumental in having Jesus Christ crucified, was a great achievement. Syria, at that time was a truly Christian land. "In fact this is the only period in which Syria has been a fully Christian country..... Not only was the country Christian, but the age was an ecclesiastical age".

It was in this age of persecution, religious prejudices, taboos, ethnical differences, and acute hatred resulting in mass killings, when this Document was dictated to an assembly of Believers, Mushrikeen and Jews, not far from a totally Christian land, where at about the same time controversies raged, which ended in a, "sentence of excommunication on the tomb of St. Peter; the ink was mingled with the sacramental wine, the blood of Christ; and no ceremony was omitted that could fill the superstitious mind with horror and affright".

It was the same period, when in India, Harsha ruled and according to a Chinese pilgrim, "The penalty of imprisonment, inflicted after the cruel Tibetan fashion, which left the prisoner to live or die was freely awarded and mutilation was often adjudged".

In spite of it all we are told that in every one of these lands their particular civilization was at its peak and yet man was in bondage and writhed with pain at the feet of other men. Man had forgotten that he and other men were all descended from Adam and Adam had been created from clay:-

"He it is Who hath created you from clay". *6: 2*

How unnatural that men should be regarded as unequal and yet inhabit the same planet. Many prophets had come and tried to teach men and women that they were equal as human beings, but it was left to the Last Prophet of Allah to establish complete equality in those who believed in Allah and him as His Messenger and Servant.

While he was dictating this Document of great consequence he was observing the principle of equality. It would take centuries for mankind to realise the effect and importance of this principle.

Rule of the Almighty

The ultimate destination of mankind, while on this planet is the mastery of elements of nature. He has to achieve vast knowledge of nature of things and elements to an extent that very few can imagine. Acquisition of knowledge at the level of entire humanity demands peace, justice and equality among mankind. This will come about when mankind rises above the level of present ignorance and becomes one Ummah. This is the most important lesson taught by the Last Prophet of Allah, while dictating this unique Document. Universal peace will be achieved when the principle of equality of man is universally accepted. The Prophet (PBUH) when dictating this Document brought the level of all men on an equal pedestal. Jews who, at the time, were looked down upon, except may be in Iran were given equality with Arabs of Quraysh and Ansar origin. Equality of man appears to be one of the main features of his Mission, and, "It is difficult to portray the events of the life of the Prophet (PBUH) unless we first understand the nature of the Mission entrusted to him"."

This Mission, according to the Quran is complete guidance of mankind in all walks of life. Man has to enter Islam completely.

> *"O ye who believe! Come, all of you, into submission".*
> *2: 208*

And the Prophet has to bring mankind into Islam-submission to the Will of Allah.

> *"(This is) a Scripture which We have revealed unto thee (Muhammad) that thereby, thou mayst bring forth mankind from darkness unto light, by the permission of their Lord, unto the Path of the Mighty, the Owner of Praise". 14: 1*

The Eternal Message of Allah happens to be placed in a world which, in certain respects, alters with changes in time and geography. And yet this Eternal Message guides men to the straight path. "The glory of Islam is that it distinguishes the universal from the changing particulars".

If we study the Quran and try to locate Eternal Commandments we will find that these happen to be all in respect of those aspects of human life and nature, which remain constant and are not subject to any great changes as a result of time and place. Those aspects of life whether at the level of an individual or at the collective level of society, which are subject to changes due to change in surroundings, have been left to the individual or the society, as the case may be, to find the best solution as long as no other Commandment is violated in the process. This means that no restrictions have been placed on "the changing particulars."

It is the same with the Sunnah of the Prophet (PBUH). He has set precedents in all walks of life but restrictions are placed only in the field of universals and particulars arc left to be decided by the individual and the society, as the case may be. He was the Messenger of the Code of Life Revealed by Allah. He was not sent as a military commander and yet he demonstrated the "why, when and how" of war, because the Ummah needed guidance in it. He was not a statesman and yet he demonstrated how justice tempered with mercy was to be administered in a society of equals. He led his army to many a battlefield, keeping in view the principles of war and compulsions of strategy and tactics dictated by geography and other factors and demonstrated all the qualities of a great commander.

His critics fail to keep his Mission in view when commenting on his activities as a soldier or as a statesman because their view of a Way of Life is limited to acts of prayers only. To say that, "Muhammad (PBUH) himself was not a warrior and had few military gifts. In battle he invariably followed behind the front line, never, if avoidable, himself engaged in hand to hand fighting", amounts to disregarding his role as a guide of commanders. The writer forgets that commanders do not engage, normally, in hand to hand fighting. They have to direct, control and deploy troops as the situation may demand.

This vague statement of a British general does not mention those qualities of martial nature which in his opinion were absent in the Prophet (PBUH). He would have probably liked to see in him qualities displayed by British generals like Kitchner, who, "sword in hand and Bible in pocket he enjoyed a career of spectacular warfare in Russia, China, India, and Africa...." Kitchner's enjoyment of war amounted to perversity, when he had defeated Mehdi's Army he arranged a victory parade, on 10th of April 1898, in which, he treated the captured enemy commander Amir Mahmud in the most cruel manner. "Dragging chains which were riveted round his ankles, and wearing a halter round his neck the defeated army commander was made to walk, and sometimes run, behind the cavalry. His hands were bound behind his back, and he was driven forward by Sudanese guards who lashed him with whips when he stumbled. Kitchner rode on a white horse in triumph". What a spectacle of British chivalry and martial excellence during the closing years of nineteenth century when European civilization was at its height.

This British general of whom many generations spoke with admiration, gave orders, that the tomb of Mehdi be razed to the ground and his bones to be cast into the Nile. Mehdi's skull which was unusually large was kept aside to be used as inkstand. One suggestion was to use it as a drinking cup. He had ordered Wingate, another famous British soldier, to "loot like blazes. I want any quantity of marble stairs, marble payings, iron railings, looking glasses and fittings, doors, windows, furniture of all sorts". A victorious general who pardoned his life-long enemies must have appeared to General Glubb, to lack martial qualities common among European generals and conquerors. The objective of the Prophet (PBUH) was to establish peace as a precedent for Believers until the end of Time. He had to demonstrate what was an ideal life. This included both war and peace. It included the life of a labourer and also that of a ruler. He demonstrated the life of a man of all walks of life, when he was being persecuted and we find no change in the way he lived, when he was the ruler of entire Arabia and his army had a successful round of exchange of arms with the Byzantian Imperial Army, at the battlefield of Mowta. As a general his strategy was not only to win the war but to succeed in the days after the war as well, and his war stands alone in the annals of military history, which brought happier days both for the winner and the vanquished although a winner in earlier battles he had accepted armistice on the enemy's terms.

It has been recorded by his biographer "When there was peace and war was abolished and men met in safety and consulted together none talked intelligently about Islam without entering it. In these two years double as many or more than double as many entered Islam as before". Throughout his life he was keen to use all his resources to bring about peaceful atmosphere in which his Message could be understood and accepted. Today, fourteen centuries after him, the world has accepted the point of view that peace alone can solve mankind's problems.

A modern writer has said, "In an age of Total War we will need Total Peace". War, however, has to be catered for." Wars do not break out of themselves, but they may change the course of history and the fate of mankind.... War has, therefore, become the greatest of social problems". For him and for Islam war had become the greatest of not only social but also political problem. He gave to the world, Islam—The Message of Peace-when war had been brought to his doorstep. This Document is of great consequence as it gives an answer to a multi-national Ummah, as to how they should face an aggressor and survive. One of the outstanding features of this Document, which cemented the citizens of Yathrib was justice with Equality for all. Peace within communities and, at international level, cannot be established without equality and equal status to men and groups of men—the nations. This equality was not acceptable either within Arabia or at the international level at that time. The Arabs of Mecca, steeped in the idea of racial superiority, their minds clouded with racial prejudices, and having a class ridden society, were in no mood to accept equality between Abu Jehl, the high born Quraishi chief and Bilal the Negro slave.

Equality for All

It was the principle of equality of man which evoked the animosity of the two neighbouring mighty empires of Iran and Byzantine, towards Islam and Muslims. The ruling classes of both these empires were securely entrenched as the high born elites, who held the birth right of princely and regal positions. The birth of an Ideology of "Equality before the Eyes of Allah," both in this and the next world, was a revolutionary reality which had to be nipped in the bud. The rest of the world was to array itself on the side of these to Empires, one after the other. The prophesy of Abbas bin Ubada was fulfilled soon enough but it was to continue being fulfilled for ever.

It was during the Second Bayah at al-Aqaba that Abbas bin Ubada al-Ansari, said to the Ansars who were swearing allegiance to the Prophet (PBUH), "O men of Khazraj, do you realise to what you are committing yourselves in pledging your support to this man? It is to war against all and sundry. If you think that if you lose your property and your nobles are killed you will give him up, then do so now, for it would bring you shame in this world and the next. But if you think that you will be loyal to your undertaking even if you lose your property and your nobles are killed, then take him for by God. It will profit you in this world and the next".

The men from Khazraj and many others who followed their footsteps are still being challenged by the enemies of Justice and equality for all. It is, outwardly, that people oppose Islam, while their real opposition is against the principle of equality of man, by those whose vested interest are in danger or being jeopardised. It was a question of life and death in that age. Religion during that age made men of religion oblivious of cruelties perpetuated in the name of religion. Minor differences or even suspicion of minor differences led men to throw others into flames. As has been remarked, "It remained for the Medieval Church, however, to put cruelty and burning and gruesome public executions on the firm popular basis of exalting religious spectacles". There can be no peace in the world unless the world led by Muslims observes laws relating to Jihad on the Path of Allah and in conducting their foreign affairs as ordained in the Quran. This Document was the first writing, directing towards the principles and the policy according to which human societies should conduct their affairs. It has been universally accepted that in the world of today there is no international law, relating to the conduct of states in matters of conflict or mutual interest, obligations and the making and breaking of treaties. There have been usages in various parts of the world, which have been overlooked more often than not and in all conflicts national interests have prevailed. "International Law, so called, is in reality national law regulating international relations of those states".

Prefect Document

Islam has a complete Code of International Law. It, however, operates at the level of the Millah of Islam, on the principle that Believers are an Ummah when considered with respect to the rest of humanity. If Muslim States observe in their inter-state relations, the Commandments of the Quran, the super powers will find it difficult to drive humanity in World Wars, as they have done twice during twentieth century. These Quranic Injunctions dictate relations between Muslim states and also between Muslim states and others. Islamic Law is the only Law which forbids states to undertake aggression of any kind; not even for the spread of religion.

This Document, apart from being the Constitutional Charter of the state of Yathrib was at the same time the document on the authority of which this state had come into existence. The person proclaiming the coming into being of this new state was Prophet Muhammad (PBUH), the last of the line of prophets, who had received Revealed Word of Allah. As a result of the contents of this Document, the state of Yathrib received all those elements which add up to the formation of a state. "A state exists as soon as the four formal elements (a people, a territory, a government and the characteristics of sovereignty) can be found in it and that recognition by other states merely recognizes the social fact", and non-recognition does not alter its status. The newly created state of Yathrib was, however, recognized soon after its establishment.

The Prophet (PBUH), immediately after the promulgation of this Document went out of Yathrib, stayed with various tribes, each of which held sovereign status within its tribal territory, and executed friendly treaties with them. Apart from establishing treaty relations with neighbouring tribes, these journeys of the Prophet (PBUH) fixed approximate limits of the territory of Yathrib. The boundaries of an Islamic State, cannot be a permanent feature. Islam cannot have and does not have fixed boundaries. Islam attracts people because of principles of justice and equality. It spreads and with its spreading are extended its boundaries. Islam has not remained static even during its days of political eclipse. The spread of Islam in Africa has been when a greater part of Africa had been occupied by European Colonial powers.

In Malay Archipellago Islam was spread by Muslim merchants at a time, when Spain held sway over the area. "They did not come as conquerors, like the Spanish in the sixteenth century, or used the sword as an instrument of conversion; nor did they arrogate to themselves the privileges of a superior and dominant race so as to degrade and oppress the original inhabitants".

It is said of Al-Mamun that when a certain Yazdan bakht a leader of the Manichaean sect came on a visit to Baghdad and held a disputation with the Muslim theologians, in which he was utterly silenced, the caliph tried to induce him to embrace Islam. But Yazdanbakht refused saying, "commander of the faithful, your advice is heard and your words have been listened to: but you are one of those who do not force people to abandon their religion". It was the same in Eastern Europe where, "The Calvinists of Hungary and Transylvania, and the Unitarians of the latter country, long preferred to submit to the Turks rather than fall into the hands of the fanatical house of Hapsburg; and the Protestants of Silesia looked with longing eyes towards Turkey...." The writer speaks in the same vein of other countries and other lands. "Even in Italy there were men who turned longing eyes towards the Turks in the hope that as their subjects they might enjoy the freedom and the toleration they despaired of enjoying under a Christian government".

As said earlier, this toleration of Muslims, in all the then known lands of the Globe, was the result of magnanimity shown by the Prophet of Islam (PBUH) when dictating this Document in Yathrib, at the time, when the first state of Yathrib was coming into existence. The Muslims have honoured the spirit of this Document throughout these fourteen centuries, which is not a mean achievement. In spite of it, and may be because of it and the resulting popularity of Islam, it "inspires perfidy of the Balkans, the hate of the Jews, the apprehension of the Hindus and the animosity of the Russians".[1] The remarks of Abbas bin Ubada Ansari have been referred to above. His prediction continues to come true and may continue much longer. The basic reason for this opposition is the fear of loss of vested interests of the ruling classes and the religious hierarchy, of many faiths which upholds these classes and are a hindrance towards universal equality of man and the resultant justice and fairplay for the masses.

The tenacity with which Muslims have held on to the principle of equality is due to the fact that, they believe staunchly in the Sovereignty of Allah, which is the core and basis of all Islamic teachings. Islam stands for the Sovereignty of Allah alone and of none else. This, in practice, means that the Eternal Laws enjoined by Allah cannot be altered. If this principle was accepted by the ruling classes they would, after that, not be able to frame laws as and when it suited their vested interests. They desire to keep the framing of laws in their own hands and thus they and their institutions set aside for framing and promulgating laws retain Sovereignty in their own hands.

People's Power

The law assures that Parliament is omnipotent and paramount. It can make or unmake laws on any matter whatsoever.... The power and jurisdiction of parliaments, says Sir Edward Coke, is so transcendent and absolute, that it cannot be confined, either for causes or persons, within any bounds.... It hath sovereign and uncontrollable authority in making, confirming, enlarging, restraining, abrogating, repealing, reviving and expounding of laws, concerning matters of all possible denominations, ecclesiastical or temporal, civil or military, maritime or criminal. This fact is contained in their Constitutions, whether written or based on practice, precedence and legal judgements.

Speaking of the Constitution of England (which included English possessions in Scotland, Ireland and Wales) Dicey, an eminent lawyer, has mentioned "three leading characteristics in the existing Constitution of England; they are now generally designated as the Sovereignty of Parliament, the rule of law and the convention of the constitution"." If a similar analysis was to be made of the Constitutional Charter of Medina, its leading characteristics, that would emerge would be firstly, the "Sovereignty of Allah and His Prophet" (PBUH), secondly, "The Rule of Law" and thirdly, "The Equality of Man." As composed to the Sovereignty of Parliament which means sovereignty of man made laws, and Convention of the Constitution, these characteristics certainly carry more weight. Mankind has, time and again, failed to convince itself that it can successfully conduct its affairs, without Guidance from Allah. Mankind, in nearly every land, "has been the victim of disastrous illusion—the illusion of our ability to emancipate ourselves from natural laws".

Whether we call them as Natural Laws, (Revealed to prophets of earlier eras) or openly admit that they are Laws given by Allah who alone is our Creator and Sustainer and Knows our needs far better than us, makes no difference. These are laws which are based on Truth from Him, who has set a destination for mankind which cannot be arrived at except by conducting ourselves in accordance with these Laws. Man has been given knowledge and intelligence, but both these qualities are limited as compared to the knowledge and Power of Allah. "It is evident that human intelligence has not increased simultaneously with the complexity of the problems involved." Today, as much as in the past, civilized humanity has shown itself incapable of directing either its individual or collective affairs. The modern world, like the Quraysh of Mecca, needs to be bold and pay homage, to the basic principle of the acceptance of the Sovereignty of Allah.

This Document, The Constitutional Charter of Medina, laid down, in no uncertain terms, that Allah alone wielded Supreme Power and that the method of invoking that power is Allah Himself and His Prophet (PBUH) is the interpreter of His Laws. This Document also lays down priorities to be adopted for the security and defence of states established by Muslims. The test of Constitutions whether they are capable of meeting the needs of their respective states has been suggested by a modern American writer as follows:-

> *"How effective is the constitution in enabling us to come to grips with periodic crises? What are the principal objectives of our national institutions? What service do they render? What are the rights and obligations of American citizenship"?*

The Constitutional Charter of Medina, as a Document, is fourteen hundred years old. If modern constitutions are examined in the light of the above mentioned questionnaire it would clearly come out that human mind has not made any perceivable advance in this respect. The history of events in Medina, subsequent to the issue of this Constitutional Charter, has been recorded in greatest possible detail. We can, as a result of its perusal, say that the periodic crises that occurred, in Medina, after the promulgation of this Document, were conveniently solved through actions based on it.

There is no doubt about the fact that at the time of its promulgation, the entire population of Yathrib had rejoiced about it and had unanimously accepted to live under its protection and abide by its laws. This Document, "brought into existence a voluntary association of all sections of Medinites-Muslims and non-Muslims, emigrants and locals, principals and clients,..." Aus and Khazraj, the two Arab tribes, were the only people who could claim that Yathrib belonged to them. They had been at war with one another but had settled their differences, lately. An agreement had been reached tentatively that in order to give the place semblance of an organized community they should choose a king. Abdullah bin Ubay the leader of Khazraj was being talked of as the future king of Yathrib when Bait-e-Aqba Thani took place. Soon after this, Muhajirs started arriving in Yathrib. They and the Ansars were a far more organized group, than any tribe could be, and Abdullah bin Ubay's crowning ceremony was soon forgotten.

There were Jews also in Yathrib. They were all engaged in trade and commerce and being rich had built themselves strong forts outside the main city of Yathrib. The Jews, however, did not either own or belong to the place. A number of theories have been advanced, but the most plausible theory is that they were immigrants from Syria as a result of one of purges that used to be carried out from time to time, to rid the Holy Land, of them. They were living under the protection of various sub-tribes of Aus and Khazraj. They did not possess any right other than what the Haleef-protecting tribe-cared to allow them. This Document had completely altered their social and political status. They were being raised to the status of citizens of Yathrib like any other person from amongst the tribes of Aus and Khazraj. This was a great elevation in their status. They were no more aliens or emancipated slaves. They would, henceforth be able to speak up to the Arabs as equals and the word Jew would soon loose the sense of inferiority which it had, hitherto, carried all the world.over.

The Prophet (PBUH) was allowing them a further concession, which would soon make them a political force to be reckoned with. He was, on certain conditions, inviting them to become a part of the Ummah of Believers. This invitation happened to be under Divine Guidance and was, therefore, all the more attractive. Although this invitation was also given to the Christians but they were so few in Arabia that the Jews would have been certain to overshadow them always.

This invitation, however, had one point which in the end was likely to be unacceptable to them. It was that they had first to accept the Sovereignty of Allah. The invitation being the result of an Ayah of Quran must have made them hesitate but they do not seem to have shown any such hesitation in the beginning. The Words of this Ayah of Quran, are:-

> *"Say, O People of the Scripture! Come to an agreement between us and you: that we shall worship none but Allah, and we shall ascribe no partner unto Him, and that none of us shall take others for lords besides Allah. And if they turn away, then say, Bear witness that we are those who have surrendered (unto Him)".* *3: 64*

The Prophet (PBUH) was trying to create a multi-national Ummah which was to form a coalition of all those who believed in Allah and thus were being asked to form a united front against the godless. He had advocated an idea, which the West have taken up lately but not with the intention of finding a united platform for all religions, but, to find out means of accelerating Christian Missionary activities in Africa and South East Asia. What would have been the shape of a society, in which, all those who believed in Allah, were to form one Ummah, and yet continue calling themselves by their old denominations, would be difficult to imagine.

Hijrah of the Prophet (PBUH) had brought about a fundamental change in the society of Yathrib. There were, in Yathrib, Mushrekeen, who were pagan Arabs and did not follow any set rules, which could fall under the heading of Laws of a Religion. There were, as mentioned earlier, Jews, who, at least in principle, followed the law of Moses (May Allah's Blessings be on him). Because of being the followers of a Revealed religion, they considered themselves as superior to the pagan Arabs, although they lived under their protection. There were some Arabs who had adopted the law of Moses but their position was strangely unidentifiable. They lived among their own families and observed Arab customary law but considered themselves as possessing a higher intellectual creed. If they were asked to choose one of the two camps, in case of a quarrel, they would have joined their particular tribe and not gone to the Jewish camp.

The arrival of the Prophet (PBUH) altered the social structure of Yathrib completely. In fact, it had started undergoing a change since the Bayate Aqba Thani. The Prophet (PBUH) had appointed twelve leaders from among the Medinites who had come to Mecca to embrace Islam. The Prophet (PBUH) had told the gathering, "Bring out to me twelve leaders that they may take charge of their people's affairs.' They produced nine from al-Khazraj and three from al-Aus". This was the beginning of Muslims bringing into existence an organized Islamic Society. "With the appointment of these twelve leaders an organized Islamic Society came into being". On their return to Yathrib, these twelve leaders conducted the affairs of Madinite Muslims, until the arrival of the Prophet (PBUH).

The Jews had not been able to set up any communal life with the few Arabs who had accepted the Shariah of Prophet Moses. The Prophet of Islam was inviting not only Arabs but Jews, Christians and all others to share with the Believers higher values of the activities of a community organized on the basis of Sovereignty of Allah and equality of man, His most Balanced creation. The result was that, even when the Believers were in a small minority, the social life of Yathrib, due to their presence, had started taking its direction from the Muslims and adopted Islamic values in an imperceptible way.

The Prophet (PBUH) and the small band of his Companions set the pace and texture of social life and thus became the centre of all communal activities. Whenever any issue demanded Allah's commandment for its settlement or the Prophet's own verdict in the matter, the Muslims did make all possible efforts to arrive at the authentic views of Islam on the basis of these two sources. The earlier Revelations of the Quran of Medina period are all relating to laws regarding various aspects of life. Many of them resulted from questions asked at these gatherings where the Prophet (PBUH) invited people to embrace Islam. He is known to have gone to a Jewish school to preach Islam to them. If there passed a group of people, by the road, he would stop and join them to invite them to Islam, even though they disliked it.

A new social structure based on the Sovereignty of Allah and equality of man was taking shape. A new culture was emerging out of this social structure. Man was being given, for the first time in his cultural life, the proper place in the scheme of things, and man's mind was awakening to his place in this universe. One can find no better key to the internal logic of a society than its conception of man and his place in nature.

This high position had been bestowed upon man by Allah Himself, in His Eternal Code of Life. The result was that the social and cultural trends of life in Yathrib, at a time when the Believers were in a small minority, took a turn towards adoption of Islamic values, and life became centralised around the personality of the Prophet (PBUH) and his Companions.

The Significance

As mentioned earlier the Constitutional Charter of Medina has importance for more than one reason. It is the earliest written document of the Government and State of Medina. Later documents like the Peace Treaty of Hudaybiya, the Victory Proclamation of Khayber, and the Overlordship Gazette Notification of Aila granted to the Christian population of that place, were all of the nature of proclamation of cessation of hostilities due to one or the other reason. This Document stands in a different position. It established a state and a government in order to meet aggression. Invasion by Quraysh of Mecca had to be stopped. Defence of a society cannot be assured without first organizing that society. When a society is organized it takes the shape of a state.

The state must have law and it must also lay down as to what was the source of law and who in future would be entitled to amend or add to this law. All these steps were being finalised through the Constitutional Charter of Medina. This process has been explained in modern terminology in the following words. "Peace among men and a civilized society, which are one and the same thing, are imaginable only within a legal order equipped with institutions to give effect to principles and norms in the form of law..." The Prophet (PBUH) was laying down that the final authority in Islam would be Allah, through revelations to him. Arabian society was losely governed by custom. There was no written law. Absence of law was a great hindrance to the establishment of a progressive and stable society. The Charter was removing this imbalance. "Whenever men group together and approve of a given standard morality, they must speak finally in terms of a law. Law permits morality to grow and as it grows the standard of law is elevated and morality is further advanced, for the two have reciprocal influence".

In this case, although hostilities had not started, war had been declared and arrangements had to be made to face the enemy. Allah had also Commanded.

> *"O ye who believe! Take your precautions, then advance the proven ones, or advance or altogether". 4: 71*

It is beyond doubt that the Document was promulgated to bring into existence the State of Medina so that it could be defended against the impending attack by the Quraysh of Mecca. Discussion leading to the declaration of its contents, if any, are conspicuously absent from both the Seerah and Hadith literature.

No Flaws : Its authenticity is, however, above doubt of any kind. It cannot be a spurious document. Once Islam and the Muslims had emerged as victorious, not only within Arabia, but had also liquidated the two strongest empires of the then civilized world, there was no need for them to concoct a document of the early period when Muslims were very few and not very strong. In actual fact once they stepped out of Arabia, they paid no particular attention to it. It is genuine both from external evidence and from the inner evidence of its contents. The idea that it is the sum total of a number of agreements arrived at on a number of occasions is so illogical that it should be ignored completely. As is well known, the events which took place after the promulgation of the Charter, developed with such after, and in such an unforseen manner that a situation had arisen where there was no need of fresh terms being issued, or new agreements gone into with any party.

The idea that the document in its present shape is the result of numerous agreements is the result of the basic misconception, that it was an agreement. One may ask "agreement between whom, because the Document was being issued with the heading "From Muhammad, The Prophet of Allah." Its contents were Legal Orders and not paragraphs of an agreement. A charter from some one in power can be amended or additions made to it by the authority issuing the original charter. From Badr onwards the Prophet (PBUH) did not have to issue new instructions to any one in Yathrib. The Jews were getting weaker every day and signs of rebellion on their part had developed immediately after Badr. They had not "followed the Believers and not fought along with them." They had not, therefore, qualified for any of the concessions granted to them through the Charter.

If anything, any fresh document, would have curtailed concessions granted to them from the incidence of rebellious behaviour of the Jewish tribe, Banu Qainuqa, immediately after Badr, the Jews were not in a position to request for a reappraisal of their relations with the ruling party.

The arrival of ultimatum from the Quraysh of Mecca was a serious affair. They were a powerful tribe and had the influence which leaders of thought possess in a society. They exercised the sole authority of laying down the religious ceremonies and the Arab way of life. They held the monopoly of carrier trade between southern Arabia and the flourishing market of Middle East, and were very rich as compared to the rest of Arabia. An attack by them, against Yathrib, would wipe out this small agricultural town of Najd. War in any case "is not a pass time. It is a serious means for a serious object".

The Meccan object was very serious. Muhammad (PBUH) had "mocked their Way of Life," and taken refuge in Yathrib to save their Way of Life they had to destroy him completely. They had awoken to the danger from the time of the second Bayah of Aqba. As already mentioned when some of the Companions started migrating to Yathrib they "assembled in their council chamber, the house of Qussay bin Kilab, where all their important business was conducted, to take counsel what they should do in regard to the Prophet (PBUH), for they were now in fear of him." It was suggested that "they should put him in irons behind bars." This was objected "on the ground that news would leak out that he was imprisoned, and immediately his followers would attack and snatch him away then their numbers would so grow that they would destroy the authority of the Quraysh altogther".

After some further discussion Abu Jehl came out with a new plan. This was "that each clan should provide a young, powerful, well born, aristocratic warrior; that each of these should be provided with a sharp sword; then that each of them should strike at him and kill him. The Banu Abde Manaf could not fight them all and would have to accept blood money which they would all contribute". Having failed to kill him they were not able to liquidate Islam in Mecca. They could not, however, let it prosper in Yathrib. They were afraid, as they said that "Their numbers would so grow that they would destroy the authority of Quraysh altogether". They decided not to permit their numbers to grow and decided to act quickly. They knew of the disappointment of Abdullah bin Ubay. His people had made a sort of jewelled diadem to crown him and make him their king, when Allah sent His Prophet (PBUH) to them; so when his people forsook him in favour of Islam he was filled with enmity realizing that the Prophet (PBUH) had deprived him of his kingship. However, when he realised, that his people were determined to go over to Islam, he went too, but unwillingly, retaining his enmity and dissimulating.

The Quraysh sent a letter to the people of Yathrib, but addressing it to Abdullah bin Ubay. The letter was, in fact, a declaration of war. It said, "you have given protection with you, to our men. You should kill these people or turn them out of Yathrib. We swear by Allah that if you do not do that, we will all attack you and having destroyed you, will capture your womenfolk". This was a very good excuse for him to use force and turn the Prophet (PBUH) and his Muhajir Companions from Yathrib. He was the head of a very powerful tribe, which appears to have been numerically stronger than others.

Its members were alive to the needs of religious revival. Out of twelve leaders chosen to look after the affairs of Muslims of Yathrib, nine belonged to his tribe. He decided to use force if the occasion demanded to kill the Prophet (PBUH) and the few Muhajir Companions. The Prophet (PBUH) heard of his decision and went to him. Very little of the conversation between them is recorded. Abdullah bin Ubay was confronted with a new reality. Islam, although a religion of peace, denoted complete submission to the Will of Allah. It meant the acceptance of the Sovereignty of Allah which in practical life was demonstrated by obeying the Laws of Allah. This is what is meant by:-

> *"I created the Jinn and humankind only that they might worship me".* *51: 56*

And one of the Commands of Allah is that He has Ordained fighting for the Believers.

> *"Warfare is ordained for you".* 2: 216

The occasion for which this Commandment has been primarily Ordained is when some other group fights against you. It says:-

> *"Fight in the Way of Allah against those who fight against you, but begin not hostilities".* 2: 190

It has to be remembered that this Ummah is One:-

> *"Verily this Ummah of yours is One Ummah".* 23: 52

The Prophet (PBUH) brought home to Abdullah bin Ubay in these words:-

> *Do you realise that if you use force the Muslims from Yathrib will fight alongside the Muhajir Muslims and you will be shedding blood of your tribe on both sides.*

He realised the mistake he was making and decided not to use force against the Prophet (PBUH) and his Companions. His change of attitude was the result of his fear of being defeated at the hands of determined fighters. History is replete with instances, where people have had recourse to peace for fear of being hurt, in the end. The philosophy of Ahimsa—non-violence—is also the product of such logic, because the same people believe in Kali Devi, the goddess, who quenches her thurst from blood of gory murders. Peace accepted by him was of this kind. When we could not use force he resorted to mischief and remained a hypocrite and a tool of the Jews until his death.

History books are silent on further details of the conversations, that took place between the Prophet (PBUH) and Abdullah bin Ubay, it would be correct to assume that the latter must have asked the Prophet (PBUH) the way Yathrib was to be defended against the Mekkans. The details of the Charter lead us to the conclusion that the Prophet (PBUH) must have replied that the Muslims would defend Yathrib and if the others would like to share that responsibility the Believers would permit them to join in this great honour.

It could also be said that, as a result of the urgent need to defend Yathrib, the Prophet (PBUH) formulated the plan of establishing the state of Yathrib, giving it a Constitution, and laying down the responsibility of defence on Believers. Abdullah bin Ubay could not help accepting this plan. The next event mentioned in history books is the Constitutional Charter itself.

The Charter was dictated under the shadow of an impending war of extreme intensity. Its defence paragraphs must belong to the same period. The concessions granted to the Jews are linked with defence paragraphs and must belong to the same period. The paragraphs covering general administration were also the demand of the time. There are no further events in the history of Yathrib, which could have resulted in the issue of further the documents. The division of the Document of Professor Sergeant in 'A, B, X, Y, etc, amounting to eight different documents can certainly be called a futile effort, made merely to create doubts and with no fruitful object.

The war that was visualised when dictating this Document lasted for nine years and had, before ending, embroiled the largest Empire of that period in it, thus initiaing the longest war of history— The war between the Crescent and Cross—which is raging even today, fourteen centuries after the Charter came into force, and is no-where near its end as yet. Islam until then had laid greater stress on the building of character of individuals. The Charter ushered in the collective life of the Ummah. The principle that Muslims formed a nation by themselves, even when they lived in surroundings, which were not purely Islamic and it was given prominence by the Charter. The contents of the Charter make it clear that even when living as a numerical minority. Believers take over the administration of the society on condition that the principle of the Sovereignty of Allah is being acted upon.

As mentioned earlier, as far as details are concerned, when dictating the Charter, greater emphasis has been paid to matters relating to the defence of the state, than to other matters. The Prophet (PBUH) as a result of the wisdom and insight granted to him by Allah, kept his mind centered on the period after the war when need would arise for rehabilitation of people. In the words of a modern military thinker, "The true national objective in war lies in the 'after war'. If the civilized world is to be saved from collapse, there is urgent need to produce true grand strategists to replace the blind exponents of mass destruction". He argues that "If you concentrate exclusively on victory, with no thought for the after effect, you may be too exhausted to be profited by the peace, while it is about certain that the peace will be a bad one, containing the germs of another war".

The author is speaking from experience of two World Wars. Britain won both of them but lost the peace that followed. The experience of modern world over the last two centuries has shown that the war to end war has yet to be fought, unless laws of war laid down by Allah are observed in total. The war that was initiated by the Quraysh of Mecca and won by the Prophet (PBUH) ended, as far Arabia was concerned, because the Prophet (PBUH) keeping the after-war period in view had done nothing, during and at the end of war, which could keep alive the hatred generated by war. Modern wars have tended to increase hatred to a point, when, a rapprochement becomes impossible. We need, therefore, to study his life, his teachings, his foreign policy and the manner in which he fought his war and then magnanimously pardoned his enemies. It will show a pattern of human behaviour unparalleled in the annals of human history.

The Prophet (PBUH) had accepted the responsibility of defending Yathrib against the threatened attack, when Yathrib had yet no state, no government and no army. He and his Companions were the total force available for this onerous task. There were no armaments, no provisions, no transport animals and no finances to provide all these instruments of war. He had, however, men, who were prepared to lay down their lives on the Path of Allah. He had trained them to such unchartered heights of Belief in Allah, that no weapon could force them to abandon their positions. He also knew his enemies. They were resourceful. They were rich merchants and could furnish their army with the most sophisticated weapons.

They also had the means to last them during a long drawn war. They had friends among Arab tribes. They could, as a result widen the zone of war and have him surrounded and they had the means and facilities to make the blockade permanent, but his Belief in Allah outweighed those considerations. It is true that "once war begins, no one can tell how it will go. There are some who urge that we should abolish all armaments, and refuse to fight on any pretext. If this view is put forward on religious grounds, I will not deal with it beyond saying that it does not seem to me in accordance with the Bible... If on the other hand, its advocates believe that it would make for peace, it is inconsistent with recent events. China offered little or no resistance to Japan, yet that did not save her from the loss of territories as large as Europe, and the slaughter of some thousands other citizens".

The position of Believers, at the time of declaration of war by Mecca, was far more precarious than any community of peaceful and peace-loving people, who are threatened by a neighbour, who does not approve of their Ideology and their Way of Life. The enemy was the same, who had persecuted them in Mecca, ignoring relation of blood and friendship. A small number, a little over seventy had migrated to Habsha, and now less than fifty males had reached Yathrib and found a place, where they hoped to live according to Allah's given Way of Life, and they were being threatened with war and possible extermination. They had no alternative but to accept war. If they decided to avoid war, where could they go. They would have become stateless. The result would have been that the Islamic Society, which was visualised by the Prophet (PBUH) as a result of Revelations to him, from Allah, would not have been possible to be established. Allah's Promise was that they would be uppermost if they were Believers, was enough for them:-

> *"It is a promise from Allah in truth; and who can be more truthful than Allah in utterance"? 4: 122*

And

> *"(It is) a Promise of Allah. Allah faileth not His Promise". 39: 20*

And Allah has promised that :-

> *"Faint not nor grieve, for ye will overcome them if ye are (indeed) believers". 3: 139*
>
> *"And verily Our word went forth of old unto Our bondmen sent (to warn) that they verily would be helped. And that Our host, they verily would be the victors". 37: 171-173*

They were indeed Believers in its fullest meaning. No group of any Ummah of days gone by had reached heights of Belief in Allah which they had proved to have reached, and were yet to prove on many an occasion.

Most Required : Documents of this nature are not issued in a vacuum. There is always a background and a pressing need for them. In fact, pressing necessity, for the execution and enforcement of such documents alone made them acceptable to people. Such documents, whether they are named as agreements, treaties, charters or constitutions, are promulgated because the very existence of those societies depends on bringing into existence means of laying down the pattern of communal life, and such documents provide and guarantee a disciplined life of the community. Apart from rights and duties of individuals and groups such documents lay down restrictions and penalties for the breach of rules of conduct, expected of those for whose guidance they are issued.

Preparations to meet the threat of war are taken in hand, when the danger is real and the entire society recognises it. War cannot be taken lightly because it "is a social phenomenon too complex to be governed by any simple formula". Except the Prophet (PBUH) himself no one was either qualified nor was there anybody who had the moral strength to accept the responsibility of making the decision to defend .Yathrib or when the decision had been taken to take defensive preparations in hand and then conduct the war. To accept the duty of defending a state and its people is a decision of great moral character. An ill prepared nation is in serious danger of losing its war. To lose a war means to surrender the "right of freedom of thought" and to lose freedom of thought means to lose the right to live according to one's chosen Way of Life, which includes one's mode of worship. The Muslims could not afford to lose the war. They had chosen the Islamic Way of Life of their free will.

It was being challenged by the people, who had persecuted them for nearly thirteen years. They were determined that if they could not win the war they would fight to the last man. The battles fought by the Believers for the defence of Yathrib were all fought with the determination that they would fight until each one of them had achieved Shahadah. The Prophet (PBUH) had trained his Companions to wish for Shahadah and he was certain that they will come up to his expectations. His historic words, just before the attack of Meccan Army started at the battlefield of Badr are a testimony of the Believers having absorbed this philosophy. He had said:-

O Lord!
If this little band of Believers
Is wiped out today
There shall be none left
To obey your Commandments
Until the Day of Judgement.

There had been wars before and there were to be wars in future as well, but this war was different both in conception and the manner in which it was expected to terminate. Both sides were fighting to defend their respective Way of Life. It could end in not only the defeat of one army or the nation it belonged to but it was to end with the end of the Way of Life to which the loser belonged. It was a war aimed at the extermination of the Muslim's Ideology and Way of Life. The idea, that all wars are fought for differences, which can be solved peacefully, does not appear to be applicable to this war. Normally it can be said that, "Just how senseless and futile an expedient it really is, can usually best be judged by those who lose rather than by those who have won". In this case it was not applicable because the losers were to forego the freedom of living in accordance with their chosen Way of Life. This

Document had been dictated keeping in mind this Philosophy of War that to remain a Believer in Allah was only possible when Sovereignty of Allah could be proclaimed and life was led in accordance with His Commandments. To achieve that it was essential, that land occupied by Believers had to be defended to the last. It was, therefore, necessary, that Yathrib had its Basic Law—its Constitution—promulgated in a manner that its defence preparations could be taken in hand legally and constitutionally. Hence the correct heading of the Document can be "The Constitutional Charter of Yathrib... Medina".

It was not an agreement with the Jews as Allama Shibli Noamani calls it. He says "The Prophet (PBUH) sent for Ansars and Jews and dictated an agreement....which was accepted by both parties". Another eminent writer Jalal-ud-Din Jaffery writes, "When the Prophet (PBUH) arrived in Medina, he had an agreement written between the Ansars and the Jews". Naeem Siddiqui, the only one out of all Urdu writers has shown a different approach to the problem. He writes, "The Prophet (PBUH) created an organisation for the arming of the State of Medina, through which he integrated the Muslims, the Jews and the unbelievers, into a new society. He had a written document of the nature of an agreement, prepared. The nature of this document was of a proper constitution and it can be correctly called as the first written constitution".

Nearly all writers of Seerah in Urdu have called the "Charter" as an "Agreement," between either the Prophet (PBUH) and the Jews, or between the Believers and the Jews. An eminent learned man like Syed Abul Hassan Ali Nadvi has termed it as an agreement of peace with the Jews. Having correctly said that, "The Prophet (PBUH) on this occasion gave a writing to the Muhajirs and Ansars, "he adds "which contained an agreement of peace with the Jews". Another eminent historian writes, "On arrival at Medina, the Prophet (PBUH) during the very first year of Hijrah considered it appropriate to execute an agreement with all nationalities on the principle of internationalism so that a national solidarity should continue in spite of the ethnic and religious differences". Khalid Alvi, referring to the Jews writes, "He (the Prophet PBUH) made an agreement with them".

It could be that the word agreement has crept in because of absence of a proper equivalent of the term "Charter," in Urdu. The mistake dates back to Ibne Hisham, due to absence of a technical term for "Charter" in that age. He has used the word Aahadahum which has been translated as "covenant." The sentence as a result reads " the covenant between the Muslims and the Medinans and with the Jews".

Muslim and non-Muslim writers of Seerah in English, who belong to the present age, have also relied on Ibne-Ishaq, in more or less the same manner as Urdu writers. Abu Bakr Sirajuddin (Martin Ling) who has written with great devotion says, "and the Prophet (PBUH) now made a covenant of mutual obligations between his followers and the Jews of the Oasis". A non-Muslim writer of Pakistan origin says that before the signing of the agreement a thorough exchange of views had taken place. This may be correct but no work of early period seems to mention a thorough exchange of views. He writes, "After a thorough exchange of views, an agreement was reached and was reduced to writing".

Muir while translating the Document uses the words "Charter of Muhammad the Prophet" instead of "Charter from Muhammad," but in introducing it he writes, "It was natural that Muhammad, holding these sentiments should desire to enter into a close and binding union with the Jews, and this he did in a formal manner shortly after reaching Medina. He associated them with himself by a treaty of mutual obligation drawn up in writing". The difference between an agreement and a Charter is very vast. An agreement is between two equals and a Charter is given from one to others. An agreement can be rescinded by either party. A Charter can be altered, amended or cancelled only by the authority which promulgated it. Apart from the heading given to the document its contents alone can guide later researchers to give their verdict on it, whether it was a treaty, an agreement or a Charter.

Treaties are between states and usually the heading says so For instance, "Security Treaty between Australia, New Zealand and United States of America". Similarly Pacts are between independent sovereign states. For instance, "Pact of Mutual Co-operation (CENTO)" was signed between a number of states including Pakistan, Turkey and Iran. Recently a new name for mutual treaties has appeared. This is called a "Convention." For instance, "Convention regarding the Regime of the Straits" Let us, once again, look at Meethaq-e-Medina in a little greater detail, particularly its heading. It says:-

> *"This Document (writing) is from Muhammad, The Prophet of Allah (PBUH.)"*

It is clear that it is neither an agreement nor a treaty because it is not between Muhammad (PBUH) and some others. It is from him and he is the Prophet (PBUH) of Allah. Those receiving the Document are being told that the person issuing this Document is doing so in his capacity as the Prophet of Allah. Then it goes on to say that it is being given:-

"To"

"Quraish and Yathribite Believers".

Believers whether from Mecca or from Yathrib were all his followers known as his Companions. No group of people in the history of mankind have shown their devotion to their leader as was shown by his Companions to Muhammad (PBUH) the Prophet of Allah. When marching out to the battlefield of Badr, the leader of Ansars of Yathrib, Saad bin Muadh said, "We believe in you, we declare your truth, and we witness, that what you have brought is truth, and we have given you our word and agreement to hear and to obey; so go forth where you wish, we are with you, and by Allah, if you were to ask us to cross the sea and you plunged into it, we would plunge into it with you, not a man would stay behind. We do not dislike the idea of meeting your enemy tomorrow. We are experienced in war, trustworthy in combat....

" Whatever else description or name may be given to this Document it cannot be called an agreement between the Prophet (PBUH) and his followers. It was being given by him to them and they were all included in it, both the Muhajirs from Mecca and the Ansars of Yathrib.

There were others as well. They were:-

"those who will follow them and fight alongside them."

It would be applicable to others as well, provided these others followed the lead of his followers, the Believers, from Mecca and Yathrib. Apart from following the Believers they had to take part in fighting alongside the Believers to qualify themselves as recipients of this august Document.

This heading ends with a brief last remark, "They will form ONE UMMAH to the exclusion of others." It means that if the others qualified as recipients of the Document, then they and the Believers, the Companions of the Last Prophet of Allah, will form an Ummah apart from the rest of humanity. It was a great honour, that was being bestowed on them but the price was also very high. They had to accept the Believers as their leaders and continue to follow them by joining in war with them against their enemies.

Thus the Document was primarily issued as the Basic or Fundamental Law The Constitution of Yathrib, so that defence arrangements could be taken in hand, on behalf of the entire population. The Believers, being the group which had sworn allegiance to him as a result of the Bayah formed the manpower of his army. The march to the battlefield of Badr proved this fact. None others were prepared to sacrifice themselves for a cause, in which they did not believe. History has recorded one more Charter given by the head of a state. This was King John of England. This Charter, however, was taken by force by the barons of the realm, because, "King John was very unwilling to grant it.

This was on the 15th of June 1215 A.C., that the Great Charter was sealed with the king's great seal. He agreed that 24 barons shall be appointed to see that he kept the promises which it contained. He agreed only because he was compelled.... He never meant to keep the promises that it contained, and he did not keep them. He sent to France for soldiers and when they came he made war on his own people. He asked his friend the Pope for help and the Pope helped him by excommunicating all barons, by London under Interdict, and by telling John that he had no need to keep his promises". The surprising part of the whole story is, that, there was not much in the Charter, which an honest ruler of an average society need to have objected to.

It may seem strange that the Pope of all the people, should have advised a Christian ruler to go back on his promises. It was, however, not the first time, nor the last time, that the head of Church had advised a prince to go back on his promises. In one case, "the Pope, who seeing his plans being nullified, by this (peace treaty) initiated the Magyars to break the peace; oaths sworn to infidels not being binding". The Charter given at Yathrib was in the spirit of Islam, the New Way of Life. It had to be in accordance with all ethical, moral and legal principles laid down by Allah, for Believers in Him and His Prophet (PBUH). The time of its issue was the most critical period in the history of Islam—a time when the threat against Islam and Muslims was the greatest. This fact must be kept in mind while studying the Clauses of the Charter.

The position in which the Muslims were placed at this time has been misrepresented by some Western writers. Preparations for defence of Yathrib have been interpreted as aggressive designs against the Mekkans. A well known British historian writes that "Muhammad had now, as it were, thrown down the gauntlet, which the Mekkans could not but pick it up. He had effectively challenged them to a full scale trial of strength". It appears that after writing a few more sentences he remembered that it was the Mekkans who had declared war. He adds; "The Meccan belief thought Muhammad would avoid them rested on a misappraisal of the relative strength and fighting qualities of the two parties". He has avoided to give the source on which he has based the superior strength of the Muslim Army.

Chapter 3

Islamic Governance Traditions

The political system of Islam has been based on three principles, viz: *Tauhid* (Unity of God), *Risala* (Prophethood) and *Khilafa* (Caliphate). It is difficult to appreciate the different aspects of Islamic polity without fully understanding these three principles. We will therefore begin with a brief exposition of them.

Tauhid means that one God alone is the Creator, Sustainer and Master of this universe and of all that exists in it—organic or inorganic. The sovereignty of this kingdom is vested only in Him. He alone has the right to command or forbid. Worship and obedience are due to Him alone, none else sharing it in any degree or form. Life, in all its multifarious forms, our own physical organs and faculties, the apparent control which we have over everything that exists in this universe, and the things themselves—none of them has been created or acquired by us in our own right. They are the bountiful provisions of God and in bestowing them upon us, He is associated with no one. Hence, it is not for us to decide the aim and purpose of our existence or to prescribe the limits of our worldly authority nor is anyone else entitled to make these decisions for us. This right rests only in God, who has created us, endowed us with mental and physical faculties, and all material provisions for our use. This principle faculties, and all material provisions for our use. This principle of the Unity of God altogether negates the concept of the legal and political sovereignty of human beings. No individual, family, class or race can set themselves above God. God alone is the Ruler and His commandments are the law of Islam.

The medium through which we receive the law of God is known as *risala* (Prophethood). We have received two things from this source; (a) The Quran, the Book in which God has expounded His law; and (b) the authoritative interpretation and exemplification of the Book of God by the Prophet Muhammad, through word and deed, in his capacity as the representative of God. The broad principles on which the system of human life should be based have been stated in the Book of God. Further, the Prophet of God has, in accordance with the Divine Book, set up a model of the system of life in Islam by practically implementing the law and providing necessary details where required. The combination of these two elements, according to Islamic terminology, is called the *Shariah.*

Let us now consider *Khilafa,* which means "representation". The real position and place of man, according to Islam, is that of the representative of God on this earth, His vicegerent; that is to say, by virtue of the powers delegated to him by God, he is required to exercise Divine authority in this world within the limits prescribed by God.

Now take, for example, the case of an estate of yours which someone else has been appointed to administer on your behalf. You will see that four conditions are invariably fulfilled in this case. First, the real ownership of the estate remains vested in you and not in the administrator; secondly, he administers your property only in accordance with your instructions; thirdly, he exercises his authority within the limits prescribed by you; and fourthly, in the administration of the trust he executes your will and fulfils your intention and not his own. These four conditions are so inherent in the very concept of "representation" that they come to mind as soon as one utters the word "representation". If any representative does not fulfil these four conditions he will naturally be blamed for abusing his authority and for breaking the covenant which was implied in the concept of "representation". This is exactly what Islam means when it affirms that man is the representative *(Khalifa)* of God on earth. Hence, these four conditions are also involved in the concept of *Khilafa.* The state that is established in accordance with this political theory will in fact be a Caliphate under the sovereignty of God and will have to fulfil the purpose and Will of God by working on God's earth within the limits prescribed by Him and in accordance with His instructions and injunctions.

Democracy at Work

The above explanation of the term *khilafa* also makes it abundantly clear that no individual or dynasty or class can be *Khalifa,* but that the authority of *khilafa* is bestowed on the entire group of people, the community as a whole, which is ready to fulfil the conditions of representation after subscribing to the principles of *Tauhid* (Unity of God) and *risala* (Prophethood). Such a society carries the responsibility of the *khilafa* as a whole and each one of its individuals shares the Divine *khilafa*. This is the point where democracy begins in Islam. Every person in an Islamic society enjoys the rights and powers of the Caliphate of God and in this respect all individuals are equal. No one takes precedence over another or can deprive anyone else of his rights and powers. The agency for running the affairs of the state will be formed with the will of these individuals, and the authority of the state will only be an extension of the powers of the individuals delegated to it. Their opinion will be decisive in the formation of the government which will be run with their advice and in accordance with their wishes. Whoever gains their confidence will undertake the duty and obligations of the Caliphate on their behalf: and when he loses this confidence he will have to step down. In this respect the political system of Islam is a perfect form of democracy—as perfect as a democracy can ever be. Of course what distinguishes Islamic democracy from Western democracy is that while the latter is based on the concept of popular sovereignty the former rests on the principle of popular *khilafa*. In Western democracy, the people are sovereign, in Islam sovereignty is vested in God and the people are His Caliphs or representatives. In the former the people make their own laws; in the latter they have to follow and obey the laws *(Shariah)* given by God through His Prophet. In one the government undertakes to fulfil the will of the people; in the other the government and the people who form it have all to fulfil the purpose of God. In brief, Western democracy is a kind of absolute authority which exercises its powers in a free and uncontrolled manner whereas Islamic democracy is subservient to the Divine law and exercises its authority in accordance with the injunctions of God and within the limits prescribed by Him.

The Objectives

This being the essence of Islamic Political Theory, we may now examine the type of state which is built on the foundations of *Tauhid* (the Unity of God), *risala* (the Prophethood of Muhammad) and *khilafa* (the Caliphate).

The Holy Quran clearly states that the aim and purpose of this state is the establishment, maintenance and development of those virtues which the Creator of this universe wishes human life to be enriched by and the prevention and eradication of those evils the presence of which in human life is utterly abhorrent to God. The State of Islam is not intended for political administration only nor for the fulfilment through it of the collective will of any particular set of people; rather, Islam places a high ideal before the state for the achievement of which it must use all the means at its disposal. And this purpose is that the qualities of purity, beauty, goodness, virtue, success and prosperity which God wants to flourish in the life of His people should be engendered and developed and that all kinds of exploitation, injustice and disorder which, in the sight of God, are ruinous for the world and detrimental to the life of His creatures are suppressed and prevented. As well as placing before us this high ideal Islam gives us a clear outline of its moral system stating positively the desired virtues and the undesirable evils. Keeping this outline in view the Islamic state can plan its welfare programme in every age and in any environment.

The persistent demand made by Islam is that the principles of morality must be observed at all cost and in all walks of life. Hence, it lays down an unalterable policy for the state to base its politics on justice, truth, and honesty. It is not prepared, under any circumstances whatsoever, to tolerate fraud, falsehood and injustice for the sake of any political, administrative or national expediency. Whether it be relations between the rulers and the ruled within the state, or the relations of the state with other states, precedence must always be given to truth, honesty, and justice over material considerations. It imposes similar obligations on the state as on the individual, viz: to fulfil all contracts and obligations, to have uniform standards for dealings; to remember duties along with the rights and not to forget the rights of others when expecting them to fulfil their obligations; to use power and authority for the establishment of justice and not for the perpetration of injustice; to look upon duty as a sacred obligation and to fulfil it scrupulously; and to regard power as a trust from God and use it with the belief that one has to render an account of one's actions to Him in the life Hereafter.

Fundamental Rights

Although an Islamic state may be set up in any part of the earth, Islam does not seek to restrict human rights or privileges to the geographical limits of its own state. Islam has laid down some universal fundamental rights for humanity as a whole, which are to be observed and respected under all circumstances whether such a person is resident within the territory of the Islamic state or outside it, whether he is at peace with the state or at war. Human blood is sacred in any case and cannot be spilled without justification. It is not permissible to oppress women, children, old people, the sick or the wounded. Woman's honour and chastity are to be respected under all circumstances. The hungry person must be fed, the naked clothed, and the wounded or diseased treated medically irrespective of whether they belong to the Islamic community or are from amongst its enemies. These, and other provisions have been laid down by Islam as fundamental rights for everyman by virtue of his status as a human being to be enjoyed under the constitution of an Islamic state. Even the rights of citizenship in Islam are not confined to persons born within the limits of its state but are granted to every Muslim irrespective of his place of birth. A Muslim *ipso facto* becomes the citizen of an Islamic state as soon as he sets his foot on its territory with the intent to live there and thus enjoys equal rights of citizenship along with those who acquire its citizenship by birth. Citizenship has therefore to be common among all the Islamic states that (may) exist in the world and a Muslim will not need any passport for entry to or exit from any of them. And every Muslim is to be regarded as eligible and fit for all positions of the highest responsibility in an Islamic state without distinction of race, colour or class.

Islam has also laid down certain rights for the non-Muslims who may be living within the boundaries of an Islamic state and these rights must necessarily form part of the Islamic constitution. According to the Islamic terminology such non-Muslims are called *dhimmis* (the covenanted), implying that the Islamic state has entered into a covenant with them and guaranteed their protection. The life, property and honour of a *dhimmi* (non-Muslim citizen) is to be respected and protected exactly like that of a Muslim citizen. There is no difference at all between a Muslim and a non-Muslim citizen in respect of the civil or criminal law.

The Islamic state shall not interfere with the personal rights of the non-Muslims. They will have full freedom of conscience and belief and will be at liberty to perform their religious rites and ceremonies in their own way. Not only can they propagate their religion but they are entitled even to criticize Islam within the limits laid down by law and decency. The rights given in this respect are not limited, but the civil law of the country is to be fully respected and all criticism will have to be made within its framework which would be applicable to all citizens of the state. These, as well as many other rights, have been granted to the *dhimmis* in Islam. These rights are of an irrevocable nature. The non-Muslims cannot be deprived of them unless they renounce the covenant which grants them citizenship. Whatever be the extent of oppression which a non-Muslim state may perpetrate on its Muslim citizens it is not permissible for an Islamic state to retaliate on its non-

Muslim subjects in the slightest degree; even if all the Muslims outside the boundaries of an Islamic state are massacred, the state cannot unjustly shed the blood of a single non—Muslim citizen living within its boundaries.

The Components

The responsibility for the administration of the government, in an Islamic state, is entrusted to an *amir* (leader) who may be compared to the president or the prime minister in a modern democratic state. All adult men and women who believe in the fundamentals of the constitution will be entitled to vote for the election of the *amir*.

The basic qualifications for the election or an *amir* are that he should command the confidence of the largest number of people in respect of his knowledge and grasp of the spirit of Islam; he should possess the Islamic quality of fear of God and be endowed with qualities of statesmanship. In short, he should have both virtue and ability. A *shura* (advisory council) is also to be elected by the people for assisting and guiding the *amir* in the administration of the state. It will be incumbent on the *amir* to administer the country with the advice of this *shura*.

The *amir* can retain office only so long as he enjoys the confidence of the people and will have to relinquish his office when he loses this confidence. But as long as he retains such confidence he will have the authority to govern and exercise the powers of government in consultation with the *shura* (advisory council) and within the limits set by the *Shariah*. Every citizen will have the right to criticize the *amir* and his government and all reasonable means for the ventilation of public opinion will be available.

The Legislation : Legislation in an Islamic state will be restricted within the limits prescribed by the law of the *Shariah*. The injunctions of God and His Prophet are to be accepted and obeyed and no legislative body can make any alterations or modifications in them or make any law contrary to them. As for the commandments which are liable to two or more interpretations the duty of ascertaining the real intent of the *Shariah,* in such cases, will rest on people possessing a specialized knowledge of the law of the Shariah. Hence such affairs will have to be referred to a sub-committee of the advisory council comprising men learned in Islamic law. Great scope will still be available for legislation on questions not covered by any specific injunctions of the *Shariah* and the advisory council or legislature will be free to legislate in regard to these matters.

***Judiciary*:** In Islam the judiciary is not placed under the control of the executive. It derives its authority directly from the *Shariah* and is answerable to God. The judges should be appointed by the government but once a judge has occupied the bench he will have to administer justice among the people according to the law of God in an impartial manner, and the organs and functionaries of the government will not be outside his legal jurisdiction, so that even the highest executive authority of the government is liable to be called upon to appear in a court of law as a plaintiff or defendant like any other citizen of the state. Rulers and ruled are subject to the same law and there can be no discrimination on the basis of position, power or privilege. Islam stands for equality and scrupulously sticks to this principle in social, economic and political realms alike.

The Machinery

The arrival of the Prophet (PBUH) at Medina in A.D. 622, marked the first step towards the establishment of an Islamic state. Considering that Medina was still inhabited by non-Muslims, atheist Arabs, and Jews, the Prophet (PBUH) in his first legislative act drew the lines, in a convention, that would regulate relations between the different factions of the citizens of Medina. In the first part of his ten years of leadership in Medina, Prophet Muhammad (PBUH) laid down the foundation of a city-state, that would grow within a few years to encompass the whole Arabian Peninsula. He started with the construction of a mosque that would serve as a school, a centre for consultations and information, a court for receiving envoys and delegations, as well as a place for worship and prayers. He constructed a market place for the Muslims to counter that of the Jews. He then directed his efforts to building a Muslim army. In the latter part of his stay in Medina, he assigned to his governors and representatives the different parts of Arabia.

Laying down the basis for the subsequent rules guiding relations of the Islamic state with other countries, Prophet Muhammad (PBUH) set good examples in his diplomatic correspondence with foreign royalty, in the dispatch of envoys to neighbouring districts, in the establishment of new rules, or the implementation of old ones. These were related to the laws of peace and war, and the modalities and contents of the agreements that, he concluded with the opposing parties. He was thus paving new roads and giving a new meaning to the concept of international diplomacy. During the succeeding periods of the four Orthodox Caliphs and the Umayyad rule (A.D. 631-750), the Islamic state witnessed an era of expansion that brought it into direct contact and interaction with the Byzantine, the Persian and the Chinese Empires and peoples. The experience and sophistication of these civilizations enriched Islamic culture and concept. It was during the Abbaside period (A.D. 750-900) that the Islamic state, reaching its peak in political influence, cultural maturity and economic prosperity, represented the universal state.

Medina Convention

When the Prophet (PBUH) and his Meccan disciples reached Medina, it was inhabited by two major tribes, the Aus and the Khazraj, which had long been feuding with each other. In addition, there were several Jewish communities in Medina. Besides the Aus and the Khazraj, not all of whom were Muslims yet, the Medina society consisted of the Muslim exiles from Mecca, the Muslim helpers from Medina and the non-Muslim Arabs and Jews. In these circumstances, Prophet Muhammad (PBUH) became the teacher, arbitrator and the centre of all powers. In this capacity he applied himself first to the task of introducing order in Medina and organizing relations among different factions on a proper basis. With this objective in mind he issued a charter, by which blood feud was abolished and lawlessness repressed. Equal rights were granted to the Jews, who committed themselves to helping the Muslims in defending the city.

In this convention, to which all the communities adhered, the Prophet (PBUH) considered the Muslims, whether exiles from Mecca (Muhajeroun) or helpers from Medina (Ansar), as one community (Ummah), while addressing each one of the Jewish communities as a separate entity. Those who allied themselves with the Muslims would have their support and be on an equal footing. The parties to the Charter of Medina would conduct war or peace collectively. No party would unilaterally conclude peace with a belligerent adversary or wage war against a third party by itself. No one among the non-believers (Mushrikin) was to grant protection (Aman) to a Quraishite or to his property, nor would he prevent a faithful from acting against a Quraishite.

The Jews would share the expenses with the faithful. As long as they were fighting, the Jews of Bani Auf were an Ummah (a community) with the faithfuls. They had their own faith just as the Muslims had theirs. The Jews of Bani-Al-Harith, the Jews of Bani Saedah, the Jews of Bani Jusham, the Jews of Bani Al-Aus, of Bani Thalabah, had the same (rights) as those of the Jews of Bani-Auf.

No one from the Quraish or from those who supported it would be granted the protection of the parties to the convention. They (the parties to the convention) would support each other against any other party that would attack Medina. Anyone leaving Medina or staying in it would be safe, except for those committing injustice or misdeed.

Thus, the main political features of the convention were:

- For the first time in the history of Hijaz, a political unity was formed of the different factions and tribes of Medina under the leadership of the Prophet (PBUH).
- The influence of the Jews, which prevailed in the past due to their manipulation of the hostilities among the Medina tribes, was to be countered and minimized.
- The Prophet (PBUH) then secured not only a fortified front against any possible attack from his declared enemies, the Quraishites, but also formed the first ring in the chain that would besiege Mecca and contribute to its weakening. From there he could divert his attention to the most immediate business of organizing the state affairs, internally and externally.

Formation of the State

In establishing the structure of the new state, Prophet Muhammad (PBUH) built a mosque that would serve as a headquarter, as well as a place of prayers. He then designated a new commercial centre for the Muslims, apart from the old one which was controlled by the Jews. By such an undertaking he laid the foundation for an economic structure of the state that would function on the basis of Islamic principles, free from the influence of the Medina Jews.

From the first day of his arrival in Medina, the Prophet (PBUH) concerned himself with the formation of a military force, well organized and trained, that would be capable of defending the state and safeguarding its interests. The Islamic army was assigned military expeditions, that would serve the ultimate political and diplomatic ends. The frequent attacks on the trade caravans, going to and coming from Mecca, were intended to weaken the Quraishite economic power. At the same time these expeditions served as training experiments as well as a show of strength to other Arab tribes in the region.

On the international front, the Prophet (PBUH) dispatched a number of envoys with messages to monarchs and leaders of the neighbouring states and tribes, acquainting them with the new faith and inviting them to embrace it. He sent a messenger to the Emperor of Persia and another to the Byzantine Emperor. The former tore the message and banished the envoy from his presence, whilst the

Byzantine Emperor received the ambassador with considerable courtesy. A third envoy, sent to a prince subordinated to the Byzantine, in the Damascus region, was cruelly murdered.

Islamic Era

At the age of forty, Prophet Muhammad (PBUH) received his Commission and started to preach the new faith of Islam. The name 'Islam' came from an Arabic expression which implied complete 'surrender' to Allah, the one and only God. He, therefore, called for abandoning the old beliefs, repudiating paganism and discarding many inherited traditions and superstitions. Beginning with his immediate family and close relatives from Quraish, the Prophet (PBUH) gradually widened his circle of activities to include all the inhabitants of Mecca and those groups who came to visit it during the seasonal pilgrimage.

Although the new religion adopted many of the traditions and values prevailing in that society, it was a potent blow to the dominant social structure and its basic values. It is comprehensible, then, that the initial mild rejection of the Meccan leaders to the new faith became a fierce resistance as it spread. Prophet Muhammad's (PBUH) adversaries pursued an escalating opposition that started with dialogue and negotiations. It was stepped up with the application of different kinds of pressure and culminated with the torture of those professing adherence to the new faith.

The heads of the Quraish clans perceived Prophet Muhammad (PBUH) 'as the head of the community, however small, like a state within a state.' The relations between the two communities and their leaders, in many aspects, followed a course similar to that, which existed between two states. In conducting these relations, the methodology used was not far from diplomatic practices prevailing nowadays. In resolving their differences, both sides resorted to dialogue and negotiations, employing 'intelligence' and 'tact' and implied promises or threats. They applied these skills in their direct contacts or through their envoys and delegations. Both parties suggested compromises, and at certain stages accepted them.

Prophet Muhammad (PBUH), in his discourses resorted to persuasive arguments and discreet preaching: 'Call unto the way of thy Lord with wisdom and fair exhortation, and reason with them in a way that is best and most gracious.' On the other hand, the leaders of Quraish, who could not use force or inflict on Prophet Muhammad (PBUH) the same mischief they had inflicted on his followers—as he belonged to a strong and respected family of Quraish—had to opt for the diplomatic practice available to them. They sent delegations to his uncle and protector, Abu Talib, on three occassions, and each time they used a different approach. Failing to find a solution, they decided to negotiate directly with Prophet Muhammad (PBUH). On these three occasions they tried again either to strike a deal or to challenge his prophetic missions, or to reach a compromise. Both parties sent delegations outside of Mecca and both met with representatives coming to Mecca in their endeavours to win alliances or to obstruct the other party's manoeuvers to do so.

Delegations within Mecca

The Quraish tribe, fearing the spread of Islam among the people of Mecca and its repercussions on their prestige, values and beliefs, decided to send a delegation to Abu Talib, the Prophet's (PBUH) uncle and protector, demanding that either he prevent his nephew from pursuing his discourse or denounce him. The delegation which consisted of some dignitaries explained to Abu Talib the harm that Prophet Muhammad (PBUH) was causing to their beliefs and traditions. They pointed out that Abu Talib, who did not embrace the new faith himself, was in disagreement with Prophet Muhammad (PBUH), as they were. However, Abu Talib apparently mollified them before they left. On the second occasion, the Quraish delegation came to Abu Talib and used a threatening tone, asking him to prevent his nephew from opposing their beliefs. They told him that if he continued to do nothing about it they would fight him.

Abu Talib conveyed this to his nephew and requested him not to burden him with a load that could prove to be too heavy for him to shoulder. The Prophet (PBUH) replied that even if the sun were placed in his right hand and the moon in his left, he would never relinquish his mission.

The third delegation from the Quraish came to Abu Talib with a third option. They suggested that he deliver Prophet Muhammad (PBUH) to them and they give him in exchange Amarah bin al-Walid, who was a wise and presentable young man from the family of Quraish. Abu Talib condemned this sort of bargaining where he 'was to deliver his adopted son to be killed', as he put it, 'while accepting their son to be fed and protected.'

In the three encounters, it is to be noted that both sides had observed the prevailing social (tribal) norms when they pursued their patterns of negotiations, namely, the obligation to stand on the side of the family and to help and defend even those members whose point of view they did not share. The Quraish recognized Abu Talib's family obligations and the latter accepted this burden despite the fact that he did not share Prophet Muhammad's (PBUH) belief. It is worth mentioning that both sides resorted to their verbal skills and persuasive arguments throughout their talks. Also both sides implied latent power in supporting their respective positions. The Quraish delegations implied the unanimity of the Quraish clans and their firm resolution. Abu Talib reckoned on his family prestige and the fact that it could not be easily challenged. Prophet Muhammad (PBUH) expressed his steadfastness and confidence in the support of God who would help His faith to ultimately prevail.

In the second phase of these encounters, the Quraish leaders decided to contact Prophet Muhammad (PBUH) directly and to talk him out of his discourse. In the first attempt they agreed on sending one of their dignitaries known for his knowledge of soothsaying and poetry. They selected Utbeh bin Rabiah, who met Prophet Muhammad (PBUH) and started his negotiation by referring to the damage the Prophet (PBUH) was inflicting on his peoples' beliefs and idols. Then, questioning his motives for rejecting the creed of his kinsmen they offered to reward him if he abandoned his mission. Utbeh conveyed to him their readiness to make him the richest man, if he sought wealth, or to concede to his leadership if he sought honour and prestige. In reply, Prophet Muhammad (PBUH) read to him a passage of the Quran related to the questions in the mind of the delegate about the Prophet (PBUH), the Quran, and the core of the new faith.

When Utbeh returned to his people he advised them to leave him to what he was striving to accomplish, assuming that if he prevailed, then his rule over the Arabs 'would be your rule and his glory would be yours' and that if he were killed by the Arabs, then 'they would have saved you the effort.' This argument did not convince the Quraish. Their leaders decided to launch another attempt. This time they invited Prophet Muhammad (PBUH) to meet them by the Kaaba. They started the negotiations by repeating their previous complaints and offers. Then they stepped up the offensive. They challenged his God's power, requesting him to move the mountain or to bring the rivers into their land or to resurrect their ancestors, so they could testify to his authenticity. Prophet Muhammad (PBUH) based his argument on the rationality and logic of his mission rather than on miraculous proofs or supernatural manifestations. He kept telling them after every request that it was not for that, that he was commissioned, but that God had sent him as His Apostle to deliver His message.

In their third attempt, the Quraish leaders sought to reach a compromise. They sent a delegation of four dignitaries, who proposed to Prophet Muhammad (PBUH) that they worship his God and he worship their gods. If either party was the true one, then both parties would benefit from their common practice. The Prophet's (PBUH) response was a firm rejection of this bid and it was expressed in the Quran as 'Say: O ye that reject the faith! I worship not that which ye worship. Nor will ye worship that which I worship... to you be your religion and to me my religion.' One can interpret this encounter and the aim of the negotiations conducted through it as endeavours to reach a compromise over the disputed matter.

Negotiations generally imply the attempt to reach a compromise, based on concessions made by both parties. The extent of the concessions made by either side may reflect inversely the power it possesses to support its argument. Often negotiations are conducted for purposes other than reaching a settlement. They may be launched by one party with the intention of exploring the status of the adversary. In some other instances, negotiations may be conducted for the mere purpose of gaining time, in preparation for another course of conflictual encounter. The Soviet Field Marshal Shoposnikov might have meant that when he said, 'If war may be said to be the continuation of politics by other means, then peace, in its turn, is no more than the continuation of conflict by other means.'

Through the interactions the Quraish leaders had with Prophet Muhammad (PBUH), they sought either to explore his plans, or to reach a kind of negotiated settlement, or to challenge him in order to expose his weak points in preparation for 'the continuation of the conflict by other means.'

Delegation Dispatched Abroad : After failing to reach a settlement with Prophet Muhammad (PBUH), the Quraish notables resorted to other means, aiming" at obstructing him and containing his successes. On the personal front, they intensified their pressure on his followers and his immediate family, the Banu Hashim. In order to expose what they expected to be his weaknesses, they sent a delegation to Medina to meet the Jewish rabbis there. Since Prophet Muhammad (PBUH) declared that the Islamic faith is the continuation and the completion of Christianity and Judaism, the Jewish rabbis of Medina could help in refuting this claim. It is mentioned that the rabbis of Medina advised the delegates to put three questions to Prophet Muhammad (PBUH). TWO of the questions were related to stories recorded in the Old Testament. If he failed to answer any of these questions, then he would prove ignorant of the Jewish faith and that would negate any connection claimed between the two religions.

When repression against the followers of Islam intensified, the Prophet (PBUH) advised those who could not secure protection to migrate to Abyssinia. This choice was based on two circumstances. The first one was that the Abyssinian Negus was the nearest Christian leader, who could offer asylum to the Muslims. The second was that the Arab pagans had connections with South Arabia which belonged at that time to Persia, an ancient enemy of the Christian power of Byzantium. The number of followers, who migrated to Abyssinia, in the fifth year of the Prophetic Mission, was eighty two. After the immigrants settled in Abyssinia, the Quraish tribe schemed to pursue them in their asylum and sent two delegates to the Abyssinian Negus. One of them was Amr bin-al-Aas, a very shrewd person, whose name appeared in a later period as a remarkable negotiator and warrior. The mission of the Quraish delegation was to convince the Abyssinian Negus to disclaim the Muslim refugees and if possible, to extradite them.

At the same time the Quraish notables decided to move farther in their sanctions against Prophet Muhammad (PBUH) and his protectors, Abu Talib and the families of Banu Hashim and Banu Al-Muttalib; (Hashim and Al-Muttalib were two brothers. Prophet Muhammad (PBUH) and his uncle Abu Talib descended from the first one). The Quraish leaders met and concluded a written agreement, which they deposited at the Kaaba and by which they vowed to boycott Banu Hashim and Bani Al-Muttalib. It was agreed that none of the Quraish would deal with anyone of the two families in trade, marriage or social contacts. It is noteworthy that this boycott agreement was not directed against individuals, who followed the new faith, but included everybody in the two families (Hashim and Al Muttalib) whether they were believers or non-believers of Islam. The reaction of Banu Hashim and Bani Al-Muttalib families was the same and the non-believers showed solidarity with the believers." The boycott agreement was an example of an inter-tribe or inter-state conduct of relations.

During the tenth year of the Prophetic Mission, Abu Talib, the Prophet's (PBUH) uncle and protector passed away and he became more vulnerable to the hostility of the Quraish. He left Mecca for Al-Taif to call its people to embrace Islam and to seek their support and alliance. There, he was met with defiance and rebuke. He returned to Mecca vowing not to submit, as long as God, Lord of the weak and helpless, was his support.

Migration to Abyssinia

In the fifth year of the Prophetic Mission, many of the Muslims migrated to Abyssinia to escape the repression of the Quraish. They left in two groups totalling eighty two persons. Ruqayah, the Prophet's daughter and her husband Othman (RA) (who was to be the third Caliph) were in the first group. The second group included Jafar bin Abu Talib, Abu Talib's son and Prophet Muhammad's (PBUH) cousin. The Muslims believed that they would be given refuge by the Abyssinian Negus, who was a Christian and believer in one God. After they were accepted in Abyssinia, the Quraish leaders dispatched a delegation of two persons to the Negus in order to convince him to extradite those who were offered asylum and to deliver them to their people in Mecca. The delegates, keen to succeed in their diplomatic mission, planned their approach carefully. They carried gifts to the monarch and his aides. First, they met with the patriarchs individually, and explained to them that they had sheltered some of their people, who had relinquished their fathers' religion, but who had not embraced the patriarchs' faith. Contrary to both religions, they had invented, as the delegates put it, a religion of their own, which was acceptable to neither party. They appealed to each patriarch to send these defectors back and to advise the king not to summon the Muslim immigrants for a hearing. When the two delegates were received by the Negus, they presented their gifts to him and repeated the claims that they had put to the patriarchs. The latter attested to the delegates' claim and proposed to the monarch to disown the immigrants and to deliver them to their people, who knew them better and were aware of their mischief. The Negus refused to disavow those who sought asylum in his country and he declined to entertain the petition of the delegates without first verifying the charges against the immigrants.' When the Muslim group was brought before the king, they were asked what made them differ with their people and abandon their religion without embracing Christianity or any other beliefs.

On behalf of the Muslim group, Jafar bin Abu Talib took the stand to answer these questions. He addressed the Negus, and said that, 'Before Islam, we were people of ignorance, worshipping idols, committing atrocities and disrupting family relations until God raised up an apostle from amongst us; we know his ancestry, his truthfulness and his credibility. This apostle called on us to believe in one God and to worship Him and commanded us to tell the truth, to keep family ties, to protect whoever sought refuge among us...we believed in him and followed his teachings, while our people, oppressed us and endeavoured to impose their faith back on us. This is why we migrated to your country and solicited you and not anyone else, seeking your protection and hoping not to be mistreated by you.' The Abyssinian Negus requested Jafar to read verses of his book and Jafar read a passage, i.e. the *Sura XIX* entitled Mariam. The Sura tells the story of Zakaria, having a son Yahya (John) at a late age and of Mariam (Mary the Virgin), who although a virgin, by the will of God had a son Isa (Jesus).

The Negus was pleased with what was said and commented that what the Prophet (PBUH) was preaching and that which Jesus proclaimed, 'both were emanating from the same source.' He told the delegation from Quraish 'You may both leave, these people I will never deliver to you.' When the Quraish delegation left the court, Amr ibn-al-Aas thought of another approach. He decided to inform the Negus that the Muslims believed that Jesus Christ was just a man—no better than a slave. He returned the next day and proposed to the Negus to summon the Muslims and to ask them what they thought of Jesus. The Negus put the question to them. Again Jafar bin Abu Talib spoke and said that they thought of Jesus what their Prophet (PBUH) had conveyed to them and that Jesus was a slave of God, His apostle and His spirit. He was the word of God delivered to Mariam the Chaste. This argument did not satisfy the patriarchs, but it did satisfy the Negus, and the report goes on to say that he dismissed the two Quraish delegates, rejecting their gifts and rebuking their mission.

Quraish Boycott

Realizing that the Abyssinian Negus had extended his protection to the Muslim immigrants, and that the Muslims in Mecca were increasing in number, the Quraish notables held a meeting where they decided to boycott Bani Abdul-Muttalib. They recorded this agreement in a written document which they deposited at the Kaaba. Such an action provoked the Bani Hashim and Bani-Al-Muttalib to ally themselves with Abu Talib and Prophet Muhammad's (PBUH) followers. This alliance included the Muslims and non-Muslims within the two clans.

The boycott continued for a period of two to three years, during which the people, besieged in their quarter in the ravine of Abu Talib, suffered from lack of food supply except for what was secretly infiltrated. One of the Quraish notables, Hisham bin Amr, who was related on his mother's side to Bani Hashim, used to load a camel with food stuff and lead it to the opening of the ravine in the darkness of the night and release it to the people in the besieged quarter. He convinced another figure of the Quraish, Zuhayr bin Abi Umayah, to raise the boycott, Zuhayr expressed his consent and reservation as they were alone in this matter, and both agreed to seek the support of other notables. After that Hisham went to a third and a fourth person and reached the same agreement with them. The group of five met together and drew a plan for abrogating the agreement.

The next day they went to the Kaaba and after the sermons Zuhayr called for the people of Mecca and addressed them, asking how they could eat their food and wear their clothes at a time when Banu Hashim were suffering and were denied the right to trade with them. He then vowed not to rest until this unjust and disruptive document was destroyed. When Abu-Jahl, one of the main adversaries of the Prophet (PBUH) interrupted his speech and insisted that the agreement be preserved, another one from the group of five came to the help of Zuhayr, then the third one came, followed by the fourth in the group. All expressed their concurrence with him. After them, Hisham bin Amr stepped forward to state that he too had never consented to the agreement from the beginning and that he would repudiate its contents. Although the number of people who condemned the agreement was not big—only five—the manner in which they spoke, one after the other, gave the impression that this was the feeling of the majority. When, in the end, one of them went to tear up the document, he found that it had already been destroyed.

Delegations to Mecca

Prophet Muhammad (PBUH) and his companions spared no opportunity to explain their religion to those, who came to Mecca and to call on them to accept the faith. He met groups of Arabs, who came to Mecca for pilgrimage and for trade. He received envoys and delegations, who arrived to inquire about the new religion and to acquaint themselves with its Prophet (PBUH).

In the ninth year of the Prophetic mission (A.D. 619), a delegation of Christians from Najran (a region south of Mecca) came to meet the Prophet (PBUH). After they had put their questions to him and listened to passages from the Quran, they left and were confronted by Abu-Jahl and a number of Quraish men, who tried their best to counter whatever impression the Prophet (PBUH) had left on the delegation. During the same period, an envoy from Hamadan (a tribe living in the northern part of Yemen) called Qays bin Amr came to meet Prophet Muhammad (PBUH) and to report back to his people. After discussing his mission with the Prophet (PBUH) and declaring his conversion to Islam, Qays expressed his own and his peoples' readiness to support the Apostle. He was requested to return to his people and to find out, if Hamadan was ready to take Prophet Muhammad (PBUH) in their midst and to support and defend him. Qays left for Hamadan and later returned alone to announce his peoples' adherence to Islam and their readiness to host him. Though, Prophet Muhammad (PBUH) expressed his appreciation for the positive response, he found it short of a firm commitment. His agreement with the Medina delegation later on proved to be based on something more concrete.

Prophet Muhammad (PBUH) maintained his contacts with people visiting Mecca. During the pilgrimage season he met the different tribes coming to Mecca, calling on them and convincing them to accept Islam. At one of these seasonal gatherings in Mecca, a delegation from Medina, representing the Aus tribe, came seeking alliance with the Quraish against the Khazraj, the other major tribe in Medina. Medina, which was known as Yathrib, was inhabited mainly by two Arab pagan tribes (Aus and Khazraj) and an influential Jewish community. The continuing hostilities between the two tribes gave rise to the dominance of the Jewish community. The delegation from Yathrib was headed by Abul Qayser Anas bin Rafie and included Iyas bin Muadh. Prophet Muhammad (PBUH), hearing of the arrival of the delegates, and their purpose, came to meet them and said: 'Would you have what is better than what you have come for?' When they asked what that was, he said: 'I am the Apostle of Allah. He has sent me for all humankind; to call upon them to worship God and to ascribe no partner to Him. And He revealed to me the book.' Then he called on the delegation to embrace Islam and read before them verses from Quran.

Iyas, influenced by what he heard, expressed his sympathy and preference for what was presented, but he was rebuffed by his superior, who told him that he was there for a different purpose. It appears that, despite the fact that Prophet Muhammad (PBUH) did not convert the group, his message was delivered and it was to be conveyed to the people of Yathrib. So when he met other delegations from that city, his views were already known to them.

First Aqaba Delegation : During the pilgrimage season to Mecca in March, A.D. 620, Prophet Muhammad (PBUH) met a group of the Khazraj tribe, who came to Mecca for the same purpose as the other Yathrib delegation had come the previous season, that is, to seek an alliance among the Quraish, against their opponents, the Aus and Jews. When Prophet Muhammad (PBUH) talked to them and explained to them the faith of Islam, it seemed as though they were not surprised with the basic idea, as they had often heard from the Jews about the awaited Messiah. They looked at each other and said, 'By God! He is the new Prophet the Jews had always threatened us with. Why should we not be ahead of them to join him?' They declared their faith in Islam and told him that, they had left their people divided in feuds and hostilities and that, they would return to them and call on them to accept the faith. They promised that if they were united around this faith, then no one among them, would have a more honourable position than the Prophet (PBUH).

They returned to Yathrib (Medina) and started propagating Masab bin Umair the new faith, aided by a Muslim who had previously emigrated to Abyssinia. The next year, five of them came back again to Mecca together with seven new converts and met the Prophet (PBUH) at Aqaba, the pass between Mina and Mecca. Here, he heard their plight and enjoined upon them the basic laws of Islam and sent one of his companions to teach them the religion and to lead their prayers. This emissary of the Prophet (PBUH) followed the wise approach and sagacious advice of the Prophet (PBUH) in preaching Islam to those voicing their opposition to it in Medina. Once, one of the Medina notables came to him and in a threatening manner ordered him to leave them alone. The emissary prudently asked him to sit and listen to what he had to say. If he found it satisfactory, he might then accept it, otherwise he could point out what he disliked. The Medina notable Osayd bin Hudhayr accepted the proposal as a fair one. He listened to what the emissary read from the Quran and declared his acceptance of the faith. He then advised the emissary to go and meet Saad bin Muadh, the man, who would be followed by all his people, if he accepted the faith.

It is worth pointing out here that throughout all the meetings between Prophet Muhammad (PBUH) and those delegations and individuals whom he strived to bring to the new faith, the Prophet (PBUH) always invoked rational argument and discreet presentation and each and every time read to them, passages of the Quran. While all the other prophets had performed miracles as proofs of their divine missions, the only proof put out by Prophet Muhammad (PBUH) was the words he voiced. The value of a word to an Arab lies in its meaning, its rhythm, its music, and its logic and its eloquence. To the Arabs, the spoken word is a covenant, that commits them to the most serious obligations. The Quran described Jesus Christ, as being the word of God descended to Mary. The first word of the Quran that was delivered to Prophet Muhammad (PBUH) when receiving his commission was

'Iqraa', which means 'read'. Those who specialize in Islamic history and literature, would appreciate the impact and deep effect the language of the Quran had on a people, who appreciate the value of the word. For them it is understandable that the only sign of Prophet Muhammad's (PBUH) divine inspiration was the Quran itself, its contents and its wordings. The first delegate from the Quraish came to meet Prophet Muhammad (PBUH) to verify that is he a poet or a soothsayer. He heard him recite the Quran and went back to his people to assert that, what he heard was not the word of a poet, or that of a soothsayer. It is said that the only miraculous proof of the new religion Islam, was the language and the content of the Quran.

Second Aqaba Agreement : During the pilgrimage season of the thirteenth year of the Prophetic Mission (A.D. 622), a group of seventy three men and two women from Medina came to Mecca and met with the Prophet (PBUH) at Aqaba. It was in the darkness of night that Prophet Muhammad (PBUH) came to meet them accompanied by his uncle Abbas, who had kept his pagan belief. Abbas addressed the Medinese, telling them of the position Prophet Muhammad (PBUH) occupied among his people and within his family and that he had been defended even by those, who did not adhere to his faith. He went on to say that despite that, Prophet Muhammad (PBUH) had chosen to join them and to ally himself with them, if they believed that they would defend him. Abbas warned them that if they could not pledge this support to him, they must leave him, where he was protected and esteemed. The group from Medina gave their assurance and offered to take an oath of allegiance to Prophet Muhammad (PBUH).

Before the Medina party committed themselves to Prophet Muhammad (PBUH), they made it clear that their forthcoming agreement would sever ties, they had with another party, meaning the Medina Jews. They asked if he would give them up once his cause prevailed. Giving them the assurance of his constant allegiance to them, Prophet Muhammad (PBUH) had them swear their fealty to him in defending him, as they defended their women and children.

Having sworn this mutual oath of allegiance, Prophet Muhammad (PBUH) requested them to solicit twelve captains from among themselves as representatives. Then, he addressed the twelve persons named by the group and stated to them that they would be the guarantors to what their people were committed to, as the Disciples were to Jesus. He would be the guarantor for his people. The twelve captains expressed their consent in confirmation of the pledge covenanted with their people.

On the basis of the second Aqaba agreement, Prophet Muhammad (PBUH) gave permission to his followers to immigrate to Medina. The migration to Medina of the Mecca Muslims was effected in successive waves. The last three to leave Mecca were Prophet Muhammad (PBUH), his close companion Abu Bakr (RA) and his cousin Ali bin Abu Talib. On 25 September 622, Prophet Muhammad (PBUH) accompanied by Abu-Bakr (RA) arrived in Medina to start a new phase in the history of Islam, which marked the beginning of the Muslim calendar year. The arrival of the Prophet (PBUH) in Medina, where Islam had spread among all the Aus and Khazraj tribes, laid the basis for the establishment of the first Islamic state.

The Manifestations : Throughout this period one discerns manifestations of diplomatic practices, which formed the basis for the more sophisticated practices observed in the succeeding period. Relations and contacts between communities and tribes resembled relations and contacts among states now-a-days. The methods, manners and means of conducting diplomacy might have been quantitatively and qualitatively limited. There have been instances where pacts, agreements or pledges were conducted and concluded verbally or in writing, after negotiations and exchange of delegations.

Nevertheless, the examples mentioned indicate a degree of maturity in diplomacy. The norms and traditions known to the Arabs of that period were the background for such practices. These were accepted and used by both communities, the Muslims and the pagans, but certain features reflected the new culture of Islam. For instance, when the two delegates from the Quraish went to the Abyssinian Negus to explain the contradictions between Islam and Christianity in terms of Jesus Christ, the Muslims debated among themselves as to what they should tell the Negus. They concluded that they should be truthful about what they believed. The debate that would ensue eleven centuries later as to whether, diplomacy could revert to deception or should be based on truthfulness, was settled in the incident mentioned above. The Muslims believed that credibility does not only pay off, but also reflects their faith, which could be translated into modern terminology as reflecting their constant policy.

Another aspect of diplomacy in that era was that when negotiations were concluded, the argument of either party would reflect the power that backed the party's position. In the case of negotiations between the Quraish and the Muslims, the Quraish delegations always backed their argument with the support and unanimity of their clans, while the only power the Muslims relied on was the strength of their argument and their belief. The third feature of this type of diplomacy was that it represented a way of life rather than a professional activity, that simply served the purpose of the mission. The Quran enjoined them to adopt a certain manner in their discourse or when effecting their responsibility. 'It is part of the mercy of God that thou dost deal gently with them. Wert thou severe or harsh-hearted, they would have broken away from about thee.' That thou have averted evil with good.' 'Call unto the way of thy Lord with wisdom and fair exhortation and reason with them in the better way.'

The Perception

The modern concept of state is, that it is an organised institution, which is run by the people through their elected representatives for the collective welfare of the people, residing in a specified territory. The ultimate power vests in the people, who are real sovereign and, therefore, masters of their destinies. They are free to legislate and enact any law, following their own desires. The constitution of the state is moulded according to the history, belief, customs and ideology of its people. All the secular states of the world, whether Democratic or Socialistic are administrated by man-made laws, and institutions, and are based on the theory of material advancement, and utilitarianism.

Concept of State

The concept of state in Islam is altogether different from the present-day concept of state. In modern times when territorial nationalism is the order of the day and material and economic considerations almost wholly shape peoples' outlook and policies, the making of an Islamic State stands out as the triumph of an ethical concept. But the Western observers may question: firstly, what the character of Islamic State is and, secondly, as to how an Islamic State can be realised in a democracy in the twentieth century. In this context it becomes necessary for us to ascertain as to what the true form, character and nature of an Islamic State is and how far it can be realised in the structural pattern of a modern society. In this context, it should be kept uppermost in the mind that Islam is not merely a religion in its narrow import. It is not a set of dogmas, mythological beliefs or mere rituals. It does not divide life into water tight compartments. There is no dichotomy in Islam between the temporal and spiritual; the structure of Islam is essentially religio-political. In this system the state forms an integral part at the apex and as Dr. Muhammad Iqbal points out "is only an effort to realise the spiritual in human organisation". *(Lectures on Reconstruction of Religious Thoughts in*

Islam, page 155). Thus, Islam presents the whole of reality to man and wants to give him guidance in every walk of life. It requires him to discriminate between the right and wrong and to accept a path because it is right and not because it is secular or non-secular. It attempts to bring the realities of this world in harmony with the ideals that provide security for this world and the Hereafter. It is a complete code of conduct. It is a way of life and a philosophy of life. It is a social, economic and political system. Hence, it is a statecraft.

It is in this context that the whole outlook and effort for raising the edifice of the state has to be different from the lines on which people ordinarily pursue the task of state building. Thus spiritual and ethical values of Islam have played a decisive role in this regard. This has been embodied in the concept of Islamic State—a state patterned on the socio-moral, religio-political principles of Islam. It is not torn by the dualism of state and church whose separation has been deemed an absolute dogma in Western Political Science. The church is not recognized in the genuine Islamic State as an exclusive institution representing religion. The concept of state religion or the Papacy or theocracy cannot give a correct picture of the character of the Islamic State. In a theocracy, the Pope assumes a special intimacy with God and nobody can reach God except his intermediary. This concept is alien to Islam. The criterion of an Islamic State is not union of the ruler and the government, but the principle of justice and religion combined with social action. Thus, in order to understand the concept of state in Islam, lct us examine the essentials of the state.

To constitute a state four elements are essential: (i) territory; (ii) population; (iii) organization; and (iv) sovereignty. In regard to the fourth element, the Islamic State differs fundamentally from all other states, and in that occupies a unique position.

No state can be termed independent unless it enjoys sovereign power i.e. the absolute right to make laws for people within its jurisdiction. This gives rise to the question, who should possess such right? In ancient times, when *might is right* was the rule the most powerful individual, through sheer brute force, used to conquer certain territories and instal himself as the ruler of the people. He called himself king and arrogated to himself the absolute right of law making and the right to set up any form of government that suited his convenience. Being himself the chief law-giver for his people, he was considered above law, and, as such, not bound by any law, not even his own. And in consequence of the enjoyment of this and other exclusive rights and privileges, he regarded himself as God incarnate. As an obvious corollary of this belief, he had full control over the life and death of his subjects who are required to give him unquestioning and unconditional obedience and to serve him blindly. The people were, thus, reduced to the position of mere serfs and chatties: they enjoyed no fundamental rights, nor could they claim, freedom of expression or liberty of conscience.

Later in history, when feudalism became the order of the day, a few feudal lords joined the monarch in claiming the right to make laws for the country, but the people remained where they were earlier so far as their rights and privileges were concerned. The monarchs along with those few lords enjoyed innumerable exclusive privileges and all that at the cost of those whom they ruled by virtue of being the law-givers for the land.

During the mediaeval period, the ecclesiastical authorities in Christian Europe tried to set up theocracy i.e. the rule based upon divine laws; but as the few Commandments which were regarded as infallible could not cover all aspects of human activities, the priests found an excuse to arrogate to themselves the right of making additional laws for the people. They also put themselves above the law, and as such enjoyed exclusive privileges, depriving the people of their just and inalienable rights.

Following the pattern of theocracy and in order to assert their so-called inalienable hereditary rights and infallibility, the mediaeval English monarchs claimed the 'Divine Right of Kings' the traces of which theory are still to be found in England, the most democratic country in the world. For that matter, the maxim "The King can do no wrong" still holds as good in England today as it was during the mediaeval and post-mediaeval period.

Even in Greek democracy, which is regarded by some as an ideal institution, the people were divided into two classes: the free (men) and the slaves. The latter, in the opinion of Aristotle, were not fit to participate in government. Their position was like that of animals whose only duty was to serve their free masters who owned them. They had none of the rights of citizens. Nor were women given any right and, so much so that Aristotle would confine to more domestic duties. The philosophers who called the Greek democracy into existence because the sole law-makers for the country and their antipathy towards women and healots resulted in social inequality. In other words, Greek democracy assured freedom only for the free, male Greeks, and was confined to Greece.

Rousseau, the well-known French philosopher, was, however, the first to enunciate the idea of popular sovereignty, and it was after the French Revolution that attempts were made to found state on this basis in Europe.

First State

The Islamic State, as is well-known, was founded by the Holy Prophet in the seventh century of Christian era; and continued with full vigour during the period of first four Caliphs *(Khulfa-i-Rashidin)*. But soon enough, its complexion changed owing to certain variations in its ideals. However, certain basic ideals like equality, liberty, justice and even toleration remained in force to a certain degree in the post-Rashidin period.

But owing to the existence of institutions like monarchy and feudalism, the fundamentals of Islamic State, could not find a foothold in European countries, although a very energetic, glorious Islamic State was in existence in Spain for several centuries. The abolition of the institutions of monarchy and feudalism in the wake of French Revolution, however, paved the way for the reception of these ideals into Europe.

Even in modern democracies which are based upon popular sovereignty, equality, liberty, justice and toleration are rarely to be found. Strange though it may sound, this contention is nevertheless based on facts. No doubt, in modern state laws are made by the representatives of the people, yet they are made in such a way as to suit the interests of either a class or a party at the cost of the opposition or they remain so defective that different interpretations are put for different sections of the people. They are so nicely twisted that they always favour the "sovereign" class. In all modern democracies, from the President or the King down to the legislature, they are all allowed, in the first instance, to enjoy some sort of exclusive privileges, for instance, exemption from taxation, exemption from appearance in the court or immunity of arrest (while performing their official duties), reservation of seats in trains or planes, or other priorities in several other respects. Secondly, the ruling party makes such laws which could suit and advance its own interest, although it may adversely affect the opposition e.g., if the Labour Government is in power, it will promulgate laws suiting the labourer and normally at the cost of the capitalists and *vice versa*.

The most flagrant example of discrimination in this respect can be found in South Africa where the original, native inhabitants were deprived of their inalienable right to franchise by the foreign ruling class. This racial discrimination was also to be found on another level in one of the most democrative countries of the world viz., the U.S.A.

Even in the most democratic country of the world, viz., England, one finds the same phenomena of inequality although little in comparison to above mentioned countries in operation: For instance, one does find discrimination, though in a lesser degree, so far as the interpretation of law and dispensation of justice are concerned.

Even in the eastwhile communist states which are regarded more advanced in this respect than their capitalist counterparts, the same phenomena of inequality, injustice and intoleration prevails on account of the same defect. The heads of communist states along with their lesser party bosses, were all above the law; nay, they imposed themselves on the people through the force of an election. As there is no check on the sovereign powers of the legislators, they deprived the people even of their liberty of conscience; and by putting an end to private enterprise and initiative, they reduced human beings to the position of an inconsequential part of a huge machine.

This defective system of law-making is primarily due to the fact that the right of sovereignty has been entrusted to human agency without any divine restriction. And it is because of basic human weakness that men when they are entrusted with the law-making power, more often than not misuse it in their own favour or in favour of the party or class which they represent. In other words, unrestricted sovereign powers have been assumed by human beings, in all the states from time immemorial resulting in exclusive privileges for the ruling authorities and deprivation of inalienable human rights of the people as a whole.

In an Islamic State, on the other hand, sovereignty belongs to God, the Almighty Allah. This does not, however, mean that in an Islamic State, all the laws are to be made by God Himself or that the Quran provides all possible positive laws and that people have nothing to do with sovereign functions. On the other hand, the laws, enacted in an Islamic State are, to be made by the people of the state, but in the light of the Quranic fundamentals. Thus, in an Islamic State, the people enjoy a partial and restricted right of law-making. They cannot, of course, make any law which runs contrary to the Quranic instructions, meant for universal application. In this sense, the people who make the laws, are not really law-makers. Nor are they above the law; they are only the executors of law and they stand at par with ordinary citizens.

First Source : There are two kinds of verses in the Holy Quran, namely decisive and allegorical, the latter being those which are capable of different interpretations. The decisive verses are the basis of the Book, and contain the fundamental principles of religion. So that whatever may be the differences of interpretation over allegorical verses, the fundamentals of religion are not affected by them.

Second Source : The *Sunnah* or *Hadith* (the tradition of the Prophet) is the second, and undoubtedly a secondary, source from which the Islamic laws are drawn. *Sunnah* literally means a way, rule or manner of acting. In its original sense, therefore, *Sunnah* indicates the doings, and *Hadith* the sayings of the Holy Prophet, but in effect both cover the same ground and are applicable to his actions, practices and sayings; *Hadith* being the narration and record of the *Sunnah,* but containing, in addition, various Prophetical and historical elements of Islam. As the Holy Quran generally deals with the broad principles or essentials of Islam the details are generally to be supplied by the *Sunnah* of the Holy Prophet. Even for the two important religious institutions of Islam, viz., prayer and *Zakat,* no details are to be found in the Quran. The details about these injunctions were only supplied by the practice of the Holy Prophet.

These are but two examples: but since Islam covered the whole sphere of human activities, hundreds of points had to be explained by the Holy Prophet by his example in word and deed, while the moral side, his was the pattern which every Muslim was required to follow. The persons, who embraced Islam, thus, stood in need of both the Holy Quran and the *Sunnah.* And it was because the *Sunnah* occupied such a tremendous though a secondary place in the super-structure of Islam that the early Muslims devoted themselves so assiduously and so energetically to collecting all traditions with every possible care that was humanly possible. In judging whether a certain *Hadith* was spurious or genuine, the collectors not only made a thorough investigation regarding the trustworthiness of the transmitters but also applied other tests for its acceptance. No *Hadith* was to be accepted, if it was opposed to or was against the plain teachings of the Quran. Being the secondary source of law, *Hadith,* is, however, to be judged by the Quran. If it agrees with the Quran, it should be accepted; if it runs counter to the spirit of a Quranic injunction, it should be rejected.

Third Source : *Ijtihad* is the third source from which the laws are drawn. The word itself is derived from the root *"Jihad",* which means exerting oneself to the utmost or to the best of one's ability, and *Ijtihad,* which literally conveys the same significance, is technically applicable to a lawyer's exerting his mental faculties to the utmost for purposes of solving difficult problems. Reasoning or the exercise of judgement, in the theological as well as in legal matters, plays a very important part in Islam. The Quran does recognise revelation as a source of knowledge higher than reason. But it also admits that the truth of the principles established by revelation may be judged by reason, and in doing so, it repeatedly appeals to reason and denounces those who do not use their reasoning faculty. It also recognizes the necessity of the exercise of judgement in the formulation of a decision. *Ijtihad* or the exercise of judgement is expressly recognised in the *Hadith* as the means by which a decision may be arrived at when there is no direction in the Holy Quran or the *Hadith.* The following *Hadith* is regarded as the basis of *Ijtihad* in Islam:

> *On being appointed Governor of Yemen, Muadh Bin Jabal was asked by the Holy Prophet as to the rule by which he would adjudicate. He replied "by the law of the Quran". "But if you do not find any direction in the Quran, how would you decide", asked the prophet. He replied, "I will apply the* Hadith *and Sunnah". "But if you don't find any guidance in the* Hadith *as well?" He was again asked. "I will then exercise my judgement and act on that," came the reply. The prophet raised his hands and said, "Praise be to Allah who guides His Messenger as He pleases".*

This *Hadith* shows not only that the Holy Prophet approved of the exercise of judgement but also that his companions were well aware of the principles, and that *Ijtihad* was freely resorted to by his followers, when necessary, even in the Prophet's lifetime.

Fourth Source : The fourth source of Islamic law is *Ijma.* The word *Ijma* is derived from *jams* which means collecting or gathering together, and *Ijma* carries the double significance of composing and settling a thing which has been unsettled and hence determining and resolving upon an affair, and of agreeing or uniting in opinion. In the terminology of the Muslim jurists, *Ijma,* means a consensus of opinion of the Mujtahids, or an agreement of the Muslim jurists, of a particular age on a point of law. *Ijma,* however, is not an independent source of law; it is only *Ijtihad* on a wider basis and like *Ijtihad,* it is always open to revision.

In the second century of the *Hijra* arose the famous schools of the great jurists who codified the Islamic law according to the needs of the time; and this codification became, the chief basis of Islamic law at that time. However, owing to the degeneration that presently set in the Muslim society (in consequence of which it could not produce jurists of the calibre of the famous four *Imams),* the community as a whole began to believe that the codification, as done by those great *Imams,* was final; and that there was no scope for further *Ijtihad* in *Shariat.* Whatever may be the justification, this belief was nevertheless contrary to the very teachings of Islam. Since the Islamic laws are to be derived from the Quran which is regarded as a universal guide for all time, it is inevitable that *Ijtihad* should continue to be exercised. It is, therefore, a mistake to suppose that the door of *Ijtihad* was closed after the four *Imams.* It has already been shown that the Quran and the *Hadith* have both directions to the effect that the Muslim world should continue to exercise its judgement in making laws itself. Since the ultimate test of the correctness of *Hadith* is the Quran itself, the conclusion is evident that Islam allows independence of thought, subject only to one thing—that the principles laid down in the Quran are not contravened.

It will thus be seen that the Muslim community possesses the partial and restricted right of law-making. It is this restriction imposed upon the framers of law in an Islamic State which has created a world of difference between this state and all other states. The beauty of the Quranic principles is that they, being of divine in origin, are equally applicable to the whole mankind, irrespective of a person's status, position, colour, race, sex, language or nationality. If a thing is declared legal, it is legal for all in any shape or form. There are to be no exceptions; and even if they are allowed, they are allowed for all under certain conditions and circumstances. We can, therefore, conclude that owing to the restricted right of legislation entrusted to the most learned scholars among the Muslim community, nobody is regarded as a legislator (in the modern sense of the word) in an Islamic State. The authority or authorities in such a state can only be regarded as the executor.

The Fraternity

In accordance with the famous verse of the Holy Quran "The believers are but a single brotherhood". The first characteristic of the Islamic state is fraternity. This verse asserts that Muslims, whatever, be their country, race, colour, or language, are members of a single brotherhood. Among the believers white and black, rich and poor, master and servant, Arab and non-Arab, stand together and enjoy equal rights and bear equal responsibilities in running the state. Such is the force of Islamic brotherhood that even blood relationship counts for nothing. An unbeliever, even if connected with a believer by blood ties, falls into a totally different category of citizenship. As regards the division of the Believers into nations and tribes, the Holy Quran says, "We made you into nations and tribes so that you may recognize each other. Verily the most honoured of you with Allah is he who is the most righteous of you" (XLIX). This verse emphasises that all regional and tribal distinctions are merely for the sake of convenience. Neither can they form the basis for the classification of rights of status of human beings nor should the separation or fusion of nationalities depend upon them. Among the Believers if any distinction is to be made at all, it should be on the basis of *Tuqwa* or piety. The flowering of Islamic fraternity perhaps, reached its climax on the occasion of *Hijrat* when the prophet knitted one *Muhajir* and one *Ansar* together in the brotherhood of Islam and they both lived under the same roof as brothers.

The Sovereignty

Since sovereignty in an Islamic State is restricted to the four corners of the *Shariah,* whose principles are universal and equally applicable to all, the obvious resultant characteristic of such a state is equality. It is, however, a mistaken notion that Islam sanctions absolute equality among its votaries. Absolute equality is denied by nature, as no two persons are equal in every respect. Any amount of effort on the part of a state to equalise the mental faculties or even physical gifts of different persons will prove fruitless. Consequently, a well-known verse of the Quran says: "Verily, We have given preference to some over others". However, the question arises, "What is the concept of equality in Islam"? It means equality before law and in matters of civic rights and obligations to the state. Above all, it means affording of equal opportunities to all, irrespective of caste, colour, race or birth; it also connotes social equality, a principle which even some of the most progressive and democratic states in the world have not been able to enthrone even in the present age. Only merit, character and devotion to the cause of Islam should enable a person to occupy the highest position in the state. A person's worth should not be judged by birth, but by efficiency, character and services to the cause of Islam.

The Liberty

The third characteristic of an Islamic State is liberty, which in its true perspective was, for the first time, presented by Islam to humanity. The greatest character of individual liberty is involved in that very *'Kalima'.* "There is no god but one God" excluded all other authority but that of God. A Muslim is free as he is not required to obey any other authority, but that of God. In other words, this would mean that he is only free within the limits, prescribed by the *Shariah*. None can encroach upon the rights of others, but at the same time can feel free within his or her own rights. Freedom of expression and liberty of conscience are the two cornerstones of Islamic polity. Even an ordinary citizen of the state can criticise the highest in the state and call him to account. However, licence in the name of liberty is not allowed; none enjoys the right of slandering people or to make fun of the authorities. It is, however, the obligation of the Islamic State not to deprive any citizen of the liberty Islam confers upon him without proving his crime in the court of law and without giving him full opportunity and facilities for his defence.

The Justice

The fourth characteristic of an Islamic State is justice. Justice in an Islamic State, should be impartial and no respecter of persons, whether high or low, prince or peasant, white or black, Muslim or non-Muslim. The Quran enjoins upon Muslims to decide a case on the basis of equality, justice and upright testimony. As such, the entire Muslim community is to be held responsible for the administration of justice. The following verses of the Holy Quran sum up the conception of justice in an Islamic State: "O ye who believe be (firm) maintainers of justice, bearers of witness for Allah's sake, even though it be against your own selves, or your parents or your kins and whether it be against rich or poor; for Allah can best protect both. Follow not the lusts (of your hearts), lest ye swerve; and if ye distort (justice) or decline to do justice, verily Allah is well-acquainted with all that ye do". (IV: 135). "If (O Muhammad;) thou judges concerning the affairs of non-Muslims, judge in equity between them (however hostile may be the attitude towards thee). For Allah loveth those who judge in equity", (V: 45). Thus the Holy Quran has emphasised again and again that however hostile, mischievous or cruel may be the person with whom the authorities have to deal, it is not permissible for them to deviate even slightly from the path of justice. In the light of the above Quranic injunctions, it becomes incumbent upon the head of the state to provide free impartial justice to all irrespective of caste, creed, colour, nationality, race, status or sex.

According to Islamic notions, the head of the Islamic State has a two-fold judicial function, one positive and the other negative. His positive functions related to the establishment of peace in the state, maintenance of concord among the various sections of the people and the protection of the weak against the strong. His negative functions concern punishment of the evil-doer and the restitution of the rights of the injured. For the dispensation of justice, the head of the state has to appoint *Qadis,* well versed in *Shariah law.* God-fearing and of irreproachable character and sterling piety.

The *Qadis* who apply divine law, consider themselves responsible not only to the head of the state but also to God Almighty and, as such, dispense justice equitably and speedily. Since the *Qadis'* court is regarded as God's court, no preferential treatment is to be given even to the highest in the state.

"The King can do no wrong", does not hold good in an Islamic State so far as the dispensation of justice is concerned. No one can claim exemption from appearance in the court or even a preferential seat in the court. Recording of deposition of influential persons through commission is not allowed by Islamic law. The Islamic law lays down easy procedure for the conduct of cases and cheap and speedy justice is to be meted out to rich and poor alike free of cost.

However, Islamic State lays greater emphasis on the prevention of crimes than on punishing the culprits after the offences are committed. Seeking legal opinion from well-known scholars has been in vogue since the very inception of Islam. The authorities allowed learned scholars to give free and legal advice to all and sundry. This institution enabled the state to assume that every citizen know the law, for it gives an equal opportunity to every person to know such legal details which he or she did not already know. Often *Qadis* who were not quite sure about some legal point, referred the case to *Mufti* and took a *Fatwa* from him.

Dual Responsibility

The fifth characteristic feature of the Islamic State is that everyone from the Caliph to an ordinary citizen is doubly responsible, viz., to God and to some sort of earthly authority. The fear of God and the punishment in the hereafter being common to all, the people are responsible to the head of the state, who, in turn, is himself responsible to the former. Hence, there is a double check upon the actions of all the citizens in an Islamic State.

In public, they do not commit any act of omission or commission for the fear of the state officials, in private, they also abstain from committing any wrong as they are conscious of the presence of Almighty. Thus, the dichotomy of distinction between the public and private life of a citizen in an Islamic State disappears altogether. The absence of the fear of God is the weakest point in all modern states, particularly in a communist state, where people, devoid of moral conscience, as they are, can commit any wrong, unnoticed by the state officials; whereas people in an Islamic State dare not do any such act of omission or commission as they are conscious of the fact that their God is having a vigilant eye over them and they shall not escape punishment.

In accordance with a verse of the Quran "We created believers" and unbelievers, the population in an Islamic State is divided between believers and unbelievers. Among the believers, there are two kinds: first those who believe in all the revealed religions and their prophets and also in Islam as the last religion and Prophet Muhammad (peace be upon him); and, secondly, those who believe in their own revealed books and prophets, but not in Islam or its Prophet Muhammad (peace be upon him). Since the Islamic State is an ideological state, it is but natural that its administration should primarily be entrusted to those who believe in its ideology and agree to sacrifice their all in running the state and making it a success.

In order to defend the frontiers of the Islamic State and to promote the cause of its ideology, military service is made compulsory upon all the able-bodied Muslims without any exception; in return, they are guaranteed maintenance allowance from the state. The second group of believers, viz., the followers of the revealed books who believe in the existence of the God but do not believe in Islam or its ideology when such people agree to live within the jurisdiction of an Islamic State, their relations are guided in accordance with the famous verse of the Quran, "No compulsion in matters of faith". The Islamic State regards them as *Dhimmis* or its own responsibility; and guarantees them full liberty of conscience protection of property, life and freedom of religious belief. Nay, it goes one step further and provides full scope for the growth of their culture and traditions and the administration of their civil affairs in accordance with their own religious laws.

An Islamic State does not believe in forcing its own culture and traditions on others or in adopting coercive measures to get the culture of the *Dhimmis* submerged into that of the Muslim, as it is usually seen under a nationalist disposition. As the *Dhimmis* are not obliged to defend the Islamic State, they are required to pay a small tax in return, known as *Jizya:* in case they offer themselves for military service, they are exempted from the tax too. No distinction is made between the Muslims and the followers of other revealed books in matters of the civic rights and the latter could qualify themselves for all offices of the state except the religious ones.

Thirdly, the unbelievers are those who either do not believe in the existence of God Almighty and in the Hereafter or associate other partners with God. The followers of this Godless cult are fundamentally opposed to all the believers of God; and are at the perpetual warfare with them.

Islam which believes in the establishment of peace by liberating mankind from all shackles of slavery is the worst enemy of the Godless cult. So long as this cult survives, Islam cannot flourish and will not be able to achieve its ideals; and, therefore, as a moral force, it is directly opposed to this evil force. As such, this Godless cult has been described in the Holy Quran as *fitna* (mischief) which must be rooted out from the Universe so that the faith of God may flourish.

Guiding Principles

As all the guiding principles of the Islamic State are derived from the Quran which, according to Muslim belief, is a divinely revealed book, some people assert that it (the Islamic State) is a religious institution. In reality, the Islamic State is not a religious institution in the sense of medieval Christian theocracy in which certain ecclesiastical authorities claimed for themselves the right of law-making. Others assert that the Islamic State is temporal as it is required to administer affairs which are temporal in character and not spiritual.

It is, however, not temporal in the modern sense of the term, since the modern state is not guided by religion, and it usually lacks moral conscience and a moral basis for administration and application of its laws. Since the fundamental ingredients of an Islamic State are derived from the Quran, it becomes a little difficult to separate religion from temporal function.

And since its chief function is to protect Islam and to promote its cause, both within and without and to administer both religious and temporal affairs. In accordance with the Quran and the *Sunnah,* this state may be regarded as both religious as well as temporal. It should, however, be made clear that the state religion of Islamic State must be Islam for whose protection and maintenance, it is called into existence and continues to exist.

It will be a falacy to compare the Islamic State with any modern state, as it fundamentally differs from all of them and stands as a class by itself. Since it is based on Quranic principles and has a definite mission to perform, it may be regarded as an ideological state. It may, however, be termed as theo-democracy, for, in such a state, under the sovereignty and paramountcy of God, a limited popular sovereignty has been conferred on the believers.

Since the Islamic State encompasses both the religious and the temporal spheres, and come into existence through a contract between the (elected) *Ameer* and the general *Ummat* (community), it is nothing if not a devise to fulfil the aspirations of the individuals themselves collectively and, to a certain extent, individually. The state is thus not marked by any suicidal controversy between the state and the individual. According to the Islamic polity, the state, the *Ameer* and the *Millat* are all animated by an ethical ideal, and it is the duty of each one of them to strive after and towards this ideal. Accordingly, the personal liberty of the individual is guaranteed to a very large extent under this system; and political power is not concentrated in the hands of one person.

Yet another feature of the Islamic State is to carry on the administration through mutual consultation. The Quran says, "those who (conduct) their affairs by mutual consultation" *(Amr a hum Shura Beina Hum);* and "(O Muhammad) consult these (i.e. in the affair. Then when thou hast taken a decision put the trust in (Him)" (Ill: 150). Thus, there should exist in an Islamic State a Majlis-i-Shura or Council consisting of representatives of the people, reflecting the total legal wisdom of the entire country. The appointment of this council is made by the *Ameer* himself from among various sections of the people; the only criteria for appointment being their intimate knowledge of the *Shariah,* their character. The Ameer-in-Council is to legislate in consultation with the *Majlis* and administer the state with their consent. Since the final authority is the Quran and the *Sunnah,* pleas should be based on, and in accordance with them. The decision is to be unanimous and the *Shura* feels collective responsibility.

The Islamic State is noted for separation of powers. Although the *Qadis* are to be appointed by the *Ameer,* the highest executive head in the state, in consultation with Shura, yet judiciary is completely independent of the Executive. The fact that *Qadi* can accept a suit against the very person of the *Ameer* without any previous permission and can try him in an open court—this feature of Islamic judiciary is an index to the independence of judiciary in an Islamic State. Nor is the *Ameer* exempted from personal appearance or to be given any preferential seat, in the court. The question of taking deposition of great and prominent personalities by means of commission does not arise in an Islamic State.

The Centralization

Another feature of the Islamic State is centralization in matters of legislation. The nature of the Islamic state which is based on Quranic principles, demands that there should be uniformity in legislation. It is only the Central Legislative Assembly which could legislate in connection with matter touching the religious aspects of life or the common problems of the state for instance, foreign policy, taxation, justice and constitution.

However, in matters of temporal administration, much can be left with the provincial authorities. In case of provincial revenues and expenditure, the provincial treasuries can work as independent units; the Provincial *Baitul Mal* is to receive and disburse the amounts realized. In early Islam too, *Zakat* realized from a certain place was used to be spent on the needs of the local people; balance, if any, in the Provincial Treasury used to be deposited with the Central Treasury, whereas deficit, if any, in the Provincial Treasury met from the Central *Baitul Mal*. The whole empire is to be divided into provincial units. The Governors, appointed by the Caliph in consultation with the *Shura* and the local people, could be transferred and dismissed from their posts.

The economic policy of the Islamic State is to be based on some positive injunctions in the Quran. It lays down, "So that the wealth should not circulate only among the rich from among you". Hence, the distribution of wealth among all classes of believers has been emphasised by the institution of property tax, known as *Zakat,* to the extent of 2½ per cent on surplus property, each hoard as well as commercial capital; and restrictions on the process of testamentary disposition, laws of inheritance and the prohibition of usuary. The Islamic State believes in the imposition of minimum taxation and the provision of maximum comforts for the people.

The believers who are supposed to pay less than the *Dhimmis* could, however, be required to pay all their surplus wealth to the state in case of emergency. Since the believers have to stake their lives and property for the defence and the maintenance of the state, they are secured due provision for their food, shelter and other necessities of life. Islamic State does not believe in class war nor does it undertake a complete socialization or democrative management of the basic instruments of production and distribution. It does allow the individuals to acquire private property so that their incentive may not be lost; but, on the other hand, it does not allow the concentration of wealth into few hands in order to perpetuate capitalism in its naked form. The economic system in an Islamic State thus stands midway between the two antagonistic systems in the present world capitalism and communism.

The objective of the Islamic State is to "establish prayer and pay *Zakat;* and enjoin good upon the people and to restrain them from committing wrong "(XXII: 41). The Quran also refers to Muslims as the best people sent down to Universe in order to do good and prevent others from committing wrong. These verses are very significant and sum up the chief objectives of the Islamic State regarding the duties of the Muslims. The first part of the first verse relates to prayers and *Zakat* which enable Muslims to practice in actual life the principle of equality, liberty, fraternity, justice and obedience to the *Imam.*

The first part of the second verse regard the Muslims as the best people and as such incapable of doing wrong. They are, therefore, required to persuade others to do good as also restrain them from committing wrong. This express Quranic injunction entails enormous responsibilities upon the head of the state as well as its people. This obligates the state not only to carry out these orders within its own jurisdiction but also beyond it if occasion arose.

It is, thus, that the Islamic State is to be at perpetual war with forces of tyranny, wickedness, and godlessness. In order to emancipate mankind from bondage, whether physical or intellectual, the Islamic State is required to wage *Jihad.* But *Jihad* or holy war is not to be fought for personal aggrandisement or national glorification. It is to be waged only for the establishment of the rule of God and for ending man's tyranny over man and man's injustice to, and man's inhumanity to man.

The first Islamic State was set up by the Holy Prophet (peace be upon him) in the city of Yathrib, later named Medina-tun-Nabi, which ultimately became shortened into Medina. This should be our model, because it is our belief that whatever the Holy Prophet (peace be upon him) did was perfect as he was not only a living embodiment of the Holy Quran but also acted under Divine guidance through revelations.

The State came into existence after the *Hijra* from Mecca, but before that the Holy Prophet had entered into a compact with the leaders of *Banu Ahws* and *Banu Khazraj,* two leading tribes of Yathrib who had embraced Islam and invited him to shift to their town. This pact was made at a place called Aqaba and was in the nature of a bilateral treaty under which the Medinites on their part, accepted the Holy Prophet (peace be upon him) as their religious and political leader and undertook to protect him from all his enemies, and in particularly the *Quraish,* and the Holy Prophet (peace be upon him), on his part, bound himself never to forsake them or to return to Mecca.

The words used translated into English read:

> *"Nay in life and death I am with you and you are with me. I will fight whom you fight and I will make peace with whom you make peace."*

The formula adopted for the oath of allegiance taken by the Medinites at the hands of the Holy Prophet (peace be upon him) was to the following effect:

> *"We pledge that we will hear and obey you, in times of our distress and in times of our plenty and shall stand by you whatever may befall us of happiness and of anguish, and that we will speak the truth wherever we be not fearing the censure of the censurers in the path of Allah."* (Bayat-i-Aqaba Thani).

City of the Prophet

The conditions prevailing at Medina at that time were one of utter chaos. Not only was there no administrative machinery to bind the tribes together but they were actually weary of their traditions of unending tribal wars. *Banu Aws* and *Banu Khazraj* were divided into twelve clans and the Jews into ten and each clan was fully autonomous. The first task, therefore, was to teach the new converts the principles of the new faith. Hence, the first thing undertaken was to construct a mosque where the community could be collected and taught the practical lessons of fraternity, equality, liberty and justice. Thus, the new community was welded into a disciplined group with a common ideology.

Having got the followers together, the Holy Prophet (peace be upon him) gave practical shape to the injunction of the Holy Quran that "the believers are but a single brotherhood, so make peace and reconciliation between your (contending) brothers and fear God that ye may receive mercy" (XLIX: 10) by obliterating the distinction between *Quraish, Aws* and *Khazraj* and pairing them together as brothers in Islam. Each of the 150 *Muhajirs* adopted by an *Ansar* as a brother with whom he was even agreeable to share his wealth but, the *Muhajirs,* not wishing to be a burden on their hosts, were content to engage themselves in various trades with the help of their *Ansar* brothers and this brought prosperity to them and really integrated themselves with the *Ansars.*

After organising his followers into a social polity the Holy Prophet (peace be upon him) applied his mind to the essential task of providing protection to the newly formed community from the *Quraish* who were still bent upon destroying the Muslims. To meet this external threat it was found necessary first to consolidate the position of the community within Medina itself which was then in habited by a large number of Jews also. The hand of friendship was extended to them and treaties of mutual security and defence were entered into guaranteeing them equal civil rights, freedom of religion and mutual protection against external aggression in return for their recognition of the Holy Prophet (peace be upon him) as the paramount executive, military and judicial authority. The Jews willingly accepted this condition and became as a body the allies of the Muslims and thus the city state of Medina came into existence as a political entity.

The Holy Prophet (peace be upon him) was not content to leave all this in a nebulous state; so a charter was drawn up meticulously recording the terms of agreement and the rights and obligations of the respective contracting parties. This became the constitution of Medina and is, perhaps, the first written constitution to be drawn up in the world. It was drawn up in two parts. The first part consisted of 23 articles dealing with matters concerning the *Muhajirs* and *Ansars* and those who were "attached to them and crusaded with them", while the second part dealt with the relationship between the Muslims and the Jews.

The basic concept of this charter was that all would accept the Holy Prophet (peace be upon him) as the Paramount Authority in all matters administrative, judicial and military, and obey his lawful orders. He was to be the commander of the combined army, the executive head of the state and the final court of appeal but not a ruler in any sense of the term as the sovereignty over the universe, according to Islam, vests in Allah alone and all without any exception are subject to His laws.

The next main concept was that the Muslims were to form a single unit of this political community, separate and distinct from the rest, and the Jews as a body were to constitute the other unit. The two together were to form a federation for the purposes of war and peace and the defence of Medina. In all other matters each federating unit was to be completely autonomous but subject to the paramountcy of the Holy Prophet (peace be upon him).

Each unit was to enjoy complete freedom of religion and governed by its own laws, customs and traditions except that the practice of blood-revenge and counter-revenge was to be totally banned and no interference on the basis of kinship or tribal affinity was to be permitted in the affairs of the state, and particularly, in the administration of justice.

This compact did not extend to purely religious wars *(Jihad)* but the Jews expressly undertook that they would not in any event grant protection to the *Quraish* or their allies. So far as the Muslims were concerned the number of *Ansar* tribes was fixed at ten and the *Muhajirs* were declared to be one tribe. Each tribe was to be treated on a par with the other in respect of their rights and duties. War and peace and the administration of justice were to be matters of common or federal concern and were to be the concern of the clan, tribe or individual. This put an end to tribal anarchy and gave birth to a sense of collective responsibility. Henceforth, everyone was to be a party to peace and war and, therefore military service was compulsory for all.

In the same way, all were collectively responsible to see that no one dared harm or encroach upon the rights of others and that everyone, according to the teachings of the Holy Quran, acted with absolute fairness, free from any bias or partiality, fear and favour, even though it be against one's own interest or the interest of one's parents, kinsmen or tribesmen (IV: I 35). Tribal affiliation was recognised only to the extent that the tribe was saddled with the responsibility of ransoming its own captives from the enemy and the payment of a debt was made obligatory on the debtors' kinsmen as well.

The Protection

The right to grant protection was to be enjoyed by everyone, high or low, and the pledge given even by the lowliest was to be binding on the entire community but no Muslim was entitled to grant protection to a *Quraish* to Mecca or to prevent anyone from taking revenge from such a *Quraish* for the cruelties perpetrated by them upon the Muslims in Mecca. If to these we add that the entire Muslim community was already firmly pledged to believe in one God, accept His sovereignty over the universe, follow His Commandments as revealed to the Holy Prophet (peace be upon him) and to obey the latter's lawful commands, then the pattern that emerges is of a community organised on the basis of the cherished principles of equality, liberty and fraternity in the real sense.

The main characteristics of this state that can be gathered from the above are:

- That it was an institution established through a democratic process namely, the free will and accord of the people desiring to form the same and to accept the Holy Prophet (peace be upon him) as the paramount authority (Pledge of Aqaba Thani and Agreement with the Jews).
- That it was a constitutional organisation set up under a written charter (Charter of Medina).
- That it was a federal structure comprising two communities, the Muslims and non-Muslims, and not two territories.
- That it was an ideological state based on the concepts and fundamental principles embodied in the Holy Quran.

What these fundamental principles are is well-known not only to every Muslim but also to the entire world, for the simple reason that Islam is a living force and a world order. Although the fundamental principles of Islam are universally known, yet it would not be out of place to recount them here.

Concept of Sovereignty

The concept of human sovereignty is completely absent from the political philosophy of Islam. The Holy Quran proclaims: "It is only for Allah to command" (XII: 40) and "to Allah belongeth the dominion of the heavens and the earth (II: 107). This has been repeated often in the Holy Quran: "To Allah alone belongeth the dominion of the heavens and the earth and all lies between" (V: 17); Knowest thou not that Allah hath power over all things" (II: 106).

Next to Allah sovereign power resides in the people, as in respect of Adam. Allah announced to the angles that He is going to create a *Khalifa* on the earth (II: 30). Again Allah said: "Oh David, We did indeed make thee a *Khalifa* on earth—so judge thou between men in truth and justice" (XXXVIII: 27). This introduces the concept of *'Niabat-i-Ilahi'* and from this flow the following consequences:

- That next to Allah the sovereign power resides in the people. As Sir Abdur Rahim put it in his book on *'Islamic Jurisprudence'*

(p. 62), Islamic law does not admit of "the sovereign power being dissociated from the people howsoever they might choose to exercise it".

- That all are equal before the law.
- That the exercise of power is a trust.
- That power has to be exercised in accordance with the Commandments of Allah and in His name.
- That everyone vested with power is accountable for his actions.
- That no one is above the law; none not even the *Khalifa,* enjoys any immunity.

This puts an end to the concept of divine origin of kings hitherto fore adopted by the Hindus, the Pharoahs of Egypt, the Sassanians of Iran and the Christians of Europe. Under this concept, the sovereign was the source of law and it was religious duty to obey his commands; but under the Islamic system, the king was not the source of law and, therefore, not above the law.

Chapter 4

The Clash of Shariah and Democracy

When America toppled Saddam Hussein, it promised to replace his ruthless and lawless regime with a government characterized by the rule of law. But what kind of law?

The draft Iraqi constitution provides for Islam as "a fundamental source of legislation"; it further stipulates that no law can be legislated that "contradicts the ruling of Islam." The application of Shariah, or Islamic law, is not mentioned, but that is the implication of these phrases.

The dispute between Sunnis and Shiites during the drafting of the constitution was only about whether Shariah should be the single source of lawmaking, or just one of several. Did the United States wage a costly war in Iraq in order to introduce Shariah? Did decision makers in Washington know that in post-Saddam Iraq there are divergent understandings of democracy and the rule of law - the Western secular and the Islamic Shariah-based understanding of constitutional law - which clash with each other?

In addition, there is no common understanding of Shariah among Muslims, because Islamic law is based on the interpretation of the Quran and has never been codified. The term Shariah occurs only once in the Quran, and in the context of morality, not law.

The post-Quranic character of the Shariah is made clear by the fact that in the eighth century, after the Islamic revelation, the four legal schools, or madhahib, of Islamic law were established on the basis of diverse interpretations of the Quran.

The call for Shariah that one hears today throughout the Muslim world, as religion becomes politicized and the law Islamized, is a call for an Islamic state based on the idea that Shariah can form a country's constitution. The global context is the political revival of religion - and along with it the idea of divine law. But is Shariah really constitutional law? And how does the call for Islamization of the law fit in with democracy?

In fact, Shariah understood as modern constitutional law is in conflict with individual human rights.

Take the question of freedom of faith. Islam respects the other monotheist faiths, Judaism and Christianity, and provides their believers with recognition as "protected minorities," but does not view them as equals. Muslims themselves are denied the right of conversion, which is regarded as "riddah," or apostasy. If Muslims convert, the Shariah calls for them to be punished with death. For that reason, Shariah cannot contribute to a legal pluralism, because any pluralism must combine diversity with basic common understandings. The commitment to universal international standards can coexist with a diversity of cultures, but only if a common concept of law is insisted upon. Respect for the global political revival of religion means recognising religious legal traditions, even ones recently revived or newly invented. But Shariah would have to be reformed before an Islamic democracy could come about that was based on the recognition of commonalities in constitutional law.

In its present form, Shariah is not eligible as a model for constitutional law. The inclusion of Shariah in the Iraqi constitution, even as "a source," gives concern over whether this is to become the model for the rule of law in the envisioned process of a transformation of the greater Middle East.

Shariah and National Law in Afghanistan

The period until 1920: The struggle for an independent and unified nation. Afghanistan's geographic placement at the crossroads of civilizations determined its fate as early as the fourth century B.C., when Alexander the Great defeated the Persian invaders who had been the first to achieve domination. A series of conquests followed with particularly devastating invasions by the Mongol leaders Genghis Khan and Tamerlane. Two thousand years of ravage and invasions stalled the establishment of a unified state, which did not come about until the 18th century. The first Afghan kingdom, more a confederation of tribes then, was established by Ahmad Shah Durrani in 1747. He was approved as the first Afghan king in Kandahar in a mass gathering of the Afghan people referred to as the 'Great Assembly' (*Loya Jirga*), which was only later again taken up when it was reactivated as the National Assembly in the early twentieth century. Afghanistan ultimately emerged as a nation in the mid-nineteenth century, by which time the new rulers had to cope with the colonial ambitions of the British and the Russians (Reynolds & Flores 2005: 1-3).

The Second Anglo-Afghan War of 1878-1880 resulted in the creation of an independent Afghan kingdom within the British sphere of influence, serving as a buffer zone between Russia and India. Its present boundaries were fixed during the reign of King Amir Abdul Rahman (1880-1901), who aimed to bring the region's tribes and ethnic groups under centralised control, unify the country politically, and establish a central government with a certain degree of standardised administration. Amir Abdul Rahman held the position of King and Chief Justice, issuing verdicts in accordance with the principles of Islamic law and traditions.

In 1896 a compilation of criminal rules based on Hanafi law was proclaimed (Vafai 1988: 24). There was no state controlled court system in Afghanistan until the 1920s. The king was vested with the authority to preside cases dealing with rebellion, embezzlement, forgery and bribery by government officials, treason, and crimes against the state and members of the royal family. In all other cases, law was dispensed by religious courts and religious judges. Statutory enactments of this area were basically designed to reiterate Islamic law. For example a guide called the 'judges principles' (*atasas ol-qod*) that drew from the classical Hanafi law was issued by Amir Abdul Rahman in the late 1880s and was designed to control the activities of the judges (Kamali 1985: 35; Vafai 1988: 24). Additionally, judges had to comply with an elementary court procedure outlined in a guideline for civil and criminal matters called 'book of governance' (*okumatiketabèe-ye h*). Amir Abdul Rahman divided the existing laws of his kingdom into three groups: Shariah law, administrative laws (*qanun*), and tribal laws. Likewise, he established three kinds of courts: the religious courts, which in fact already existed, that dealt with religious and civil matters; criminal courts administered by chiefs of police (*kotwals*) or by judges; and a board of commerce consisting of merchants, who settled business disputes (Vafai 1988: 11-12). Tribal groups had always had their own ways of dispute settlement. This was done in particular through the local assemblies (*jirgas*) following a specific procedure.

Amir Abdul Rahman reigned with an iron fist. The country was stable with little or no internal unrest. Afghanistan remained, however, a fragmented country with local governors acting with virtual autonomy. In addition, the country was held in a stranglehold by a corrupt and fanatic system of Islamic clerics (*mullahs*), absolutely opposed to any advancement that could potentially weaken their power. This held especially true in the tribal hinterlands of Afghanistan.

After Amir Abdul Rahman's death, his son Habibullah succeeded him. Habibullah (1901-1919) eased the system of compulsory conscription, dismantled his father's secret intelligence service, and put an end to some of the most brutal forms of corporal punishment. At the same time, religious organisations regained some of their former influence (Ewans 2001: 80).

The new king also founded a state council for tribal affairs and gave the tribal chiefs more autonomy in the administration of regional affairs. He ensured that the quality of education was improved by setting up schools of higher education based on the French model as well as military academies and teacher training institutes. The first hydroelectric power plant was also built during his reign. The legal system, which was until then based on uncodified Islamic law, was compiled under Habibullah: a four-part compilation of Islamic law encompassing the civil and criminal principles of the Shariah was published, the so-called 'Supreme Commandments' (*siraj ol-ahòkam*), to be used as a framework of reference by judges (Kamali 1985: 35).

During World War I, Habibullah aligned himself with the British. This was a dangerous decision because the population was strongly opposed to the British and their domination of their country. Many Muslims were reticent about supporting an infidel empire, such as that of the British, against the former seat of the Caliphate, the Ottoman Empire. Habibullah was accused by his people for having failed to achieve full independence from all foreign powers and was assassinated on 20 February 1919 in a hunting resort far from Kabul. When Amanullah, Habibullah's son, succeeded to the Afghan throne in 1919 (1919-1929), the country was plagued with ethnic divisions, tribal conflict, and corrupt religious fanaticism.

The Period from 1920 until 1965: The Struggle between Modernity and Traditionalism

1919-1933: The First Afghan Constitutions

Amanullah's first act as a king was to declare war on the British to end their domination in Afghanistan. On 3 May 1919, the third and last Anglo-Afghan war started and ended with the Treaty of Rawalpindi signed on 8 July 1919. Amanullah was determined to reform Afghan society. From 1919 to 1923, a series of political, legal, and judicial initiatives were taken at his initiative with the aim of resolving the fractures of Afghan society (Kohlmann 1999). Slavery was formally abolished; campaigns of reconciliation against the violent divisions between Sunni and Shiis were undertaken; and the status of the non-Muslim minorities was improved by abolishing their *jezye* tax (a special poll tax levied from non-Muslims in Islamic societies).

Amanullah sought to bring Western secular law to his homeland. He was looking in particular at Kemal Atatürk in Turkey and Reza Shah in Iran. In April 1923, he enacted Afghanistan's first formal written constitution, the constitution of the government of Afghanistan, the *am-name-ye asasi-ye dulat-enez alie-ye afghanestan* (Vafai 2001: 93). This first legal text, consisting of 73 articles, included a list of basic freedoms that the Afghan people had never been awarded, such as freedom from torture, freedom from unlawful search and seizure, personal freedoms, and guarantees of justice from government officials. Islam was inscribed as the official religion of the state, but the constitution also granted protection to the followers of other religions. The equality of all Afghan citizens, access to political rights, personal freedom, freedom of the press, and the right to education were guaranteed.

The Constitution of 1923 prohibited extrajudicial or extra-legal punishment; courts were to be the only legitimate institution to deal with all disputes within society. The independence of the judiciary and the courts was recognised, and any kind of intervention in court procedure was prohibited. A special High Court was established temporarily to deal with crimes committed by members of government and ministers. Elementary education was declared compulsory for all Afghan citizens. Amanullah also introduced the right of women to education, permission for female students to travel abroad for higher education purposes, abolished child marriage, and put restrictions on polygamy. He furthermore issued a new administrative code, transferring jurisdiction of family matters from the religious courts to civil courts (Vafai 1988: 12). Afghanistan's first constitution triggered the enactment of a plethora of other legislation (*am-namenez*) related to administration, education, social institutions, trade, and industry. More than 51 *am-namenez* were published between 1919 and 1927.

In 1925, a penal code, the *am-name-yenez omumi-ye jaza*, was published (Vafai 1988: 25). It contained 308 articles and was primarily based on Shariah principles, with some influence from the French penal code of the time.

Article 1 of the Afghan Penal Code (1925) categorised crimes into three categories, as is done in the classical Shariah: *hòodud* (class of punishments that are fixed for certain crimes, including theft, fornication, consumption of alcohol, and apostasy); *asqes* (retaliation); and *tazir* (punishments that are administered at the discretion of the judge).

The *am-namenez* concerning the court procedure, *am-name-ye tashkilat-e asasinez*, required judges and the Shariah courts to issue decisions in accordance with the provisions of the penal code. A group of religious scholars (*ulama*) also compiled a guide for judges (*at-e amaniyetamassok al-qod*). It consisted of two parts, a civil and a criminal part (Kamali 1985: 37). The first enactment of a military penal code, the *am-name-ye jaza-yenez askari*, was another major step towards more legal certainty, especially considering that the Constitution of 1923 embraced the principle of the rule of law in criminal matters.

Amanullah's reforms were, however, responded to with hostility. The advent of civil, secular law was not accepted by Amanullah's assorted enemies among the *mullahs*, who saw their power fading in a more educated society. They accused the *am-namenez* of being unIslamic and in violation of God's laws. When Amanullah attempted to change the free day of the week from Friday to Thursday and ordered the unveiling of women and the compulsory wearing of European dress, the enraged *mullahs* joined forces with the tribesmen, who resented Amanullah's meddling in their affairs, and gradually began to destabilise his government.

Amanullah had to make concessions. In the late 1920s, he agreed to end female education by the age of twelve, to rescind the prohibition on child marriages, to allow polygamy, and to strike down the freedom of religion as set forth in the *am-namenez* (Kohlmann 1999). His efforts to provide Afghanistan with a modern legal framework were perceived as too radical by his fellow countrymen. His constitution and the changes he endeavoured to introduce underestimated the strength of traditionalism and conservative opinion.

Despite his many attempts to unify the country and help it overcome its ethnic and religious fractures, these grew only worse as the country became subject to fanatically competing leaders with extremist ideologies. In early 1929, Amanullah abdicated and went into temporary exile in India. His attempt to return to Afghanistan failed, as he could not secure the support from his people. From India, the ex-king travelled to Europe and settled in Switzerland, where he died in Zurich in 1960.

In contrast to Amanullah, his successor Nadir Shah (1930-1933), a military general in Amanullah Khan's reign, adopted a more conservative path. His policies are reflected in the Constitution of 1931, which overruled many of the Amanullah reforms and numerous *am-namesnez*. Against the backdrop of near anarchy in the country following Amanullah's abdication, a new constitution, the *osòul-e asasi-ye dulat-e alie-ye afghanestan* was promulgated on 31 October 1931 (Ewans 2001: 101).

It contained 110 articles and clearly endorsed the traditional supremacy of Shariah in Afghanistan. This is manifested in the numerous references to the Shariah, which essentially amounted to proclaiming Shariah as the law of the country. Islamic law continued to dominate judicial practice, and the limited number of statutes that still existed was mainly concerned with procedural and administrative matters. The Constitution of 1931 was also clearly more conciliatory towards the tribal establishment and in clear contrast with its predecessor in its emphasis on adherence to Islam in legislation and government affairs.

The progressive views of Amanullah and the conservative approach of Nadir Shah created discontinuity in the legal and social order; the contradictory objectives of the constitutions of 1923 and 1931 gave further rise to disorientation and dissatisfaction. The need for corrective measures to bring about a balance between the expressions of the modernist and conservative ideological currents in the country was strongly felt.

1933-1964: Modernity and Traditionalism Revisited

In 1933 Nadir Shah was assassinated. His son Zahir Shah succeeded him at the age of 18. While officially Zahir Shah was proclaimed king, from 1933 onwards Afghanistan was effectively ruled by his uncle Hashim, who took the position of royal prime minister (1933-1946). Hashim was keen to implement the strict rule of the Shariah (Ewans 2001: 104).

Nonetheless, the proliferation of newspapers and journals, although under strict censorship, allowed for the exchange of ideas among the Afghan elite regarding the interactions between modernity and the rule of Islam in society and the life of the individual. Archaeological excavations conducted by the French fostered some ideas of a glorious pre-Islamic past, and encouraged secular ideas among

Afghan intellectuals. The Afghan economy advanced with the introduction of Western banking institutions, the enhancement of exports of agricultural products, and transit trade through Russia. External relations expanded with other countries such as Japan, Germany, Italy, and the United States. In 1946, Hashim retired following the wish of the royal family and was replaced by Sardar Shah Mahmoud Khan, another uncle of Zahir Khan, as prime minister (Ewans 2001: 105).

Sardar Shah Mahmoud Khan (1946-1953) was a more tolerant and liberal ruler. He had political prisoners released and allowed a certain degree of freedom of the press. Relations with the United States improved, many projects were undertaken in construction, and the educational system started to develop once again. Despite all his efforts, the country was moving toward destabilisation. In 1953, Sardar Shah Mahmoud Khan was replaced by his cousin, Mohammad Daoud Khan, who took over the position of prime minister. Through cooperation with the Soviet Union and the United States, the economy was further developed. While the American influence was visible at the University of Kabul, the Russians pressed for another institute of higher education and established the Kabul Polytechnic. The Afghan army was reformed and modernised with Russian weapons after America twice refused the proposal made by Afghan authorities to supply the Afghan military with arms (Magnus & Naby 2002: 47).

The Constitution of 1931 remained in force, in turn ensuring the prominent position of the Shariah as enshrined within it. From 1933 until the promulgation of a new constitution in 1964, a mixed pattern in legislation developed, leading to confusion over the relationship of state law to Shariah, especially in cases of ambiguity and conflict between them. The courts generally applied the Arabic manuals of the Hanafi school of law and the Ottoman *Mejelle*, i.e. the codified version of the Hanafi school of law for civil transactions, excluding family law (Kamali 1985: 36). An early departure from this pattern came about with the promulgation of the Commercial Code of 1955 and the Commercial Procedure Code of 1963, both of which were not based on the Shariah but on Western models.

This period can be seen as a time in which attempts were made to bring together the modern and conservative elements in Afghanistan. When members of the royal family appeared unveiled at the annual ceremony marking Afghanistan's independence, for instance, the religious establishment protested seriously. Daoud, who was well versed in matters of theology, though, insisted that veiling was not required in Islam. When the mullahs persisted with their campaign, they were thrown into jail without getting any public support. This was an altogether quite different outcome of events than had been the case with the fiasco of Amanullah's attempted reforms thirty years earlier.

The Period from 1965 Until 1985: Communism and the Republic of Afghanistan

1964-1973: Zahir Shah and Tentative Constitutionalism

Daoud was forced to resign in 1963. Shortly thereafter, Zahir Shah promulgated Afghanistan's third constitution, which was approved by the *Loya Jirga* (the National Assembly) on the 1st of October 1964. This constitution was conceived over a period of eighteen months and reflects to a certain degree public consultations and debates from this period in its contents. The 1964 constitution paid attention to issues of institution-building and democratic structures, namely the role of and structure of a parliamentary democracy and the independence of the judiciary. Indeed, the 1964 Constitution introduced for the first time (at least on paper) the separation of powers to the Afghan legal system.

The constitution excluded members of the royal family from political offices, but retained considerable powers for the king (Amin 1993: 17). As head of the state, he embodied national sovereignty and was the guarantor of the basic precepts of Islam and of the country's independence. The king was supposed to be a follower of the Hanafi doctrine. According to Article 15 of the 1964 constitution, the king was accountable to no one and had to be respected by everyone.

Article 2 of the constitution declared 'the sacred religion of Islam' as the religion of Afghanistan. Equality of all human beings, secrecy of people's communication, and freedom of expression were declared to be fundamental rights. A fundamental step towards more political participation was taken in Article 32 of the constitution. It allowed for the first time the formation of political parties. The aims and activities of a party, as well as its ideology, had to be in accordance with the values embodied in the constitution. Financial resources should be available to create a political party, and a party formed in accordance with the provisions of the law could not be dissolved without judicial proceedings and the decision of a competent court.

Article 103 of the constitution introduced a new institution, that of the Attorney General, to conduct investigation of crimes. The office of the Attorney General was similar to the American institution of Attorney General, indicating that to a certain extent the Constitution of 1964 was influenced by the U.S. Constitution. The Attorney General was to be established as an independent body of the executive power of the government, reporting only to the executive. The judicial branch was not to interfere in its activities.

Although the Constitution of 1964 concentrated most state authorities in the person of the king, it was still the most liberal constitutional document ever in Afghanistan. Parliament was to consist of two houses; the House of the People (*Wolesi Jirga*), elected by the people of Afghanistan in free, universal, secret, and direct elections in accordance with the provisions of the law for a period of four years; and the House of the Elders (*Meshrano Jirga*), one-third of its members to be appointed by the king and the remaining two-thirds to be elected in free, universal, secret, and direct elections. The government was required to publish all legislation in an official state publication called *jaride rasmi* (Afghan Official Gazette); the Gazette was to be distributed to the courts and other legal institutions.

The judiciary was to consist of a Supreme Court and other courts, with the task of adjudicating all litigation brought before them. The judges, who could be held accountable by the newly established Supreme Court, were appointed by the king. A Supreme Court was established, with branches for civil, commercial, criminal, military, and national security cases. For the first time, a juvenile court was established in Kabul to adjudicate in cases where the defendant had not yet reached the age of fifteen (Lau 2003: 52).

The 1964 constitution was the first to provide a clear definition of 'law' and to establish a formal order of priority in favour of statutory law.

Law is a resolution passed by both Houses, and signed by the king. In areas where no such law exists, the provisions of the Hanafi jurisprudence of the Shariah of Islam shall be considered as law.

Although the rights and duties given to the Houses of Parliament by the 1964 constitution were important and could have been the basis for people's participation in politics, in reality, the Houses remained largely ineffective, and no significant body of statutory law emerged. The Constitution of 1964 had established a powerful parliament and, thus, reversed the hitherto prevailing role of a more powerful executive. Consequently, the two engaged in a power struggle, both failing to adjust to their new roles under the constitution.

Thus, like its predecessors, the third Afghan constitution was not implemented. No law for the formation and organisation of political parties was drafted, nor did any independent political party emerge, much less gain permission to be registered in Afghanistan (Rubin 2002: 73). The king's democratic experiment failed because he did not allow the constitutionally-mandated liberties to take root, as is evidenced by the fact that there was no law on political parties or on provincial councils and municipalities and by the fact that no attention was paid to the judicial reforms requested under the 1964 constitution. The conflict between the legislative and executive powers further exacerbated the instability and problems plaguing the Afghan political scene.

On 1 January 1965, the People's Democratic Party of Afghanistan (PDPA), which was known as the 'Khalq' party was formed by Noor Mohammad Taraki. Like all other parties in Afghanistan, the PDPA was an unofficial, clandestine party that was not registered with the government. The PDPA soon split into two parties because of disagreements between its leaders Taraki and Babrak Kamal. Whereas Taraki remained head of the 'Khalq' party, Karmal established the 'Parcham' party in 1967. Most of the supporters of Khalq were Pashtuns from the rural areas in the country. The Parcham supporters came mostly from urban citizens and supported social-economic reforms in the country. The Khalqs accused the Parchams of being under the allegiance of Zahir Shah. Meanwhile, the influence of communism began to become ever more visible, both groups being consistently pro-Soviet, and being strongly supported by the Russian embassy and Soviet advisers in Kabul.

A Criminal Procedural Code was enacted in 1965; it consisted of 500 articles addressing in particular the arrest, detention, interrogation, and trial of the accused. The code also covered the implementation of punishments, the temporary duration of imprisonment, and the differentiation between the role of the police and prosecutors and the supervision of their duties and responsibilities. It is not entirely clear whether this new Code was inspired by Soviet law. In any case, it signified the introduction of a secular piece of legislation, which brought the Afghan legal system closer to Western legal traditions.

1973-1978: The Creation of the Republic of Afghanistan

On 17 July 1973, Mohammad Daoud Khan - the cousin of Zahir Shah and his former prime minister - carried out a military coup with the support of a small number of troops and a handful of military officers associated with the PDPA while Zahir Shah was in Europe. For the first time in its history, Afghanistan was proclaimed a republic. Meanwhile, the communist party was increasingly influencing various parts of Daoud's government by pushing its own allies and supporters into key administrative positions. This triggered opposition by the religious establishment and fostered the emergence of Islamic groups. Daoud clamped down on these Islamist groups. In 1974, the leader of the Muslim Brotherhood, Mohammad Niazai, was arrested along with some 200 followers (Ewans 2001: 131). Determined to get public support for his government, Daoud decided to crack down on the communist parties as well.

Had Afghanistan's ruler legalised the functioning of political parties and political parties been institutionalised through periodic elections, competition for power and influence could have taken place through the ballot box. In the absence of institutionalised and democratic mechanisms for political change, however, the competition between leftist and Islamic groups soon assumed the shape of armed conflict.

In 1976 a new penal code (PC) was enacted based primarily on Islamic principles, but drawing also on European criminal codes. (7) Article 1 of the Penal Code of 1976 defines the scope of application and sets forth as follows:

This law regulates offences that call for discretionary (*tazir*) penalties. Any person who commits a crime calling for fixed punishment (*addh*, pl. *odudh*) or retaliation (*asqes*) or the payment of blood money (*diyat*), will be punished according to the principles of the Hanafi school of law.

That meant that the *odudh* crimes were not within the scope of application of the penal code. However, whenever a *addh* crime could not be established by Hanafi evidence law, the punishment for that crime would fall within the scope of the 1976 penal code, if evidence was sufficient *vis-à-vis* the standards set by the code. The penal code, thus, provided for an alternative procedure, making *odudh* crimes punishable under the principle of *tazir*, with prison sentences of various durations.

The unstable legal situation led to the enactment of yet another constitution on 24 February 1977. Daoud was elected president for a period of six years. The new constitution transferred all authorities of the king under the 1964 constitution to the president of the state. Daoud also occupied the position of prime minister, foreign minister, and minister of defence. The power over the judiciary, which until then had been vested in the person of the king, was also transferred to the president, and the position of Chief Justice granted to the Minister of Justice.

The Constitution of 1977 differs considerably from the previous three constitutions. Alongside the emphasis on Islam, the 1977 constitution introduced for the first time the notions of nationalism and socialism. Article 22 of the 1977 constitution designated Islam as the religion of the state without reference to the prominence of the Hanafi school of law, as had the previous constitution (1964). Article 64 went further than the previous constitution, however, as it contains a repugnancy clause, subjecting all laws to a process of assessment on their compatibility with the basic principles of the sacred Islamic religion. Yet, in other respects the law was more liberal.

For instance, Article 28 repeated the principle of equality of gender, stating that: '[T]he entire people of Afghanistan, both men and women without discrimination and privileges, have equal rights and obligations before the law.' The addition of the passage 'both men and women' was completely new and had never been in any Afghan legal document so far. Articles 39 and 40 of the 1977 constitution granted freedom of assembly for all citizens of Afghanistan provided the assemblies are unarmed. A one-party system led by Daoud's party (the National Revolutionary Party) was created by Article 40 of the 1977 constitution. A national assembly called the *melli jirga* replaced the former Parliament of the 1964 constitution by substituting the two houses (House of People and House of Elders) with only one assembly.

In the same year, the Afghan Civil Code (CC), modelled on the Egyptian Civil Code of 1949, was enacted as a further piece of legislation aimed at modernising the legal system. The code encompasses 2,416 articles that regulate all aspects of civil law, including family and inheritance law. The code blends Shariah-based law (mainly in the field of family and inheritance law) and modern secular law to solve the existing problems and thereby secure social stability in the community.

The code was in particular influenced by the French civil code, for example in matters regarding the age of capacity for transactions and the requirement for registration of documents concerning marriage, divorce, parentage, and kinship. To clarify the relationship between different sources of law, Article 1 of the code provides that in cases where there is an explicit regulation in the law, independent interpretation of the court (*ejtehad*) is not allowed. However, if no such explicit rule exists, the court may fill the gaps with the rules of the Hanafi school of law. Finally, despite its prominent role in Afghanistan, the Civil Code of 1977 did not allocate any role to customary law.

1978-1985: The Saur-Revolution, the Mujahedin, and Soviet Invasion

In April 1978, yet another coup, the so-called Saur-, or April-Revolution (*thavr*), was staged by parts of the PDPA. Daoud and his family were killed and power was handed over to a joint military-civilian Revolutionary Council, with Taraki serving as its head, president, and prime minister. The constitution was amended by a declaration the following day on 28 April 1978. All governmental affairs had to be executed through decrees and procedures of the Revolutionary Council. Decree No. 8/1978 implemented a stringent land reform, redistributing the land and severely limited the ownership of land. Any land considered as surplus was confiscated without compensation and redistributed to landless peasants and farmers. Modern Soviet type cooperatives were designed to replace the traditional rural economic relationship. In the field of civil law, on 17 September 1978 Decree No. 7 was promulgated. It abolished the bride price, or transfer of money from the groom to the bride's family, called *walwar* in Afghanistan; set the minimum age for marriage at 15 and 18 for girls and boys, respectively; and prohibited child and forced marriages.

Meanwhile, Islamic resistance groups (the *mujahedin* movements) had started to form themselves outside Afghanistan. After the arrest of Niazai in 1974, some of his supporters, such as Hikmatyar and Rabbani, had fled to Pakistan. In 1974, they had split away from the main party, with Hikmatyar establishing the Islamic Party and Rabbani, the Islamic Society party. Besides these two groups, numerous other *mujahedin* movements were also formed. These groups would later play a central role in the resistance against the communist rule and against the Russian military invasion (Magnus & Naby 2002: 151).

In 1979, internal conflicts within the PDPA escalated. Factional conflicts and the strong presence of the *mujahedin* movements in Pakistan and inside Afghanistan persuaded the Russians to act. Basing themselves on the Soviet-Afghan Treaty of Friendship of 5 December 5 1978, which allowed for military intervention by the Russians in the event of any threat to their interests in the area, Russian troops invaded Afghanistan on 27 December 1979. Karmal, the leader of the Parcham party mentioned above was installed as head of the Democratic Republic of Afghanistan.

Some 850,000 Afghan refugees had fled the country by May 1980, with an estimated 750,000 Afghans applying for asylum in Pakistan and an additional 100,000 in Iran (Ewans 2001: 158). The Russian invasion was strongly condemned by the international community. The

Heads of the Organisation of the Islamic Conference, gathered in Saudi Arabia, where they declared the invasion to be a threat to international peace and stability. The U.N. General Assembly passed seven resolutions condemning the invasion, all without practical effect. In the meantime, however, seven *mujahedin* opposition groups had come together in Peshawar in Pakistan and merged into the so-called Afghanistan's Islamic Union of Mujahedin on 16 September 1981 (Ekhwan 2002: 15).

Meanwhile, in Kabul, Karmal was concerned with gaining internal legitimacy among the Afghan people. He promised a government in which all factions and parties would be embraced and represented; a new constitution with provisions for elections and a multiparty system; land reform; amnesty for returning refugees and political prisoners; freedom of religion; and the establishment of Islamic institutions that could act as advisory bodies to the government. To appease public opinion, he restored the old black, red, and green national flag that was replaced after the Saur-Revolution by a flag without the green colour representing Islam.

On 21 April 1980, the fifth Afghan constitution was promulgated. It contained 68 articles. In order to avoid a direct clash with public opinion, the Constitution of 1980 did not explicitly mention Communism or Marxism in its provisions.

Instead, it just pointed to the objectives, views, policies, organisation, and responsibilities of various administrative institutions in the government according to the PDPA program. Article 54 of the 1980 constitution upheld the institution of the Supreme Court and reorganised the court system by providing for provincial and city courts, as well as special courts to try specific cases such as military cases. In March 1980, the Law on the Organisation and Jurisdiction of the Courts was passed; it was amended less than two years later on 22 December 1981. This law specified the court procedure and set out the hierarchy of the courts. Articles 12 and 13 of this law mandated the establishment of a bar association to 'provide legal assistance for the defence of accused persons'. Karmal also created a Department for Islamic Affairs, which was to act as an advisory body for the government on Islamic affairs.

Despite these initiatives, the government continued to lose credibility. This was particularly so given its rampant disregard of national and international legal and human rights standards it purported to support (e.g. ICCPR, CESCR, CERD, and CAT). During this period, there were frequent human rights violations at the highest levels of power, ongoing illegal detentions of political activists and religious leaders, and the well-publicised executions of members of opposition groups, in the absence of any trial or pretence of justice. In consequence, Afghanistan became an area of instability in the region, ravaged by internal conflict and foreign intervention.

A March 1985 human rights report prepared for UNCHR details accounts of deliberate bombing of villages, massacres of civilians, and execution of prisoners of war belonging to resistance groups (Ermacora 1985: 12)

In the mid-eighties the war was particularly intense. The Afghan government, supported by Soviet troops, was involved in major combat all around the country, with the government focusing all its attention on its military campaigns rather than anything else. On 26 September 1982, the heads of the Islamic states conferring in Nigeria suspended the membership of Afghanistan from the Organisation of the Islamic Conference.

Foreign countries such as China, the U.S., Saudi Arabia, and Iran considerably helped the resistance groups within and outside Afghanistan. The alliance of the seven *mujahedin* groups, however, revolved only around their common struggle against the Russians and the Kabul regime. Besides this, the resistance groups had little in common and were involved in persistent factional disputes. From the very beginning, they were as much prepared to co-operate with each other as to fight each other. Neither their shared Muslim faith nor the concept of the need for a holy war (*jihad*) to oust the Russians was strong enough to outweigh their personal, tribal, and ethnic interests. All efforts to foster their commonness and bind them together into a unified movement failed. This lack of unity meant that the *mujahedin* were unable to coordinate their activities inside Afghanistan or carry out a unified strategy for their common objectives. In fact, this was one of the main reasons behind the unsuccessful attempts of the *mujahedin* to overthrow the communist regime in Kabul.

In April 1985, Karmal held a *Loya Jirga* in Kabul, inviting 1,800 representatives from around the country. With only 600 members attending, the assembly failed to garner much legitimacy as a genuinely representative body. The elections of August 1985 were yet another unsuccessful attempt by Karmal to legitimise his government (Ewans 2001: 165), as was the creation of a National Reconciliation Commission that was to design a new constitution. All his attempts to incorporate a broader participation of the non-communist groups into his government failed.

The Period from 1985 Until 2001: From Civil War to Democracy

1985-1992: Afghan Civil War

In autumn 1985, the Russians replaced Karmal with Najibullah, who was the head of the secret service department of the communist regime. His instalment to power was a political decision aimed at creating a stronger and more decisive government able to protect the continuity and power of the communist regime, even after the eventual military withdrawal of the Russians (Ewans 2001: 168). The international community's efforts to put an end to the Russian occupation moved very slowly, and no agreement had been reached so far. It was not until 28 July 1986 that the Soviet leader at the time, Gorbachev, facing heavy international pressure, announced that the Russian troops would be withdrawn, and that this withdrawal would be completed by October 1986.

In fact, Soviet troops only left Afghanistan on 15 February 1989. This represented a great challenge for the communist regime in Kabul. Najibullah had to stay in power without the support of the Soviet troops. Towards the end of 1987 the government of Najibullah, in an effort to reconcile the conflicting parties, drafted a new constitution, which was adopted on 29 November 1987 by the *Loya Jirga*. The new constitution was similar to the Constitution of 1964 in its adherence in Article 2's reference to the sacred religion of Islam. According to Article 94 of the 1987 constitution, eight different governmental institutions were given the power to propose, introduce, amend, or repeal laws. The constitution also introduced the Constitutional Council of Afghanistan as a supreme institution for the interpretation of laws and international treaties in accordance with the constitution of the country. It was also to act as a consultative body for the president in legislative matters.

In 1990, Najibullah called upon the *Loya Jirga* to ratify a new constitution. In comparison to the two previous constitutions of 1980 and 1987, the 1990 constitution did not make use of communist terminology. Islam and nationalism were back on the front page. Article 1 proclaimed Afghanistan to be an 'independent, unitary and Islamic state'. Article 5 set forth provisions for a multiparty system. Article 25 gives due attention to the private sector for the establishment of private enterprises, and Article 20 encourages foreign private investment.

The PDPA was reformed and renamed the Homeland Party. In November, Najibullah met with leaders of the *mujahedin* and representatives of the former king Zahir Shah to seek a political solution to the ongoing conflict. U.N. Secretary General Perez de Cuellar proposed his plans for an international consensus for a peaceful settlement in Afghanistan in May 1991. It aimed at Afghanistan's independence and self-determination, a ceasefire, halting the flow of weapons into the country, and a transitional mechanism leading to free and fair elections. The Kabul regime, Iran, and Pakistan accepted the resolution. The alliance of the seven *mujahedin* groups in Peshawar was, however, unable to consent on the composition of the future government in Afghanistan.

In this situation of negotiations, one of the strongest allies of the Kabul regime, Dostum, an Uzbek who had control of some of the northern provinces, seized the opportunity and joined forces with the resistance militias of Ahmad Shah Massoud, a Tajik to take the city of Mazaar-e Sharif, one of the key provinces in the north of Afghanistan. This move was the death warrant for the peace plan of the United Nations and Najibullah's regime. Some parts of the Kabul regime joined ranks with the *mujahedin*. The advantage shifted decisively in their favour. They believed that victory was theirs and saw no need to stick to any U.N. peace plan that would include a role for Najibullah and his supporters (Ewans 2001: 177).

On 18 March 1992, Najibullah resigned and accepted the formation of a transitional government led by the *mujahedin* in close co-operation with the United Nations, despite the fact that the resistance groups were still struggling over power-sharing arrangements. Until then, the civil war that was waged in fact between the different *mujahedin* groups, rather than against communists, had been limited to some parts of the country. After the collapse of the Kabul communist regime the armed conflict spread into Kabul and the rest of the country. Government administration, legal institutions, universities, schools, and all other educational and social institutions did not function any longer and were simply closed down.

1992-2001: The Taliban and the Rise of Fundamentalism

The collapse of the Najibullah regime and the seizure of power by the *mujahedin* symbolised the end of a functional state structure in Afghanistan. A 51-member council called the Islamic Jihad Council (*shura-ye jihadi-ye eslami*), consisting of thirty field commanders, ten *mullahs*, and ten intellectuals, was established to rule the country for a period of two months. The Council was succeeded by an interim government that held power for four months. The problems were enormous: on the one hand, the new government had to deal with a state apparatus that lacked legitimacy; on the other hand, the resistance parties were not able to establish a functioning government.

In the course of the civil war almost all the state institutions had been looted or destroyed (Ewans 2001: 181). The Ministry of Justice was used as a military base, and all legal documents and laws stored at the ministry had been destroyed during the five years of *mujahedin* domination.

No new constitution was drafted, nor had the constitution of the previous regime been repealed; not a single decree was issued during the *mujahedin* rule to identify the sources of law for the judiciary and other legal organs; no central legislative activities took place during this period of time; and there was uncertainty as to the applicable laws in all fields (Lau 2003: 5). The difficulties were exacerbated by the ongoing civil war. This enhanced the rule of traditional law, i.e. classical Islamic and customary law (especially the *Pashtunwali*, an ethical customary code of the Pashtuns), since they represented the only continuity in the country. In more remote areas, where statutory laws had never arrived, the principles of Islamic and customary law had always been the primary sources for the resolution of legal and social conflicts (Lau 2003: 4).

Afghanistan was more fragmented than ever when the Taliban, a movement of indoctrinated students of Islam from the refugee camps in Pakistan, emerged in 1994. As head of the government, Rabbani controlled Kabul, its outskirts, and the northeast of Afghanistan. The West (the province of Herat) was controlled by Ismael Khan. The East (the Pashtun provinces) was under the leadership of an independent group of *mujahedin* commanders in Jalaalabad, who occasionally fought against each other. A small region south and east of Kabul was controlled by Hekmatyar. The northern six provinces were under Dostum's command. And, finally, the Hazaras controlled the province of Bamian. Furthermore, dozens of warlords and leaders of militia groups exercised their control and harassed the population throughout the country (Rashid 2000: 21). Even international aid organisations feared entering Afghanistan, as the country was drowning in a savage civil war.

The successful expansion of the Taliban movement saw them control almost 90 per cent of the country by 1998. This, however, did not lead to the re-establishment of a strong state. The government activities of the Taliban were limited to the provision of security by incorporating local combatants into their own military structure and to the introduction of a bizarre and harsh version of Islamic law, with implications in all areas of law, such as public executions and a vigorous application of the *hòodud* punishments (Schetter 2002: 113).

An announcement on Radio Kabul on 28 September 1996 stated that 'thieves will have their hands and feet amputated, adulterers will be stoned to death and those drinking alcohol will be lashed'. TV, video, satellite dishes, music, and games, including chess and football, were pronounced un-Islamic (Rashid 2000: 50). The Taliban also established a 'Department for the Enforcement of Virtue and Suppression of Vice', *amr bi-l-maruf va nahi-ye an-al-monkar*, that was given unlimited authority for the enforcement of all the decrees issued by the Taliban government. A decree issued in 1997 by Mullah Omar, the founder of the Taliban movement, declared that all the laws against the principles of Hanafi Islamic jurisprudence were not applicable. The Taliban announced via the radio that after the seizure of Kabul, they would abolish all the laws and regulations of the communist regime and reintroduce the system of law that was in place during Zahir Shah's reign (1964-1973), with the exception of the provisions related to the king and the monarchy.

They also claimed to support the principles of representative, non-discriminatory government based on the principles of the Shariah (Ewans 2001: 205). That never happened; the Taliban regime violated all principles of the Constitution of 1964. Throughout their rule, the Taliban executed *hòadd* and *asqes* punishments that had not been applied in the recent legal history of Afghanistan. In practice, the option of paying blood money to the victim's family in lieu of corporal punishment was not used very often. Amputation of hands and legs for theft and stoning of adulterer and adulteress were executed. The Taliban meant to deter people from committing crime and, therefore, ordered executions and amputations to be held in public in the sports stadium of Kabul.

One of the Taliban's first acts was the execution of former president Najibullah who had been living on U.N. premises since 1992. There was no trial, and the public display of Najibullah's dead body revolted many people outside and within the country.

Under the Taliban, discrimination against women peaked. They issued numerous edicts to control literally every aspect of women's behaviour, in both the public and private spheres. They were forbidden to take employment, to appear in public without a male relative, to participate in government or other public debate, and to receive secondary or higher education. As a result, women were deprived of the means to support themselves and their children. Only female doctors and nurses were allowed - under strict observation of the religious police - to work in hospitals or private clinics. These edicts were issued by the Ministry for the Promotion of Virtue and the Prevention of Vice and enforced through summary and arbitrary punishment of women by the religious police.

The Taliban claimed that they were prepared to provide for education and employment opportunities for women as soon as the social and financial circumstances were convenient. Unfortunately, such conditions for the implementation of a sound Islamic program for women were never implemented, with some subsequently claiming that it had never existed in the first place.

The Taliban received support in the form of donations from foreign sponsors, located mostly in Saudi Arabia, Pakistan, and the United States. New recruits from the religious schools (*madares)* located in Pakistan were urged to join the Taliban movement to fight against the *mujahedin* groups in the north of the country. On 20 March 1996, more than 1,000 religious scholars and tribal leaders gathered in Kandahar to discuss the policies and platforms of the Taliban regime for the future. On the 4th of April, the assembly ended with a call of the Afghans announcing a *jihad* against the Kabul government still run by the *mujahedin* groups. Mullah Omar was named 'Commander of the Faithful', a title abolished a century earlier by Amanullah (Ewans 2001: 195).

In May 1996 Osama bin Laden, whose Saudi Arabian citizenship had been revoked in 1994, arrived in Jalalabad. He had been travelling to the Pashtun border areas between Pakistan and Afghanistan since the early eighties, where he had established training camps for the resistance forces against the communist regime. He cooperated with the Taliban who offered him their protection. Bin Laden provided the Taliban with extensive financial and human resources. After the bombing of the U.S. embassies in Kenya and Tanzania in 1998, Bin Laden became the world's most wanted terrorist. The Clinton Administration responded to the bombings of their embassies with cruise missiles directed against training camps that had been run by Bin Laden in Afghanistan since 1981. Ironically, these camps had at an earlier point in their history been supported by the U.S., Saudi Arabia, and Pakistan for training Afghan opposition soldiers to fight the Soviet occupiers.

With the assassination of Massoud on 9 September 2001 and the attacks of 9/11 in the U.S., the situation changed dramatically. The Bush Administration held Bin Laden responsible for the terrorist attacks of 9/11 and accused the Taliban of sheltering him. Consequently, starting on 7 October 2001, the United States began air strikes against the Taliban as part of a campaign aimed at putting an end to the rule of the Taliban regime, an objective that was soon achieved. This was done ostensibly in support of the so-called Northern Alliance of the *mujahedin* groups, since the Taliban regime had only been internationally recognised by Pakistan, Saudi Arabia, and the United Arab Emirates.

2001-present: Democracy and the Future of Afghanistan

On 27 November 2001, a Conference was held in Bonn, Germany, which brought together representatives of the resistance groups, consisting of the main civil war parties and warlords, pro-Zahir Shah technocrats and intellectuals, and two other small Afghan groups based in Pakistan and Iran (Wardak 2005: 65).

Although the present anti-Taliban groups could not be considered to represent the Afghan people, the 'Agreement on Provisional Arrangements in Afghanistan pending the Re-Establishment of Permanent Government Institutions', also known as the 'Bonn Agreement', provided a framework for the process of state formation to create a broad-based, multi-ethnic, and representative government in Afghanistan. Executive powers were vested in Hamid Karzai, a Pashtun, as head of the Interim Administration of Afghanistan on 22 December 2001. Karzai was reconfirmed as the head of the Interim Administration by the 1,550 members of an Emergency *Loya Jirga* held in Kabul on 10 June 2002.

On 14 December 2003, a nine-member commission presented a new draft constitution to the Constitutional Loya Jirga (the constitutional assembly for the new Aghan Republic). The text of the constitution had been drafted following public consultations that took place over a period of several months. After almost three weeks of heated debates, the *Loya Jirga* approved the new constitution; it was signed on 26 January 2004 by Karzai. This cleared the way for the restoration and implementation of the rule of law, and hopes were expressed for an imminent end to the power of the warlords and the anarchy gripping the country.

The Bonn Agreement set June 2004 as the target date for the formation of a fully representative and elected Afghan government. However, that timeframe was repeatedly changed. When on 31 March 2004, the second international conference on Afghanistan's future took place in Berlin ('the Berlin Conference'), a work plan was issued for the Afghan government to hold free and fair elections in autumn 2004. Prior to the elections, the full exercise by citizens, candidates, and political parties of their political rights under the 2004 Constitution was to be ensured.

These rights included, among others, freedom of organisation, freedom of expression, and the principle of non-discrimination, as well as paying particular attention to the participation of women as both voters and candidates. In the end, the decision was taken to hold presidential elections in October 2004, delaying parliamentary, provincial, and district voting until April 2005 (International Crisis Group 2005).

Thus, the first presidential elections in Afghanistan were held on 9 October 2004. According to U.N. officials, nearly 10 million voters were registered in the country. Since no census of Afghanistan has ever been taken, it is not possible to know how many eligible voters there actually were. Nearly 42 per cent of the registered voters were women, but it should be noted that that figure drops to less than 10 per cent in some provinces in the southeast. In addition, 740,000 Afghan refugees in Pakistan and nearly 600,000 Afghans in Iran were registered to vote in the elections. Amongst seventeen challengers (including a female physician), the interim president Karzai was elected and sworn in as first elected Afghan president on 8 December 2004.

The first parliamentary elections in 36 years in Afghanistan, scheduled for April 2005, were finally held on 18 September 2005, with 2,800 candidates, amongst which 344 women ran for the 249 seats of the Lower House. In contrast to the 80 per cent turn out rate for registered voters during the presidential elections, reports indicate that only about 50 per cent of the 12.4 million registered voters cast their vote during the parliamentary elections.

A new Electoral Law with 57 articles, adopted on 27 May 2004, regulated the conduct of elections. Article 20 of the law provides for a single, non-transferable vote (SNTV) system under which candidates may run either individually or be nominated by a party. Under this system, party lists are not admitted. Political parties may endorse or nominate candidates, but they are not allowed to use party symbols on the ballot, making it difficult for voters who wish to vote along party lines to identify their chosen candidates on Election Day. It must be noted that political parties have a serious credibility problem in Afghanistan. They are often associated, on the one hand, with the Communist Party and the Soviet invasion and, on the other hand, with the Islamist military groupings who formed to fight the Soviets and whose infighting produced much of the instability and bloodshed of the 1990s. Consequently, many Afghans do not trust political parties and see them as pursuing self-interested policies for their particular ethnic group, clan, or tribe. This is one of the primary reasons the SNTV system, which allows for a focus on individuals rather than parties *per se*, was chosen for use in the first elections in Afghanistan after so many decades of strife.

The SNTV has, however, been criticised as being ill-suited for a country like Afghanistan. According to international observers, to be successful under this type of voting structure, a party must have sufficient control over its support base in each contested district to instruct it how to allocate votes among the party's candidate. Otherwise, the party risks having too many votes cast for one candidate, beyond the minimum needed for election, and too few for others. A system that encourages party development and participation in the political process would have been more desirable given Afghanistan's nascent democracy (International Crisis Group 2004).

As in the past, the 2004 Constitution provides for two houses in the *Loya Jirga*. The Lower House (the *Wolesi Jirga*) has 249 seats, with members directly elected by the people. Each of the 34 provinces is a single constituency in the *Wolesi Jirga*. Ten seats are reserved for the *Kuchi* (nomads) community (Electoral Law, §2, Art. 20), with the remaining 239 seats distributed among provinces in proportion to their population, with each province having at least two seats. Each member of the *Wolesi Jirga* enjoys a five-year term expiring on the 22nd of June of the fifth year (2004 constitution, Art. 83). Mohammad Yunos Qanuni, the former Minister of Interior and Education, was elected head of the Lower House.

The Upper House (the *Meshrano Jirga*) consists of a mixture of appointed and elected members (total 102 members). Sixty-eight members were selected by the 34 directly elected provincial councils, and another 34 were appointed by President Karzai (2004 constitution, Art. 84). President Karzai's appointments were vetted by an independent U.N.-sponsored election board and included seventeen women (50%), as required by the Constitution. Sebghatulla Mojadeddi was appointed President of the *Meshrano Jirga* by President Karzai.

The new National Assembly has the potential to play a vital role in stabilising Afghanistan, institutionalising political competition and giving voice to the country's diverse population. By being accountable to the Afghan people, it can demand accountability of the presidential government. However, the success of this institution remains delicately poised, particularly because of the absence of a formal role for political parties, essential for mediating internal tensions.

Meanwhile, at the London Conference on 31 January-1 February 2006, donor nations pledged to help rebuild Afghanistan over the next five years with a sum of 10.5 billion dollars (equivalent at the time to 8.7 billion Euros). Some 80 per cent of this amount represents new money, with the remainder made up of outstanding portions of earlier pledges.

The key elements of the so-called Afghanistan Compact set out specific targets for improving security, governance, the rule of law and human rights and for enhancing economic and social development. A further vital and cross-cutting area of work is eliminating the narcotics industry, which remains a formidable threat to the people and state of Afghanistan, the region, and beyond.

At the Afghanistan Conference in Rome in July 2007 international donors pledged to support the training of judges, the building of new prisons, and the enactment of other measures to strengthen Afghanistan's judicial system with an additional 360 million dollars. President Karzai told the conference that urgent priorities included low salaries, poor infrastructure, and the training of personnel.

However, the security situation has deteriorated in past several years. According to a report by the United State Institute of Peace, the year 2009 was the most violent on record for Afghans and international forces since 2001, and Afghan and international public confidence is diminishing.

Contrary to their pledge in 2007, the Afghan government and its international allies are mainly focused on two issues, namely combating corruption within the Afghan government and resolving the ongoing conflict with the Taliban. All other issues have become secondary. The lack of security, economic development, effective rule of law, and coordination of effort will, however, always stand in the way of sustainable progress in the country. These problems are interrelated, none of which can be addressed without simultaneously addressing the others.

On 1 December 2009 the Obama administration announced that the U.S. would send another 30,000 troops to Afghanistan, but also start withdrawing troops as per July 2011. It is unclear whether such an increase in troop presence will boost security in Afghanistan if no serious attention is given to the promotion of the rule of law, development, institution-building, and economic growth.

The presidential election of 20 August 2009 is another illustration of the growing instability in Afghanistan. With more than 40 presidential nominees, about 5 million people cast their votes. The outcome of the election was marked with fraud and voting irregularities; no single candidate managed to obtain 51 per cent of the total votes. As the allegations of widespread fraud gained ground, a runoff election was scheduled to take place on 7 November 2009. On 1 November 2009, Karzai's main challenger Abdullah pulled out of the runoff election. Karzai, who won 49 percent of the total votes in the first round of the election, was thus announced the elected president by the Independent Election Commission of Afghanistan. Although the election was over, the irregularities and fraud connected to the election process raised suspicious about the legitimacy of the government. The reappointment of Dostum (as the Army Chief of Staff) and Qahim (as the First Vice President), two prominent warlords accused with human rights violations and war crimes, has raised even more concerns about Karzai's government and his leadership.

On 28 January 2010 the latest Afghanistan Conference took place in London. The conference was meant to bring together the international community to 'fully align military and civilian resources behind an Afghan-led political strategy'. A radical increase of civilian and military security forces is planned with the aim of reaching 171,000 members in the Afghan Army and 134,000 Afghan policemen by the end of 2011, bringing thus the total security force numbers to over 300,000. Furthermore, measures were announced to tackle corruption, including the establishment of an independent Office of High Oversight and an independent Monitoring and Evaluation Mission. According to agreements made at the conference, development assistance shall be better coordinated in the future, with the aim of increasingly channelling funds through the Government of Afghanistan. Interestingly, the Afghanistan strategy of the international community embraces also the support for the Afghan Government to integrate ex-warlords by offering economic incentives to those who 'renounce violence, cut links to terrorism and agree to work within the democratic process'.

Meanwhile, the planned parliamentary elections for May have been postponed until September 2010. The election commission cited several reasons for its decision: security concerns, logistical challenges, and a budget shortfall to name a few. The postponement of elections was hailed by Western donors, as it allows more time to put election reforms in place in order to avoid the repeat of the widespread fraud that marred the 2009 presidential elections. The postponement may also give the electoral institutions additional time to carry out the necessary preparations for the elections and to make improvements to the electoral process based on lessons learned during the presidential election in 2009.

Constitutional Law

The 2004 constitution proclaims in its very first article that 'Afghanistan is an independent, unitary, and indivisible Islamic republican state'. Article 3 contains a repugnancy clause stating that no law may be repugnant to the beliefs and ordinances of the sacred religion of Islam (literally: '*mokhalef-e mokam-e din-e moqaddas-e eslamtaqedat va ah*') or to other values embodied in the constitution. This is not new, since all Afghan constitutions, except for the 1980 constitution, contained such a clause. This version of the constitution, however, fails to define what is to be understood as the 'beliefs and ordinances of the sacred religion of Islam' or what the expression 'Islamic Republic' encompasses.

Article 130 of the Constitution of 2004 in fact stipulates the priority of statutory law over Islamic law, noting that only when no explicit provision in state law exists shall Islamic law be applicable. The article further reads:

The courts, in cases under their consideration, shall apply the provisions of this constitution and other laws. Whenever no provision exists in the constitution or the law for a case under consideration, the court shall, by following the principles of the Hanafi jurisprudence and within the limitations set forth in this constitution, render a decision that secures justice in the best possible way.

It is, however, not clear whether these constitutional postulates imply that the ethical values of Islam govern the interpretation of the laws, or whether the constitution and state-enacted law set the framework within which Islamic law must operate (Yassari 2005: 48).

Closely linked to these questions is the question as to who is to interpret the constitution. The proposal to establish a genuine 'Supreme Constitutional Court' was rejected in the drafting process of the 2004 constitution. Consequently, the constitution, as it is currently formulated, foresees two distinct institutions with competency in interpretation matters.

In the first place, Article 157 sets forth that an 'Independent Commission for the Supervision of the Implementation of the Constitution' should be created. Yet, according to Article 121 of the same law, it is the Supreme Court that has the competence to 'review laws, legislative decrees, international treaties and conventions on their compliance with the Constitution and to interpret them, in accordance with the law [...]'. This constitutionally instituted dichotomy may cause serious problems in the future (Yassari 2005: 49). However, as an Independent Commission for the Supervision of the Implementation of the Constitution was never established, this problem is not acute and the task of interpreting and supervising the implementation of the constitution is conducted by the Supreme Court of Afghanistan.

While articulating that 'Islam is the sacred religion of Afghanistan', Article 2 of the 2004 constitution also asserts that followers of other religions are free to exercise their faith and perform their religious rites within the limits of the law. Furthermore, Article 130 sets forth that with reference to cases under court consideration, if no relevant statute is found the Hanafi school of law is to be utilised to the exclusion of all the other schools of Islamic jurisprudence. However, a new development in this constitution is the recognition, for the first time, of Shii law as a source of law to be used in cases where Afghan Shii are involved. Article 131 of the constitution provides:

In cases involving the Shii followers, the court shall, in disputes concerning personal status matters, apply the Shii school of law in accordance with (statutory) law. In other disputes, where no provision can be found in this Constitution and other laws, the courts shall adjudicate the case in accordance with the rulings of the Shii school of law. It should be noted that in the first part of the article, the constitution makes explicit reference to matters of personal status, as opposed to other areas of the law, such as criminal and constitutional law. The latter portion of the same article, however, offers some freedom of interpretation, as it provides that whenever both parties to a legal dispute (other than in matters of personal status) are Shii followers and no ruling can be found on the basis of legal standards articulated in the constitution or other statutes and acts, the judge may apply the rules of the Shii school of law. Thus, whenever existing statutes, such as the civil code, do apply the scope of application, Shii law is excluded (Kamali 2005: 30).

In response to Article 131 of the 2004 constitution a Code of Personal Status of Shii Afghans was promulgated in July 2009. This law had been quietly making its way through Afghanistan's parliamentary system since 2007, when President Karzai finally signed the bill in March 2009, with the intention to gain the support of the Shii minority for the August 2009 election, without however paying attention to its content and potential backlash. Whereas there was generally a consensus among Afghans that the law as such was a positive development, giving rights and recognition to a historically excluded and persecuted minority, the content of some provisions of the bill that included several restrictions on the rights of Shii women caught the attention of national Afghan and international human right groups and the international media, causing the law to soon be dubbed the 'rape law' by Western journalists. Although the law was circulated and shared with some local authorities and members of the civil society, it however received minimal public debate. According to a report of the Afghanistan Research and Evaluation Unit, public inclusion was missing from the process of law making entirely, revealing the weak links between policymakers and their constituents. It also showed a continued emphasis on ethnicity, sect, and faction as a basis for political alliances and organisation, rather than on partisan platforms that speak of issues of public interest (Oates 2009). After strong public reactions, the bill was amended and some of the contested regulations, such as the rules on temporary marriage, were omitted; the amended Code of Personal Status with its 236 articles came into force on 27 July 2009.

The 2004 constitution requires the head of state to be a Muslim. He is the patron of the religion of Islam and, as such, must protect the 'basic principles of the sacred religion of Islam, and the constitution and other laws' of Afghanistan. The constitution has, however, omitted in this regard a reference to the Hanafi school of law, meaning then that there is no requirement that the president be a follower of the Hanafi doctrine. The article further prescribes that the president, unlike the construction of the king under Article 15 of the 1964 constitution, is not beyond accountability. Article 69 expands upon this principle in its articulation of the impeachment procedure and removal from office of the president when he is charged with treason, crimes against humanity, or any other serious crime.

Article 116 foresees a three-tier court system with a Supreme Court, appeals courts, and district courts. The constitution does not, however, give detailed rules on the structure of the courts. According to Article 123, the rules related to the structure, authority, and performance of the courts and the duties of judges shall be regulated by statutes.

In January 2005, a temporary Supreme Court of Afghanistan was established. President Karzai appointed nine judges to the court, all of them Islamic scholars, including one Shii scholar. Fazl Hadi Shinwari, an Islamic scholar known particularly as being ultra conservative was appointed as Chief Justice. The temporary Supreme Court operated until the parliamentary election in September 2005 and the formation of a new *Loya Jirga*. In summer 2006, President Karzai appointed several new, more moderate members to the Supreme Court. However, he also chose to re-nominate Shinwari as Chief Justice. Despite controversy surrounding the validity of Shinwari's legal credentials, his nomination was allowed to continue, but ultimately failed when voted on in Parliament. Karzai then chose his legal council, Abdul Salam Azimi, to succeed Shinwari. Azimi's nomination passed, and the new court was sworn in on 5 August 2006.

With regard to women's rights, the Constitution of 2004 contains an equality clause. According to Article 22, any kind of discrimination and privilege between the citizens of Afghanistan is prohibited. The citizens of Afghanistan - whether man or woman have equal rights and duties before the law. While the express wording of this article does not differentiate between men and women, legal rules contained in the Civil Code 1977 and the Penal Code 1976, as well as actual social practice, in particular in accordance with customary law, do. The equality clause must, thus, be seen as an article that is to be included in any modern constitution, but one that does not reflect the way women and their position in society are conceived in male-dominated and war-ravaged Afghanistan. It remains highly doubtful that women will be able to successfully rely on this article for the protection of their rights in the foreseeable future.

Law of Personal Status

The current Afghan Civil Code dates back to 1977; it contains provisions on family and inheritance law that are essentially a codification of the Hanafi school of law, with inclusion of some provisions of the Maliki school of law. Family law provisions cover matrimonial law, polygamy, child custody, and divorce. The enactment of the Civil Code constituted a step forward from its antecedent, the Marriage Law of 1971, which was silent on polygamy. Moreover, its provisions on child marriage and divorce did not match any of the family law reforms that had taken place elsewhere in the Middle East, the Maghreb, and Pakistan in the 1950s and 1960s. In contrast, the Civil Code of 1977 introduced reforms on child marriage, polygamy, and divorce. These amendments do not, however, sufficiently address the social need for more effective measures, and they do not further either the equality clause contained in Article 22 of the 2004 constitution or the principles outlined in the CEDAW to which Afghanistan is a signatory.

An enormous gap exists between the professed support for the principle of equality and the reality of tribalism in Afghanistan's traditional society. The importance and prominence of customary law, and especially the customs and principles that are known collectively as the *Pashtunwali*, which enjoy quasi-legality and apply to virtually every aspect of daily life, should not be understated. These rules pertain mostly, but not exclusively, to the commission of crimes, especially those committed against persons and/or property (International Legal Foundation 2004: 7). Such conflicts are primarily resolved by an exchange of women from the family of the perpetrator of the crime to the family of the victim. Women involved in this exchange (*bad* or *badal*) do not have any say.

Custom-based and traditional attitudes towards women are difficult to change. Many women in Afghanistan cannot even hope to dream of enjoying something even resembling equal rights, despite the fact that the twentieth-century constitutions all boldly proclaim the opposite.

Marriage

The Civil Code of 1977 accords women the right to choose a husband without the prior consent of their guardian, in accordance with the Hanafi school of law. With reference to child marriage, Articles 70 and 71 of the civil code specify a marriageable age of eighteen for boys and sixteen for girls, but dilutes in the meantime the effect of its own provision by providing that a 'valid marriage contract may be concluded by the contracting parties themselves, or by their guardians and representatives' (CC, Art. 77). The law, thus, falls short of addressing abusive exercise of the power of guardianship whereby parents, brothers, and uncles often impose their will on minor, and even adult, boys and girls. More recently, the Supreme Court has approved of a new standardised marriage contract (*-namenekah*), with the explicit aim of curbing forced and child marriages. It remains to be seen whether in absence of any sanction people will abide by it. This will also depend on the observance of the requirement of registration. The 1977 civil code introduced a registration requirement for all marriages. According to Article 61 of the civil code, every marriage has to be registered.

The competent body for the registration of marriages is currently the district court of the area where the parties reside. However, according to Afghan officials and current reports, in most parts of the country, marriages are neither certified nor registered. Only 5 per cent of the marriages have been registered (Ertürk 2006: 8). This means that the vast majority of Afghans are not officially registering their marriages. The registration of births, marriages, divorces and deaths are indispensable for determining the population number and ensuring legal security in a modern state. Due to the lack of reliable registration, it is not possible to collect statistics with regard to the marriage of minors for example. Likewise, in marital disputes, due to the lack of official documents, it is hard to prove the existence of a marriage.

The lack of registration is partly explained by the fact that non-registration does not affect the validity of the marriage: a marriage is considered religiously valid without registration. The participants of a workshop on family law, conducted by the Hamburg Max Planck Institute in 2006 in Kabul, argued that a further reason why people do not register their marriages is their distrust in courts. Accordingly, it is against the Afghans' way of thinking, habits, and traditions to begin their marital life by going to a court, even if it is only in order to register the marriage. The other reason for not registering marriages is the fact that there is no need for it in daily life. Presenting certified documents is rarely necessary in Afghanistan. Thus, a simple but effective method for promoting registration would be a compulsory presentation of the marriage certificate to employers and landlords. For this purpose, trustworthy, extrajudicial registration authorities should be set up all over Afghanistan.

A further important issue in marriage law is the so-called bride price (*walwar*), which has to be differentiated from the Islamic dower (*mahr*). *Walwar* is a customary tradition whereby the groom or his family has to pay to the head of the bride's household a sum of money (or commodity) supposedly to reimburse the parents of the bride for the financial loss they suffered while raising their daughter. *Walwar* originates in the tribal tradition of Afghanistan, and viewed from the Pashtun perspective, it is a matter of honour: the higher the *walwar*, the higher the esteem of the husband's family for the bride. Some have argued that the concept of *walwar* is wrongly considered as 'selling girls', since this view ignores the socio-cultural background of the institution. The idea underlying *walwar* is to provide some financial relief to the girl's parents who purchase gold and silver ornaments, clothes, household utensils, etc. as dowry for their daughters. However, even if the dowry may be paid for out of the *walwar*, this is not a legal or customary obligation; *walwar* very often does not benefit the girl's family nor does it flow into the expenses for the wedding ceremony, also paid for by the family of the groom (Kamali 1985: 85).

The amount of commodities or money acceptable as *walwar* differs from province to province, as do the social attitudes with regard to this practice. In the 1980s, Kamali recorded amounts varying between 20,000 and 200,000 Afghanis depending on the geographic areas; a uniform figure could not be given. Likewise, a report conducted by the Max Planck Institute for Private Law in Hamburg in 2005 revealed equally variable amounts of payment of *walwar*. Data revealed, for instance, that the *walwar* for a virgin girl ranged 2,000 U.S. dollars (about 85,000 Afghani) to 40,000 U.S. dollars (1,700,000 Afghani) for the first marriage of a girl. This amount might be even higher if the man was already married; it would double for the third marriage and increase further for the fourth marriage. It is important to add that the amount of *walwar* can also vary according to chastity, beauty, education, and the social class or economic standard of the girl's family.

The need to purge the Afghan way of life of this tradition detrimental to society at large was strongly felt. Accordingly, *walwar* has been prohibited in all family law legislation prior to the Civil Code of 1977. The Marriage Law (1921) explicitly forbade the practice of *walwar*, as did its successor, the Marriage Law of 1926. Both statutes failed, however, to specify any means of enforcement or sanction in case of infringement. The Marriage Law of 1949 contains similar provisions. According to its Article 5, the bride is denied any further gift (including *walwar*) in addition to her dower. Article 6 provides the groom with some means of action and stipulates that the government is authorised to take action in a situation where, after the completion of a valid marriage, the guardian of the bride refuses to allow the bride to join her husband because of his refusal to pay extra money. This provision, however, had hardly a scope of application since normally the bride price is to be paid before the conclusion of the marriage.

Subsequent legislation repeated the prohibition of *walwar*, but as its predecessors, the Marriage Act 1971 failed to specify the competent court to hear cases on the matter, the penalties involved, or the way the violator should be prosecuted. The absence of sanctions made Article 15 inapplicable in practice. The intention of the legislator to eliminate *walwar* did not include any effective measure for the enforcement of the prohibition or sanctions for violation. The civil code also does not address the issue, thus failing to tackle one of the most burning issues in Afghan legal reality. With no effective measure to sanction its breach, the practise is still widespread in Afghanistan today.

In a country suffering from widespread poverty and unemployment this institution must be reconsidered in view of the fact that many men cannot afford it and are forced to sell their land or travel abroad to earn money for it (Yassari 2005: 58-59). Ironically, economic reasons also play a significant role in the persistence of *walwar*. The girl child can become an asset exchangeable for money or goods. Families see committing a young daughter (or sister) to a family that is able to pay a high price for the bride as a viable solution to their poverty and indebtedness. The custom of *walwar* may motivate families that face indebtedness and economic crisis to 'cash in' the 'asset' as young as 6 or 7, with the understanding that the actual marriage is delayed until the child reaches puberty. However, there is no guarantee that this is really observed and some reports indicate the danger of little girls being sexually abused not only by the groom but also by older men in the family, particularly if the groom is also a child (Ertürk 2006: 8).

Polygamy

The civil code confirms the validity of polygamy, but makes it contingent on conditions such as just character of the husband, his financial ability to maintain more than one wife, existence of a lawful benefit, and consent of the new wife (CC, Art.s 86, 89). Polygamy remains permissible under the requirements of Article 86 of the civil code, which reads as follows:

Polygamy can take place when the following conditions are fulfilled: 1) when there is no fear of unequal treatment as between the wives; 2) when the husband has sufficient financial means to maintain his wives. This includes food, clothing, housing and adequate medical care; 3) lawful reason, such as the first wife remaining childless or her suffering from diseases that are difficult to cure.

Since judicial permission prior to a polygamous marriage is not required to certify that the husband has indeed fulfilled these requirements, these conditions are not likely to be very effective. Judicial intervention is only possible after the polygamous marriage has been concluded. Consequently, when an Afghan man enters a polygamous marriage, violating any of the legally prescribed conditions, the second marriage will be valid (Ertürk 2006: 11). It will only give the wife (be it the first or the second) a right to judicial separation on the basis of harm (*dòarar*) in cases where the husband failed to fulfil the stipulated conditions (CC, Art.s 87, 183).

These rules, once again, fail to address the social realities of Afghanistan, placing the burden of proof entirely on the wife. It is extremely difficult for an Afghan woman to prove that her husband is unjust and has inflicted injury on her. The current legislation cannot, therefore, be considered a real remedy for the difficulties Afghan women face. Since polygamy in the Afghan society is considered to be less of a social stigma than divorce, divorce is very rare and discouraged by social pressure. Moreover, it is questionable whether the entitlement to divorce is a real option to many Afghan women. In many cases, a woman may prefer putting up with the polygamous marriage of her husband than to petition for a divorce that would likely leave her without financial means.

Divorce

Until the introduction of the Civil Code in 1977, divorce was exclusively governed by Hanafi law. Any legislation that addressed the subject prior to this time was of a piecemeal nature and essentially left the Shariah law intact. The Civil Code, thus, represents the first attempt to comprehensively codify the Shariah law of divorce. It provides for four types of marriage dissolution:

First, there is the repudiation of the wife by the husband. The provisions of *alaqt* are codified in Articles 135-155 of the civil code and reflect the Hanafi rules. Under the Civil Code (1977), the husband's unilateral right to divorce, without giving any reasons and without recourse to the courts, has been retained. The husband's may pronounce the *alaqt* verbally, in writing, or even by gesture (CC, Art.s 139, 135). Witnesses are not required and the repudiation does not need to be registered. The code is completely silent on that matter. The possibility of the husband to divorce his wife with no further formalities leaves a big legal insecurity for the women as to their marital status.

The second form of divorce is the judicial divorce initiated by the wife *(tafriq)* (CC, Art.s 176-197). This kind of divorce must be based on specific grounds that are borrowed from the Maliki school of law.

The grounds for judicial separation include: the husband suffering from an incurable disease; his failure or his inability to maintain his wife; absence/desertion for three years without a lawful excuse; the husband's imprisonment for ten years or more, in which event she can ask for a divorce after the first five years of imprisonment; and harm *(dòarar)* which can denote both physical and psychological injury.

Thirdly there is the divorce against payment *(khol)* (CC, Art.s 156-176). This kind of divorce is initiated by the wife whereby she provides financial consideration in exchange for her divorce. *Khol* represents the only form of dissolution whereby the wife has the right to initiate divorce proceedings without pleading a special reason such as harm or injury as grounds for divorce.

Under Hanafi law, however, it can only be effectuated with the husband's consent, severely limiting the scope of this right. The rules on *khol* in the Afghan code fail to take note of the family law reform measures that other Muslim countries have introduced. An Afghan woman's attempt to utilise *khol* under the Civil Code can, therefore, be frustrated simply by the husband's refusal to agree to her proposal.

Finally, there is the annulment of the marriage (*faskh*) (CC, Art.s 132-134), the legal dissolution of the marriage contract on the basis of an absence of a key requirement for the legality of the contract. This can be the case when one of the two parties has not consented to entering into the marriage, when psychological illnesses (such as insanity) are detected, or when the dower is inadequate (Kamali 1985: 184). It is clear that the Afghan Civil Code does not meet the standards envisaged in the Bonn Agreement or the equality clause of the 2004 constitution. Therefore, in order for the Civil Code to reflect these standards, it needs to be revised, not only with reference to polygamy and divorce, but also with regard to all of its provisions that do not comply with these standards.

Code of Personal Status of Shii Afghans

The Code of Personal Status of Shii Afghans (CPS) is composed of 236 articles. Article 1 states, that the code was drafted in response to Articles 131 and 54 of the Constitution of 2004 to regulate the personal status of Shii Afghans. Accordingly, the Supreme Court must appoint eligible Shii judges to implement the code. Whenever issues arise that are not addressed by the provisions of the CPS, the court shall decide in accordance with the Shii Ja'fari school of law as espoused in the writings (*fatwas*) of its most renowned and recognised religious authority the so called 'source of imitation' (*marja-e taqlid*).

According to Article 123 of the CPS, the husband is the head of the family. This kind of regulation is found in almost all family codes in Islamic countries. However, Article 123 further provides that the court may appoint the wife as head of the household, if it is established that the husband is intellectually unable to assume this position. Also, the much contested Article 132 Section 4 of the first draft of the code, which provided that the wife had to be sexual available whenever the man so wished, was omitted in the final version, as was the chapter on temporary marriage, which is recognised under Shii law, but prohibited under all Sunni schools of law. Furthermore, the marriageable age for women is 16 and for men 18, which is remarkable, considering the Shii rules allowing for marriage from the age of puberty (9 for girls and 15 for boy).

Criminal Law

As mentioned earlier, according to the Bonn Agreement, all legislation that does not conflict with the regulations stipulated in the existing legal codes or with the international legal obligations to which Afghanistan has committed itself shall remain in place. Thus, to this extent, the Penal Code of 1976 is still applicable. Furthermore, the Law on Detection and Investigation of Crimes of 1978 (LDIC), the Counter Narcotics Code of 2005, the Juvenile Code of 2005, and the Police Law of 2005 are applicable. The Criminal Procedure Code of 1965 (CPC), as amended in 1974, has been replaced by a new Interim Criminal Procedure Code (ICPC) that was ratified by the Ministry of Justice on 25 February 2004. The Code has 98 articles and was prepared by the Italian Justice Project Office, an Italian organisation responsible for oversight and implementation of legal reform projects funded by the Italian government in Afghanistan. Regrettably, these sets of laws do not always operate well together. For example, Article 98(3) of the ICPC states:

Upon promulgation of this law, any existing laws and decrees contrary to the provisions of this code are abrogated.

This article has been causing confusion and various problems for legal practitioners in the executive and the judiciary. For a police officer, a prosecutor, or a judge, it is extremely difficult to know which article(s) of the LDIC or CPC is contrary to the provisions of the ICPC and which is not (Gholami 2007).

Furthermore, according to some reports, substantive criminal law in Afghanistan continues to be governed in large part by Islamic law and in certain areas by customary law. Some of the punishments awarded for *addh* offences, such as, for instance, the stoning to death of an adulterer if certain evidential requirements are met, do conflict with both the 2004 constitution, which prohibits the imposition of punishments 'incompatible with human dignity', and Afghanistan's international legal obligations.

This is also true for the *Pashtunwali* justice system, which is based on the principle of *bad*, or the exchange of women between families when a crime is committed as compensation for the crime (Lau 2003: 22). However, it is not known whether the present administration intends to modify these aspects of Islamic and customary criminal law. It is in these areas that the most flagrant conflicts with international human rights standards still exist, and this is, together with family law, the two areas of law likely to be the most sensitive to reform.

Other Legal Areas, Especially Economic Law

The first Afghan Commercial Code was enacted in 1955. It contained 945 articles encompassing regulations on the merchant, (CoC,

Art.s 1-115), commercial companies (CoC, Art.s 116-470), commercial documents (CoC, Art.s 471-588), and commercial transactions including commercial agency and insurance (CoC, Art.s 589-945). Islamic law did not influence Afghan commercial legislation, as this legislation was based on the Turkish Commercial Code, which was, in turn, based on Western secular legislation, especially on German and Swiss law.

Traditional Afghan society with its tribal structures found it hard to adapt to the provisions of the code, as it did not match their needs, nor could they fulfil the requirements of the code. Article 117 of the Commercial Code (1955) defined, for example, various kinds of companies that had to be registered at the High Court of Appeal in Kabul, with the Ministry of Justice publishing all relevant information (e.g. trade mark, name of the company, and other specifications) in the Official Gazette.

The areas of intellectual property, banking, money exchange, and industrial property had never been codified and also required urgent regulation in order to attract foreign investors and industries. Accordingly, several statutes were published to cover these areas of commercial activities. The following statutes still exist and are applicable according to the Bonn Agreement: the Commercial Code of 1955; the Commercial Procedure Code of 1963; the Law of the Chamber of Commerce of 1951; and the Law for the Registration of Trade Marks of 1960. Since 25 years of civil war have turned the economy into a war economy (Schetter 2002: 109), it is difficult to assess the effect of statutory commercial law in Afghanistan today.

In 2002, a new Investment Law was enacted. It aims to attract and secure foreign investment in Afghanistan. It was amended in December 2005. According to Article 2, the State is committed to maximising private, both domestic and foreign, investment and to creating a legal regime and administrative structure that will encourage and protect foreign and domestic private investment in the Afghan economy in order to promote economic development, expand the labour market, increase production and export earnings, promote technology transfer, improve national prosperity, and advance the people's standard of living.

The only requirement to invest in Afghanistan is to maintain a valid bank account and to pass a criminal background check. Investments in Afghanistan can be 100 per cent foreign owned.

In September 2003, a new Banking Law was passed by Presidential Decree. It contains 101 articles and is clearly investor-friendly as long as contracts are followed. There are, however, scant provisions for enforcement in case of any default. Afghanistan lacks special courts for banking matters, and there is no recognition of foreign judgments. Interestingly, the law makes no reference to the principles of Islamic Banking. Islamic banking and interest-free banking are still in their infancy in Afghanistan. The civil war has played its part in bringing about this situation. There are currently no Islamic banks in the country, and there is no legislation covering the institutional and procedural aspects of this kind of banking. The war and the period following it have brought even the regular banking system to the brink of collapse (Kamali 2005:26).

International Treaty Obligations and Human Rights

The Constitution of 2004 contains a long list of guaranteed basic human rights of the citizens of Afghanistan. Afghanistan has also ratified the following international treaties: CEDAW, CRC, CAT, CERD, CESCR, and the ICCPR.

During the past twenty-five years, though, Afghan society has been through an extraordinary amount of violence. Throughout this period, serious abuses of human rights and war crimes by all sides in the conflict have taken place, including massacres, looting of houses and property, rapes, revenge killings, illegal imprisonment, the torture and murder of prisoners, and assassinations of political opponents (Amnesty International 2002). The legacy of war, poverty, and religious fanaticism has particularly affected Afghan women, who have suffered from both cultural and structural inequalities and violence in Afghan society for centuries. The persistence of this situation over the past quarter of a century has produced what Wardak calls a 'culture of human rights abuses' that is justified, and even positively sanctioned, in the shadow of warlordism in Afghanistan (Wardak 2005: 73).

After the fall of the Taliban regime, the Afghan Independent Human Rights Commission (AIHRC) was established on 2 June 2002 in response to Article 58 of the 2004 constitution. The AIHRC is the product of a national consultative process between Afghan human rights activists, the Interim Administration at the time, and the United Nations. Creation of the Commission was also encouraged and supported by Resolution 134/48 of U.N. General Assembly in 1993, and the Paris principles. The Commission, with its eight branch offices throughout the country, aims to protect and promote human rights across Afghanistan. In accordance with the 2004 constitution, the AIHRC functions as a permanent institution for the monitoring and, where necessary, investigation of the human rights situation in

Afghanistan. AIHRC is funded by donor countries assisting Afghanistan, and, as such, forms an important part of national income for the country. The AIHRC is currently chaired by Sima Samar, a well-known women and human rights advocate and activist within national and international forums. Before chairing the Commission, she was elected as the Vice-Chair of the emergency *Loya Jirga*.

Since its establishment, the AIHRC has regularly reported on violation of human rights, related in particular to women, children, and civilian casualties and death as a result of ongoing clashes between the NATO and Taliban and perpetrators of war crimes in Afghanistan. Their latest report, the Report on the Situation of Economic and Social Rights in Afghanistan of November/December 2009 aims to assess the status of economic and social rights in Afghanistan in the year 1387 (2009) against the national and international obligations of the government with respect to these rights.

The report highlights that one of the most significant challenges in Afghanistan is still the worrying security situation. Despite existing commitments, strategies, and policies developed to improve the socio-economic situation of Afghans, many men, women, and children continue to suffer from extreme poverty, high unemployment, systemic discrimination, and a lack of access to healthcare, schools, and adequate housing. Implementation and enforcement of legislation to protect social and economic rights also remains limited due to weak judicial institutions.

The social reality of human rights protection in Afghanistan thus reveals a depressing picture of almost complete legal impunity. Not only do grave past violations of human rights remain unpunished, but abuses continue without any immediate prospect of bringing the perpetrators to justice. Any reform of the legal system to bring it in line with international human rights standards or with the provisions of the new constitution will require as an essential prerequisite the existence of a stable, functioning, and capable state, both able and willing to enforce laws (Lau 2003: 4). At present, this is sadly not the situation in Afghanistan.

The Afghan legal system and its evolution throughout the last hundred years have been coloured by three factors: its traditional and tribal government and local customary laws; Islamic law; and the development of statutory laws by the central state authorities.

The relationship between Islamic law and customary law is complex. Local customs and customary law continue to have a very prominent role. Despite official statements to the contrary, people usually resort to the chiefs and eldest of their communities, whom they frequently refer to as the 'white beards' (*rish-e sefid*), for dispute resolution. Generally, when a dispute arises, the parties agree on whether the dispute is to be resolved 'Shariah-wise' or in accordance with customary law, e.g. mainly the *Pashtunwali* (International Legal Foundation 2004: 7). There are very few reports and data on the application of customary law in Afghanistan. Decisions of the *jirgas* are conveyed orally, and there are no written reports. In many cases, customary law strictly contradicts Islamic law. This is especially so in cases where women, without their consent, are given into marriage to settle disputes between families.

Historically, there has been simultaneous coexistence and competition between Shariah and customary law. While Islamic law, namely the Hanafi school of law, substantially controls matters of personal relationship and most aspects of inheritance, local custom prevails in land tenure. In criminal matters, both sources of law can govern the case.

All Afghan constitutions, except the Constitution of 1980, endorsed the traditional supremacy of Shariah in Afghanistan. This is manifested in the numerous references made to the Shariah, proclaiming it as the law of the nation. This can be explained by the fact that Afghans have always had recourse to Islamic law. It has been the single constant to have steadily survived a century of law reform and legal insecurity. Note, for instance, a reminder of Afghan's political and legal history: the burst of modern legislation under Amanullah between 1919-1929 was abrogated by the succeeding regime; the Western-oriented reforms of the 1970s were eventually completely undone in the communist era; and the attempts to turn the legal system of the country from its religious tribal and customary basis to an imposed emphasis on a general Sovietisation of the legal system after 1978 failed.

Since the latter half of the nineteenth century, a number of efforts have been made to modernise and secularise the existing legal system, or at least specific areas of the law. Statutory legislation is a latecomer on the scene, meant to supplement the Shariah especially in areas that were not covered by the latter. Legislation in traditionally Shariah-dominated fields such as family law, law of property, contracts, and evidence mainly sought to codify the substantive Shariah rules for purposes of easy reference by judges and lawyers. In this respect, they are seen as merely a restatement of Islamic law (e.g. CC, Art.s 497-750, reflecting Hanafi contract law). Other pieces of legislation, such as the Commercial Code on the other hand, are genuinely secular codifications.

These legislative initiatives have frequently been accomplished only through the employment of drastic, even violent, measures (Reynolds & Flores 1993: 1). Ironically, the general effect has been to generate strengthened support for Islamic and customary law at the local level. Furthermore, Afghan legislation (secular and otherwise) has been limited both in its quantity and in its quality. The result is disjointed legislation, with many gaps and unregulated areas of law. Röder calls the legal landscape 'a patchwork' of various norms (Röder 2009: 257). While the nation may be a unified state in a strict sense, the law is in practice a fragmented *mélange* of secular, customary, and religious law variously applied according to local acceptance of central legislation and modified by shifting conditions of governmental authority. Legal pluralism is the hallmark of legal reality in Afghanistan.

Without exception, all surveys of the Afghan legal system have made note of the fact that Afghanistan's statutory laws and regulations exist solely on paper (Weinbaum 1980: 51). Most of the literature also points to the fact that for ordinary people and villagers, who form the vast majority of the population, tribal/customary and Islamic law are far more significant and actually better known than state legislation (Amin 1993: 66). The limited practical value of Afghanistan's statutory laws has to be attributed to the decline and demise of central political authority in Afghanistan as a result of the civil war, but also to the lack of training of legal professionals and the inability to adapt statutory law to Afghanistan's particular circumstances. This means for instance that judges either do not know the law well, or know it, but are reluctant to apply it. The *de facto* subdivision of the legal system into official statutory law and unofficial mainly unwritten law is characteristic of the Afghan legal history ever since attempts were made to introduce statutory laws. The difficulty of implementing statutory laws also has very practical considerations: many of the statutes have for a long time been unavailable, due to the destruction of archives and the complete breakdown of administrative order during the years of civil war.

Hence, in Afghanistan it is not the implications of Shariah or Shariah-based law which, at least for the moment, prevents the application and implementation of international legal and human rights standards, but the lack of a system by which the rule of law may be established so that the legal system is capable of - practically, socially, politically - guaranteeing and enforcing laws effectively. Although the Government is committed to carrying out its duties imposed not only by Afghanistan's domestic laws but also by the country's international obligations, the greatest challenge to action is the lack of security and the fragile peace balance in the country.

A functional legal system in Afghanistan, which is applied by the professionals and accepted by the population, requires incorporation of certain aspects of Islamic and customary law, within the limits imposed by human rights considerations. It is impossible to reject the existing body of tribal laws in its entirety, as this will damage the legal reform process; but at the same time, discriminatory practices, especially those against women, must be abolished. This, in turn, means bringing about a gradual change of popular attitudes on part of the population at large concerning the application of those rules that infringe upon basic human as well as basic Islamic rights. This is the *conditio sine qua non* for change. As long as practices such as *bad* and *walwar* are not seen as disgraceful and against human dignity, imposing a system from above will not be successful in Afghanistan. In changing these practices, history, traditional structures, and the failures of the past must be taken into consideration.

Chapter 5

Islamic Shariah Law and Democracy

During a drunken poker game last Friday night at one of my friends' houses, an interesting debate was born. The recent ousting and killing of Libyan dictator Muammar Gaddafi is a good thing for the world, absolutely nobody is disputing that. What my friends and I debated over beer and cards, however, was what the ramifications of this really are and whether this would actually cause the people to embrace democracy, or if the government would get hijacked by another despot. President Barack Obama, in a statement issued by the White House shortly after Gaddafi's death said, "After four decades of brutal dictatorship and eight months of deadly conflict, the Libyan people can now celebrate their freedom and the beginning of a new era of promise." Mr. President, I respectfully ask that you don't jump the gun just yet because the embracing of democracy by a country that practices the law of Shariah is never a given.

Shariah law is basically a form of religious Islamist law, or, more simply, a code of conduct. While the law itself has vast interpretations by different schools of Muslim thought, one thing is agreed upon by virtually all of them – Shariah law is a reflection of what Muslims believe to be the will of God for the rest of humanity.

This immediately should raise red flags for any country attempting to instill a democracy, as you suddenly have a conflict of interest over religion and politics. It's not just that, however. In order to truly understand how important the law of Shariah is to Islamic countries, one must understand that to the overwhelming majority of people in countries like Libya, no matter if they are peace-loving Muslims or those of the fundamentalist variety, "God's will" is one of the most important things to them, and this fact is what makes it so hard to instill a true democracy in an Arabic nation.

According to The Washington Post, Mustafa Abdul-Jalil, head of Libya's National Transitional Council, said that the new vision for Libya has "an Islamist tint, [and that] Islamic Shariah law would be the 'basic source' of legislation and existing laws that contradict the teachings of Islam would be nullified." Special attention deserves to be paid to the last bit in that quote.

Shariah law does include certain elements that are indicative of democracy, most of which being the election of officials by the people. It is the definition of democracy that is the question and how that concept is applied when viewed in conjunction with Shariah law.

According to Ali Khan, a professor at the Washburn University School of Law, Shariah law contains elements that "are fully compatible with democracy, provided that religious minorities are protected and the incumbent Islamic leadership remains committed to the right to recall." As history has shown us, "incumbent Islamic leadership" hasn't always been so committed to recall. It is primarily for these reasons why I take Obama's optimism for Libya with a grain of salt. It's not that the people don't want to be free, because by and large they do. It's more about the difficulty of implementing a democratic, western system, in a region that has never been open to western practices that holds the "law of god" higher than anything. Shariah law, as backwards as most of its tenets are, is an institution in Islamic society.

I hope it does work in Libya and that the Arab Spring sets a precedent for many other nations in similar situations, but causing a collective shift in how people view democratic law in light of Shariah is easier said than done.

The Clash of Islam and Liberalism

Islam is not merely a religion. It is also - and perhaps, foremost - a state ideology. It is all-pervasive and missionary. It permeates every aspect of social cooperation and culture. It is an organising principle, a narrative, a philosophy, a value system, and a vade mecum. In this it resembles Confucianism and, to some extent, Hinduism.

Judaism and its offspring, Christianity - though heavily involved in political affairs throughout the ages - have kept their dignified distance from such carnal matters. These are religions of "heaven" as opposed to Islam, a practical, pragmatic, hands-on, ubiquitous, "earthly" creed.

Secular religions - Democratic Liberalism, Communism, Fascism, Nazism, Socialism and other isms - are more akin to Islam than to, let's say, Buddhism. They are universal, prescriptive, and total. They provide recipes, rules, and norms regarding every aspect of existence - individual, social, cultural, moral, economic, political, military, and philosophical. At the end of the Cold War, Democratic Liberalism stood triumphant over the fresh graves of its ideological opponents. They have all been eradicated. This precipitated Fukuyama's premature diagnosis (the End of History). But one state ideology, one bitter rival, one implacable opponent, one contestant for world domination, one antithesis remained - Islam.

Militant Islam is, therefore, not a cancerous mutation of "true" Islam. On the contrary, it is the purest expression of its nature as an imperialistic religion which demands unmitigated obedience from its followers and regards all infidels as both inferior and avowed enemies.

The same can be said about Democratic Liberalism. Like Islam, it does not hesitate to exercise force, is missionary, colonising, and regards itself as a monopolist of the "truth" and of "universal values". Its antagonists are invariably portrayed as depraved, primitive, and below par. Such mutually exclusive claims were bound to lead to an all-out conflict sooner or later. The "War on Terrorism" is only the latest round in a millennium-old war between Islam and other "world systems".

Such interpretation of recent events enrages many. They demand to know (often in harsh tones):

Don't you see any differences between Islam on the one hand and Judaism and Christianity on the other?

Islam is a young religion, less than 1400 years old. When Judaism and Christianity were at this phase of their development, they resembled Islam today: they were rife with militancy, obscurantism, misogyny, missionary belligerence, and all-pervading, dogmatic intolerance.

Don't you see any difference between terrorists who murder civilians and regular armies in battle?

Both regulars and irregulars slaughter civilians as a matter of course. "Collateral damage" is the main outcome of modern, total warfare - and of low intensity conflicts alike.

There is a major difference between terrorists and soldiers, though:

Terrorists make carnage of noncombatants their main tactic - while regular armies rarely do. Such conduct is criminal and deplorable, whoever the perpetrator. But what about the killing of combatants in battle? How should we judge the slaying of soldiers by terrorists in combat?

Modern nation-states enshrined the self-appropriated monopoly on violence in their constitutions and ordinances (and in international law). Only state organs - the army, the police - are permitted to kill, torture, and incarcerate.

Terrorists are trust-busters: they, too, want to kill, torture, and incarcerate. They seek to break the death cartel of governments by joining its ranks.

Thus, when a soldier kills terrorists and ("inadvertently") civilians (as "collateral damage") - it is considered above board. But when the terrorist decimates the very same soldier - he is decried as an outlaw.

Moreover, the misbehaviour of some countries - not least the United States - led to the legitimisation of terrorism. Often nation-states use terrorist organisations to further their geopolitical goals. When this happens, erstwhile outcasts become "freedom fighters", pariahs become allies, murderers are recast as sensitive souls struggling for equal rights. This contributes to the blurring of ethical percepts and the blunting of moral judgment.

We must bear in mind that Islam is a relatively young religion, at a stage of its development similar to 11th century Christianity: belligerent, missionary, exclusive, and committed to Jihad (doing battle with one's frailties, foibles, and weaknesses in order to get closer to God). In the Medieval Church, the various orders of ascetic monks reified this ideal of attaining goodness and holiness by suppressing one's humanity and renouncing the world and its temptations. In this sense, they were a mirror image of today's Islamic militants. Many of them indeed went on to participate in the Crusades (warrior-monks such as the Knight Templars and the Hospitaliers).

Would you rather live under Shariah law? Don't you find Liberal Democracy vastly superior to Islam?

Superior, no. Different - of course. Having been born and raised in the West, I naturally prefer its standards to Islam's. Had I been born in a Muslim country, I would have probably found the West and its principles perverted and obnoxious.

The question is meaningless because it presupposes the existence of an objective, universal, culture and period independent set of preferences. Luckily, there is no such thing.

In this clash of civilization whose side are you on?

This is not a clash of civilizations. Western medieval culture is inextricably intertwined with Islamic knowledge, teachings, and philosophy – the direct descendants of antiquity.

Christian fundamentalists have more in common with Muslim militants than with East Coast or French intellectuals.

Muslims have always been the West's most defining Other. Islamic existence and "gaze" helped to mould the West's emerging identity as a historical construct. From Spain to India, the incessant friction and fertilizing interactions with Islam shaped Western values, beliefs, doctrines, moral tenets, political and military institutions, arts, and sciences.

This war is about world domination. Two incompatible thought and value systems compete for the hearts and minds (and purchasing power) of the denizens of the global village. Like in the Westerns, by high noon, either one of them is left standing - or both will have perished.

Where does my loyalty reside?

I am a Westerner, so I hope the West wins this confrontation. But, in the process, it would be good if it were humbled, deconstructed, and reconstructed. One beneficial outcome of this conflict is the demise of the superpower system - a relic of days bygone and best forgotten. I fully believe and trust that in militant Islam, the United States has found its match. In other words, I regard militant Islam as a catalyst that will hasten the transformation of the global power structure from unipolar to multipolar. It may also commute the United States itself. It will definitely rejuvenate religious thought and cultural discourse. All wars do.

Aren't you overdoing it? After all, al-Qaida is just a bunch of terrorists on the run!

The West is not fighting al-Qaida. It is facing down the circumstances and ideas that gave rise to al-Qaida. Conditions - such as poverty, ignorance, disease, oppression, and xenophobic superstitions - are difficult to change or to reverse. Ideas are impossible to suppress. Already, militant Islam is far more widespread and established that any Western government would care to admit.

History shows that all terrorist groupings ultimately join the mainstream. Many countries - from Israel to Ireland and from East Timor to Nicaragua - are governed by former terrorists. Terrorism enhances social upward mobility and fosters the redistribution of wealth and resources from the haves to haves not.

Al-Qaida, despite its ominous portrayal in the Western press - is no exception. It, too, will succumb, in due time, to the twin lures of power and money. Nihilistic and decentralized as it is - its express goals are the rule of Islam and equitable economic development. It is bound to get its way in some countries.

The world of the future will be truly pluralistic. The proselytising zeal of Liberal Democracy and Capitalism has rendered them illiberal and intolerant. The West must accept the fact that a sizable chunk of humanity does not regard materialism, individualism, liberalism, progress, and democracy - at least in their Western guises - as universal or desirable.

Live and let live (and live and let die) must replace the West's malignant optimism and intellectual and spiritual arrogance.

Edward K. Thompson, the managing editor of "Life" from 1949 to 1961, once wrote:

"'Life' must be curious, alert, erudite and moral, but it must achieve this without being holier-than-thou, a cynic, a know-it-all or a Peeping Tom."

The West has grossly and thoroughly violated Thompson's edict. In its oft-interrupted intercourse with these forsaken regions of the globe, it has acted, alternately, as a Peeping Tom, a cynic and a know it all. It has invariably behaved as if it were holier-than-thou. In an unmitigated and fantastic succession of blunders, miscalculations, vain promises, unkept threats and unkempt diplomats - it has driven the world to the verge of war and the regions it "adopted" to the threshold of economic and social upheaval.

Enamored with the new ideology of free marketry cum democracy, the West first assumed the role of the omniscient. It designed ingenious models, devised foolproof laws, imposed fail-safe institutions and strongly "recommended" measures. Its representatives, the tribunes of the West, ruled the plebeian East with determination rarely equalled by skill or knowledge.

Velvet hands couched in iron gloves, ignorance disguised by economic newspeak, geostrategic interests masquerading as forms of government, characterized their dealings with the natives. Preaching and beseeching from ever higher pulpits, they poured opprobrium and sweet delusions on the eagerly duped, naive, bewildered masses.

The deceit was evident to the indigenous cynics - but it was the failure that dissuaded them and others besides. The West lost its former colonies not when it lied egregiously, not when it pretended to know for sure when it surely did not know, not when it manipulated and coaxed and coerced - but when it failed.

To the peoples of these regions, the king was fully dressed. It was not a little child but an enormous debacle that exposed his nudity. In its presumptuousness and pretentiousness, feigned surety and vain clichés, imported economic models and exported cheap raw materials - the West succeeded to demolish beyond reconstruction whole economies, to ravage communities, to wreak ruination upon the centuries-old social fabric, woven diligently by generations.

It brought crime and drugs and mayhem but gave very little in return, only a horizon beclouded and thundering with vacuous eloquence. As a result, while tottering regional governments still pay lip service to the values of Capitalism, the masses are enraged and restless and rebellious and baleful and anti-Western to the core.

The disenchanted were not likely to acquiesce for long - not only with the West's neo-colonialism but also with its incompetence and inaptitude, with the nonchalant experimentation that it imposed upon them and with the abyss between its proclamations and its performance.

Throughout this time, the envoys of the West - its mediocre politicians, its insatiably ruthless media, its obese tourists, its illiterate soldiers, and its armchair economists - continue to play the role of God, wreaking greater havoc than even the original.

While confessing to omniscience (in breach of every tradition scientific and religious), they also developed a kind of world weary, unshaven cynicism interlaced with fascination at the depths plumbed by the locals' immorality and amorality.

The jet-set Peeping Toms reside in five star hotels (or luxurious apartments) overlooking the communist, or Middle-Eastern, or African shantytowns. They drive utility vehicles to the shabby offices of the native bureaucrats and dine in $100 per meal restaurants ("it's so cheap here").

In between kebab and hummus they bemoan and grieve the corruption and nepotism and cronyism ("I simply love their ethnic food, but they are so..."). They mourn the autochthonous inability to act decisively, to cut red tape, to manufacture quality, to open to the world, to be less xenophobic (said while casting a disdainful glance at the native waiter).

To them it looks like an ancient force of nature and, therefore, an inevitability - hence their cynicism. Mostly provincial people with horizons limited by consumption and by wealth, these heralds of the West adopt cynicism as shorthand for cosmopolitanism. They erroneously believe that feigned sarcasm lends them an air of ruggedness and rich experience and the virile aroma of decadent erudition. Yet all it does is make them obnoxious and even more repellent to the residents than they already were.

Ever the preachers, the West - both Europeans and Americans - uphold themselves as role models of virtue to be emulated, as points of reference, almost inhuman or superhuman in their taming of the vices, avarice up front.

Yet the chaos and corruption in their own homes is broadcast live, day in and day out, into the cubicles inhabited by the very people they seek to so transform. And they conspire and collaborate in all manner of venality and crime and scam and rigged elections in all the countries they put the gospel to.

In trying to put an end to history, they seem to have provoked another round of it - more vicious, more enduring, more traumatic than before. That the West is paying the price for its mistakes I have no doubt. For isn't it a part and parcel of its teachings that everything has a price and that there is always a time of reckoning?

From Venezuela to Thailand, democratic regimes are being toppled by authoritarian substitutes: the military, charismatic left-wingers, or mere populists. Even in the USA, the bastion of constitutional rule, civil and human rights are being alarmingly eroded (though not without precedent in wartime).

The prominent ideologues of liberal democracy have committed a grave error by linking themselves inextricably with the doctrine of freemarketry and the emerging new order of globalisation. As Thomas Friedman correctly observes in "The Lexus and the Olive Tree", both strains of thought are strongly identified with the United States of America (USA).

Thus, liberal democracy came to be perceived by the multitudes as a ruse intended to safeguard the interests of an emerging, malignantly narcissistic empire (the USA) and of rapacious multinationals. Liberal democracy came to be identified with numbing, lowbrow cultural homogeneity, encroachment on privacy and the individual, and suppression of national and other idiosyncratic sentiments.

Liberal democracy came to be confused and confuted with neo-colonial exploitation, social Darwinism, and the crumbling of social compacts and long-standing treaties, both explicit and implicit. It even came to be associated with materialism and a bewildering variety of social ills: rising crime rates, unemployment, poverty, drug addiction, prostitution, organ trafficking, monopolistic behaviour, corporate malfeasance, and other antisocial forms of conduct.

Communism, Fascism, Nazism, and Religious Fundamentalism are as utopian as the classical Idea of Progress, which is most strongly reified by Western science and liberal democracy. All four illiberal ideologies firmly espouse a linear view of history: Man progresses by accumulating knowledge and wealth and by constructing ever-improving polities. Similarly, the classical, all-encompassing, idea of progress is perceived to be a "Law of Nature" with human jurisprudence and institutions as both its manifestations and descriptions. Thus, all ideas of progress are pseudo-scientific. Still, there are some important distinctions between Communism, Fascism, Nazism, and Religious Fundamentalism, on the one hand, and Western liberalism, on the other hand:

All four totalitarian ideologies regard individual tragedies and sacrifices as the inevitable lubricant of the inexorable March Forward of the species. Yet, they redefine "humanity" (who is human) to exclude large groups of people. Communism embraces the Working Class (Proletariat) but not the Bourgeoisie, Nazism promotes one Volk but denigrates and annihilates others, Fascism bows to the Collective but viciously persecutes dissidents, Religious Fundamentalism posits a chasm between believers and infidels.

In these four intolerant ideologies, the exclusion of certain reviled groups of people is both a prerequisite for the operation of the "Natural Law of Progress" and an integral part of its motion forward. The moral and spiritual obligation of "real" Man to future generations is to "unburden" the Law, to make it possible for it to operate smoothly and in optimal conditions, with all hindrances (read: undesirables) removed (read: murdered).

All four ideologies subvert modernity (in other words, Progress itself) by using its products (technology) to exclude and kill "outsiders", all in the name of servicing "real" humanity and bettering its lot.

But liberal democracy has been intermittently guilty of the same sin. The same deranged logic extends to the construction and maintenance of nuclear weapons by countries like the USA, the UK, France, and Israel: they are intended to protect "good" humanity against "bad" people (e.g., Communists during the Cold war, Arabs, or failed states such as Iran). Even global warming is a symptom of such exclusionary thinking: the rich feel that they have the right to tax the "lesser" poor by polluting our common planet and by disproportionately exhausting its resources.

The fact is that, at least since the 1920s, the very existence of Mankind is being recurrently threatened by exclusionary ideas of progress. Even Colonialism, which predated modern ideologies, was inclusive and sought to "improve" the Natives" and "bring them to the White Man's level" by assimilating or incorporating them in the culture and society of the colonial power. This was the celebrated (and then decried) "White Man's Burden". That we no longer accept our common fate and the need to collaborate to improve our lot is nothing short of suicidal.

Freedom or Theocracy?: Constitutionalism in Afghanistan and Iraq

> *"Afghans are victims of the games superpowers once played: their war was once our war, and collectively we bear responsibility."*
>
> *"In the approved version of the [Afghan] constitution, Article 3 was amended to read, 'In Afghanistan, no law can be contrary to the beliefs and provisions of the sacred religion of Islam.'... This very significant clause basically gives the official and nonofficial religious leaders in Afghanistan sway over every action that they might deem contrary to their beliefs, which by extension and within the Afghan cultural context, could be regarded as 'beliefs' of Islam."*
>
> *"The lopsided [electoral] victory by Iraq's Shiite Muslim alliance gives it the biggest voice in shaping the nation's new government and constitution.... Will Shariah, or Islamic law, become the main reference for national policy on divorce, censorship, the role of women in society, broadcasting and public morality, as many Shiite clerics and their followers insist?"*

During the past four years, the United States has replaced two dictatorial regimes in majority Islamic countries with more democratic governments. These interventions enforced the "Bush doctrine," the declaration of President George W. Bush after the murder of nearly 3,000 Americans by Saudi and Egyptian terrorists on September 11 that all states "harbouring" or supporting terrorists would see their leaders deposed and pro-American ones installed.

The Bush doctrine, its adherents plausibly argue, has profoundly advanced the cause of human rights in Afghanistan and Iraq. Specifically, it liberated Afghans and Iraqis from dictatorships with two of the worst human rights records in the world, replacing them with constitutional democracies ostensibly devoted to respecting individual rights.

Activists for human rights and religious freedom have been more critical concerning the United States' role in the political processes of Afghanistan and Iraq. They argue that the paradoxical effect of President Bush's policies is to have replaced two unstable, marginalized regimes with what may become enduring and universally recognized Islamic fundamentalist states, albeit with greater democratic credentials. The new constitutions of Afghanistan and Iraq have enshrined Islam as the official religion and source of legislation, which no social policies may contravene. This codification of religious fundamentalism was an inevitable byproduct, some observers contend, of the delegation of the nation-building process in both countries to religious extremists who enjoyed devoted followings of armed militiamen.

This article explores this debate by analysing legal developments in Afghanistan and Iraq, with a particular focus on Afghanistan's new constitution, ratified in early 2004 before the first post-Taliban elections were held. The Afghan constitution symbolizes the unmistakable liberation of Afghanistan's people from the despotic and even genocidal rule of the Taliban, but its many provisions requiring compatibility of government policy with an unwritten code of Islamic law may allow grave human rights violations to continue, and frustrate democratic demands for respect for international human rights standards and the country's civil law traditions.

Accelerated judicial reform will be necessary to ensure that the provisions in the constitution for judicial review of laws for conformity to religious doctrine will not be utilized to implement theocratic rule, which is the result that many powerful Afghans, possessing armed militias used to intimidate their political opponents, are working towards.

Afghan modernizers and fundamentalists have enjoyed varying degrees of foreign support and intervention throughout the twentieth century. Depending on how the new constitution is interpreted, the past support of the U.S. and its allies to some of the most radical elements of the fundamentalist camp may have assured their enduring victory.

Part I of the Article explores the historical context in which Afghanistan's new constitution was drafted and ratified, and the unique responsibility of the U.S. and the Soviet Union in creating that context.

Part II traces the rise and fall of the Taliban theocracy, which murdered thousands of political opponents and religious minorities, and intensified the fundamentalist oppression of Afghans instituted after the fall of the communist Afghan regime.

Part III describes how after the rout of the Taliban, the U.S. accepted Afghan fundamentalists into prominent positions from which they could control the process by which Afghanistan would draft and ratify its new constitution and develop a post-Taliban legal system.

Part IV proposes some test cases for judging the implementation of Afghanistan's new constitution and judicial reform efforts from the perspective of democracy and individual rights, including new bans on blasphemy and political secularism that are ripe for systematic abuse, plans to revive fundamentalist punishments avoided by most modern states such as stoning and amputation, and the ongoing oppression and enslavement of Afghan women and girls.

The article concludes by drawing some parallels between the Afghan constitutional process and the ongoing process of transitioning Iraq from a nominally socialist dictatorship with a genocidal record into a so-called "Islamic democracy." Many Iraqis, and almost all residents of majority Kurdish areas of northern Iraq, report being better off as a result of the U.S.-led operation to remove Saddam Hussein from power. But as in Afghanistan, the Iraqi delegates handpicked by the U.S and the U.N. to draft a constitution have established Iraq as a religious state. At the behest of powerful fundamentalists with private armies, the drafters of the interim Iraqi constitution included language providing for judicial review of legislation for conformity to an unspecified, but probably fundamentalist, version of religious law. At the same time, more than 100,000 Iraqis have died violently since the war began; Iraqi fundamentalists are murdering and raping members of the indigenous Christian population at an accelerated pace, prompting tens of thousands to flee the country; and Iraqi women are facing new restrictions on their freedom of movement and dress, as well as deprivation of their rights in marriage and divorce.

The actions and public statements of Iraq's most prominent religious leaders, to which the likely leaders of the new Iraq will defer if present trends continue, raise precisely the same sorts of concerns as the fundamentalist policies that have continued in Afghanistan.

Historical Context of the Rise of the Taliban Theocracy

Pre-Constitutional Afghanistan

Like many countries, Afghanistan had no written constitution prior to the twentieth century. The land was ruled either as a province of another empire, or independently by an Afghan monarch or local tribal leaders. For many centuries, the legal system had its basis in a combination of Shariah law and ancient customs such as the *jirga*, a council of tribal elders convened to settle important issues, and Pashtunwali, the Pashtun code of conduct emphasizing conservative family values and the seclusion of women from public view. Around the turn of the 20th century, Afghanistan opened up to secular influences and women's rights by abolishing some forced marriages, raising the minimum marriageable age, liberalising women's access to divorce and rights of inheritance, and prohibiting extravagant gifts to a bride's family that could be used in essence to purchase a girl from her parents.

Constitutional Monarchy

The events leading up to and following the adoption of the first Afghan constitution would be repeated many times in Afghan history: a set of policies looking towards the future and the West infuriated fundamentalists, whose opposition was violently suppressed but eventually succeeded, with foreign intervention, in deposing the regime responsible for the new policies.

On April 9, 1923, Amanullah Khan, the Amir of Afghanistan, secured the ratification by a Loya Jirga of Afghanistan's first written constitution. The 1923 constitution set forth a blueprint for modernising Afghanistan and assuring greater rights for Afghan women and religious minorities within the framework of Islamic governance. It guaranteed that all Afghan subjects would have "equal rights in accordance with Shariah and the laws of the state." Some Afghans interpreted this provision as entitling Afghan women to citizenship and equal rights. The constitution promised greater rights to religious minorities such as the Hazaras, who as Shia Muslims had been labelled as infidels and massacred and enslaved in the nineteenth century for this reason. It abolished torture, slavery, and forced labour; created a legislature, although the Amir would appoint the Prime Minister and many of its members; and decreed that followers of religions other than Islam, such as Hinduism and Judaism, were entitled to the protection of the state. Elementary education became compulsory for all Afghan "citizens."

Despite its modernising aspirations, the 1923 constitution established what would be considered theocratic rule by contemporary standards. A "theocracy," literally speaking, would be the direct rule by a divine being on Earth; this possibility having been disavowed by mainstream Christianity and Islam, most theocracies in fact consist of "government by priests or men claiming to know the will of God." By this definition, Afghanistan's 1923 constitution was theocratic by virtue of the authority it invested in men claiming to know the will of God. The constitution made the "sacred" and official religion of the state, and enshrined the King as the "servant and the protector of the true religion of Islam." It instructed legislators to give "careful consideration" to the "requirements of the laws of Shariah." Perhaps most importantly, it provided that in Afghan courts of justice, "all disputes and cases will be decided in accordance with the principles of Shariah and of general civil and criminal laws." The judiciary, in this instance as in others, served as the key instrument of fundamentalist Islamic theocracy.

Taking on centuries-old customs, Amir Amnullah Khan introduced ambitious legislative reforms improving Afghan women's rights. The Amir declared that Afghan women would no longer "be treated as second-class Muslims." In 1921, he enacted a Family Code banning child marriage, marriages between close relatives, excessive dowries, and the exchange of women as "blood money" in payment of interfamilial disputes. He opened girls' schools and sent women students abroad for higher education. After 1923, the Amir introduced Afghanistan's first civil code, which abolished polygamy and marriages to all girls under the age of 18. His wife Soraya appeared unveiled in public and participated actively in politics, citing the example of women in the "early years of Islam."

Not satisfied with the constitution's gestures towards theocracy, and disappointed with King Amanullah's record as the "protector" of Islam, Afghanistan's religious elite quickly moved to overthrow and reverse his modernising reforms. The head of a prominent religious family, which served as "king makers" in Afghan society, immediately denounced the 1923 constitution as a "communist" document. A rebellion reached the outskirts of the capital Kabul, and was only repelled when the Amir mobilized his new air force to strafe and bomb the advancing insurgents, and then executed the revolt's leaders.

Rebels having nearly toppled his regime, the Amir called a Loya Jirga to amend the 1923 constitution in several important respects designed to pacify Afghanistan's religious elite. One amendment made the Hanafi school of Islamic law the official religious rite of

Afghanistan. Additional concessions from the Amir included "watering down" the rights of women, reintroducing torture when "in accordance with the rules of the Shariah," and allowing a Council of Islamic Scholars to "decide whether new laws were in accordance with Islamic law."

After Amir Amanullah became King of Afghanistan in 1926, he announced further sweeping reforms aimed at helping Afghan women. He endorsed expanding Afghan girls' access to education, proclaimed his opposition to the compulsory veiling of women, and imposed Western dress within the capital of Kabul. In response, Afghan religious leaders once again led conservative Afghan tribes in rebellion. Under siege, King Amanullah abdicated the throne in early 1929. Historians tend to blame the King's overhasty reforms for his downfall, especially those dealing with mandatory veiling, the seclusion of women, and forced and underage marriages. But the West failed to support the King who admired its values, and Britain actively worked to overthrow him. Many Afghans and even the British press believed that the British Empire was behind Amanullah's fall from power, given the Empire's poor relations with him.

King Amanullah's successors quickly overturned his reforms. But in doing so, they did not return Afghanistan to a pre-modern or pre-constitutional condition. Instead, they established an Islamic constitutional monarchy that, despite its theocratic aspects, also retained some of the 1923 constitution's gestures towards reform.

A Loya Jirga in 1930 created Afghanistan's next stable government and pronounced Nadir Shah as Afghanistan's King. The King promulgated the second Afghan constitution in 1931. With a few minor changes, it endured as Afghanistan's governing charter for more than 30 years.

Like the 1923 constitution, it embraced tradition while looking tentatively towards the future. On the side of tradition, it made the Hanafi school of Islam the state religion, established a requirement that all legislation conform to the Shariah, and gave religious authorities the power to review Afghan laws and governmental policies for correspondence to Shariah law.

But it also guaranteed compulsory elementary education, freedom of the press within the limits of the Shariah, and a limited role for democratically elected officials to participate in the drafting of legislation. Afghan women became eligible to vote in elections, although the authorities later declared this provision to be incompatible with Islamic law. King Nadir Shah's government enforced Afghan women's obligation to wear the all-covering *burqa*, a tent-like covering that obscures the entire person and leaves only a mesh opening to see through. The new King reinvigorated *purdah* (the Persian word for "curtain"), or the prohibition against women participating in public life or having contact with any men other than their husbands or those close relatives whom they are forbidden to marry. In Afghanistan, these "restrictions severely limit women's activities, including access to education and employment outside the home. Many [women] are largely confined to their homes."

The King was assassinated in 1933, leaving his throne to his 19-year old son Zahir. King Zahir Shah would preside over the slow improvement of living conditions in Afghanistan for over 40 years after his father's death in 1933. As Prime Minister, the King's first cousin Muhammed Daoud Khan strove to develop Afghanistan's economy by securing vast amounts of economic and military aid from the neighbouring Soviet Union. The U.S. also initiated several important development projects in Afghanistan, but declined to supply military aid.

In 1959, Prime Minister Daoud created a major cultural crisis when the wives and daughters of the Afghan royal family appeared unveiled for the first time since Amanullah's reign. Many religious leaders publicly condemned this display, but Daoud argued that Islam did not make the veiling and seclusion of women obligatory. Other educated women, particularly in Kabul, then began to abandon the veil, including growing numbers of nurses, midwives, and teachers.

In response, the more conservative mullahs provoked riots and acid attacks on unveiled women, until Daoud had about 50 of them jailed and charged with treason and heresy. Daoud's government quelled an armed uprising in Kandahar with advanced weaponry obtained from the Soviet Union. Daoud finally released the mullahs from custody, and they brought the unrest to a halt, agreeing that each Afghan family would be allowed to decide for itself whether its women would practice *purdah*.

In the 1960s, Afghanistan's third constitution propelled the nation further towards democracy and respect for human rights, but like its 1923 model it would eventually fall to a combination of foreign intervention and the violent opposition of local radicals. This time, the communists and fundamentalists would divide the country between them. King Zahir Shah set out to establish a constitutional monarchy that would provide for more democratic input and thereby build public support for the regime.

Despite Daoud's large victories in winning superpower development aid and ensuring greater participation for Afghan women in public life, the King successfully pressured him to resign as Prime Minister in 1963. The next year, a Loya Jirga ratified a new constitution, drafted with French assistance. Afghanistan's 1964 constitution "limited the monarch's absolute power through the creation of a parliament and the clear separation of powers." The King could no longer enact laws without the approval of both houses of parliament. But he retained broad executive powers, including the powers to declare war and command the army; to appoint the Prime Minister and one-third of the Afghan Senate, dissolve the parliament, and veto legislation; and to appoint the members of the Supreme Court. The lower house of the Afghan parliament and one-third of the Afghan Senate would be elected to four-year terms by direct elections, subject to the King dissolving parliament and calling new elections at any time and for any cause.

The 1964 constitution loosened the requirements of previous Afghan constitutions that the state be governed in accordance with Shariah law. Like the 1923 constitution, it recognized Islam as the "sacred" and official religion of Afghanistan. But the 1964 constitution did not require that all Afghan laws conform to Shariah as such, stating that "there shall be no law repugnant to the basic *principles* of the sacred religion of Islam and the other values embodied in this constitution." Similarly, the constitution no longer anointed the King as the "protector of the true religion of Islam"; instead it urged him to "protect the sacred *principles* of the religion of Islam." These references to general "principles" provided the legislature with greater leeway to enact laws that presented some tension with the tenets of Islamic law taken literally. Finally, the 1964 constitution no longer gave Shariah equal status with Afghanistan's "general civil and criminal laws," but made it authoritative only where no statute existed in the area.

One victory for religious conservatives in the 1964 constitution would have important consequences in post-Taliban Afghanistan, and that is the empowerment of the judiciary to enforce the Hanafi school of Islamic Shariah jurisprudence as Afghan law. The Hanafi school is perhaps the least accommodating of the four major schools of Shariah law to the autonomy of women and children, as it has traditionally been construed to allow marriages to be contracted by a guardian on behalf of a minor child and to forbid women from securing a divorce under most circumstances. The 1964 constitution stated that where no law existed in an area, "the provisions of the Hanafi jurisprudence of the Shariaat of Islam shall be considered as law," and required Afghan court, to render justice in cases not controlled by the constitution or statutory law "by following the basic principles of the Hanafi jurisprudence of the Shariaat of Islam."

Although many subsequent commentators have stressed that the 1964 Constitution granted greater rights to Afghan women, the document did not make substantial advances in reforming women's rights within the legal or judicial system. The 1964 constitution gave all Afghan "people" equal rights and obligations before the law, as the 1923 constitution had given all Afghan "subjects" equal rights and duties before the law.

Following the example of the 1923 constitution, women's equality and most of the other rights recognized in the 1964 constitution, including the right to liberty, property, freedom of speech and association, education, and employment, could be limited by provisions of the law.

The 1964 constitution did innovate by granting Afghan women unprecedented opportunity to participate in government. Women won the right to vote in parliamentary elections, be elected to parliament, serve as members of government, and even become government ministers. These rights became a reality for the first time in Afghan history, as women helped vote several of their number into parliament, and a woman became Minister of Public Health in 1965.

Ultimately, the 1964 constitution's most enduring legacy may be that radical elements in Afghan society misused its freedoms to prepare the way for dictatorship and the deaths of countless Afghans. Afghan communists, some of whom had been barred from Kabul University or recalled from study or work in the U.S. for expressing their radical ideas, became free to organize.

Although the Kabul area elected a few Afghan women and leftists as representatives in the first elections under the 1964 Constitution, the parliament as a whole was dominated by the rural landowners and conservative religious leaders who could afford the high costs of running for office, which led many progressive young students and middle-class Afghans in Kabul to despair of democracy, and seek more radical solutions. In 1965, Muhammed Taraki and Babrak Karmal founded the People's Democratic Party of Afghanistan (PDPA), the Communist Party of Afghanistan "in all but name."

The PDPA attracted a growing membership among young students and intellectuals in Kabul University and the urban Afghan middle class. Afghan voters elected three PDPA members to the Afghan parliament in 1965, including Karmal. The Principal of Kabul Teachers College, Hafizullah Amin, joined the PDPA and was elected to parliament in 1969. Each of these three men - Taraki, Karmal, and Amin would go on to assume the helm of dictatorial left-wing Afghan regimes.

Prominent Afghan fundamentalists lacked the public support necessary to be elected as such to the parliament as PDPA members were, but they organized disciplined cadres of followers during the 1960s and 1970s. The ideas of the Egyptian fundamentalist Sayyed Qutb, the "intellectual light" of the Muslim Brotherhood, "attracted particular interest" in the Kabul Shariah faculty, which Kabul University opened in 1952.

Al-Aznar of University in Egypt, which had taken the Kabul Shariah faculty under its wing, was a centre of the Muslim Brotherhood's fundamentalist political activity. The head of the Kabul Shariah department, Professor Ghulam Muhammed Niazi, was deeply influenced by the Muslim Brotherhood's campaign for Islamic fundamentalist rule while studying at al-Aznar University. The fundamentalist program of the Muslim Brotherhood and its progeny of jihadist groups is, in brief, a holy war that would replace the corrupt monarchs of Muslim countries with Islamic states that would govern all aspects of life, strictly segregating men and women and providing "humanity a complete cure for all its ills."

From his perch as professor of Shariah law, Professor Niazi led the fundamentalist movement in Afghanistan. He established cells in Kabul and Paghman dedicated to formulating strategy, and developed contacts with sympathetic government officials. Joining Professor Niazi in his campaign for an Islamic revolution in Afghanistan were two other graduates of al-Azhar University, whose fundamentalism would determine the course of Afghan history for generations: Burhannudin Rabbani and Abdul Rasul Sayyaf. Mr. Rabbani, who had translated the writings of Sayyed Qutb into the Afghan language of Dari, succeeded Professor Niazi as Amir of the Islamic Association of Afghanistan in 1972. Around this time, a young student leader at Kabul University named Gulbuddin Hekmatyar joined the Muslim Brotherhood and shortly became famous for throwing acid in the faces of unveiled Afghan women. Rabbani, Sayyaf, and Hekmatyar would each go on to lead the fundamentalist revolt against the Afghan constitutional monarchy, then the Afghan communists, and finally against the Soviet occupation of Afghanistan.

Eventually, each of them would govern entire mini-states, but none of them could ever quite manage to bring all of Afghanistan under his faction's control.

Socialist and Communist Dictatorship

Despite Afghanistan's slow but steady progress in promoting democratic input and women's rights under Zahir Shah, Afghan leftists demanded immediate and sweeping change. But the socialist and communist ideology to which they turned sparked implacable opposition in Afghanistan's conservative religious leaders, setting the stage for the decades-long struggle between Soviet-backed leftist governments and Pakistani-based fundamentalist *jihadi* fighters

With extremists organising feverishly, the Afghan economy entered a tailspin in the early 1970s. Government corruption and a three-year drought from 1969 to 1972 brought on a famine that killed between 100,000 and 500,000 Afghans. The Afghan famine provided an opening for former Prime Minister Daoud, still popular with the Afghan military, to overthrow the monarchy in 1973. Young officers trained in the Soviet Union executed the coup. Afghanistan became a republic, and Daoud its first President. Half of his cabinet ministers in were communists allied with the Parcham faction of the PDPA led by Babruk Karmal, and hundreds more communists entered government ministries and provincial officialdom.

Daoud saw the fundamentalists as the greatest threat to a modern Afghanistan, so he arrested Professor Niazi and 200 other fundamentalist plotters in Kabul. By one account, this action began the war between leftists and fundamentalists that continued for almost 20 years, until the near-obliteration of the leftists and the communist movement after the dissolution of the Soviet Union and the *mujahideen* victory in 1992. The fundamentalists who had fled to Pakistan from Daoud's mass arrests, including Rabbani and Hekmatyar, helped organized a holy war against Daoud's regime from their new base in Pakistan. The most successful operation was an incursion from Pakistan into Afghanistan's Panjshir valley led by Ahmed Shah Massoud, who would become one of Rabbani's best commanders. The revolution failed, however, and the fundamentalist movement splintered into factions led by Rabbani and Hekmatyar.

The 1977 constitution granted President Daoud near-absolute powers, a common theme among Afghan regimes following the fall of the monarchy. It was otherwise a profoundly leftist document, contemplating dramatic economic and judicial reforms. All laws contrary to the "basic principles" of the religion of Islam remained unconstitutional, and judges in the Afghan courts would decide cases before them not governed by statutory law according to Hanafi law. But for the first time in Afghan history, the country's constitution specifically stated that "women and men," and not simply all Afghan "subjects" or "people," were entitled to equality before the law and protection against discrimination. A unicameral legislature elected by all Afghans over the age of 18, half of which would be reserved for farmers and the working class, would draft legislation.

The 1977 constitution was never truly implemented, because even as it was being prepared, the Soviet Union became concerned that Daoud was being drawn into a pro-American stance with Saudi money, and began pressuring the divided Afghan communists to unite to overthrow him, which they did. When Daoud issued an order for his communist opponents to be arrested, it triggered a revolution.

During its long reign, and despite massive foreign aid, the monarchy had done little to improve Afghanistan's standing as one of the poorest, least healthy, and worst educated countries in the world. In the late 1970s, even after some of Daoud's reforms, 50% of Afghan children died before reaching the age of five, 80% of Afghan children received no education, and "the per capita income, at $157, was one of the lowest in the world."

In April 1978, communist military officers turned Afghanistan's air force and tanks against the Daoud regime. The air force bombed the presidential palace, killing President Daoud and many members of his family. The first decree of the leaders of the revolution bestowed ultimate authority on the head of the PDPA, Nur Muhammed Taraki. Another decree gave men and women equal rights, prohibited forced marriages, established a minimum marriageable age of 16 for girls, and reduced the bride price to a low fixed minimum amount to discourage the widespread sale of young Afghan girls by their parents. "The Government called for women to enjoy freedom, to dress as they please, work in the civil service, armed forces and other institutions and enjoy other equal rights." Taraki's regime introduced universal education for boys and girls and a campaign against illiteracy, and enacted a "far-reaching redistribution of land" from large landlords to peasants.

President Taraki's government rapidly lost control of the country to anti-regime forces, which in early 1979 led several Afghan provinces in open rebellion, including Nuristan and Hazarajat. Iranian fundamentalists, fresh from establishing the Iranian theocracy under

Ayatollah Ruhollah Khomeini, inspired a revolt in the large Afghan city of Herat close to the Iranian border, drawing on outrage there against the government's efforts to promote Afghan women's literacy. An army officer named Ismail Khan organized a mutiny of the Afghan armed forces in the Herat area. In response, the government bombed the city and waged a devastating assault with tanks and helicopters, killing up to 20,000 people and razing many buildings. These events prompted Prime Minister Amin, who had gained influence over the Afghan security services, to seize power, killing his former comrade Taraki.

In July 1979, U.S. President Jimmy Carter signed a National Security Directive authorising secret American aid to the Pakistan-based rebellion against the Afghan government. President Carter's National Security Adviser advised him at the time that this aid would likely result in a Soviet invasion, and later boasted of "drawing the Russians into the Afghan trap." On December 27, 1979, Soviet forces in and around Kabul captured the main government ministries, neutralized key Afghan army units, and fanned out to other major Afghan cities such as Herat and Kandahar. Soon the Soviet occupying army reached 85,000 men. Before the Red Army's defeat almost another 700,000 men would follow.

The Soviets installed PDPA founder Babruk Karmal as President of Afghanistan. Karmal promulgated a new constitution in 1980 that purported to establish the rule of the Afghan people and recognize a similar list of individual rights as those recognized in previous constitutions. The constitution no longer enshrined Islam as a bulwark of the government's legitimacy. All political parties other than the PDPA were outlawed. With the Red Army occupying the nerve centres of Afghan society, moreover, the Soviet leadership, rather than the PDPA or the Afghan people, was the real power in Afghanistan during the 1980s.

Karmal and his Soviet handlers reaffirmed and expanded the efforts of Daoud and Taraki regimes before them to promote greater equality for Afghan women. The communists "officially sanctioned a wider public role for women, whose status improved." By 1985, 65% of the students at Kabul University were women, and Afghan women worked in most government agencies, social organisations, factories, the national airline, and the health care sector. By the time the communists lost power, "women accounted for 70 percent of teachers, 50 percent of government workers, and 40 percent of medical doctors." Women worked as police officers, members of the military, and journalists. Afghan women increasingly appeared unveiled in public, as their counterparts in Soviet Central Asia had done decades previously. Communist reforms intruded into Afghan family life when the communists banned the purchase and sale of young girls as wives, and provoked rage by demanding that fathers allow their daughters to learn to read. The regime's family courts were "mostly presided over by female judges" and protected women's rights in marriage and divorce and to equitable child custody and support.

Whatever hope existed for true equality between Afghan women and men, rich and poor, was lost in the genocidal war between Soviet and Afghan communist forces and the fundamentalist insurgents backed by the Western and wider Islamic worlds. Both sides abandoned laws and constitutions in a common descent into wanton violations of human rights.

U.S. President Ronald Reagan and Pakistani dictator Zia ul-Haq directed billions in American military aid for the *mujahideen*, mostly to "the more extreme Sunni fundamentalist faction led by Gulbuddin Hekmatyar." Hekmatyar used the money to organize a tightly disciplined faction for the day when he would "impose an authoritarian Islamic state that would sequester women and punish Moslems who don't practice their faith." With great violence, his party forced Afghan women refugees in Pakistan to bury themselves in *burqas*. Several Afghan women were murdered in Pakistan simply for failing to cover their hair.

Saudi Arabia favoured the armies of Abdul Rasul Sayyaf, whose party "recruited thousands of fighters from Arab countries." Like Hetmatyar, Sayyaf had little indigenous support in Afghanistan, but grew powerful because of the prolific Saudi money and foreign weaponry at its disposal. In 1980, Sayyaf recruited a number of "Afghan Arabs" to the Afghan cause, including Osama bin Laden, who was working with the CIA at the time. The CIA supported Pakistani efforts to "recruit radical Muslims from around the world" to fight in Afghanistan. Over 35,000 radicals from Muslim countries, mostly Arabs, signed up to fight in the "holy war," and 65,000 had "direct contact" with the war. Over 12,000 Arabs and others received training in "bomb-making, sabotage and urban guerrilla warfare" in camps the CIA helped build. These Arab fighters would develop into the *al Qaeda* terrorist organisation and become the military backbone of the Taliban movement.

By 1987, the communists and fundamentalists had killed more than one million Afghans by some estimates, and had driven another seven million from their homes. The Soviets carpet bombed major

Afghan cities such as Herat and Kandahar into ruins, wiped half of Afghanistan's villages off the map, and destroyed much of the country's farmland. Nevertheless, the Afghan resistance continually replenished its dead with new recruits from the millions of refugees in Pakistan and Iran, and armed them with fresh infusions of American and Saudi aid. The *mujahideen* gained control of up to 90% of the countryside and became "immensely wealthy" by making it the world's second largest opium producing land.

Although the scale of the bombing and shelling of Afghan cities and towns posed the greatest threat to human rights, the *mujahideen*'s fundamentalist policies promised to overturn decades of progress towards including Afghan women in public life. During the 1980s, women rarely walked the streets in rebel-controlled regions of Afghanistan. "Those who leave their homes wear the chador [or *burqa*], a voluminous shroud covering the wearer from head to toe, and may only survey the world through a 4-by-4-inch rectangle of netting extending from the tip of the nose to the eyebrows." In Pakistani refugee camps run by the rebels, women were denied access to areas containing men, and prohibiting from seeing male doctors. (When the Taliban continued these policies, the U.S. cited them to help justify the war.)

In 1987, the new Soviet leader Mikhail Gorbachev decided to withdraw entirely from Afghanistan. The Soviets planned to leave the country to Najib Allah, the former head of the Afghan secret police, who had taken over from Karmal as the Afghan communist leader in 1986. Najib Allah convened a Loya Jirga in 1987 to signal the moderation of the communist regime's policies.

The 1987 constitution it passed once again enshrined Islam as the sacred religion of Afghanistan and provided that no law could be contrary to its "principles" and the other values in the constitution. It guaranteed equal rights to men and women and among religious minorities in a similar manner to previous constitutions, and provided for a number of individual rights to be defined in accordance with the law. The ruling communist PDPA party lost its majority of seats in parliament after elections held in 1988 pursuant to the new constitution, and a member of Daoud's pre-communist government became Prime Minister. Najib Allah even reserved seats in parliament for *mujahideen* leaders, and invited them to lay down their arms and participate in a mixed government, an offer that they refused.

The Soviets completed their withdrawal from Afghanistan in 1989. The day after the last troops had returned, Gorbachev proposed a ceasefire between the communists and fundamentalist parties to U.S.

President George H.W. Bush, with the two superpowers agreeing to halt shipments of weapons until democratic elections under U.N. supervision could be held. The Bush administration and the Afghan rebels refused to negotiate, with the result that for years, the *mujahideen* supplied by the U.S. continued devastating rocket attacks on Afghan towns and cities, killing up to 40 people in each blast.

Nevertheless, the Afghan communist regime of Najib Allah survived, sustained by a combination of rebel infighting and billions of dollars in Soviet military aid. Najib Allah convened a Loya Jirga in 1990, promising to achieve national reconciliation and moderate the communist face of the Afghan government. The resulting 1990 constitution proclaimed Afghanistan a multiparty state to be governed according to laws in conformity with the principles of Islam, including the right to own and inherit property pursuant to Shariah law. The commanding heights of the economy remained state property, but private investment was allowed, at least in theory. The National Assembly, selected by a mixture of direct elections and appointments as under previous constitutions, approved laws prior to the President's signature, with a Constitutional Commission exercising limited review.

Fundamentalist Rule

As many had predicted, the victory of the Afghan rebels brought civil war, fundamentalist outrages, and thousands of atrocities against civilians. The "Islamic revolution" triumphed in Kabul in April 1992. The military defence of Kabul unravelled due to the collapse of the Soviet Union in 1991 and the defection of Afghan communist military commander Rashid Dostum to the rebels in March of 1992. But after the communist regime fell, the war continued. With no communists left to fight, the *mujahideen* leaders were left to wage a bitter struggle for power among themselves, as Najib Allah had predicted in 1990.

The *mujahideen* perpetrated frequent massacres and "indiscriminate killing," as well as "rape, torture and looting." Joined by General Dostum's tanks, Hekmatyar's forces finished the job of destroying Afghanistan's housing stock and architectural heritage by rocketing the Afghan capital Kabul into ruins. Almost 20,000 Afghans were killed or injured during the fighting in 1993. In 1994, the United Nations reported that Kabul, spared the type of bombing to which Kandahar had been subjected by the Soviets, had become "the most destroyed city in Afghanistan." The warring factions killed about 50,000 Kabulis and committed many "medieval atrocities."

The victorious fundamentalist armies subjected Afghan women to some of the worst treatment in Afghan history. The State Department reported that the *mujaheddin* were responsible for "innumerable cases of rape." Human Rights Watch described 1992-1995 as the worst period in Afghan history, replete with "mass rapes" and the indiscriminate slaughter of civilians. *Mujahideen* fighters kidnapped many Afghan women for purposes of sexual slavery, as a "method of intimidating vanquished populations and of rewarding soldiers."

While the soldiers of the victorious rebel armies ran wild, discipline was reserved for Afghan women. In 1994, the Supreme Court of the Islamic state of Afghanistan issued a series of rulings requiring a woman to "wear a full-body veil" and stating that she "must not leave her house without her husband's permission," and "must not look at strangers." Other courts issued rulings ordering that women be stoned to death for adultery or other crimes.

The "valiant and courageous Afghan freedom fighters" also persecuted religious minorities viciously. On February 11 1993, the military forces of President Burhanuddin Rabbani and his ally Abdul Rasul Sayyaf occupied a Kabul suburb populated largely with minority Shia Hazaras. Their armies killed "'up to 1,000 civilians', beheading old men, women, children and even their dogs, stuffing their bodies down the wells."

Finally, Afghanistan under *mujahideen* rule became known for training and harbouring international terrorists. Ramzi Yousef, who masterminded the 1993 World Trade Centre bombing, had fought under the command of Abdul Rasul Sayyaf, the junior partner in Rabbani's *mujahideen* government. The U.S. government issued a report in the 1990s in which it cited Saudi-backed *mujahideen* commander Sayyaf for "continuing to harbour and train potential terrorists." Sayyaf's faction maintained close contact throughout the 1990s with Osama bin Laden, and welcomed him back to Afghanistan in 1996.

Rise and Fall of the Taliban Theocracy

The Atrocities and Tyranny of the Taliban

Almost three years after the fall of the communist government, the *mujahideen* had failed to establish an effective central government or national judicial system. Instead of establishing law and order, their forces were killing, raping, and looting at will, and had "blocked food and medical supplies desperately needed by [the Afghan] people." An estimated 100,000 Afghans died in Kabul alone prior to the Taliban takeover in 1996. All told, about 400,000 Afghan civilians died in the civil wars and humanitarian disasters of the 1990s.

In early 1994, according to their own legend, a group of former *mujahideen* fighters and Islamic students, or Taliban, joined together to fight the "Muslims who had gone wrong," and started by freeing young boys and girls from local warlords who had kidnapped them for rape. As the future President of Afghanistan, Hamid Karzai, testified before Congress, the "Taliban emerged when Afghans were desperately looking for a savior," and their "emergence was supported by the majority of the Afghan people" who hoped that they would "end the bloodshed" and bring "peace and stability." The Taliban selected Muhammed Omar as their leader, a village mullah from a backward area of southern Afghanistan who had fought in the American-backed *jihad* against the post-Soviet Afghan government of Najib Allah.

The U.S. and its allies in Pakistan and Saudi Arabia initially supported the Taliban movement. Their critical military, financial, and diplomatic aid to the Taliban transformed a ragtag gang of fighters into a sophisticated army with tanks, artillery, bombers, and an intelligence capability. With fresh infusions of foreign financing and manpower for each new offensive, the Taliban defeated every major *mujahideen* commander.

The Taliban captured Kandahar in 1994 largely by bribing local commanders with over $1.5 million probably provided by Saudi Arabia via Pakistan. They doled out more cash to buy control of Uruzgan and Zabul provinces, and occupied Herat with tens of thousands of Pakistani recruits and "arms, ammunition, and vehicles provided by Pakistan and Saudi Arabia." In 1996, Saudi and Pakistani intelligence orchestrated the triumph of the Taliban revolution by helping ensure the fall of Kabul and Jalalabad.

As many as 8,000 more residents of Kabul died in the fighting and the ensuing Taliban atrocities. In response, many of the *mujahideen* leaders whose factions had opened the way for the Taliban revolution by abusing the Afghan population for years formed the Northern Alliance. But angered by the looting and routine violence against civilians that had characterized *mujahideen* rule, some Kabul residents initially welcomed the Taliban, even after thousands of Kabulis died in the battle for the city.

The Taliban persecuted the Shia Muslims, who then made up as much as 20% of the Afghan population, even more brutally than had the *mujahideen* under Rabbani and Sayyaf. A mutiny in Mazari-Sharif opened the door to Taliban occupation of that city; although 3,000 Taliban died in an uprising that followed, the Taliban retook the city in 1998, backed by Pakistani intelligence officers and even Pakistani troops. The victorious Taliban slaughtered up to 8,000 civilians in a frenzy of killing and rape directly mostly at the Shia Hazara. The Hazara holdout of Bamiyan was the last major city to fall, with more mass murders of Shias the result, including of hospital patients roused from their beds. The post-Taliban governor of Bamiyan has estimated that 20,000 Shias and others died in this way. Iran mobilized its army to intervene against the massacres and systematic rape of Shias, but backed down under pressure from the U.N. Security Council. The genocidal killing continued into 2001, as Pakistan continued to deliver military aid to the Taliban in violation of U.N. sanctions.

The Taliban aimed to install a government and legal system that would revive a life like pious Muslims had lived "1,400 years ago." The Attorney General of the Taliban declared: "The Constitution is the Shariah so we don't need a constitution." The Taliban believed that the principal purpose of the anti-Soviet *jihad* had been the establishment of Shariah law, and indeed that is how the *mujahideen* leaders who had been fighting for Shariah from bases in Pakistan even prior to the communist coup in 1978 explained their war at the time.

Saudi Arabia, the primary backer of the Taliban along with Pakistan, served as the model for the Taliban state. Saudi Arabia is a fundamentalist monarchy, whose constitution demands allegiance to its founding King and his "children's children" in the name of religion. Its government tortures members of religious minorities and its religious police administer beatings to women who reveal their faces, hair, or bodies in public. The Saudi government helped create the Taliban, encouraged them to give refuge to bin Laden, and tutored them in theocracy. The Saudi Ministry for the Propagation of Virtue and the Prevention of Vice trained a similar Taliban agency in enforcing Saudi-style laws, including the near-total covering of women.

The resulting system of Taliban law involved severe criminal sanctions, enforced with great capriciousness and corruption, against any activities viewed as sinful or otherwise harmful. The Taliban's prohibitions addressed activities prohibited by religious tradition as harmful to the person (drugs and alcohol, gambling, and usury); sexuality and Western fashions (music and dancing, British or American hairstyles, the shaving of men's beards, women's high-heeled shoes, and fashion magazines); "idolatry" (photographs, paintings, statues, and sorcery); and other relatively harmless activities that might lead to gambling or distract from prayer (television, sports, kite-flying and the keeping of birds as pets). Proving the old adage that the law often falls behind advances in technology, however, the Taliban did not prohibit use of the Internet until July 2001, half a decade after banning kite-flying in 1996.

The mode of enforcement of the Taliban's prohibitions proved as uncompromising as the bans themselves. Torture by various methods was routine and vicious under the Taliban. Violations of the Taliban dress code and inappropriate male-female contact were cause for being beaten black and blue with clubs or rifle butts. Implementing Taliban law required stoning adulterers and amputating the hands of criminals, medieval punishments which had been abandoned by most Muslim countries.

While Afghan men suffered conscription into the Taliban army, bitter fighting in the north of the country, imprisonment or murder for their religious or political affiliation, and denial of virtually any access to entertainment or unrelated members of the opposite sex, they enjoyed some ability to go to school, find a job, and travel. The Taliban kept Afghan women, by contrast, largely shuttered indoors. Upon taking power in Kandahar in 1994, the Taliban forbade the education of girls and the employment of most women outside of their homes. After becoming the rulers of most of Afghanistan in 1996, the Taliban's religious police decreed that women must wear all-covering *burqas*, which many Afghan women could not even afford (as they cost about two months' wages), effectively sentencing them to house arrest. The Taliban ordered women to stay in their homes as much as possible, ended the rudimentary female education and employment that the *mujahideen* had allowed to continue, and allowed women to see only female doctors, while banning women from practicing medicine.

Building A New Afghan Government

The Bush administration, in response to the terrorist attacks of September 11, 2001, demanded that the Taliban cease harbouring Osama bin Laden and the *al Qaeda* terrorist organisation, and threatened war and the destruction of their government if they refused. But the Taliban declined to hand over bin Laden, the Saudi terrorist leader and *mujahideen* fighter suspected of masterminding or inspiring the 9/11 attacks; bin Laden had contributed about $100 million to the Taliban by that time. A Taliban spokesman, however, indicated that the regime would hand bin Laden over for trial, provided that the U.S. provided evidence of his responsibility for the 9/11 attacks, which the

U.S. had provided only to its "key allies." On October 7, 2001, the U.S. began bombing *al Qaeda* terrorist targets and Afghan military, electricity, and communications facilities. Special forces units on the ground provided the targeting coordinates for U.S. aerial bombing, which destroyed the Taliban tanks and troops that had held off the Northern Alliance opposition for years. Hundreds of Taliban conscripts and hardcore troops died in the fighting, including many prisoners of war summarily executed by Northern Alliance gunfire or suffocation in sealed truck containers. Thousands of Afghan civilians died in the U.S. bombing raids and the ground operations that mopped up after them. Whole families were cut down, sometimes as a result of apparently indiscriminate bombing based on innacurate or misleading information.

Driving the Taliban before them, the luminaries of the anti-Soviet *jihad* retook their former positions in Herat, Bamiyan, and Kandahar, the prize of Kabul going to the forces of former President Rabbani, now led by Ahmed Shah Massoud's successor Muhammad Fahim. Former *mujahideen* deputy foreign minister Hamid Karzai, leader of the largest Pashtun tribe, entered Afghanistan after September 11 to raise a Pashtun rebellion against the Taliban, joining Gul Agha Shirzai in taking Kandahar.

The occupation of Kabul by the Northern Alliance created a political crisis for the U.S. and the U.N., which had urged their forces to hold back from taking the city until a broad-based government could be formed. Under pressure from the U.S. and other nations, Northern Alliance commanders and other Afghan military factions agreed to participate in U.N.-sponsored talks held in Bonn, Germany. Almost two dozen Afghan delegates, mostly drawn from the Northern Alliance and the circle around former King Zahir Shah, signed an accord called for the creation of an Interim Authority to rule Afghanistan until a Transitional Authority government could be selected in a Loya Jirga six months later, and a "fully representative government" freely elected two years after that. Although loyalists to the former King Zahir Shah initially voted that he return to power, the U.S. and U.N. secured the delegates' agreement to appoint Pashtun anti-Taliban leader Hamid Karzai as Chairman of the Afghan Interim Authority.

Over 1,000 elected and 700 selected delegates to the June 2002 Emergency Loya Jirga established the Islamic Transitional Authority of Afghanistan and elected Hamid Karzai as its President. Despite the support of a majority of delegates at one point, the former King of Afghanistan Mohammad Zahir Shah withdrew his name from consideration for the presidency, prompting Human Rights Watch to accuse the U.S. of "'brazen' interference in the loya jirga, [which was] promoted as the birth of Afghani democracy." Some delegates also objected that *mujahideen* commanders who had killed innocent Afghan civilians were wielding too much control over the Afghan political process. "We were told that this loya jirga would not include all the people who had blood on their hands," said one delegate to applause.

Warlord Theocracy and Human Rights Violations

Bonn's aspirations for government under law and with respect for human rights have yet to be realized throughout Afghanistan. Of course, the Karzai administration inherited a miserable and barely functioning country from the Taliban and Northern Alliance forces who had controlled it through 2001: average life expectancy was only 40 years, 70% of Afghans were malnourished, more infants died in childhood and more mothers died in childbirth than in almost any other country ever recorded in human history, and millions of children had been orphaned in the various wars since 1978. But none of these poor health statistics can justify the sorts of human rights violations that have occurred in Afghanistan since the Taliban's fall.

The Karzai government began as "an island in a sea of uncompromising warlords" who field large militias outside the framework of the Afghan National Army and exercise totalitarian theocratic powers. Most rural areas and even major cities are not under the firm control of the central government, especially at night. According to a member of the Afghanistan Independent Human Rights Commission, "trials do not take place in accordance with law. In provinces, warlords are the law, the judge, the government."

Abdul Rasul Sayyaf, a Wahhabi fundamentalist sent to Afghanistan in the 1980s by Saudi Arabia to promote its ideology, controls much of Kabul province. The governor of Kabul province and many of the city's police and intelligence officials are loyal to him, his troops patrol western Kabul, and even President Karzai himself is reportedly "often forced to bow to [his] demands." International peacekeepers in Kabul "have publicly accused... troops under his control of being responsible for a series of murders, abductions and extortion incidents in that sector of the city, aided by a cadre of loyalists in the police department." Following mainstream Saudi ideology, his forces "continue to enforce strict Islamic social codes including restrictions on women's education and dress." Sayyaf's forces have tortured villagers and old people for such crimes as listening to music. He views any attempt to question his authority as a form of blasphemy, and had two newspaper editors arrested on blasphemy charges and sentenced to death for criticizing his tactics.

The authorities in Kandahar, Afghanistan's second largest city, continue to implement the rural Pashtun traditions that the Taliban proclaimed to be requirements of Islam. Young girls are forced into marriage under pain of imprisonment; one received a five-year sentence for refusing to go along with an arranged marriage. The police jailed another woman for refusing to enter into a marriage with a man to whom she had been promised by her parents when she was only two years old. Kandahar's post-Taliban legal officials imprisoned a woman who escaped after being held as a sex slave for seven years; she had been sold for about $200 during Taliban times to a man who raped her repeatedly. Because of cases like these, the head of a major nongovernmental organisation working in Afghanistan reported that she could "see no change for most women" in Kandahar since the Taliban lost power.

In the north, a campaign of ethnic cleansing against Pashtuns has raged. Soldiers and armed militia in northern Afghanistan have rounded up and shot dozens of Pashtun men at a time, raping many Pashtun women and young girls, a crime that can lead to the murder of its victim by members of her own family in conservative rural Afghanistan. The militia of former communist commander General Dostum raped whole families of women, including girls as young as 10. A U.N. official called the abuses against ethnic Pashtuns "systematic and wide scale." Thousands of Pashtuns fled their homes, some living in caves to keep warm.

For most of the past four years, a "hardline Islamist" ruled Herat, a historically more liberal city near the Iranian border that is widely viewed as a litmus test for human rights after the Taliban. The security forces of Governor Ismail Khan borrowed a page from neighbouring Iran, which Khan called "the best model of an Islamic country in the world," using beatings and torture to silence political opponents, journalists and human right activists. Women complained that his regime resembled that of the Taliban, as their mode of dress was confined to two options: *burqas* or full-body veils (known as *chadoris*) that expose only the face. The police in Herat ordered that 10 forced gynecological examinations be conducted every day to test the chastity of girls or women arrested on suspicion of immoral conduct. Although President Karzai promoted Ismail Khan from Governor to the Ministry of Mines in September of 2004, he continued to field a militia, and thousands of petty warlords with similar ideologies continue to hold power in their respective fiefdoms.

The principal engine of theocratic tendencies on a national basis has been the Afghan courts, the policies of which have been indistinguishable in some respects from the Taliban's. As a respected religious scholar among *mujahideen*, Sayyaf persuaded Afghan transitional president Hamid Karzai to declare Afghanistan an "Islamic" state after the Loya Jirga, and to ensure that "Afghanistan's justice system will be based on the Quran and Shariah law." Sayyaf, the Northern Alliance's "No. 2 political leader," threatened guerilla war against the government if his demands were not met. Foremost among these demands is gender apartheid.

Sayyaf prevailed upon President Karzai to appoint as Chief Justice of Afghanistan's Supreme Court Fazal Hadi Shinwari, a fundamentalist member of Sayyaf's political party who is not even trained in Afghan constitutional or statutory law. Shinwari has "called for Taliban-style punishments and brought back the Taliban's dreaded Ministry for the Promotion of Virtue and Prevention of Vice," which "deploys squads to stop public displays of 'un-Islamic' behaviour among Afghan women." A list of laws and policies being enforced in Afghanistan reads like the Taliban's handbook: women cannot speak in private with men, young people can be arrested if they marry without their parents' consent, women are forbidden to travel without supervision of a male family member, married women are denied the ability to attend high school, education of women together with men is banned, and women are restrained from singing in public. Most women remain confined to their homes as many Afghan men, backed by the judiciary, continue to treat women "according to the old Taliban ways."

Shinwari's influence stretches far beyond the Supreme Court. He has "appointed most of Afghanistan's current judiciary — mostly clerics in rural areas — as well as many of the country's provincial governors, especially near Kabul." He used this power to appoint Afghans with only informal religious training and little experience to the bench, including almost 130 of his political allies to the Afghan Supreme Court, while women judges with decades of experience in the Afghan judiciary were denied posts. As a result, the Afghan courts are "dominated by religious conservatives who have more in common with the Taliban than with Karzai."

The U.S. promised that an Afghan commission on judicial reform would rein in Mr. Shinwari's theocratic excesses. But due to the fundamentalists' control over the political process, judicial reform long stood at a standstill, even backsliding into increasing control by extremists. The Judicial Reform Commission was dissolved in 2002, "reportedly obstructed by religious hard-liners." The Supreme Court is itself violating the constitution by being packed with too many justices. Moreover, little or nothing has been done to ensure that judges are qualified, that criminal defendants have access to defence attorneys, that lawyers have access to books containing the laws currently in effect, or that endemic corruption ends. Prison conditions are horrifying, and torture is common. Far from secular reformists gaining ground, Sayyaf himself is said to be next in line to be Afghanistan's Chief Justice.

The New Afghan Constitution

The Constitution Drafting Process

The Bonn agreement provided for a Constitutional Commission to draft a new constitution for review and adoption by a Constitutional Loya Jirga to be convened by October 2003. President Karzai appointed a nine-member Constitutional Drafting Commission, which included two women, and a 35-member Constitutional Review Commission, which included seven women. President Karzai appointed Vice President Nematullah Shahrani, a prominent conservative, to head both commissions, a signal to many that the constitution would establish a national religion and mandate strict religious law.

Past Afghan constitutions failed to ensure national unity and long-term stability, partially because the population as a whole felt excluded from the drafting process. To involve the Afghan people in the framing of their constitution, the Afghan government and international community planned to submit the draft document to a broadly representative Constitutional Loya Jirga, which was held in December 2003. In addition, the U.N. helped organize a public consultation process to include thousands of ordinary Afghans. Still, most rural Afghans never heard of the constitutional process underway in their country until it was already over.

The Ideological Battle for the Future of Afghanistan

Given the decades-old struggle within Afghan society between secularists and fundamentalists, the role of religion in the new constitution was bound to be contentious. Fundamentalists such as Rabbani and Sayyaf used their representatives on the Constitutional Commission and the Supreme Court to fight for a constitutional mandate of theocracy. Experts warned that these leaders wanted their "conservative interpretation of Shariah law incorporated into the next

Afghan Constitution." International human rights activists, on the other hand, advocated a constitution that respected religious difference and closed the door on the totalitarian fundamentalism that killed so many Afghans in the 1990s.

A commission of human rights activists and Islamic law scholars recommended that the new constitution shy away from mandating one man's version of Shariah or Islam, and retain instead the flexibility of the 1964 constitution's requirement of governance in conformity with the "basic principles of Islam." Amnesty International and Human Rights Watch recommended other improvements to the draft constitution in terms of religious freedom and due process.

Afghan activists also demanded strong protection for women's rights. Afghanistan's Deputy Minister for Women's Affairs argued for an express ban on all forms of discrimination against women and a clear requirement of universal education of Afghan women. A conference convened in Kandahar of women leaders from across Afghanistan went further, demanding an "Afghan Women's Bill of Rights" that included equal representation in parliament and the Constitutional Loya Jirga, compulsory education through high school with opportunities for higher education, full property and inheritance rights and participation in economic life, access to modern health services and reproductive care, freedom to decide whom to be married to, enforcement of criminal laws against violence and sexual abuse, and an end to the exchange of women as compensation for crimes by one family against another (known as *Bad*).

The draft constitution, unveiled to the public in early November 2003, proclaimed Afghanistan an Islamic state with a national religion. Under the draft, no law could be "contrary to the sacred religion of Islam," Afghan judges must rule in accordance with the provisions of the conservative Hanafi school of jurisprudence of Shariah law, the justices of the Supreme Court must swear to rule in accord with the "provisions" of religion, the President must swear an oath to safeguard religion, and the nation's educational curriculum would be religious in nature.

These articles represented a significant departure from the 1964 constitution, which required Afghan law to be consistent merely with the general "principles" of Islam rather than a government official's view of what the "religion" itself provides. Under the new draft, "anything that is against Islam could not go forward," because conservatives forces were empowered to "say virtually whatever they want is against Islam."

The draft constitution's almost complete silence on women's rights proved to be its most disappointing and even embittering flaw in the eyes of many activists for women's rights and the rule of law. The draft guaranteed women almost 17% of the seats in the Afghan Senate, but it did not explicitly guarantee women equal rights with men or prohibit discrimination against women, even though similar provisions are contained in several constitutions of majority Islamic countries in the Middle East, the Central Asian former Soviet republics, and South Asia. Nor did it provide Afghan women with rights of equal access to employment, education, and health care, or with any protections against forced marriages, family violence, and sexual abuse. Instead it provided all Afghan "citizens" with equal rights and protection against discrimination, without stating clearly that women are citizens. For these reasons, a Gender and Law Working Group convened by the Ministry of Women's Affairs prepared a number of recommended amendments to the draft constitution, including an anti-discrimination clause, guarantees of equal rights and full citizenship for women; an end to forced marriages and trafficking in women; and a provision outlawing slavery and "slave-like practices."

The Afghan Constitution: Freedom or Theocracy?

On January 4, 2004, the 1,500 Afghan delegates to the Constitutional Loya Jirga (CLJ) ratified the new constitution. The changes to the initial draft reflected a series of hard-fought compromises negotiated among several factions and hundreds of individuals. World leaders, including the President of Afghanistan, the representative of U.N. Secretary-General to Afghanistan, the U.S. Ambassador to Afghanistan, and the U.S. President, immediately hailed the new constitution as a triumph for human rights. President Karzai called it "the most enlightened in that part of the world." The U.S. Ambassador to Afghanistan praised the document as "one of the most enlightened constitutions in the Islamic world."

The Afghans who participated in the constitutional drafting process, and the international community, crafted a charter for their country that stands as an unqualified improvement over the Taliban's unwritten code of theocratic oppression. Among other improvements, the constitution remedied the draft's failure to enshrine women's rights. It now provides that: "Any kind of discrimination and privilege between the citizens of Afghanistan are prohibited. The citizens of Afghanistan - whether man or woman - have equal rights and duties before the law." This clause revives precedents in the 1977 and 1987 constitutions that specifically guaranteed that Afghan women would enjoy equal rights before the law and protection against discrimination. Moreover, the new constitution envisions a level of participation by Afghan women in their country's parliament that surpasses any historical precedent in that country, or indeed in most other countries. On paper, women are guaranteed over 25% of the seats in the lower house of parliament, and almost 17% of the upper house.

But a close examination of the tight relationship the constitution establishes between religious doctrine and the judiciary reveals that the claim that the new constitution is the most "enlightened" in the region, even in the entire Islamic world, is implausible. Although women are equal "before the law," the intention of the Afghan courts and many of the constitution's drafters is that the laws will treat them very differently in many respects, and deny them many liberties available to men. And while they may be ensured a say in parliament, their ability to pass laws improving women's plight in their country will be strictly limited by a veto power the constitution grants to radical fundamentalists in the Afghan judiciary. The constitution also omits elementary protections available to women in other countries where they have not been subjected to the kind of treatment suffered in Afghanistan for many years, such as a ban on slavery and slave-like practices, or a requirement that both parties consent to a marriage.

Many Afghans and international human rights groups have accordingly tempered their praise of the constitution. They have expressed fears that several provisions could be used to enforce medieval interpretations of Islamic Shariah law, suppress religious expression and political speech, and perpetuate Afghan laws and customs that ruthlessly oppress Afghan women. An agenda to accommodate a fundamentalist future for Afghanistan permeated the CLJ, and prevented the new constitution from realising the promises of the U.S. and U.N. that Afghanistan would henceforth abide by international human rights standards.

The warlords and fundamentalist leaders, who issued death threats against more moderate Afghan men and women to deter them from participating in or even attending the CLJ, prevailed on several critical issues that the assembly addressed. Their death threats and vote buying ensured that the "majority" of CLJ delegates were tied to the "warlord controlling the province they came from." Nor did the intimidation end at the doors of the CLJ. The chairman of the CLJ, a former *mujahideen* leader, announced that female delegates should not "try to put yourself on a level with men. Even God has not given you equal rights,... because under his decision two women are counted as equal to one man."

The chairman called for delegates who circulated a petition proposing the removal of the word "Islamic" from the name of the country to be "identified and punished" as infidels, an offence worthy of the death penalty during Afghanistan's recent history.

At the CLJ, the warlords that have ruled most of Afghanistan since the fall of the Taliban succeeded in transforming a clause providing that no law could be contrary to the religion of Islam "and the values of this Constitution" into one that says that "no law can be contrary to the beliefs and provisions of the sacred religion of Islam." Afghan experts and human rights activists regard the new clause as much more subject to abuse by fundamentalists who seek to impose Taliban-like theocratic rule, because the "provisions" of Islam were precisely what the Taliban claimed to be enforcing. Female CLJ delegates and human rights activists therefore view this provision as introducing a strict version of Shariah law by the "back door." The "beliefs and provisions" clause means "that Islamic law is the supreme law of the land," and its content will inevitably be left for a Supreme Court staffed by "hard line Shariah jurists" to interpret. Under the new constitution, the Supreme Court, whose Chief Justice has consistently pushed for a theocratic state in which his interpretation of Islam would hold sway, "can review compliance with the Constitution of laws, legislative decrees, international treaties, and international conventions, and interpret them, in accordance with the law." The constitution grants the Supreme Court, which the Chief Justice has packed with many sympathetic judges who lack training in Afghanistan's civil and secular laws, the "power to reject virtually any law or treaty as un-Islamic."

While failing in some respects to adequately protect human rights, the new constitution doesn't do enough to prohibit Taliban and other war criminals from keeping or winning government posts, and using them to impose fundamentalist rule. Such efforts had precedents in Nazi Germany and Imperial Japan, and would be revived in post-Saddam Hussein Iraq. The new constitution bars only those actually "convicted" of crimes against humanity from becoming President, a Minister, or member of the National Assembly or Supreme Court. The ineffectiveness of this provision results from the fact that despite "the enormous scale of war crimes, crimes against humanity and other serious human rights violations committed in Afghanistan,... no one has yet been tried by a competent court for crimes committed during the long years of conflict in the country." Rather than convening trials, in late 2003 coalition forces "released the Taliban's foreign minister from custody, and prominent Afghan officials... invited him and other Taliban to run for office in the upcoming elections, something that millions of Afghan women are still too afraid to do." After the Karzai government took office, "many former Taliban officials were sitting in the same government positions they held when Mullah Mohammad Omar was still in charge." Other Taliban officials have been wooed with "'the offer of a place in the government.'" Amnesty International thus declared the constitution's efforts to deny power to war criminals "meaningless."

In several other respects, implementation of the rights guaranteed in the constitution seems a distant dream. Shortly after the new constitution was adopted, U.N. Secretary General Kofi Annan's special envoy to Afghanistan warned that "there is no rule of law in this country yet." The Afghan Independent Human Rights Commission received complaints of hundreds of murders in 2003, most blamed on government officials and militia commanders. The Commission has found that "innocent people are put in jail for a very long time and for no reason." There is no sign of these practices having been put to an end by the adoption of the new constitution.

Test Cases for Theocracy Under the Sixth Afghan Constitution

Theocracy is a recurring problem in human history because the corruption and depredations of government by mere men make their countrymen long for a morally infallible ruler. But when political leaders use their military power to promote their own intolerant beliefs, the result has often been mass slaughter and widespread atrocities against members of other faiths, as occurred in the Crusades, counter-Reformation Europe, the European colonies of the New World and Africa, the Ottoman Empire during and after World War I, post-colonial India and Pakistan, and Sudan since 1989. But even mass killings have failed to preserve many theocracies from persistent rebellions led by subjects who chafe under the human rulers' arrogant misrepresentation of their own narrow views as the mandate of heaven.

In the same way, the Taliban, and before them the fundamentalists among the *mujahideen*, forced Shia Muslim Afghans and secularists either to suffer repression or to take up arms against their rulers, which massacred them in return. In the near future, Afghans may be driven into a similar bind by theocratic policies promulgated under cover of constitutional legitimacy. Whether this happens may depend on the success of the warlords and the fundamentalists who dominate the Afghan judiciary in imposing fundamentalist policies that are as damaging to human rights as those that provoke so much opposition in neighbouring Iran that mass killings and systematic torture have been deemed necessary to quell it.

Outlawing Secular Political Parties

A significant challenge to Afghans, especially women, seeking to implement their right to participate in parliamentary elections will be possible legal restrictions that could be used to silence political parties represent ethnic or religious minorities, secularists, or women. The new constitution bans political parties whose aims are "contrary to the principles of [the] sacred religion of Islam," as well as those that primarily appeal to members of an under-represented ethnic, linguistic or religious group. Afghan authorities understand the "principles" of Islam to include precepts of Shariah law "agreed upon by the major schools of jurisprudence (fiqh)"; as a result, any political party that "calls for full equality before the law of women and men could by this reasoning be defined as contrary to Islamic principles." A key test case for the constitution will therefore be whether the political parties clause will be misused in this way.

Curtailing Political Debate

Another important test of the Afghan constitution's ability to provide for peaceful and democratic change will be whether it protects freedom of speech and debate. The new constitution restricts free expression that intrudes upon religious sensitivities. A prominent member of Afghanistan's Supreme Court has declared that: "In the constitution there is an article that says things that go against Islam are not allowed." The Supreme Court has ordered two prominent journalists and the former Minister of Women's Affairs to stand trial on spurious charges of blasphemy after they criticized Afghanistan's warlords. Blasphemy is still an offence that is potentially subject to the death penalty under Afghan penal laws, and fundamentalist Afghans frequently issue death threats against people charged with it. The Supreme Court actually sentenced the two reporters to death, and a female writer was also sentenced to be executed, although none of these sentences has been carried out yet. Such prosecutions could represent a serious threat to the development of Afghan democracy.

Persecuting Religious Minorities

Particularly under the Taliban but throughout Afghan history, the country's rulers have oppressed and murdered religious minorities, especially Shia Muslims among the Hazaras. The new constitution provides that "followers of other religions are free to exercise their faith and perform their religious rites within the limits of the provisions of law." But as with many other aspects of the constitution, whether and to what extent religious minorities will be protected depends on what the "provisions of law" limiting religious freedom may be. The Chief Justice of the Supreme Court has declared that: "The Islamic government, according to Shariah, is bound to punish those who get involved in anti-Islamic activities. We can punish them for propagating other religions - such as threaten them, expel them and, as a last resort, execute them, but only with evidence."

The Chief Justice believes that there are three ways to deal with adherents of minority religions: "One, is you politely invite him to join the Muslim faith. Two, if he refuses, insist that they obey the laws of Islam. And three, if he rejects that, [the Chief Justice] says, 'I have no choice' and points to the sword above his desk, and says, 'behead him.'" The Chief Justice has also warned that anyone who preaches or describes Christianity to Afghans may face the death penalty. If these statements are translated into legal doctrine, the constitution's protection of religious freedom may prove to be very weak.

Enforcing Medieval Punishments

Stoning for Adultery

The Chief Justice of the Afghan Supreme Court has made clear that he wants to see "adulterers whipped or stoned to death, the hands of robbers amputated and murderers publicly executed." Although the Old Testament of the Bible contemplates the stoning of adulterers and other criminals, the Quran does not, and most modern states have abandoned the practice. Resuming the stoning of adulterers, as a local district court did when it ordered an Afghan woman to be stoned to death in late April 2005, would make Afghanistan's laws even more theocratic than those of neighbouring Iran, which abandoned the stoning of adulterers in 2002 after sentencing two women to be stoned to death the previous year. President Karzai has repeatedly insisted that Afghanistan will be governed by Shariah law, which many Afghans understand to provide for stoning in cases of adultery. Aides to Karzai have insisted that stoning will not be resumed on President Karzai's watch, and the Constitution provides the President with the authority to reduce and pardon penalties, but only "in accordance with law." But Karzai does not necessarily control what goes on in all of Afghanistan, and there is no guarantee that Karzai will always be President to veto court-ordered stonings. And because the Supreme Court is ultimately vested with the power to interpret the law and verify compliance with

Islam, the Chief Justice may override a Karzai pardon in an emotionally or politically charged case. A renegade warlord, fundamentalist politician, or Supreme Court power grab could therefore return Afghanistan to the days of torturing and killing women under the pretext of piety.

Amputating Hands for Theft

The Chief Justice has pronounced that "a hand being chopped for theft" is necessary for "obvious and justified reasons - ridding society of crime." Even President Karzai has expressed qualified support for the idea, noting that there are "strict rules" governing such punishments and it "is extremely, extremely difficult in the real interpretation of Shariah to cut off somebody's hand. The hand-cutting part is only applicable, only applicable, if the society has been provided with all the means of work and earning and making a life." This is somewhat reassuring, at least in those cases where President Karzai remains in control and convinced that "all the means of work" were not available to a defendant. But warlords, the Supreme Court, and future presidents may not be so gentle. Although amputation may seem preferable to some compared to life imprisonment under constant threat of rape, the sentence meted out to petty thieves in the U.S. under some circumstances, its revival would raise serious questions about Afghanistan's compliance with its international treaty obligations.

Discriminating against Women

Virtually every world religion elevates men to the position of lordship over women, placing most forms of religious fundamentalism on a collision course with equal rights and full participation by all citizens in a democratic government. Like their fundamentalist counterparts in other nations, many powerful leaders in post-Taliban Afghanistan have a record of holding Afghan women to a far higher standard of pious conduct than men are expected to obey. Afghan women must shoulder most of the burden of preventing lust and extramarital sex, by donning *burqas* and denying themselves access to most public spaces. They must submit to marriages against their will and not of their choosing, even under circumstances in which men would be free to refuse. The continuation of such practices will prove all the promises of equal rights for Afghan women before the law to be illusory.

The Burqa and Forced Covering

All of us remember how the U.S. condemned the *burqa* as the ultimate symbol of the oppression of women under the Taliban and the terrorists' ideology of "hate." A State Department press release issued during the Afghan war called the *burqa* an "infamous and intolerable" form of torturing and imprisoning women in a "voluminous, tent-like full-body outer garment that covers women from head to toe." Despite all the pain and discomfort it may cause, the allies of the U.S. in Afghanistan are still requiring women under their power to wear the *burqa*. Although American television gleefully reported that Afghan women had thrown out their *burqas* when the Taliban left, Afghan warlords are still requiring them to wear it. Most women still wear the *burqa*, not so much out of fidelity to their religious faith and the requirements of the Quran - which does not even mention veils, let alone *burqas* - but because they are forced to do so by the dictate of local warlords or the fear of marauding militiamen. "In post-Taliban Afghanistan, women have been raped for daring to think they could now go without the *burqa*." Future Afghan governments will decide whether the *burqa* is part of the "beliefs and provisions of Islam," or on the contrary is incompatible not only with Islam but with the international human rights treaties to which Afghanistan is a party. The issue will likely be resolved by the Afghan courts, which extreme fundamentalists like Sayyaf and his allies on the Supreme Court look poised to control for the indefinite future.

Involuntary Seclusion of Women

Women in Afghan society remain burdened by laws and practices that keep them out of the public sphere. Religious leaders with no legal training act as judges, imprisoning young people for such crimes as dating, falling in love, or marrying without parental permission. A woman may commit a crime simply by having a conversation or being seen in public with an unrelated man. The former governor of Herat announced on radio and television that the police and Department of Vice and Virtue "must stop men and women who are unmarried from walking together on the street" and "are obliged to beat them." This iron curtain of male-female segregation is hardly compatible with the full participation of women in a "broad-based and representational" government, which the U.S. has defined to include women.

Forced and Underage Marriage

More than two years after the Taliban fell, Afghan women are still being denied their rights in marriage and to divorce under both international and Islamic law, much more often than women in many other Islamic countries are. In July 2002, for example, almost 800 women per day applied for divorces to the judicial authorities of the

Afghan government. But instead of being granted their divorces, some were imprisoned, including a dozen women subjected to forced marriages under the Taliban. The judiciary continues to apply its version of the Hanafi school of Islamic law to deny women the right to divorce under most circumstances, granting relief from forced marriages only in "rare" cases. Women who run away from home without their husband's permission can be sentenced to several years in prison.

Teenage girls are still routinely forced into marriages with men they have never met, often much older than they are. About 50% of Afghanistan's marriages are compulsory. Afghan families often sell their daughters for excessive dowries equivalent to thousands of dollars, in a country where the average income is about $200. Many young women have resorted to setting themselves on fire to escape this contemporary form of slavery. Over 100 Afghan women died of self-immolation in the first ten months of 2004. Afghanistan's high rate of forced marriages is fuelling this unprecedented epidemic of fiery suicides. Although President Karzai has declared that there "can't be any worse oppression" than forced marriage, the Afghan government contributes to it by imprisoning girls and women married against their will, if and when they flee. Girls and women have no legal alternative to suicide, as they are arrested and jailed for fleeing child marriages or abusive families. A jailer in Kabul told a reporter that: "If a girl in Afghanistan runs off with a boy or tries to escape from her family, that is a crime." Moreover, Afghan tribal councils continue to resolve criminal cases "by ordering that the alleged perpetrator provide the family of the alleged victim with a young girl or girls, usually below the legal marriage age, in order to compensate for the alleged crime." The girl "is then forcibly married to a male member of the victim's family." Thus, the Afghan criminal justice system "is more likely to violate the rights of women than to protect and uphold them." The U.S. has tolerated these policies of the government and warlords it funds and helped gain power, even though it cited the "high rates of depression and suicide among Afghan women" as a reason to go to war against the Taliban.

International law recognizes forced marriage as a form of slavery to which Afghanistan must put an end if it aspires to membership in the community of civilized nations. For example, a treaty that Afghanistan signed on to in 1966 obliged States parties to abolish slave-like practices in which a "woman, without the right to refuse, is promised or given in marriage on payment of a consideration in money or in kind to her parents, guardian, family or any person...." Likewise, the Universal Declaration of Human Rights states that women and men have equal rights before, during and after marriage, and that "marriage shall be entered into only with the free and full consent of the intending spouse."

Finally, Afghanistan's international obligations under the Convention on the Elimination of Discrimination Against Women are to guarantee that women have "the right to choose a spouse freely" and enjoy "the same rights and responsibilities in marriage and at the time of termination of marriage."

Marriages of very young Afghan girls are a particularly grave problem. Young girls are still routinely promised in marriage to bring in an income to a poor family, or to satisfy a financial or "blood" debt. As a consequence, many young girls are pressured into marriages in their early teens and even as early as seven. The practice is not restricted to Afghanistan, but is common in rural parts of India and Africa.

The minimum marriageable age in Afghanistan is 16 by statute. However, the courts refuse to enforce this law. Nearly two years after the Taliban fell, Amnesty International reported one case in which a court refused to take any action on a criminal complaint against a 48 year old to whom an eight-year old girl had been forcibly married. This court may simply have been implementing government policy, for the Deputy Chief Justice of the Afghan Supreme Court has claimed that the "only source of legislation in Afghanistan is Islamic shariah law," which some jurists interpret to allow a "father to contract binding marriages for both his sons and his daughters so long as they are minors (up to the age of nine or onset of menstruation for girls and puberty, up to age fifteen at the latest, for boys)." Although some jurists maintain that a girl may repudiate such a marriage upon attaining puberty by application to the court, social conditions tend to vitiate this right.

International law condemns child marriages in the same breath as other forced marriages. Very young girls cannot be said to give their free and full consent to a marriage as required by the Universal Declaration of Human Rights. Theoretically, therefore, Afghan courts could find further support in that treaty for enforcing their domestic law against child marriages.

But the new constitution's deference to religious law make it more likely that the courts will rule that the prohibitions on child marriage in international law and Afghan statutes are invalid because they contradict a fundamentalist view of the "beliefs and provisions" of Islam. Such a ruling would further diminish Afghan girls' and women's prospects for true "liberation."

An Iraqi Theocracy?

Despite many differences, there are important similarities between the situations in Iraq and Afghanistan. Both Iraq and Afghanistan are majority Muslim countries, with populations of similar sizes, occupied by the U.S. and its coalition allies as a result of their complicity in international terrorism.

As in Afghanistan, regime change in Iraq has ended the rule of a vicious tyrant. Like Mullah Omar, Saddam Hussein presided over mass murder on a systematic basis (although in Iraq this occurred with support from most of the U.N. Security Council, not under conditions of international isolation as in Afghanistan). And similar struggles are underway in both countries between religious fundamentalists, who would implement a medieval version of religious law, and reformers who seek to modernize and secularize their society so as to guarantee the rights of women and ethnic or religious minorities.

From the Ba'ath to A Religious State

Any discussion of human rights in Iraq's recent history must begin with the crimes committed by Saddam Hussein over the past few decades with the cooperation and support of several foreign powers. Saddam's Baath Arab Socialist party seized power in a U.S.-backed coup in 1963, and summarily executed thousands of Iraqi intellectuals identified as suspected leftists on lists provided by the CIA. After taking the helm of the Baath party in 1979, Saddam launched two wars, against Iran in 1979 and Kuwait in 1990, which claimed the lives of more than 600,000 Iraqis. In the late 1980s and early 1990s, Saddam's military put down Iranian-backed rebellions from the Kurdish and Shia communities in Iraq, killing 100,000 to 200,000 people. In order to commit these crimes, Saddam's government secured massive financial and military support from an array of foreign powers, including the Soviet Union, France, China, Saudi Arabia, Kuwait, and the U.S.

Despite the disastrous wars, rebellions, and crimes against humanity under Saddam's rule, Iraq's population increased by almost five million people from 1980 to 1990. Life expectancy increased by almost 14 years on average between 1975 and 1990, as the government helped ensure that 90% of the population had access to safe drinking water and modern facilities for sanitation and health care. The 1991 Gulf War reversed much of this progress, as the U.S. deliberately bombed water purification, sewage, and electricity facilities, and lobbied for comprehensive economic sanctions to be imposed by the U.N. Security Council which eventually led to the deaths of one million

Iraqis, including 500,000 Iraqi children. Expressing outrage at Iraq's poor human rights record, floating questionable assertions about the threat its unconventional weapons and ties to *al Qaeda* posed to international peace and security, and rejecting Iraq's offers to allow U.S. military access to suspected weapons sites and to hold free elections, the Bush administration decided to invade the country and depose Saddam Hussein. The war claimed the lives of up to 60,000 Iraqi soldiers, along with about 100,000 innocent Iraqi civilians as of September 2004. The Iraqi death rate more than doubled, as the rates of disease, malnutrition, and infant mortality soared. War and looting destroyed Iraq's hospitals and water infrastructure along with most public buildings. The unemployment rate for Iraqis doubled to 60 percent, the remains of the water and sanitation systems collapsed, and more than 3,000 schools were bombed, looted, or otherwise destroyed. Hundreds of thousands of people became homeless.

The Iraqi government appointed by the multinational forces enshrined religion as the basis of the new Iraq. After the end of "major combat operations," the U.S. established a Coalition Provisional Authority (CPA) and an Iraqi Governing Council (IGC) to manage the country. The U.S. handed 60% of the seats on the Iraqi Governing Council to Shia Muslims with long-standing ties to the theocrats in Iran. These council members subsequently used their power to promulgate fundamentalist laws for the country, repealing more secular laws guaranteeing women's equality that had been enforced by the previous regime.

Article 7 of Transitional Administrative Law (TAL), which is intended to serve as an interim Iraqi constitution until a more permanent one can be ratified in late 2005, states that: "Islam is the official religion of the State and is to be considered a source of legislation. No law that contradicts the universally agreed tenets of Islam, the principles of democracy, or the rights cited in Chapter Two of this Law may be enacted during the transitional period." According to a prominent commentator on religious freedom, every Arab state whose constitution establishes an official religion in this way has an abysmal record of respecting civil and political rights; such clauses are used to implement "state-coerced Islamization, discrimination and even state-sanctioned persecution of religious minorities, as, for example, in Iran, Saudi Arabia and Sudan." The clause mandating compliance with all laws with the requirements of Islam goes beyond what previous Iraqi constitutions contemplated in fusing religion and the state, and hands religious fundamentalists veto power over the political development of the country. In effect, it establishes religious scholars as the authorities on what Iraq's supreme law provides, outlaws secular government, and threatens to create a theocracy in Iraq.

The public statements of the Iraqi fundamentalist leaders most likely to implement the TAL confirm that its provisions make theocracy a distinct possibility. Iraq's interim prime minister virtually declared allegiance to Ayatollah Ali Hussein al-Sistani, describing him as standing at the "forefront" of all of the country's other religious authorities on the occasion of the handover of sovereignty from the CPA. The alliance of Ayatollah Sistani and the Supreme Council for the Islamic Revolution in Iraq resembles the movement of Ayatollah Khomeini of Iran in that it demands that fundamentalist religious law be used to deny equal rights to women and religious minorities. The alliance receives large donations from the spiritual capital of Iran and uses them to maintain private armies, along with a website detailing the characteristics of the planned fundamentalist state. Although Ayatollah Sistani has promised to be less active in politics than Ayatollah Khomeini believed that clerics should be, the latter also made reassuring statements to the West about democracy, religious freedom, and women's rights, behaving quite differently once securely in power. The Iraqi Ayatollahs have been even less moderate in tone than Khomeini, in some respects; they openly "'use religion in order to assume power,'" in the words of the former head of the IGC.

In the January 2005 election, a coalition of Iraqi Shia fundamentalist parties claimed about half of all votes, and promptly declared that religious law would be implemented. The coalition will control more than 130 seats in the 275-member Iraqi National Assembly charged with drafting a permanent constitution. Its architect and inspiration, Ayatollah Sistani, has pledged that the coalition will insist upon making Islam the sole source of legislation in the permanent constitution and prohibiting any law that is contrary to his version of Islam. The close ties of leading Iraqi politicians to the Iranian theocracy do not bode well for Iraqi freedom. With opposition to the Iranian government's most conservative religious policies reportedly widespread, some elements in the country's leadership have resorted to torturing and executing thousands to maintain power. Should Iraq follow the lead of its larger neighbour, a similar drama may play out for decades to come, as it has in many other theocracies known to history.

Chapter 6

Theocratic Challenge to Constitution Drafting in Post-Conflict States

Over the past few decades, principles of theocratic governance have gained enormous public support in developing polities worldwide. The countries experiencing this resurgence of religious fundamentalism are diverse, spanning the globe from central and southeast Asia to north and sub-Saharan Africa and the Middle East. The Khomeini-led revolution in Iran is perhaps the quintessential manifestation of this broad trend, but newspaper headlines report almost weekly on religious fundamentalist insurgency in countries as diverse as Morocco, Pakistan, and Indonesia. Moreover, a process of "Islamisation" of laws has taken place in dozens of sub-national jurisdictions: twelve northern Nigerian states led by Zamfara state; Zanzibar, an island formally part of Tanzania that enjoys wide legislative autonomy; the states Kelantan and Terengganu in Malaysia, where the Parti Islam Semalaysia formed a government in the 1990s; and Pakistan's Northwest Frontier Province, where the Muttahida Majilis-i-Amal party has ruled since 2003. Religious parties have gained a tremendous popular following in countries as diverse as Egypt, India, Bangladesh, Nigeria, Algeria, and Turkey. The sweeping win of the pro-Islamic AK Party in Turkey's July 2007 general election further illustrates this trend. Meanwhile, religion continues to play a key role in European politics, from Catholic Ireland and Poland to Orthodox Serbia. Evangelical Pentecostalism has become prevalent in Latin America. A similar trend can be seen in North America, where religious fundamentalism, primarily the Christian Right, has become a significant political force.

The theocratic wave is a major source of friction in today's world. Iraq and Afghanistan are two obvious examples, but there are, alas, many others. The mass atrocities in Darfur are linked to Islamic fundamentalists coming to power in Sudan in the late 1980s. In northern Africa, a vicious decade-long war between the French-backed government of Algeria and the Islamic Salvation Front erupted after Islamists won the first multiparty election in that country in the early 1990s. In the Horn of Africa, Somalia, Eritrea, and Ethiopia are entangled in a bloody religion-related cycle of sectarian violence. Hezbollah (the "party of God") now threatens to overthrow the state's fragile multiparty coalition in Lebanon. The struggle between the nationalist Fatah movement and the religious Hamas movement has effectively split the Palestinian people. Moreover, this theocratic surge has other indirect effects on conflict areas: because political stability in Morocco and Algeria has become a primary interest of the West in the post-9/11 reality, international efforts to resolve the conflict over Western Sahara—approximately two-thirds of which is controlled by Morocco and the other third, also known as the Sahrawi Arab Democratic Republic, is actively supported by Algeria—have sunk into oblivion. In short, it is hard to overstate the significance of the fundamentalist turn in late twentieth and early twenty-first century politics.

In this Chapter, I explore several key aspects of constitutionalism in a theocratic world. I begin by identifying the challenges posed by the theocratic surge to canonical power-sharing, consociational models for mitigating tensions in multi-ethnic polities. Second, I define the concept of "constitutional theocracy" and its emergence as a new form of governance over the last few decades.

The Theocratic Challenge to Conventional Power-Sharing Mechanisms

The literature on constitutional design and engineering is voluminous. Its canonical tenor suggests that when constitutionalisation is seen as a pragmatic "second order" measure—as opposed to instances of constitutionalisation involving a more principled, first order "we the people" outlook—it may help institutionalize attempts to mitigate tensions in ethnically divided polities through the adoption of federalism, secured representation, and other trust-building and power-sharing mechanisms. Surprisingly, however, although there are many examples of discussions of the mitigating potential of constitutional power-sharing mechanisms to ease rifts along national, ethnic, or linguistic lines, scholars of comparative constitutional design have given little attention to the increasing divisions along secular/religious lines. From an analytical standpoint, the secular/religious divide differs in at least four respects from these more obvious and commonly addressed markers of identity. First, more than any other divisions along a scriptive or imagined lines, the secular/religious divide cuts across nations otherwise unified by their members' joint ethnic, religious, linguistic, and historical origins. In this sense, the secularism/religiosity factor, or other closely associated distinctions such as universalism versus parochialism, is closer in nature to less visible categories such as income deciles, social class, or cultural milieu than it is to other kinds of markers such as race, gender, or ethnicity. Nationalist Catalans, Flemish, or Quebecers see themselves as autonomous people with a unique cultural heritage, language, and history that is distinct from that of Spaniards, Valons, or Anglophone Canadians, respectively. By contrast, most cosmopolitan and traditionalist Egyptians define themselves as members of the same nation, speak the same language or dialects of it, treasure the Pharaoh dynasty, and share the same ancestral ties. Importantly, however, some Egyptians are close adherents of religious directives, while others follow them more casually.

Second, the territorial boundaries of the secular/religious divide are often blurred. Although residents of certain regions within a given country may be more prone to holding theocratic views than residents of other regions, this divide is not neatly demarcated along territorial lines, as is often the case with ethnic or linguistic boundaries. Proponents of theocratic governance may reside in peripheral towns, or in blue collar neighbourhoods at the outskirts of large urban centres. But they may also reside within a few bus stops from bastions of modernism such as art galleries, universities, shopping malls, or government buildings. This is in stark contrast to, say, Sri Lanka, where the vast majority of Tamils live in one region of the island; or, better yet, Cyprus, where the territorial divide between the Greeks and the Turks is clearly demarcated. Territory-based power-sharing mechanisms—or any other kind of joint governance structures that are based on the allocation of powers or goods by a regional key—may not be an efficient means for analysing, let alone reducing, tensions along secular/religious lines.

Third, the assumption that whole peoples share unified interests is questionable at best. Akin to early writings about the postcolonial world that tended to view post-colonial countries as a homogeneous block, populist academic and media accounts in the West tend to portray the spread of religious fundamentalism in the developing world as a near-monolithic, ever-accelerating, and all-encompassing phenomenon.

In contrast to the Western portrayal of religion as private and relatively benign, "politicized" religions are depicted as being a threat to reason and a hindrance to progress. The Islamic world in particular has been the target of much of this critique, described by leading public intellectuals as a monolithic entity committed to a fundamentalist, anti-Western agenda. The post-9/11 popular media followed suit by portraying Islamic societies as united by their religious zeal and antiliberal sentiment. In practice, however, the picture in most predominantly religious polities—Islamic, Jewish, Roman Catholic, or Hinduist is much more complex and nuanced, reflecting deep divisions and strife along secular/religious lines, as well as widely divergent beliefs, interpretations, and degrees of practice within religious communities.

In fact, most countries that have experienced a revival of religious fundamentalism over the past few decades have long been caught between identities, worldviews, and commitments that are at once secular and religious, universalist and particularist. In virtually all of these countries, the very nature of the sociopolitical order has been highly contested; civic ideology, an often relatively cosmopolitan lifestyle, and diverse policy preferences are all often striving to establish or maintain their hegemony vis-a-vis embedded symbols of tradition, religiosity, and exceptionalism.

Principles of theocratic governance may pose a threat to the cultural and policy preferences of secular-nationalist elites in these countries. After all, theocratic governance has seldom appealed to members of the often cosmopolitan urban intelligentsia and the managerial class and state bureaucrats may see it as an impediment to progress and modernisation. Theocratic governance is also often at odds with principles of modern economy and may threaten the interests of major economic sectors and stakeholders. And it would be an understatement to say that theocratic governments are not the type of regimes that find favour with supranational trade and monetary bodies such as the International Monetary Fund, the World Bank, or the World Trade Organisation. Additionally, with few exceptions, theocracy has been, and remains, abhorred by the military—perceived as a symbol of secular nationalism in many developing polities.

Fourth, and perhaps most importantly, is the uneasy union of constitutionalism and theocratic governance. Unlike the cases of race, gender, ethnicity, or language, there seems to be an embedded tension between fundamentals of theocratic governance and principles of modern constitutionalism. Principles of theocratic governance often stem from and adhere to alternative sources of authority and legitimacy. The rule of God, not the rule of law, is the ultimate tenet here. In other words, the holistic nature of theocratic governance is not prima facie conducive to constitutional compromise, power-sharing pacts, separation of powers, checks and balances, relative judicial independence, and other essentials of modern constitutionalism. What is more, principles of divine authority and theocratic governance are often at odds with international human rights regimes and principles, perhaps most tellingly in the contexts of religious freedoms, gender equality, or reproductive liberty.

These conflicting pressures and interests have led to intense constitutional maneuvering in predominantly religious polities. All of these countries face the sources of friction inherent in a constitutional theocracy—a potentially explosive combination by its very nature, and one that poses new challenges to conventional constitutional ideas about secularism, religious freedom, and the relationship between religion and the state. How can a polity therefore reconcile the principles of accountability, separation of powers, and the notion of "we the people" as the ultimate source of sovereignty when the fundamental notion of divine authority and holy texts make up the supreme governing norm of the state? Who should be vested with the ultimate authority to interpret the divine text, and on what grounds? What ought to be done when principles of modern constitutionalism and human rights collide with religious injunctions and support for theocratic governance? And, more generally, how can a polity advance principles of twenty-first century government or run a modern economy when it treats ancient texts and pious authorities as a main source of legislation?

In short, the theocratic challenge is inherently more difficult to overcome through constitution drafting than, say, divisions along ethnic or linguistic lines. This undermines the applicability of traditional power-sharing, "consociational" constitutional models commonly proposed as a way of mitigating tensions in troubled multi-ethnic polities. Conflict settings where internal strife is high and state capacity is low merely exacerbate these difficulties. An unfortunate "textbook" example of such difficulties is the Palestinian National Authority, where the struggle between the nationalist Fatah movement and the religious Hamas-led government has brought the polity to the brink of civil war. These tensions were reflected in both the 1997 Basic Law and the 2003 Draft Constitution that was included as part of the "Roadmap to Peace," proposed by the United States, the United Nations, Russia, and the European Union. In the latter document, often referred to as the "Third

Draft of the Constitution of the State of Palestine," Islam was adopted as the official state religion, though it also explicitly stated that Christian or other "monotheistic religions" would be accorded full respect and acknowledgment.

Specifically, Article 7 adopted "[t]he principles of Islamic Shari'a" as "a major source for legislation," avoiding a more forceful conceptualisation of the role of Islamic law in Palestinian society. Then came the surprise landslide victory by Hamas in the January 2006 parliamentary elections. Shortly thereafter, the Palestinian Legislative Council (PLC) approved the establishment of a constitutional court—a move undertaken by Fatah in its last days as a majority in the PLC in an attempt to constrain Hamas when it took over Parliament. A new nine-judge court was to be convened with judges appointed by President Mahmoud Abbas of the Fatah, which would have the power to rule illegal those laws judged to violate the Basic Law. Theoretically at least, Abbas effectively would have been in a position to veto laws passed by Hamas legislators. In its first legislative move in Parliament, however, Hamas—led by the then newly elected, but now ousted Prime Minister Ismail Haniyeh, and by Hamas leader-in-exile Khaled Mash'al—voted to invalidate all legislation passed by the outgoing Fatah following the 2006 election, including the creation of the constitutional court.

An unstable coalition government was established in March 2006, but tensions continued, at times violently. In early 2007, the strain between Hamas and Fatah escalated into a violent struggle, claiming the lives of over ninety Palestinians in Gaza and the West Bank. A truce was then reached in the holy city of Mecca in February 2007. According to the agreement on the distribution of cabinet positions, nine posts were to go to Hamas, including the more "ideologically sensitive" portfolios of education, justice, and the Waqf portfolio overseeing collectively-owned land and real estate held in trust for Muslim religious or charitable purposes. Six "practical" ministries were given to Fatah, including agriculture, transportation, health, and public works. Three key ministries—foreign affairs, finance, and interior, which controls security—would be held by independents.

This agreement was derailed, however, when a violent Hamas-led takeover of the Gaza Strip took place in June 2007. President Mahmoud Abbas reacted by dismissing the coalition Hamas-Fatah government and by appointing a moderate Fatah politician to head the new Palestinian Authority government. As this example illustrates, there is not a dull constitutional moment west of the Jordan River, or indeed wherever a deep rift between secular-nationalist worldviews and religious-fundamentalist aspirations cuts across a demos not otherwise divided along ethnic, territorial, or linguistic lines.

The Emergence of Constitutional Theocracy

The limited relevance of traditional power-sharing, consociational models for addressing the secular/religious divide suggests that we ought to look elsewhere for explanatory guidance. At the uneasy intersection of two present-day trends—the tremendous increase of popular support for principles of theocratic governance and the global spread of constitutionalism—a new legal order has emerged: constitutional theocracy. In contrast to a "pure" theocracy, power in constitutional theocracies resides in lay political figures operating within the bounds of a constitution, rather than from within the religious leadership itself. Basic principles such as the separation of powers are constitutionally enshrined. The constitution also typically establishes a constitutional court that is mandated to carry out some form of active judicial review.

At the same time, constitutional theocracies defy the Franco-American doctrine of strict structural and substantive separation of religion and state. Akin to models of "establishment" or "state religion," constitutional theocracies both formally endorse and actively support a single religion or faith denomination. Moreover, that state religion is enshrined as the principal source that informs all legislation and methods of judicial interpretation. Unlike the handful of European countries with a state church, the designated state religion in constitutional theocracies is often viewed as constituting the foundation of the modern state; as such, it is an integral part, or even the metaphorical pillar, of the polity's national metanarrative. In this way, religion often determines the polity's boundaries of collective identity as well as the scope and nature of some or all of the rights and duties assigned to its residents.

Constitutional theocracies, however, do more than simply grant exclusive recognition and support to a given state religion: Laws must conform to principles of religious doctrine and no statute may be enacted that is repugnant to these principles. In most instances, a well-developed nexus of religious bodies, tribunals, and authorities operates in lieu of, or in tandem with, a civil court system. The opinions and jurisprudence of these authorities and tribunals carry notable symbolic weight and play a significant role in public life. Importantly, however, the entirety of this nexus of laws and institutions is subject to judicial review by a constitutional court or tribunal. This tribunal consists of judges who are often well-versed in both general and religious law, and can speak knowledgeably on pertinent matters of law to jurists at Yale Law School as well as at the al-Azhar centre of Islamic learning in Cairo.

The "ideal" model of a constitutional theocracy can be summarized by outlining four main elements: (1) adherence to some or all core elements of modern constitutionalism, including the formal distinction between political authority and religious authority, and the existence of some form of active judicial review; (2) the presence of a single religion or religious denomination that is formally endorsed by the state as the "state religion"; (3) the constitutional enshrining of the religion, its texts, directives, and interpretations as a or the main source of legislation and judicial interpretation of laws—essentially, laws may not infringe upon injunctions of the state-endorsed religion; and (4) a nexus of religious bodies and tribunals that not only carry symbolic weight, but that are also granted official jurisdictional status and operate in lieu of, or in an uneasy tandem with, a civil court system. All in all, hundreds of millions of people, perhaps as many as a billion people, now live in polities that either fall squarely within the definition of a constitutional theocracy or that feature many of the substantive characteristics and tensions of such a legal order.

Five Models of Religion and State Relations

The separation of church and state was seen by Enlightenment thinkers as a means of confining dangerous and irrational religious passions to the private sphere. In the modern West, the longstanding French policy of laicite is arguably the clearest manifestation of the desire to restrict clerical and religious influence over the state. By enacting its 2004 ban of Muslim headscarves in public schools, the French Parliament illustrated France's "suspicion of religion and its attempt to avert the growth and influence of an incipient Muslim fundamentalism in that nation." But although the strict separation approach is the one most familiar to scholars of constitutional law and politics in the United States, expanding our horizons comparatively reveals at least five other constitutional-institutional models for delineating the relationship between religion and state; these models are of crucial importance for our analysis of the phenomenon of constitutional theocracy. I briefly discuss each in turn.

The first model involves states that have separated religion from state in what may be called separationist reformism. The Mustafa

Kemal Ataturk-led secularisation of predominantly religious Turkey is perhaps the most well-known example of separationist reformism in the twentieth century. Following the demise of the Ottoman Empire, the Kemalist secular-nationalist elite decided to abandon Islamic culture and laws, in favour of secularism and modernism. Accordingly, both the 1961 and the 1982 constitutions established an official state policy of laicism.

In Thailand, the immensely popular Theravada Buddhism has had to make way for a civic ideology centering on the Thai monarchy and advanced by a tripartite coalition of the military, state bureaucracy, and business elites, which has dominated Thai politics since the early twentieth century.

Similar in its effects was the Soviet regime's policy that forced Armenia to abandon its formal ties with the Armenian Apostolic Church, which had been recognized as Armenia's state religion from the fourth century until the early twentieth century. In Ethiopia, the introduction of strict antireligious laws followed a military junta's ferocious overthrow of Emperor Haile Selassie, descendant of King Solomon and Queen Sheba, who was a sacred figure for the Rastafarian movement in Jamaica. Selassie was also, and most importantly, negotiator of autocephaly and a longtime patron of the Ethiopian Orthodox Church. In a notably more civilized fashion, Portugal (1976), Spain (1978), (74) and Italy (1984) all adopted new constitutions or constitutional amendments that disestablished Catholicism as their state religion.

In contrast to the disaggregation of state and religion, a second pertinent constitutional model is a weak form of religious establishment—for example, establishment through the formal, mainly ceremonial, designation of a certain religion as "state religion." Several European countries illustrate this model. An evident case in point is the designation of the Evangelical Lutheran Church as a "state church" in Norway, Denmark, Finland, and Iceland—arguably some of Europe's most liberal and progressive polities. Norway's head of state, for example, is also the leader of the state church. Article 2 of the Norwegian Constitution guarantees freedom of religion, but also states that Evangelical Lutheranism is the official state religion. Article 12 requires more than half of the members of the Norwegian Council of State to be members of the state church. Similarly, Greece and Cyprus formally designate the Greek Orthodox Church as the state church. In England, the monarch is "Supreme Governor" of the Church of England and "Defender of the Faith."

The Crown has a role in senior ecclesiastical matters and, by the same token, the church is involved in the coronation of a new monarch, and senior bishops are represented in the House of Lords. A third response to the tension between secularism and religiosity is the selective accommodation of religion in certain areas of the law. Here, the general law is secular, yet a degree of jurisdictional autonomy is granted to religious minorities, primarily in matters of personal status and education.

Countries such as Israel, Kenya, India, and South Africa grant recognized religious and customary communities the jurisdictional autonomy to pursue their own traditions in several areas of law, most notably family law. For example, each religious community in Israel has autonomous religious courts that hold jurisdiction over its respective members' marriage and divorce affairs. Kenya has enacted a set of statutes to recognize the diversity of personal laws pertaining to different groups of citizens. India has long been entangled in a bitter debate concerning the scope and status of Muslim and Hindu religious personal laws, versus the individual rights and liberties protected by the Indian Constitution.

An increasingly prevalent yet seldom discussed fourth model is essentially a mirror image of these "religious jurisdictional enclaves"—what we might call secular jurisdictional enclaves. Here, most of the law is religious; however, certain areas of the law, such as economic law, are "carved out" and insulated from influence by religious law. Virtually all Islamic countries maintain criminal and economic codes that are based on French civil law, British common law, or other sources of law introduced by, or otherwise borrowed from, European nations, alongside a variable status for fiqh (Islamic law and jurisprudence).

An interesting case in point here is Saudi Arabia, arguably the country whose legal system comes the closest to being fully based on fiqh. Shari'a law is bad for business, however. Whereas Saudi courts apply Shari'a in all matters of civil, criminal, or personal status, Article 232 of a 1965 Royal Decree provides for the establishment of a commission for the settlement of all commercial disputes. Although judges of the ordinary courts are usually appointed by the Ministry of Justice from among graduates of recognized Shari'a law colleges, members of the commission for the settlement of disputes are appointed by the Ministry of Trade. In other words, Saudi Arabia has effectively exempted the entire finance, banking, and corporate capital sectors from application of Shari'a rules. Foreign investors have not protested the move.

Following the same rationale, Saudi Arabia has recently embarked upon a comprehensive modernisation of its judicial system. Among the overhaul's main tenets is the creation of specialized courts in criminal, commercial, labour, and family issues instead of a general judge-made Shari'a-based interpretation in these matters. Additionally, "[t]he judiciary council that used to act as the highest court and was controlled by some of the most reactionary clerics in the kingdom, has been relegated to administration." A new ten-member Supreme Court will be filled mostly with royal appointees, not merely with religious clerics, thereby allowing the kingdom to extend its pragmatic, flexible application of Shari'a to various aspects of public life.

Another example is the city of Dubai, which was recently ranked the United Arab Emirates's number one tourist destination. A suite in the Burj A1 Arab, one of the world's finest hotels, costs up to $11,000 per night. Upon its completion, Burj Dubai is soon to become the tallest freestanding structure in the world. Dubailand, twice as big as Disney World, is the world's largest amusement park. The United Arab Emirates, of which Dubai is a part, has the seventh highest GDP per capita of any country in the world. As in Saudi Arabia, although the Shari'a is the main source of law, economic law is civil and is therefore not subject to religious injunctions.

In a similar vein, Islam has been the state religion in the Maldives since the twelfth century. Adherence to Islam is required for citizenship. Furthermore, there is no secular legal system; rather, the local version of Shari'a law, as it is interpreted by state authorities and the Majlis, is the law of the land. Yet the Maldives continue to boast some of the world's finest hotels, catering to jet-set tourists attracted to the Maldives's world class coral reefs. A special presidential decree exempts the thriving tourist industry, which accounts for over 20 percent of the country's GDP, from several non-tourist-friendly religious imperatives.

Another approach to balancing the tensions inherent in constitutional theocracy is a mixed system of religious law and general legal principles. It is well known that Afghanistan has long been torn between conflicting values of tradition and modernism. From 1994 to 2001, the country was ruled by the radical Islamist Taliban, but the U.S. led military campaign removed the Taliban from power and installed a more moderate regime representing an array of groups hitherto in opposition: moderate religious leaders and the country's elites and intellectuals in exile. The new constitution of Afghanistan came into effect in January 2004, and it states that Afghanistan is an Islamic Republic; that the "sacred religion of Islam is the religion of the Islamic Republic of Afghanistan;" and that "no law shall contravene the tenets and provisions of the holy religion of Islam in Afghanistan." Courts are allowed to use Hanafi jurisprudence—one of Sunni Islam's more liberal interpretive schools—in situations of constitutional lacunae. At the same time, the constitution also enshrines the right to private property and resurrects a woman's right to vote, as well as to run for and serve in office. The 2004 constitution also establishes a Supreme Court composed of nine judges appointed by the president for a term of ten years. All members of the Court "[s]hall have higher education in legal studies or Islamic jurisprudence."

A second example of a mixed system is the legal system of the Comoros, which rests on two tenets: Islamic law and an inherited Napoleonic French legal code. Islam has increasingly dominated the political sphere and the May 2006 elections were won by Ahmed Abdallah Mohamed Sambi, a Sunni Muslim cleric nicknamed the "Ayatollah" for his time spent studying Islam in Iran. But the French civil code prevails in most areas of commercial life. The Constitutional Court, the ultimate arbiter of constitutional questions, consists of seven judges who are all well-versed in both the French civil law tradition and the Shafi'i school, which stresses reasoning by analogy.

Akin to the constitutions of over two dozen predominantly Muslim polities, Article 2 of Yemen's constitution, adopted in 1994, declares that Islam is the religion of the state. Article 3 further provides that Shari'a is the source of all legislation. Non-Muslims are forbidden from running for or holding elected office. The same constitution, however, calls for an independent judiciary, and establishes a separate commercial court system and a Supreme Court, which draws upon a combination of Shari'a interpretations and principles of modern constitutional law. Consequently, unique constitutional amalgamations of religious and modern principles emerge, such as Article 31 of the constitution, stating: "Women are the sisters of men. They have rights and duties, which are guaranteed and assigned by Shari'ah and stipulated by law." Another amalgam occurs in Article 46, according to which, "Criminal liability is personal. No crime or punishment shall be undertaken without a provision in the Shari'ah or the law."

The Islamic Republic of Iran is commonly considered to be a fundamentalist theocracy, with governing principles and practices that bear very little resemblance to prevailing principles of western constitutionalism. In practice, however, its system of government features many elements of a constitutional democracy. The preamble of the 1979 Islamic Republic Constitution enshrines the Shari'a as the supreme law—superior even to the Constitution itself. Articles 2 and 3 declare that authority for sovereignty and legislation has a divine provenance (from the Shari'a) and that the leadership of the clergy is a principle of faith. According to Article 6, the administration of the state is to be conducted by the wider population: the general public participates in the election of the President, the Majlis representatives (members of parliament), and municipality councils. Article 8 further entrenches principles of popular participation in deciding political, economic, and social issues.

Most notably, Iran has seen the emergence of the Guardian Council—a de facto constitutional court armed with mandatory constitutional preview powers and composed of six mullahs appointed by the Supreme Leader and six jurists proposed by the head of the judicial system of Iran and voted in by the Majlis. The Supreme Leader has the power to dismiss the religious members of the Guardian Council, but not its jurist members. More stunning still is Khomeini's strategic initiative in 1988 to amend the Iranian Constitution in order to institutionalize the regime's Discernment Expediency Council (majma-e tashkhis maslahat nezam) to serve as the final arbiter between the Consultative Assembly (Majlis) and the Guardian Council (shoray-e negahban). This new body—as of October 2005 the ultimate judicial body in Iran—aids the government in asserting its pragmatist approach to public policymaking (based on the concept of "national necessity") over the Guardian Council's more doctrinal, rigid interpretive approach to pertinent religious directives. In summary, even in the least likely settings, constitutional framers have been able to hedge or mitigate the tension between modern day needs and principles of theocratic governance through innovative constitutional design and reconstruction.

Constitutional Courts as SecularisingAgents

The growing popular support for principles of theocratic governance poses a major threat to the cultural propensities and policy preferences of secular, cosmopolitan, moderate elites in these countries. A common strategy for addressing some of the difficulties presented in the ongoing friction between traditional religious outlooks and principles of modern constitutionalism is the construction of constitutional courts armed with judicial review powers. This strategy has little effect in failed state settings, but in other pertinent settings, it may have some bite. It is well-established in the literature that constitutionalisation and the establishment of judicial review may increase the international reputation and credibility of regimes. But this is only part of the picture.

In countries struggling with the complex issue of constitutional theocracy, constitutional courts may also be viewed as the guardians of secularism, modernism, and universalism against the increasing popularity of theocratic principles. In order to govern effectively, politicians and ruling elites in predominantly religious polities must confront the challenge of constitutional theocracy while simultaneously maintaining popular support for their regimes. Indeed, an increasingly common strategy by those who wield political power—and represent the groups and policy preferences that object to principles of theocratic governance—is the transfer of fundamental collective identity questions of "religion and state" from the political sphere to the courts. Consequently, constitutional courts have been assigned the sensitive task of dealing with contentious political "hot potatoes."

The result has been an unprecedented judicialisation of foundational collective identity, particularly issues relating to religion and state, and the subsequent emergence of constitutional courts as important secularisingagents in these countries. Why is it that constitutional courts are so appealing to secularist, modernist, cosmopolitan, and other antireligious social forces in polities facing deep divisions along secular/religious lines? First, there is a "blame deflection" logic at work. From the politicians' points of view, delegating contentious political questions to the courts may be an effective means of shifting responsibility, and thereby reducing the risks to themselves and to the institutional apparatus within which they operate. The calculus of this "blame deflection" strategy is highly intuitive. If a delegation of power to the courts will increase the credit and/or reduce the blame attributed to the politician as a result of the policy decision of a delegated body, then a delegation of this sort can benefit the politician.

At the very least, the transfer of contested political issues to the courts offers a convenient retreat for politicians who have been unwilling or unable to settle contentious public disputes in the political sphere. It may also offer refuge for politicians seeking to avoid difficult or "no win" decisions and/or avoid the collapse of deadlocked or fragile governing coalitions. In other words, transferring these contested issues to the courts allows secularist leaders to talk the talk of commitment to religious values without walking the actual walk of that commitment. Second, the constitutionalisation of religion subjects certain aspects of religious affairs to state monitoring. With state funding comes statutory regulation. Akin to the legalisation of otherwise unregulated and unauthorized norms and practices, the constitutionalisation of religion may help prevent the evolution of an "underworld" of religious authority and institutions. The "legalisation" point has another related aspect to it. Historically, religious law operated primarily as private law. Its traditional location was in non-centralized religious institutions in which the judgment of individual jurists was autonomous and final, and certainly not subject to appeal. Cases were voluntarily brought to religious tribunals by private parties, not by a public prosecuting authority, and there was no state enforcement mechanism. The whole enterprise was run as an informal, yet socially and morally binding, arbitration system. For example, as Martin Shapiro has noted, non-appellate "kadi justice" in Islamic jurisprudence reflects the absence of central political authority.

By contrast, the formal constitutionalisation of religion brings religious law to the fore of the public law domain, where the state with its central political authority, regulatory hierarchies, and appellate procedures has always been a key stakeholder. Delegation and legitimation, however, are not all that attracts certain polity members to the lure of the constitutional court. Rather, the very logic of modern constitutional law—with its state-driven legitimacy and authority, procedural rules of engagement, methods and styles of reasoning, and often measured approaches to politically charged questions—seems intrinsically appealing to a moderate approach to issues of religion and state. Constitutional courts' very conception of the rule of (state) law, with its deep-rooted orientation toward European legal tradition and what Max Weber characterized as formal and rational reasoning, necessarily weakens the potential accommodation of alternative hierarchies of traditional or religious interpretation. The emergence of proportionality as the prevalent interpretive method in comparative constitutional jurisprudence also makes constitutional courts appealing to relatively moderate or secular elites. By its very nature, proportionality favours middle-of-the-road, balanced, judicious and pragmatic solutions to contested issues. Extreme or radical positions are not likely to fare well under proportionality.

A constitutional court's reluctance to grant support to radical religious views may also derive from its interest in retaining its status as the one and only legitimate interpreter of laws vis-a-vis the perceived menace of alternative interpretation systems—namely, traditional religious authorities, which are well-established within the circles of the traditional supporters of theocratic governance and have been steadily gaining support among new crowds. The deep structural reluctance of constitutional courts to recognize the legitimacy of alternative, primarily religious, interpretation systems is one of the main reasons for their near universal appeal to the urban intelligentsia, the "managerial class," and proponents of civic nationalism.

There are also more prosaic reasons why proponents of threatened secularist worldviews and policy preferences may turn to the courts. Most constitutional court judges have had a general legal education and are familiar with Western law's basic principles and methods of reasoning. More often than not, the judge's educational background, cultural propensities, and social milieu are closer to those of the urban intelligentsia and top state bureaucrats than to any other social group. Constitutional courts are established and funded by the state and their judges are appointed by state authorities, often with the approval of political leaders. Consequently, the judge's record of adjudication is well known at the time of his or her appointment. And, as the recent history of comparative constitutional politics shows us, the recurrence of unsolicited judicial intervention in the political sphere in general—and unwelcome judgments concerning contentious political issues in particular—have brought about significant political backlashes, targeted at clipping the wings of over-active courts.

Among the more common power-constraining strategies are the following: executive overrides of controversial rulings; political tinkering with judicial appointment and tenure procedures to ensure the appointment of compliant judges and/or to block the appointment of undesirable judges; court-packing attempts by those who hold political power; disciplinary sanctions; impeachment or removal of objectionable or over-active judges; the introduction of jurisdictional constraints; or clipping jurisdictional boundaries and powers of judicial review. All of these factors make it unlikely that constitutional court judges in a given polity can continue to hold views that are consistently at odds with the views of the secular-nationalist political elites.

And when judges do not comply, the political reaction may be fierce. In late 1997, for example, a serious rift developed between Pakistani Prime Minister Nawaz Sharif and the Chief Justice of the Supreme Court, Sajjad Ali Shah, over the appointment of new judges to the court. The constitutional crisis came to a dramatic end when the chief justice was suspended from office by rebel members of the Supreme Court. A crisis of a similar nature occurred in January 2000, when Pervez Musharraf insisted that all members of the Supreme Court pledge allegiance to the military administration. The judges who refused to take the oath were expelled from the Court. In a similar fashion, in March 2007, Musharraf ordered Chief Justice Iftikhar Chaudhry to resign, presumably for being over-independent and therefore "unreliable" from the government's point of view. Protests by Pakistani lawyers and opposition groups led to fierce clashes with police.

Ultimately, Chaudhry was reinstated by the Pakistani Supreme Court in July 2007, a ruling Musharraf had to accept as his bid for continuing grasp on power now depended upon the support of secularist Benazir Bhutto, whose followers instigated the pro-Chaudhry demonstrations. However, as is well known, in November 2007 Musharraf declared a state of emergency in Pakistan, suspended the constitution, dismissed Chief Justice Chaudhry for the second time in eight months, and appointed several loyalist judges to the Pakistan Supreme Court. The entire maneuver was driven, in no small part, by Musharrafs concern that the Court might declare Musharraf ineligible to serve as President of Pakistan as long as he continues to head the Pakistani armed forces.

Following two and a half years of conservative jurisprudence in religious matters by the newly established Afghan Supreme Court, President Hamid Karzai opted for a shake-up of the Court's composition. In 2006, he appointed several new, more moderate members to the Court. In addition, the reappointment of the conservative Chief Justice Faisal Ahmad Shinwari—a conservative Islamic cleric with questionable educational credentials—did not pass parliamentary vote. Karzai then chose his legal counsel, Abdul Salam Azimi—a former university professor who was educated in the United States to succeed Shinwari. The new, distinctly more moderate Court was sworn in August 2006.

Consider also Egypt, with its history of political interference with the judicial sphere. The most blatant example is the 1969 "massacre of the judiciary," where more than 200 senior judicial personnel were dismissed by a presidential decree for being overly independent. Along the same lines, disciplinary hearings were held against Egypt's Supreme Constitutional Court Judges Hisham al-Bastawisi and Mahmoud Makki for openly accusing the government of electoral fraud in the November 2005 elections. In March 2007, President Hosni Mubarak introduced a set of constitutional amendments that effectively gave more power to the president, banned the establishment of religious parties (a blatant anti-Muslim Brotherhood move), and loosened controls on security forces in its "war on terror." Among the reforms introduced was the removal of judicial scrutiny of electoral lists, ballots, and procedures.

A careful examination of the constitutional jurisprudence of apex courts in Egypt, Israel, Malaysia, Nigeria, Pakistan, and Turkey-six polities that have been facing the challenge of constitutional theocracy for decades—demonstrates how courts have become key secularisingagents for elites despite intense scrutiny from the more religious segments of the public.

Moreover, each example country illustrates the remarkably creative interpretive techniques adopted by judges confronted with concrete legal disputes that reflect and encapsulate the greater issues emerging from constitutional theocracy. Egypt, Israel, Malaysia, Nigeria, Pakistan, and Turkey have all experienced a growth in the influence of religious political movements, with a commensurate increase in the levels of popular support that they receive. At the same time, these countries differ in their formal recognition of, and commitment to, religious values. In Pakistan, the law underwent full Islamisation in 1973 and again in 1985.

Article 227(1) of the Constitution of Pakistan stipulates that "all existing laws shall be brought in conformity with the Injunctions of Islam as laid down in the Holy Quran and Sunnah, in this Part referred to as the Injunctions of Islam, and no law shall be enacted which is repugnant to such Injunctions." In theory, this means that legislation must be in full compliance with principles of the Shari'a. Similarly, Article 2 of the Egyptian Constitution, as amended in 1980, states that principles of Muslim jurisprudence (the Shari'a) are the primary source of legislation in Egypt, while Israel defines itself as a "Jewish and democratic state." Malaysia is a federal country that endorses Islam as its official religion, and political Islam has been continuously gaining political support and clout at the state level. Nigeria is a secular federal country that grants some legislative autonomy to its states, thereby allowing the states to adopt religiously-influenced laws. Finally, modern Turkey characterizes itself as secular, adhering to the Western model of strict separation of state and religion.

Accordingly, there are considerable differences in the interpretive approaches and practical solutions adopted by the six countries' respective high courts in dealing with the core questions of religion and state. Despite these dissimilarities, however, there are some striking parallels in the way that the constitutional courts in these, and some other similarly situated countries, have all positioned themselves as important secularisingforces within their respective societies. Egypt's Supreme Constitutional Court has played a central role in dealing with the core question of the status of Shari'a rules—arguably one of the most controversial and fundamental collective identity issues troubling the Egyptian polity. Constrained by Article 2 of the Constitution, Egypt's Supreme Constitutional Court has developed its own moderate interpretation of religious rules and norms.

Similarly, the Supreme Court of Pakistan has been able to advance a holistic view of the constitution that emphasizes the interdependence and harmony of its various sections. In response to the possible conclusiveness of [section] 227(1), the Court developed its "harmonisation doctrine," according to which no specific provision of the constitution, and that includes [section] 227(1), stands above any or all other provisions. The constitution as a whole must be interpreted in a harmonious fashion so that specific provisions are read as an integral part of the entire constitution, not as standing above it. In addition, the Court retained its overarching jurisdictional authority, including its appellate capacity over the newly established Shariat Appellate Bench at the Supreme Court. This has proved itself time and again to be a safety net for secular interests vis-a-vis the formal Islamisation of law.

The Israeli Supreme Court responded to the increased tension between Israel's dual commitment to universal (democratic) and parochial (Jewish) values by subjecting the jurisprudence of religious courts to the general principles of administrative and constitutional law. Over the last two decades, the Court pursued a distinctly liberalisingagenda in core matters of religion and state. At the same time, it has also protected the "Jewishness" pillar of the state's collective identity against alternative national narratives, as illustrated in the Court's controversial 2006 ruling in the Family Unification Case.

In Malaysia and Nigeria, their pertinent differences in formal accommodation of religion notwithstanding, national high courts have drawn upon federal/provincial jurisdictional boundaries to override legislative manifestations of popular religious drift at the provincial/state level.

Finally, the Turkish Constitutional Court (TCC) has played a key role in preserving the strictly secular nature of Turkey's political system amid the growing popularity of theocratic governance principles. This has been done, inter alia, by continually outlawing anti-secularist political forces and parties. For example, the TCC dissolved two major Islamic parties, the Welfare (Refah) Party and the Virtue (Fazilet) Party, in 1998 and 2001, respectively. In May 2007, the TCC went on to annul the parliamentary vote that designated the pro-Islamic AK Party nominee—foreign affairs minister Abdullah Gill—as president. A less frequently acknowledged yet equally telling example is the TCC's jurisprudence restricting the female dress code in the public education system.

A detailed analysis of the comparative "religion and state" jurisprudence of these six courts illustrates the key role that constitutional courts play in protecting and preserving the secular nature of their respective polities against the growing support for theocratic governance. Although they operate within different constitutional traditions, frameworks, and constraints, these courts have been able to advance secular or secularisingresponses to fundamental religion and state questions. In so doing, they have been able to impose effective limitations on the accommodation of religious values in public life.

This brief Chapter points to three main lessons. First, the theocratic challenge has become a significant factor in world politics as well as constitutional law. It stretches well beyond current media hot spots like Iran, Iraq, and Afghanistan. Any attempt to examine the complexities of constitution drafting in post-conflict settings without paying close attention to the ever more relevant secular/universal versus religious/particularist divide is bound to come up short. Second, the canonical literature concerning constitutionalism as an effective means for mitigating tensions in multi-ethnic or multi-linguistic states does not adequately address the theocratic challenge. It rests on four main presumptions: territorial concentration and demarcation; social and demographic cohesiveness among members of a given group; unified interests, worldviews, and policy preferences among group members; and an underlying vision of constitutionalism as a viable forum of compromise.

Although these assumptions provide a plausible set of working hypotheses with respect to dividing factors such as nationality, ethnicity, or language, they are less relevant in capturing the realities of the secular/religious divide. Of particular significance here are the inherent tensions between principles of modern constitutionalism and the rule of law on the one hand and fundamentals of theocratic governance on the other. Third, the emergence of a new legal order—constitutional theocracy, which is now shared in one form or another by dozens of countries in the developing world—provides important insights into the sociopolitical role of constitutionalism in predominantly religious settings. Regimes throughout the new world of constitutional theocracies have been struggling with these foundational quandaries, forced to navigate between cosmopolitanism and parochialism, modern and traditional metanarratives, constitutional principles and religious injunctions, contemporary governance and ancient texts, judicial and pious interpretation.

More often than not, the clash between these conflicting visions results in fierce struggles over the nature of the body politic and its organisingprinciples. An uneasy alliance emerges, comprising political leaders, state bureaucrats, economic stakeholders and the managerial class, intellectuals, jurists, and the military. Each of these groups necessarily brings to the table their own worldviews, interests, and communities of reference. Consequently, they seek to tame the spread of religious fundamentalism and diffuse attempts to establish a full-fledged theocracy. Constitutional courts find themselves at the forefront of this struggle, as they attempt to address constitutional theocracy and translate its uneasy bundle of contradictory aims and commitments into practical guidelines for public life.

The bottom line is this: constitutional theocracies are a Galapagos-like paradise for scholars of constitutional design in today's world. They reflect sociopolitical order under constant duress. Striking tensions are often seen between the rule of law and the rule of God, cosmopolitanism and parochialism, economic interests and public will, modern government and religious authorities, new constitutions and ancient texts, judicial and pious interpretation. A unique hybrid of seemingly conflicting worldviews, values, and interests, constitutional theocracies thus offer an ideal setting—a "living laboratory" as it were—for studying constitutional law as a form of politics by other means.

Bibliography

Abou El Fadl, Khaled. *Rebellion and Violence in Islamic Law.* Cambridge, UK: Cambridge University Press, 2002.

Abu-Rabi, Ibrahim M : *Intellectual Origins of Islamic Resurgence in the Modern Arab World,* Albany: State University of New York Press, 1996.

Bakhtiar, Laleh: *Encyclopedia of Islamic Law: A Compendium of the Major Schools.* Chicago, IL: Kazi Publ., 1996.

Beckett, Katharine Scarfe : *Perception of the Islamic Word,* Cambridge University Press, New Delhi, 1992.

Chaudhri, Sajedul Bar : *The Profile of an Islamic State,* Dhaka, Islamic Foundation Bangladesh, 1984.

Chaudhri, Sajedul Bar : *The Profile of an Islamic State,* Dhaka, Islamic Foundation Bangladesh, 1984.

Daniel Pipes : *In the Path of God: Islam and Political Power,* New York: Basic Books Inc., 1983.

Daniel Pipes : *In the Path of God: Islam and Political Power,* New York: Basic Books Inc., 1983.

Enayatullah Mashriqi *: Quranic System of Law*, Akhuwat Publications, Rawalpindi, Pakistan.

Ferrari, Silvio and Anthony Bradney: *Islam and European Legal Systems.* Aldershot: Ashgate, 2000.

Fluehr-Lobban, Carolyn. *Islamic Law and Society in the Sudan.* London: Frank Cass & Co., 1987.

Gerber, Haim. *State, Society, and Law in Islam: Ottoman Law in Comparative Perspective.* Albany, NY: State University of New York Press, 1994.

Goldziher, Ignaz : *Introduction to Islamic Theology and Law.* Princeton, NJ: Princeton University Press, 1981.

Haeri, Shahla. *Law of Desire: Temporary Marriage in Shi'i Iran.* Syracuse, NY: Syracuse University Press, 1989.

Haleem, M. Abdel: *Criminal Justice in Islam: Judicial Procedure in the Sharî'ah.* London: I.B. Tauris, 2003.

Ilyas Ahmad : *The Social Contract and the Islamic State*, Kitab Bhavan, New Delhi, 1981.

Inayat Ullah Khan El-Mashriqi : *God, Man and the Universe*, Akhuwat Publications, Rawalpindi, Pakistan.

Johansen, B.: *Contingency in a Sacred Law: Legal and Ethical Norms in the Islamic Fiqh*, Leiden 1999

Keddie, Nikki R. : *Roots of Revolution: An Interpretive History of Modern Iran*. New Haven: Yale University Press, 1981.

Kelsay, John. *War and the Imperatives of Justice in Islamic Law*. Cambridge, UK: Cambridge University Press, forthcoming.

Laroui, Abdullah : *The Crisis of the Arab Intellectual,* University of California Press, California, 1976.

Liebesny, H.J.: *The Law of the Near & Middle East: Readings, Cases & Materials* Albany 1975

Makdisi, George. *Religion, Law and Learning in Classical Islam*. Aldershot: Ashgate/Variorum, 1991.

Muhammad, Taha Maḥmud : *The Second Message of Islam,* Syracuse, N.Y.: Syracuse University Press, 1987.

Nasr, Seyyed Hossein : *Science and Civilization in Islam,* Cambridge, UK: Islamic Texts Society, 1987.

Peters, Rudolph : *Jihad in Classical and Modern Islam,* Princeton, NJ: Markus Wiener Publishers, 1996.

Rashed, Roshdi : *Encyclopedia of the History of Arabic Science*. London and New York: Routledge, 1996.

Rosen, Lawrence. *The Anthropology of Justice: Law as Culture in Islamic Society*. Cambridge, UK: Cambridge University Press, 1989.

Sheik, Mufti Allie Haroun : *Islamic Principles on Family Planning,* Adam Publishers, New Delhi, 2001.

Syed, Abdul Latif : *The Concept of Society in Islam and Prayers in Islam,* Goodword Books, New Delhi, 2003.

Taha, Mahmud Muhammad: *The Second Message of Islam,* Syracuse, N.Y.: Syracuse University Press, 1987.

Underhill, E. : *Mysticism : a Study in the Nature and Development of Man's Spiritual Consciousness,* Oxford, New York, 1956.

Vogel, Frank E. *Islamic Law and Legal Systems: Studies of Saudi Arabia*. Leiden: E.J. Brill, 2000.

Walker, Benjamin : *Foundation of Islam : the Making of World Faith,* Rupa & Co., New Delhi, 2001.

Wansbrough, E. John : *Quranic Studies: Sources and Methods of Scriptural Interpretation*. Oxford: Oxford University Press, 1977.

Index

I

J

L

M

N

P

R

S

T

W

❑❑❑